Ancestors and Friends

The Two Painter Brothers: mutual portraits of Henri (*right*) and Rudolf (*left*) Lehmann

ANCESTORS
AND FRIENDS

JOHN
LEHMANN

1962
EYRE & SPOTTISWOODE
LONDON

First published 1962
© *1962 by John Lehmann*
Printed by Cox & Wyman Ltd, Fakenham
Catalogue No. 6/2468/1

Contents

Illustrations

Acknowledgements are due to the Trustees of the British Museum for permission to reproduce the mutual portraits of Henri and Rudolf Lehmann, and Rudolf Lehmann's drawings of Lamartine and Joachim; to Photo Bulloz for the portraits of Franz Liszt and of Princess Christine Trivulzio Belgiojoso by Henri Lehmann; and to Archives Photographiques (Paris) for the self-portrait of Théodore Chassériau and the two drawings by Henri Lehmann from the Musée Bonnat in Bayonne.

Introduction

The basic material of this book is letters: old family letters which have emerged into the light since the end of the last war. A few years ago I happened to come into possession of my family's surviving papers, and among them was a large accumulation of letters that passed between my grandparents in the early years of their marriage, a century ago and more, together with many letters from their relations and their friends of the time, who included some of the most notable contemporary figures in art, literature, music and science. A large number of these had been published by my father in both public and private compilations; the greater proportion, however, I had never seen before.

At the same time, curiously enough, my attention was drawn to a little book, published in Paris soon after the war, which revealed for the first time the letters which had passed between my great-uncle Henri Lehmann, the painter, and his friends Franz Liszt and Madame d'Agoult, in the late thirties and forties of the last century.

The more I read these various letters, the more I felt the desire to explore further, in whatever published and unpublished diaries and memoirs I could find, and to recreate as far as I could the social circles in which these ancestors of mine had played their parts. I had the curious feeling, which grew stronger as my work went on, that all their vanished lives were asking to be brought back, that they might be able to speak with their own voices again. And it seemed to me that, in satisfying this desire, I could at the same time throw some illumination, of general interest, on what was thought and said behind the scenes in a world which appears at one time very distant from and at another very close to our own.

These studies, then, are built round the story of a family,

ranging in time from just before Waterloo to a few years after Sedan, with the scene shifting from Hamburg to Paris, Rome, Edinburgh, London and Cannes. If the reader complains that the picture is sketchy here and there, I must apologize; but where there were no documents, I have refrained from invention.

The translations from letters and diaries, where they were originally in French or German, are by myself throughout.

Apart from my extensive use of unpublished family papers and letters, I have relied for my material on my father's *Memories of Half a Century* and *Charles Dickens as Editor*; on Dr. William Chambers's *Memoir* of his own and his brother Robert's lives and his *Story of a Long and Busy Life*; on Vicomte Henri Delaborde's *Notice sur la Vie et les Ouvrages de M. Henri Lehmann*, read at the Académie des Beaux-Arts in 1883; on my great-uncle Rudolf Lehmann's *An Artist's Reminiscences,* and Lady Priestley's *The Story of a Lifetime*. I have constantly consulted Mme. d'Agoult's *Mémoires*, Mrs. Charlotte Haldane's *The Galley Slaves of Love* and Mr. Kenneth Robinson's *Wilkie Collins: a Memoir*. Among other works to which I am indebted are Amaury Duval's *Ingres*, Henri Lapauze's *Ingres, Sa Vie, Son Oeuvre*, James Payn's *Some Literary Recollections,* Gladys Storey's *Dickens and Daughter,* and C. L. Graves's *Life of Sir George Grove*. Finally, for the letters that passed between my great uncle Henri, Liszt and Mme. d'Agoult, my essential source has been *Une Correspondance Romantique*, edited by Solange Joubert and published in Paris in 1947. My grateful acknowledgements are due to Mme. de Hautecloque, literary executor of her sister Mlle. Joubert, and to Messrs Flammarion, the publishers.

John Lehmann

London 1962

PART ONE
'Clear Placid'

I

In 1814 the Free City of Hamburg was under the military occupation of the French. When Russian troops advanced to lay siege to it, Marshal Davoust ordered all the inhabitants, except the young and the well-to-do, to leave the city.

At that time, my great-grandfather Leo Lehmann, a young portrait-painter who had already made a considerable reputation for himself, had recently married. As the situation in Hamburg grew more threatening, he sent my great-grandmother, Frederika, who was expecting her first child, to take refuge with friends in Kiel. There she gave birth to a son, Heinrich. In order to join her, Leo disguised himself as a working man, pushing a wheelbarrow, and so managed to outwit the French guards at the boundaries of the city.

In course of time, six other children were born: Emil, Sebastian, Rudolf, Frederick, Elizabeth and Marie. Apart from Heinrich, only three of these concern this narrative: Rudolf, Frederick my grandfather, and Elizabeth. Leo's mother-in-law, whom Rudolf describes as a stately matron with much natural wit but scanty education, had been left very well off by her husband. She lived in a fine old house stretching back to one of the canals that intersect Hamburg, and as it was far too large and lonely for her, she let it to Leo and his family, and kept a suite of rooms on the first floor for herself. The children were rather frightened of her: Rudolf remembered the awe with which he would peep through the keyhole of the great drawing-room, always wrapped in mysterious gloom, with its furniture in brown holland. Once every week the formidable old lady invited three of her female cronies to play cards with her, and the children were allowed to tiptoe in to say good night and be given a sugarplum on their way to bed. On one occasion the scene made an indelible impression on them: only three of the old ladies were playing, for the fourth had fallen under the table. They had made her comfortable with pillows where she lay, and continued their game.

Leo had to work hard to keep his family and maintain the social position that was expected of him as one of Hamburg's most distinguished artists. His wife was an extremely energetic and determined woman, and she kept house on the strictest principles of economy. The children were told that they need not be ashamed of patches in their clothes – only of holes. Leo's heart was in his miniature painting, but to make both ends meet he had to spend a great deal of his time giving drawing lessons away from home. So it was that his studio was gradually encroached on by the other needs of the household. It became the family breakfast-room, then a seamstress was established in it, and later still it was given over to the children for their out-of-school work. Somehow or other Leo managed to continue to paint his portraits there in the intervals.

In 1831, at the age of seventeen, Heinrich, who was to be known thereafter as Henri, was suddenly seized with a determination to become an artist himself. His mother's family, the Dellevies, were still in Paris, and two of his aunts had married wealthy bankers there. As they had many connections in the literary, artistic and musical worlds, it was decided to send Henri to Paris to find a master in whose *atelier* he could work.

He set off by the *diligence*, a tedious, bone-shaking, nerve-racking journey of six days. As soon as he arrived his aunts took him in, and during the first few days he spent in Paris he was dazzled to meet many of the most famous figures, both French and German, who frequented their salons: Humboldt, Heine, Meyerbeer, Guérin, Léopold-Robert, Ingres, and many others.

Baron Gérard, a close friend of the family, suggested that Henri should join the *atelier* that Ingres had recently opened. The famous painter agreed, and very soon the young German became one of his most devoted and promising disciples.

At that time the art students were divided into two camps, the followers of the unfortunate Baron Gros, later driven to suicide by hostile criticism when the wind of fashion changed, and the followers of Ingres. When the two factions met in the streets, they would abuse and jeer at one another, and often came to blows.

Jean August Dominique Ingres was, in 1831, already over fifty years old and had passed the zenith of his creative powers. He had made his name in his youth, particularly while he was working in Rome, as a draughtsman of genius. His pencil portraits, so many of which date from his early Italian period, are marvels of delicate precision and linear vitality. Like David, who had been his master, he admired the antique, but he learned more from Raphael and believed that David's fanatical following of Greek and Roman sculptural models was leading him to a dead end. A classicism pure in contour and serenely balanced, not slavishly imitative but ever aware of the accidents of nature, was his ideal. He fulminated, with quite unreasonable violence, against Delacroix and the new vogue of the Romantics.

This passionate belief in the tradition of classicism deeply affected all the artists who came under his influence, none more than the young Henri Lehmann. His early drawings, and above all his portraits in oils, have a strong stamp of the master; though rarely as free in rhythm as Ingres's supreme works, they compel by their linear force and also, it seems to me, by a certain quality of introspective poetry that is entirely their own.

Henri had indeed a sensitive, idealistic disposition, always dissatisfied, always hoping to achieve more by patient study and work. He was conscious of having two sides to his nature, and wrote in his diary at this time: "It is a curious, perhaps a lucky gift, that I never betray to the world my tendency towards anxiety of spirit and melancholy. My nature is like a calm expanse of water that is nevertheless disturbed; the passer-by sees strange lights, will-o'-the-wisps dancing on it, because the moment anyone approaches me this dance begins, ironic, biting words start to my lips and sometimes amuse the listeners." And in a letter to his father at about the same time he wrote: "My aunts don't find those names that mother used to give me – 'tempest!' 'terror!' – justified at all. I am now just as you told me you used to be, dear father; as soon as I am alone, I become serious, inclined to melancholy, readier to weep than to laugh." With his blue eyes set deep under his broad forehead, his natural elegance of carriage and the care he took about his dress, he made an unusual impression. A fellow artist remarked that when he saw him for the first time, at the Ecole des Beaux Arts, he looked like a foreign prince on a visit to the place.

In an astonishingly short time he began to make his mark. When he was only twenty his picture of the *Departure of Tobias*, exhibited in the Salon of 1834, made a considerable stir; and three years later another biblical picture in the taste of the day, *The Marriage of Tobias and Sarah*, was bought by a well-known collector even before the Salon opened. This picture not only established his reputation as one of the outstanding younger artists, but allowed him to think at last of realizing a long-cherished ambition: to study in Rome, whither his beloved Ingres had already departed to direct the French Academy. His decision appears both to have surprised and impressed his friends, for commissions were beginning to come in abundantly and he had already painted several of the remarkable portraits which appear today as his most outstanding achievement.

Two years before, in 1835, he had written to his parents and suggested, with characteristic generosity, that he was prepared to share his studio with any one of his brothers who felt the same urge as he had to become a painter. It was Rudolf, five years younger than Henri, who decided to accept the invitation. The brothers were at last re-united in Paris in March 1835. No. 1 rue de la Michodière was a dilapidated old house, on each story of which two separate workmen's families were lodged. On the fifth floor, under the roof, was Henri's studio: part of it was curtained off to make a bedroom, the two *lits de sangle* filling nearly the whole space. At the end of his life, long after Henri's death, Rudolf wrote: "I still cannot think without gratitude of

my brother's touching devotion, who, in his straitened circumstances, voluntarily saddled himself, at the age of twenty-one,
with the care of a younger brother."

As Ingres was absent in Rome, Henri, determined that his
brother should not be contaminated by the influence of any of
the other masters of the day whose *ateliers* were open to pupils,
sent him to a private academy, kept in the rue Saint André des
Arts by a Monsieur Boudin, who happened, oddly enough, to
be an ex-sergeant of Napoleon's Grande Armée.

There, under the keen eye of his brother, Rudolf started his
studies in earnest, drawing every day from the antique in the
Louvre, and from the casts in the adjoining *moulage*, and copying
pictures of Giulio Romano, Leonardo da Vinci, Giovanni Bellini
and Raphael. Eventually he obtained admission to the classes of
the Ecole des Beaux-Arts. When, however, Henri had his first big
success with the *Marriage of Tobias and Sarah* and proposed to set
out for Rome, Rudolf decided to go with him. Before leaving,
they made up their minds to return to Hamburg to join in the
celebration of their parents' silver wedding. While they were
there, alarming news arrived of a cholera epidemic in Rome.
The brothers therefore decided to travel first of all to Munich,
then at the height of its fame as an artistic centre, and wait there
for the epidemic to subside. It was not till nearly two years later
that Rome seemed safe enough. Henri went ahead, either at the
end of 1838 or in the early weeks of 1839, to prepare the way for
his brother, who followed only some months later.

II

Among my own family papers, traces of great-uncle Henri are
rare. I never remember my father mentioning him, perhaps
because he was in his twenties when Henri died in Paris. We only
possessed two small paintings that could be indubitably ascribed
to him, though I have a hazy recollection of an album of drawings

that may have been his work. This disappeared after my father's death, I do not know to what destination. Great-uncle Henri remained a mysterious character. It was only quite recently that a volume of letters between him, Mme d'Agoult and Liszt, published in Paris soon after the last war, was brought to my notice by my cousin the late Marie Nordlinger, the friend of Proust. Through this book I was led to all the discoveries I have made about his life, and with which the following pages are concerned.

It is not known where, or when Liszt and Mme d'Agoult first met Henri. It may have been at his aunt's house in Paris, where many musical celebrities were among the guests; but more probably in Rome itself, at the Villa Medici, the seat of the French Academy, where certainly, with Ingres as Director, Henri was a regular visitor from the very beginning of his stay. At any rate, by June of 1839 they had become so intimate that Henri called them "*mes chers, chers, chers*", and Mme d'Agoult could write to him: "All the things that go to make up my inner life – the life that is hidden from the world – all the things that fill my soul and fortify it against the empty joys of the world, and the sufferings that are even emptier, you so perfectly guessed, felt and understood that you are no longer in the slightest a stranger for me, or rather you never were a stranger; you came and took your place beside us as if it was the most natural thing in the world, it was as if we had always been expecting you, as if we had known you before and you were simply coming back after being absent for a while."

The "galley slaves of love" – as George Sand maliciously called them – had known one another for six years, and had fallen in love almost at first sight. By 1839 it was already four years since Marie d'Agoult had abandoned her home, her husband and her children to live with Liszt. Though she had not lived with the Comte d'Agoult since the sudden death of her child Louise in the autumn of 1834, the elopement caused a sensation in Paris: Marie was of striking beauty, of noble birth herself, and had already begun to create a *salon* of musicians and men of letters around her. After the first raptures, things had not gone too well: they were still in love, but Franz's restlessness, his vanity, his inability to resist the advances of women who flattered and fascinated him, created an increasing tension between them, a tension from which Marie, who was far more deeply in love and far more vulnerable, suffered profoundly. They had three children, Blandine, Cosima (who was to marry Richard Wagner), and Daniel who had just been born. The time was near when Franz would resume his life of concert tours from country to country, ostensibly at least to provide for these children whom he adored; but the long absences were to make the spiritual distance between him and Marie ever greater.

Eight years before, when he was twenty years old and already famous in Paris and the great cities of the Empire, had occurred the decisive experience of his musical life: he had heard Paganini play the violin and had then and there resolved to make himself in the world of the piano what Paganini was in the world of the violin. Among his ambitions, this seems to have come even before his own composing; and the concert tours were an essential part of the campaign to realize his dreams.

When he reached Rome Henri, being unable, as a citizen of Hamburg, to be a *pensionnaire* in the French Academy, had taken a studio in the Palazzetto Borghese (next to the famous Palazzo), which had originally been built for the families of Pauline Borghese's courtiers and attendants. The top storey, with its open terrace, had been converted into studios, and there Henri settled down in the midst of a mixed confraternity of German and French artists. There too, next to his own, he prepared a little studio for Rudolf.

Henri had returned with joy to sit at the feet of his beloved master. When Rudolf was introduced to Ingres a few months later, he saw before him "a small thick-set man, inclined to be stout, dark, with a sallow southern complexion, tragic eyes somewhat like a fine St Bernard dog's, a low forehead, a short aquiline nose, long upper lip, and a very determined mouth; his face was rather round in shape and clean shaven". Life as Director of the French Academy does not seem particularly to have suited Ingres. It was some years before he could settle down to serious work at all. He wrote in one of his *cahiers* that he was unhappy, that he longed for the moment when he could return to a quiet life among friends in Paris; that he was disenchanted with everything except music and a few old intimates. Rome had changed, he lamented; where was the generous city of yore, so open-minded and liberal towards artists? Now all doors were closed, and he felt humiliated to have to beg for everything. Troublesome duties and distractions ate up his time, his peace of mind. Only the devotion of his wife and his *pensionnaires* consoled him. The contrast between the struggles and simplicity of his early years in Rome and his new official circumstances seems to have had an almost totally inhibiting effect on him. He was provided with carriages, horses and liveried servants, all at the French government's expense, in addition to a liberal entertainment allowance; but in vain. He could never be persuaded to make proper use of the grand reception rooms of the Villa Medici, as his predecessor Horace Vernet had done, and so give his *pensionnaires* a chance to find an entrée into the rather exclusive circles of Roman society.

The establishment was conducted on the dreariest and most parsimonious lines by Madame Ingres. According to Rudolf, "the Sunday evenings when she received company were of the gloomiest. Ingres was a musical enthusiast, and himself a passionate (though indifferent) violinist." He would insist on roping in some of the musical *pensionnaires* to play with him, foremost among them at that time Gounod, a thin, emaciated looking young man in his early twenties, between whom and Ingres a fervent master-disciple relationship had developed. Ingres was notoriously intolerant and biased about other artists all his life, but in Gounod's eyes the great master could do no wrong, and he would never admit that there was any truth in the accusations of despotic authority that were so frequently made against his master. On these Sunday evenings, the rest of the *pensionnaires*, together with the few guests invited – among whom anyone of the female sex scarcely ever figured – had to range themselves on the benches that ran along three sides of the room. There was very little other furniture, and in the dim lighting it was practically impossible to see anything of the magnificent tapestries, representing the history of Esther and Ahasuerus, with which the walls were hung. "The company had to listen, more or less reluctantly, to a succession of string quartets very indifferently performed, of which Ingres never had enough, until ten o'clock when the weakest of teas was served. The same cake appeared on these occasions unimpaired Sunday after Sunday, until a bold wager between two frolicsome *pensionnaires* brought it to a timely end. One of them had boasted that he would bravely walk up to the tea-table and cut the cake, when the other promised to reward him with a congratulatory handshake. We all sat in breathless expectancy when the pantomime was successfully enacted. We watched Mme Ingres' astonished face. She protested violently, but to no purpose, against the size of the portions, calling out: '*Laissez donc – ces messieurs n'aiment pas ce gâteau!*'"

It was not only Rudolf who suffered during those almost unendurable evenings. The artist Amaury Duval, who had known the Academy under Vernet's direction, has left a description of the first Sunday when Ingres presided: "*Quel changement, grand Dieu!* Was it the same place, the same salon that I saw before me? That salon where I had found so brilliant and so elegant a society? Everything was sombre and gloomy: one lamp at each corner of the enormous room that the tapestries with which it was hung made even darker; one lamp on the table, and by the table Mme Ingres with her knitting in her hands; M. Ingres in the middle of a group, talking in grave tones. But not the shadow of anyone of the female sex, only black suits, nothing that could charm the eye . . . Then began the first of the famous *soirées* of the Academy, whose procedure was repeated every Sunday and which I never saw varied during the whole of my stay in Rome. Ambrose Thomas made his way to the piano. Everyone took a seat in silence, M. Ingres in the middle of the salon, his head lifted, preparing to listen. Then the silence was total. Woe to anyone whose chair creaked! . . . Other performers followed Thomas, always playing *musique vertueuse*, as M. Ingres called the music of Mozart, Beethoven and Gluck. At the end, all took their leave, for the most part no doubt regretting the glittering *soirées* of Horace Vernet, I at least always happy to have seen my master and heard these masterpieces so skilfully played."

In spite of these cheerless occasions, and Ingres' general incapacity to cope with the demands of his official position, he remained of course, in the eyes of Henri and of many of his distinguished visitors, including Franz Liszt, the *grand maître*, the modern exponent of the classical school of painting *par excellence*. In addition, Liszt thought more highly of his prowess with the violin than Rudolf. In the autumn of 1839, Liszt sent a letter to the *Revue Musicale*, in reply to a letter from Berlioz, describing his meetings with Ingres in Rome in characteristically rhapsodic terms. "A man whose genius" he wrote, "supported by the most exquisite taste and a virile enthusiasm, has produced the finest achievements of modern painting, M. Ingres, admitted me in Rome into the most intimate friendship, the recollection of which still makes my heart swell with pride. I found in him what his public reputation had already prepared me for – and even more. M. Ingres, as you know, passed his youth in constant study and courageous struggle. He overcame neglect, misunderstanding and poverty only by obstinate toil and the heroic determination that came from unalterable belief in his own powers. Today, when he has reached mature years, he rejoices, without any trace of vanity, in a reputation achieved without the aid of base intrigues. The great artist who understands all the secrets of antiquity, whom Apelles would gladly have hailed as his brother, is not only an incomparable painter but also an excellent musician. Mozart, Haydn, Beethoven, speak the same language to him as Phidias and Raphael. . . .

"One day, which I shall never forget, he accompanied me on a visit to the halls of the Vatican museum. We walked through those long galleries where the numberless monuments of Etruria, of Greece, of Ancient Rome and Christian Italy are gathered: we passed before all those yellowing marble statues, all those paintings that time has half effaced. As we walked, he spoke. I and my friends listened to him as eager disciples. His burning words seemed to create all those masterpieces afresh. His eloquence transported us into distant centuries; line and colour took on new life before our eyes; the forms that time and vandal hands had disfigured appeared again in all their pristine purity and revealed the beauty of their youth. A poetic mystery was taking place before our eyes: it was the genius of our age evoking the genius of ancient times. . . . And then, when evening came, and we had returned home and were sitting between the green oak trees of the Villa Medici, after we had talked for a long time of these great wonders, I led him in my turn towards the open piano with a kind of gentle violence, and said to him: 'Come, dear Master, do not let us forget our beloved music, the violin is waiting for you'. . . . O, if you had heard him then! With what religious devotion he interpreted the subtleties of Beethoven's thought! With what tender strength he handled his bow! What purity of style, what truth of feeling! In spite of the respect he inspires in me, I could not help throwing myself on his neck. And I was happy to feel how he pressed me to his breast with a paternal tenderness."

Mme d'Agoult enclosed this panegyric in a letter to Henri, asking him to show it to Ingres as she felt certain the *Revue Musicale* was not available in Rome. Henri described the master's reaction in his next letter to her: "I went up to his room directly after dinner – the letter made an indescribable impression on the two of them. He wanted to 'hide under the chairs', and intends to let you know all he feels by Thursday's post . . . He embraced me for three whole minutes, and wants me to pass on the embrace to Franz. 'I kiss you for him,' he cried, 'he talks of music and names me! A man like that! But he's like a brother! Heavens, how happy I am' – and so on, and so on. He was almost weeping."

The correspondence between Henri and Marie d'Agoult, as far as we can judge from the letters that survive, began when Mme d'Agoult, who had been in poor health since Daniel's birth, left Rome to take the waters at Lucca, in the middle of June 1839. Liszt, Blandine (known amongst themselves as "Mouche" or "Moucheron") and Cosima went with her, and they all installed themselves in the Villa Massimiliana, which was built on the slope of a hill overlooking the valley of Lucca. The infant Daniel was put out to nurse with peasants at Palestrina, in the hills twenty miles or so east of Rome. His mother seems to have had a curiously detached attitude towards him, and one cannot help feeling that the unfortunate boy, whose life was so short, grew up with a crippling sense of parental indifference. Henri was charged with keeping an eye on him, a duty which he discharged with punctilious devotion. Every so often he would make the journey out to Palestrina, by trap or on horseback, to see the child and his nurse, who impressed him by her fine Roman looks, set off by the Albanian costume she wore.

When I first read the letters between Henri, Mme d'Agoult, and Liszt, I was considerably puzzled by the fact that they always addressed Henri as "Clear Placid", or "Clear" for short. We can guess that he gave the impression, when at ease with friends, of a gentle and peaceful reflectiveness, with undertones of melancholy; but why the nickname *in English*? Then I remembered Mme d'Agoult's enthusiasm for Byron: the third canto of *Childe Harold* provided the clue, for there the poet apostrophizes the Lake of Geneva as "Clear, placid Leman!" The pun must have occurred to Marie or Franz one day early on in their friendship, the name stuck. Their own nickname, "les Zyi", remains impenetrable.

The letters are filled, as the letters of close friends always are, with brief hints and allusions, often a little obscure, to their many acquaintances in the literary and artistic worlds of Rome and Paris. They are particularly interesting for the light they throw on Mme d'Agoult's constantly changing relations with George

Sand, and the ambiguous role played by George Sand's clinging and jealous devotee, Carlotta Marliani, the Italian wife of the Spanish consul at Paris.

It also emerges from these letters that Henri had a special gift for caricature. He must have given dozens of his satirical sketches to Mme d'Agoult alone; but all of them, alas, appear to have vanished. I cannot at any rate find any trace of them.

In the first letter, from Florence, on June 24th, Mme d'Agoult writes: "We miss you a great deal, yes, a great deal. I pine for Rome, Florence seems to me rather mean and shabby. The continual racket deafens me, I had become so accustomed to the deep, sublime stillness of the ancient city." Little Blandine, she tells Henri, had charmed away all misfortunes on the journey. They had stopped at Assisi. "I shall not say anything about the paintings. You know them better than I do, and in any case you know that I don't pretend to have any views about painting. I think it extremely difficult for women to have opinions of any importance about the plastic arts. We are too subjective, our education takes us too far away from physical realities (as it does from moral realities as well): we don't know how to *see*. Then again, in spite of the keenness of my likes and dislikes, I feel that I have nothing but an intuitive appreciation of beauty, there's no real basis to my taste: I like things because I like them, and that's all there is to it."

This is an interesting admission from one who, only a few years later, was to cause such a stir in the intellectual world with her critical studies of art as well as literature. She goes on to describe how a painter, "that young aristocrat who lives in the Palazzo Albani", had accompanied them on horseback from Civita Castellana, where they met him, as far as the waterfall of Terni. "We had quite an argument about your Madonna. One of his criticisms was that one of the hands of the Infant was badly drawn, to which I answered that it was quite impossible, as the pupils of M. Ingres were incapable of drawing badly." In Florence she had again met an old friend, the Italian sculptor Lorenzo Bartolini,

25

who had known Ingres in David's *atelier*. "You can't imagine how happy I made him by talking about M. Ingres and telling him all about our happy evenings in the Villa Medici. He could only speak of him with the deepest emotion, and repeated twenty times that the dream of his life was to spend it with M. Ingres." At the end of the letter she says that she and Franz have been driven nearly mad with boredom in the middle of the hubbub of the celebrations, and urges Henri to come and join them as soon as possible. Till then, "good-bye, dear Placid. Please always be 'Clear', always 'Placid', but not so much so that you forget us."

In a postscript, she tells him of a little tragedy that had occurred: they had lost their dog Othello, when they reached the pension where they were staying. "The poor dog disappeared, he was seen leaving Florence on the road to Rome, perhaps he's walked all the way back to Rome – cases have been known which are just as extraordinary. Please tell everyone you know, so that if they see a black dog *à jabot à l'anglaise* they'll know that it belongs to us, and that they'll be handsomely rewarded. We are terribly cast down by it."

Henri's first letter evidently crossed hers. He tells her that ever since they left he had been working without stop, in order not to think about the separation too much; that Sainte-Beuve, who had become one of their circle, had long been an admirer of and admired by Liszt, and was much attracted by Marie, had been to see him and he had asked him to dinner in return. "He was absolutely charming, as you know he can be. In conversation he seems to me like a firefly. He hides himself behind the most banal and obvious remarks, and then suddenly something happens and there'a a spark, a flash that betrays him. He has a curious idea about the effect of a long stay in Rome. He says that Rome makes bigots of people, fanatics. He took as examples Ingres's passion for Raphael, a certain Swedish sculptor's passion for "Greekness", Princess Wolkonsky's devotion to the religious side of Rome, the way masses of young Poles come to believe in the most extraordinary miracles, in fact he compares Rome to a series of

26

enormous catacombs, where everyone can hollow out a rock-home of his own. I remarked that unfortunately these homes were tombs; whereupon he amiably fluttered his wings and a new spark was given off to help us find a new road."

At that time Sainte-Beuve, already in his middle thirties, had made his mark as a critic of a new kind. neither being content with purely personal reactions, nor trying to set up absolute literary standards by which to judge every writer, ancient or modern, whatever the background to his work. In spite of the acid contempt in which Proust held him for his failure to appreciate either Stendhal or Baudelaire, and his patronizing attitude towards the latter, his method was fundamentally liberating. In Lytton Strachey's words, "he saw that the critic's first duty was not to judge, but to understand." He was already at work on his famous *Histoire de Port Royal*; but the *Causeries du Lundi*, by which posterity has chiefly remembered him, were not to appear in the *Constitutionnel* for more than another decade.

Henri adds, in this letter, a story which illuminates his relations with Ingres: "A few days ago I wanted to take M. Ingres the sketches he asked me to show him, and he invited me to drink coffee with him on Sunday so that we could look at them *tête-à-tête*. Well, I went along this morning, and I had the good fortune to persuade M. Ingres to accept a drawing with which he seemed delighted and which he promptly put in a frame in the place of an engraving. He is suffering quite obviously from some derangement of his mind, because he said he'd never seen such beautiful drawings as certain sketches which I was afraid of showing him, I thought them so mediocre. After we'd talked for a long time, above all about you and Moucheron, he invited me to go up to his studio where I found a host of things to admire and felt even more overcome by the sadness of seeing such a man no longer producing anything. I think he would be very much touched and flattered, if you were to write him a few lines with your news."

Ten days later Henri writes again, having just received Mme d'Agoult's letter. "I simply can't tell you what joy your adorable letter gave me, when I found it here on my return from Palestrina. First of all, let me put your mother's heart at rest, by telling you that Prince Daniel is in perfect health, that he's growing and putting on weight and has become very talkative. I got there before sunrise: I took those good people by surprise, turning up on a weekday so early, and I found their house and themselves as clean as they were when you saw them. As you can imagine, they asked me to give their infinite salutations *per sua excellenza*, they called Liszt *il nostro principe*. I shall give you some more precious details when I see you."

Henri goes on to say that her letter has made him feel that he has at last a place where he belongs, in the hearts of people who will always be his friends, and adds: "Your letter made someone else happy too: it's M. Ingres, who I really believe is a little bit in love with you – I think Franz will allow this rival *sur tous les rapports*. He never stops going into ecstasies about your wit, your charm, your goodness, the nobility of your manners and your features, and he does me the honour of insisting that I have caught all this perfectly. He has seen the portraits I did of you, he is delighted with them, and he insisted on me showing them to Mme Ingres. He even blasphemed and said that my portrait of Franz was better than his, and wanted me to tell you that." Henri took up a rather callous attitude about the dog, and added hastily at the end of his letter: "Othello has probably been stolen or will come back to you. I cannot wait to see you again . . ."

Very soon after this, Henri joined his friends at the Villa Massimiliana, and worked away at their portraits. When they left Lucca to go to the seaside at San Rossore, where they had rented a fisherman's cabin, Henri returned to Rome. Long, intimate letters began to be exchanged between the three of them: their friendship seemed to be growing ever closer. While at Lucca, they had formed an extraordinary plan, for Henri to persuade one of his sisters to join him in Rome and look after the children there. Nothing, of course, came of it: the two girls stayed with their mother, and Henri continued to keep an avuncular eye on Daniel.

Henri's first letter after his return describes the immediate visit he made to Palestrina to see how the boy was getting on. "I found Daniel had grown immensely, one could almost say he was beautiful except for his nose which remains quite inexplicably small. He has magnificent blue eyes, and displays a liveliness all the more extraordinary when you realize I'm only comparing him with his mouk-sister, catching hold of my beard and making tremendous efforts to get some sounds out. Nurse and papa as agreeable as ever. When I had him undressed to make quite certain that his little body was as healthy as his head, I saw that the nurse was hiding in her breast a charm or relic that had fallen out of his baby-clothes. So you see, he is under the special protection of some saint and you can assure yourself that all is well."

Henri goes on to tell Marie how much he was missing her. "I not only lived with you, I entered so intimately into your life that I'd begun to take it for granted that your personality was an extension of my own, using without thinking what came from you, and so imagining myself to be much richer intellectually than I really am. All this has suddenly disappeared, and yet I no longer have that horrible sensation of being like a dog that has lost its master – the feeling I described to you after our first separation – no, I am absolutely certain of you now." He then gives her an amusing picture of his journey back to Rome. "My pedantic nature makes me feel obliged to tell you about my voyage. On the boat social life was pretty strictly divided, at one end the high aristocracy, some French, Polish and German noblemen (I've got some delicious caricatures to show you), and at the other end some youthful spirits, both noble and *bourgeois*, who made fun of the others and were delighted with my caricatures. In between these two groups, the middle class who passed the time with this sort of conversation: a lady, an inveterate *naturaliste*, told us how she was in the habit of letting her feet stick out of the end of her bed in the morning, and how this habit resulted in them being seen by an indiscreet gentleman who suddenly came in, but she wasn't upset because her feet were of remarkable beauty — and then the Countess of Barbarossa, probably trying to restore the tone of the conversation, remarked: 'They tell me there are a great many hills in Rome.' I replied that at the last count there had been seven, but this made no impression whatsoever on her topographical intelligence."

In her reply Mme d'Agoult writes from Pisa: "If I was one of those estimable people (like yourself) who only write when they've got something to say, I'm not so sure, my good Clear, that I'd be writing to you today. We've just spent a fortnight at San Rossore, days of marvellous beauty, purity, harmony; but one can't describe things like that, one can only indicate to certain fine, poetic creatures, of which you are one, where to look in their own memory to find similar emotions, parallel joys." She tells him she finds Daniel's short nose quite inexplicable, but "things that can't be explained are best". Then she describes a plan that she and Liszt had dreamed up together – perhaps the last happy plan they ever had. "Now we have another project! To build a Swiss chalet in the forest here: simple country furniture, flowers, horses, a cook, and we'd spend eight months every year with *selected* friends who come as near as possible to the ideal of Zyotic perfection – which means as like Clear Placid as possible! All this has to be put in motion after the tours of England and Russia, that is in eighteen months or so. For the moment, I've taken rooms on the Arno, and Franz (you observe the sympathy) on the Piazza Santa Catharina al Angelo." The reference about Franz's "sympathy" is to the picture of St Catherine, on which Henri was at work at that time.

In the same letter comes the first reference to the storm that was brewing between her and George Sand. Mme d'Agoult had been staying with George Sand at Nohaut when she installed the young playwright Mallefille, ostensibly as tutor to her son Maurice, in fact as her lover. Very soon after, Chopin was substituted for the unfortunate Mallefille, and the novelist and her new lover went off to Majorca together. Mme d'Agoult had a great deal of sympathy for George Sand's unhappy restlessness, but her sharp intelligence could not fail at the same time to savour the comedy of such nymphomaniac behaviour. She began to write maliciously gossiping letters to her friends about the rapid succession of George Sand's lovers. Wind of this must have got about; perhaps George Sand was already feeling guilty about having told Balzac of the tension between Franz and Marie and having encouraged him to write his novel *Béatrix* about them; in any case she ceased to write to Mme d'Agoult. Both women now had excessively ambivalent feelings about one another, but Marie did not want to break entirely with George Sand, and rather imprudently wrote a long letter to Carlotta Marliani enclosing a letter to George Sand. Would Carlotta forward this letter, in which she asked George Sand the reasons for her silence? Carlotta, who no doubt had long felt secretly jealous of Mme d'Agoult and her relationship with her heroine, would not. This stung Mme d'Agoult, and in the letter to Henri, of the 26th September 1839, she writes: "Apropos Sand, la Marliani has sent me back my letter, telling me she wouldn't undertake to forward it, that she hoped I'd change my mind as the effect of my letter would quite certainly be the opposite of what I desired, and so on. Whereupon I sent the letter direct to Mme Sand, explaining why it was late; and at the same time wrote again to la Marliani to tell her that I was no longer at that charming age when one is sorry today for what one did yesterday and regrets tomorrow what one has done today, etc. etc., and that in any case what I wanted above all was an explanation, etc. etc. I ought to have an answer very soon."

In his next letter, Henri remarked: "It doesn't surprise me that la Marliani returned your letter. One of us three foretold this when you sent the letter off. I'm very curious to know what she answers." It was a long time before Mme d'Agoult heard from George Sand – her silence, she wrote to Henri, remained "as inexplicable and unexplained as Daniel's nose" – but meanwhile Carlotta Marliani had written to George Sand warning her that Mme d'Agoult was a dangerous friend and that she ought to have nothing to do with her in the future. The imbroglio grew deeper; George Sand wrote a spiteful letter about Marie to Carlotta, and then wrote a long, disagreeably two-edged letter to Marie who cannot have failed to sense the malicious undertone. Their friendship never recovered; and yet it never entirely came to an end.

In these circumstances, Henri's gentle, affectionate loyalty must have been very consoling. "Let me tell you at once, my good Marie," he wrote, "what ineffable pleasure your charming letter gave me. I found it at the Café Greco, and I enjoyed the full savour of it on the Pincio, as the sun was setting. So it is that I am filled with feelings of grateful friendship and have to write and tell you at once – thank you! At the moment I'm horribly *sur mon carré*. Franz knows what that means! If only he could come and restore my courage a little, put me in tune, for my whole machine which you are pleased to find so full of harmony is horribly *out* of tune. There are moments when there's nothing in me but regrets and fears. I only see faults in everything I do, and I ask myself why on earth I'm a painter, everything I do to shake off these gloomy thoughts is in vain, I shall just have to wait until the mood has passed." He tells her that he very nearly abandoned his work and came to join them in Pisa, one day when he was "so exhausted, so sad, oppressed like a day when the sirocco is blowing, that I tried to find forgetfulness with a book in the delicious grounds of the Villa Borghese, the charm of which you can't imagine when nature's in a good humour, but in its crushing stillness only showed me the image of myself and was scarcely the right place to quicken my deflated spirits." Does she really mean everything she says in her letters, he asks her? It would be easy to suspect she was making fun of him, if he didn't know that she always spoke to him without irony. "In short, only my thoughts of you keep me alive; waiting for your letters, planning to write to you, dreaming of seeing you again, reading your books, occupying myself with all the little commissions you give me!" A young fellow-artist, Paul Chevandier, had been to see him: "the sympathetic, the Byronic Chevandier turned up the other day, and seeing my name written on my door, cried out 'Can this be where "Clear and limpid Leman" lives?' At these words of Zyotic memory my door so inexorably closed against all comers opened for him. He has rented a house way out in the country, where he intends to live next summer surrounded by horses, dogs, and friends."

In the same letter Henri gives a vivid glimpse of his relationship with Ingres. "During the pleasant evenings I spend alone with him, he sometimes makes some interesting confessions. He spoke about a sick man's arm (in his picture *La Maladie d'Antiochus et Stratonice*) of which he had made two hundred sketches and which he had repainted fifty times. He told me that the nervous trouble which torments him so often first came when he was struggling with the piece of drapery that goes from the knee to the foot of his Christ in the *Trinità dei Monti* church. 'For fifteen days, from dawn to dusk, I painted and repainted that piece of drapery, my eyes always on the same colour. At other times, it just comes at once. For instance, my *Homer*: I learnt of the commission in my *atelier*, and by the time I'd got home I'd decided on the composition. But when it won't come, it's better to start all over again. As for that arm, I'm sure it's better now than it's ever been. I can prove it, because I've tried *every other possible way of painting it.*'

"What will-power, what patience – and what lack of imagination! He asks very eagerly for news of you. So that I can read him extracts from your letters, always put in a few phrases with that in mind, will you? The show of guilt and remorse he puts on when he admits that he owes you a letter is thoroughly comical; I'm certain you'll get it as soon as his painting is packed off. Apropos of that, he tells me that although he generally has his letters rewritten by '*la langue française*' (as he calls his secretary), he likes to write them all by himself in certain cases, 'because my ideas have a certain originality, which disappears when they're polished up . . .' What absurd naïveté in a great man! Once again he has accepted one of my drawings, and with the most touching tenderness: like the first one, it is framed and hangs over his work table."

A week later Liszt and Mme d'Agoult were in Florence, and about to separate: she to go back to Paris with her two girls, whose education was becoming an urgent matter, and he to set out on the series of long concert tours that were to absorb so much of his time and energy during the next few years – and complete his estrangement from Marie. Her journals let us see how heavy her heart was: in four years all the happiness for which she had abandoned her former life had been spent. She could not escape from feelings of guilt about having abandoned her daughter Claire, and feared she might never be allowed to see her again. Worse, she knew that Franz could not refrain from being constantly unfaithful to her. One evening, while they were at the Villa Massimiliana together, she and Franz and Henri were on the terrace alone, and Franz had said: "I realize with sorrow that an epoch in my life has come to an end. Nothing will ever bring back these last three years; there's nothing for me to learn any more, nothing to set my heart on; plans have taken the place of a free, spontaneous life. I have reached the age when one feels that nothing is good enough. I realize, bitterly, that I'm not what I would have liked to be. When one has broken everything around one, one has broken something in oneself too." That night, Marie wrote in her journal with near despair: "He seems to be deeply distressed about his failure to give me more happiness. He is not aware of what I am so well aware of, the atrophy of my brain, the presentiment of age, the death of the will."

Marie saw before her a difficult and lonely return to Paris, at the mercy of her ill-wishers to whose ever-smouldering spite she feared George Sand had added fuel. She told Henri that she had had another letter from La Marliani, "to say that it was she who wrote to George to warn her that I wasn't a sincere friend. A conclusion she drew from one or two letters I sent her in which I spoke rather flippantly of George. So I have written back, on a seriously, friendly note, but making no bones about my profound indignation; insisting again on having a direct explanation from George. Franz doesn't believe a word of what she says. He maintains that it's an indirect move on the part of George who, he thinks, was furious about certain remarks I made on the subject of Mallefille and Chopin." To this Henri replied: "The Sand-Marliani affair staggers me. The shabbiest kind of scandal-mongering flourishes in the highest social and intellectual circles: a depressing discovery! I am convinced that your presence in Paris will put an end to it all, exactly as you wish. Try to keep George as a friend, her intelligence is too rare and too remarkable – and her heart too, I almost believe. That profound understanding of unhappiness, that zeal for the good of humanity don't come from the head. Her violent imagination obliges her to experiment, to try all sorts of things; should she not be glad to recover what she must recognize to be supremely excellent? And once she's recovered it, no doubt she'll never abandon it again! See her, talk to her, let her talk, and beware of your mutual friends. I think you owe it to your friends and your dignity to forgive her and offer her your hand in friendship again."

It would seem, from certain hints in subsequent letters, that this perhaps over-generous advice was not entirely welcome to Mme d'Agoult; but an occasion was soon to come when the roles were reversed and she gave the impression of rather enjoying letting Henri realize how easy it is for a third party, who is not an injured party, to counsel forgiveness.

In *Béatrix* Balzac had written a *roman à clef* where the originals behind the imagined characters were perfectly obvious to any reader, in spite of – perhaps even more because of – the slight changes he had made in appearance and background. Mlle des Touches, who had taken the professional male name of Camille Maupin, was a rather idealized portrait of George Sand, the man-woman who "swims, hunts, rides, smokes and drinks", who writes and "can analyse a book or a heart", and has "not the smallest weakness"; Béatrix, the Marquise de Rochefide, her rival, a spiteful portrait of Mme d'Agoult; and Gennaro Conti a decidedly unsympathetic sketch of Franz Liszt, the composer and divine opera singer who is "insatiable for applause", who "shams everything, and trifles with everything", who "can act joy as well as grief, and succeeds to perfection", and "can get admiration whenever he chooses". Balzac paints Mme de Rochefide's physical beauty in glowing colours, and the envy which this beauty aroused in the older woman's breast, but "Camille knew how shallow her soul was, and how mean her pride, to which she had justly given the name of obstinacy", and Béatrix herself knew herself to be inferior to Camille, "not merely in the sum total of intellectual qualities known as talent, but also in those qualities of the heart known as passion". In one point Balzac did not distort the living truth: as Camille and Béatrix battle for possession of the soul of the beautiful and innocent young Breton nobleman Calyste, he observes that "there was between the two women a duel without truce, in which the weapons were cunning, feints, generosity, false confessions, astute confidences".

During the few days they spent in Florence before they parted, Liszt and Mme d'Agoult were very much occupied with the plans for a Beethoven monument. Liszt had been horrified to hear that only 259 francs had been subscribed in the whole of France. "It's a disgrace!" Marie wrote to Henri. "Franz could scarcely contain himself." He thought of Bartolini, who was working on a bust of Marie. He happened to be in Florence, and Liszt hurried to see him. "He promises to make a beautiful monument for 50,000 francs, and it could be ready in two years. So Franz is writing to the Committee with the offer of making up the necessary sum himself, on condition that they commission Bartolini. If the proposal is accepted (and they can't refuse it except through downright stupidity) he'll give three concerts (in Vienna, Paris and London), and if there's still not enough he'll find it out of his own pocket. I'm enchanted that he's had this idea. It is right that Liszt should be responsible for Beethoven's monument." Henri found Liszt's initiative "magnificent", but reported that Ingres, who shared his enthusiasm for Liszt's attitude, had a poor opinion of Bartolini and thought the idea was very risky. He was right: the scheme came to nothing, for in the end the Committee refused to accept Bartolini's rather laboured designs.

It sheds a touching light on Franz and Marie's affection for the young painter, that they thought of him so warmly during their last hours together in Italy. Before leaving with the children for Livorno, Marie wrote to him: "How can you dare to suggest that I should make fun of you, dear Clear? The affection that Franz and I have for you is much more complete, much deeper and much more constant than you can imagine. All the time, whatever we're talking about, your name is mentioned. Whenever we're discussing anyone, we end up by saying: 'But he's not as nice as Lehmann.' The other day, while we were taking a walk on the Camp Santo, Franz suddenly said to me: 'Of all my friends, Lehmann is the one I love most.' I was as happy to hear him say that as I would have been if he had told me the most wonderful news. I felt I even loved him a little bit more himself at that moment, for having given you pride of place in his heart."

To which the enraptured Henri replied: "I can't tell you how much two sentences in your letter moved me. I received it just as I was going to send my letter to Franz in Munich, and I reopened it and, in my excitement, forgetting that one should never abandon oneself to a revelation of one's feelings when one writes so badly, I poured out all my emotion to him. Reflection has now had time to take over. I scarcely dare tell you how grateful I am. Let me confess anyway that I blushed in full view of everyone in the Café Greco when I read what Franz had said to you, and I hurried out overcome with shame. To learn that he loves me better than everyone else and to learn it from you, you who say you love this friendship, you who have chosen me as the confidant of your sorrows – that's indescribably wonderful! I passed the whole day trembling like a plant after the passage of a storm and refreshing rain, and then when my vanity had sated itself, a feeling of compassion overcame me, a profound sadness! Through a thousand memories, I came to imagine the moment when I should see the two of you again, I broke out in a cold sweat, I couldn't listen to Beethoven's music at M. Ingres' house, every note spoke to me of you and made me miss you again. I went home ill with happiness . . . Thinking that Franz would be in Vienna till the end of November, I must tell you that I had already sketched out a little miniature in oils of you and Mouk, a very practical little affair that can be carried around *per piccoli uomini e viaggianti*, but your letter put a stop to the project, because for little things like that the occasion is everything; you'll have the miniature later on. Today 1 made a drawing which will, I hope, be a zyotic souvenir for the *distintissimo*. It has no artistic value, in fact it's rather bad, but it recalls you in your blue morning dress, passing your hand through the loose strands of your hair and bringing them together under your chin; it's a trifle, but I think it's just right.

"To talk to you about my picture I'd have to be rather less superstitious: when I talk about my work I immediately think I'm not going to do it as well. Give me another fortnight of silence. But I must admit to you that I feel strong at this moment; I believe that with three years of independence, money, solitude and *séquestrement moral*, I could make my Dante one of the most beautiful poetico-plastic creations of our epoch, everything comes down to a question of Time, nothing but that. Then at certain moments, I swear to myself that, having sold my picture and so bought my freedom for a while, I'll play the *rapin* again, the palette-cleaner, the dogsbody for a year in M. Ingres' studio, to finish a certain part of my education as a painter. Heavens! If you are going to take charge of me in Paris, as you promise, you should know the feebleness of my spirit; you only know it 'clear' and 'placid'! Only from you do I get letters that so warm my heart. Good-bye, adorable Zy."

III

There is no doubt that my great-uncle, devoured by doubts and anxieties about his capacities as a painter, missed his friends very much, particularly after these declarations of confidence and affection. The long, intimate letters continue, Mme d'Agoult's full of the gossip of Paris, the progress of the row with George Sand, and her own gradual settling in with her circle of loyal friends about her.

When Liszt received the drawing of Marie, he sent Henri a rapturous letter from Vienna, where he was momentarily laid up with fever. "I wept and wept, as you can imagine. I can't let it out of my sight. As I write to you, it is here, on my bed, close to me, I never want to be separated from it. Only, when we see one another again in Paris, I want you to put your name on it. It's no doubt childish, but I don't know why, it would give me pleasure." He tells Henri that his return to Vienna has been an incredible success, that his concerts were sold out four days ahead, and that he believes that this success will contribute even more than his previous visit to Vienna towards establishing the high European reputation he covets. "My hand is trembling," he continues, "perhaps you can't read this? My doctor has just left in a rage at finding me writing to you, and absolutely forbids me to go on. It is true that I'm very weak and full of fever. All the same, don't worry, there's nothing fundamentally wrong with me. It's quite simply a case of extreme fatigue combined with considerable nervous irritation.

"Good-bye, my dear, my very dear friend. I shall write to you again soon. Till then, I embrace you from the bottom of my heart. I am always yours – for life.

"Once again, your portrait is sublime, just exactly what I want."

Meanwhile an event had occurred which to some extent consoled Henri for the departure of Liszt and Mme d'Agoult. He had for some time been making preparations to receive his brother Rudolf, and now at last, in mid-November, he heard that he was on his way from Venice. He writes to Marie: "I went to find out about the arrival of Tuesday's *diligence*, though convinced that my brother couldn't be arriving that day. Half an hour later he was in my arms! On Monday we made an expedition to Frascati, Grotta Ferrata, Castel Gandolfo, Albano. Splendid weather, extraordinary warmth for the 18th of November. Combining duty with pleasure, I went off to Palestrina on Tuesday . . . Imagine roads without any paving, sheer bogs after October's rain, and a *cavalucero* with a prejudice against galloping that I had to prevent every moment from coming a cropper! Nevertheless, I rode along slowly for fifteen miles with the sweet, sad sound of the dead leaves scattered on the ground accompanying me; in front of me the view of the Campagna. Rome and the chain of the Sabine Hills seemed to me a wonderful enchantment during the six hours that I spent on my return journey next day." He tells Marie that Daniel is becoming a charming infant, and beginning to get quite a "mouk" look of his sisters. "After my visit to Daniel and a supper of eggs and hot soup *chez la sora Lavinia*, I went to bed. A downpour like the flood woke me up at four o'clock, I started off in complete darkness, my steed, led by a peasant, slipping all over the ancient paving stones. After two hours' going, dawn began to break and the rain to grow less. I realized that my horse had some spirit, and although it had nothing but a rope for a bridle and something quite unmentionable for saddle, I determined to leave my guide there and set off for Rome at a gallop. At ten o'clock I'd reached the Forum of Trajan, and at midday, after eighteen miles on horseback and eighteen hours without anything to eat, I was devouring a meal with a good appetite! I describe this little *tour de force* to you, so that you can appreciate all the better your comfortable sofa, your cosy fire and your excellent carriage."

Henri had no intention of finally leaving Rome and the jealous guidance of the master he worshipped for a long time to come;

but he had promised Marie that he would be with her in Paris for a short visit at least early in the New Year. "Your description of how low Paris has sunk frightens me," he writes to her, "but *alea jacta est*, I shall cross the Rubicon come what may." And he wrote to his friend Bohn, a fellow painter from Germany, to ask him to find him a room and a studio in the rue Pigalle, or thereabouts, where Mme d'Agoult intended to stay and George Sand had already installed herself. The two friends discussed in their letters how the new "Zyotic" apartments should be furnished. Mme d'Agoult had been recommended to have a "cabinet" in Moorish style, and a salon in Renaissance style. She inclined towards the former, but could not make up her mind about the latter. "If you have any Moorish ideas," she writes to Henri, "let me know. I think perhaps that little divans covered with tiger-skin would be attractive. As for the Renaissance salon, we'll see – I'm a little afraid of the vast expense, and the fashionableness of it too. Everyone wants Renaissance style today." Henri wrote back: "I don't think Moorish would be right for a grand *salon de réception*, but appropriate for a *salon boudoir* – that is, a Zyotic retreat full of flowers, pipes and coffee, to which the adorers will have entrée at all hours. But the main salon must be Renaissance. The expense you're afraid of will turn out to be less in the end, and one can't go wrong if one imitates what is really beautiful."

In the end, on Ingres' recommendation, Mme d'Agoult enlisted the services of a fashionable interior decorator, Monsieur Duban, who furnished her two salons with a care and a luxurious taste that delighted her: "M. Duban is looking after my little affairs as if it was a question of building the Louvre."

To be the centre and hostess of a famous Parisian *salon* in the heyday of the romantic age was a distinction that was worth fighting for, and that few women were sufficiently brilliant, perceptive and well-connected at once in the social and artistic worlds to achieve. Some idea of what a great *salon* could mean may be gathered from Balzac's description in *Béatrix* of Mlle des

Touches's house as Calyste first saw it: "Here, spread before the ravished eyes of this ignorant youth . . . lay the Parisian glories of a new world; just as here he heard an unknown and sonorous language. Calyste here listened to the poetical tones of the finest music, the amazing music of the nineteenth century, in which melody and harmony vie with each other as equal powers, and singing and orchestration have achieved incredible perfection. He here saw the works of the most prodigal painting – that of the French school of today, the inheritor of Italy, Spain and Flanders, in which talent has become so common that our hearts, weary of so much talent, cry out loudly for a genius. He here read those works of the imagination, those astounding creations of modern literature, which produce their fullest effect on a fresh young heart. In short, our grand nineteenth century rose before him in all its magnificence as a whole – its criticism, its struggle for every kind of renovation, its vast experiments, almost all measured by the standard of the giant who nursed its infancy in his flag, and sang it hymns, to the accompaniment of the terrible bass of cannons."

The extent to which Mme d'Agoult's mind was dominated by fear of the damage which George Sand could do her at this crucial moment of her return to Paris without Liszt, is shown by the continual references in her letters to Henri. From Lyons she had written to him with the news that La Marliani had sent her a letter "all sweetness and amiability", insisting that a few words of conversation when they met would clear everything up. Mme d'Agoult resolved to show no bitterness – to show them that she was above scandal-mongering – but she evidently found it hard to keep up, for there was yet another outburst in her first letter from Paris: "Further instalment of the Marliani business. After two days I wrote to tell her that I was here, that I couldn't visit her because I was afraid of finding people there and so break the incognito I want to keep up, that I begged her to send her husband, etc. etc. She replied that she was in bed, that her husband would come and let me know the times when I could find her alone, and so on. He came that evening. After having talked about everything under the sun, I said to him: 'Well, it seems to me your wife has lost her head. She writes me letter after letter and I don't understand a single word of them, etc. etc.' Whereupon he came out with a new version. He and his wife, he said, hadn't the least idea what was wrong with Mme Sand. His wife had reproached herself with showing one of my letters to Mme Sand, saying 'Perhaps by my indiscretion I have been the involuntary cause of the coolness between them. But as you have observed so truly yourself,' Marliani went on, 'when people are as intimate as you three are, one expects to have letters shown round, and it's obviously childish of my wife to worry about that.' I accepted this new version, and refused to get into petty bickering about it. I simply put the question in its simplest terms: Mme Sand has stopped writing to me; I want to know the reason why, she should give me an explanation or else we should forget that we have ever known one another. Marliani, who they say is very false anyway, seemed scarcely an enthusiast for Mme Sand, and refused to admit any knowledge of her affairs, or any responsibility for or complicity in her acts." She goes on to tell Henri that as far as she can make out George Sand's reputation is falling, that many friends are abandoning her, and that the Poles accuse her of slowly murdering Chopin, and ends up with a desolate cry: "Where are our happy mornings at the Villa Massimiliana? Our happy evenings in Rome? Where is *he*? Where are you? Why on earth have I come here?"

Ten days later she tells Henri that she has met George Sand at La Marliani's house and that they embraced one another, but she adds at once: "Your advice is marvellous!!! If you were here, I'd explain to you why I can't follow it." And a few days later she writes again: "All this Marliani mischief is getting unbearable. I think we're heading straight for a total rupture with George. Those two women lie as they please, but I maintain a Roman pride in the face of their lies . . . Good-bye, dear Clear.

Please come soon. *L'agréable présence* would do me so much good. I am terribly lonely at heart."

While waiting impatiently for Henri's arrival, she concentrated all her efforts on gathering a circle of absolutely loyal friends about her. Foremost among these was Charles Didier, the handsome young journalist who was one of George Sand's rejected lovers; the ever faithful Sainte-Beuve; Louis de Ronchaud, well-to-do young poet and art-historian, who was certainly at one time deeply in love with Marie, but remained a devoted friend to the end of his life (in one of his letters Henri refers to him as *"Louis le baron protecteur"*); the novelist Eugène Sue; Ferdinand Eckstein, a Dane known as "Baron d'Eckstein" who edited *Le Catholique* for some years; Bernard Potocki, a Polish expatriate and son of the Chief of Police in Warsaw, an old friend whose attentions to Marie began about this time to be more pressing; and, occasionally, the poet Alfred de Vigny.

This noble, fastidious, stoic character had just published another revised edition of his extraordinarily small, yet uniquely beautiful collection of poems, and a few years before his most enduring prose work, *Servitude et Grandeur Militaire*. He had been a frequenter of Mme d'Agoult's social gatherings at a much earlier date, before her marriage had broken up. On one occasion she had invited him to read his new poem, *La Frégate*, to her guests, but it had baffled them and as he left he had said to her: "My frigate has been shipwrecked in your *salon*, Madame."

There was also a new friend, who was destined to play an important part in Marie's life during the next few years. Shortly after reaching Paris, she wrote to Henri telling him who she was seeing: "I've re-established very close relations with Charles Didier, who loves you. His wife is most distinguished, and a useful acquisition for my feminine *alta solitudine* . . . I've made the acquaintance of Delacroix, who spoke very warmly to me of M. Ingres. I didn't conceal my enormous admiration for him: the news did not make him frown. He gives me the impression that he is about to take Chopin's place (in George Sand's favours)."

And she adds, casually, that she has seen "M. Bulwer, *aimable secrétaire d'Ambassade*". Henry Lytton Bulwer was the elder brother of the author of *The Last Days of Pompeii*, and attached at that time to the British Embassy at Paris. He was said to look not unlike Chopin, and Marie wrote to Franz that he was "very kind, full of charm, and above all infinitely gentleman-like in his tastes, his feelings and his manners". He was fascinated by her, he wanted to become her lover, and if she had been free he would have been eager to marry her. But Marie, it seems, soon made it clear to him – as she had made it clear to Louis de Ronchaud and Bernard Potocki – that in her life there was only one man and his name was Franz Liszt. Nevertheless, she allowed herself to tease Liszt about Bulwer, and (without giving names) asked whether she might have *une petite permission d'infidelité*. If she hoped to rouse Liszt to jealousy, she was horribly disappointed: he replied that of course she could, that nothing like that mattered, and he trusted her absolutely to tell him if anyone began to mean more to her than he did. "If you feel you need to, or if it gives you pleasure, or even distracts you to talk to me about Bulwer, do so, I shall be satisfied and flattered, otherwise I will never mention the matter. Truth!"

To this Marie desperately answered: "What you say about the *permission d'infidelité* . . . is full of feeling and fills me with respect for you, although your way of looking at it will always be incomprehensible to me. It is as impossible for me to conceive it as it is for a fish to fly in the air and I can only accept it as an inexplicable fact."

Meanwhile she had reconciled herself to some extent with her brother, Maurice de Flavigny, who acted as an intermediary between her and her husband. Charles d'Agoult remained fair-minded and even affectionate, and harboured no desire for social or personal revenge. But the conditions both of them made for a final reconciliation were impossible to her: that she should return to live under her husband's roof, but *without* Blandine and Cosima. When he heard of this, Liszt told her immediately that

45

she should never consent to live with Charles again, but that he thought it advisable that the children should be looked after by his mother. And to Madame Liszt they went, no doubt greatly to their own advantage; for Marie does not seem to have been the most attentive of mothers. It was about this time, just before Henri's arrival in Paris, that she wrote to him with a quite extraordinary callousness about the wretched Daniel: "What you tell me of Daniel makes me very happy. All the same, I absolutely forbid you to go back to see him before you leave. It's really madness, and at bottom a madness that can lead nowhere. The sad truth is that Providence alone can look after that child, and the best I can do is to think about it as little as possible." It does Henri credit that he refused to accept this liquidation of Daniel, and replied: "In spite of your veto, I shall go back to Palestrina, it's very easy and I don't see why one should allow the hazards that beset dear little Daniel to grow greater rather than less."

Just before Henri set out for Paris, Mme d'Agoult sent him a last, brief letter: "Only two words, dear Clear, because I'm convalescent. I have been very ill. What vile stories I shall have to tell you, Clear! You'll blush to hear what unworthy friends I have had – it will make you furious. But the zyotic sun is not sinking, and these wicked people can throw mud in the air as much as they like, they won't stop it shining. My brother is here. We have revived the intimacy of our happiest days. I never would have thought it possible in spite of everything! It's a sweet triumph for my heart.

"Give M. and Mme Ingres my warmest wishes for the new year. Adieu. This is the last word I shall write to you."

Neither Madame d'Agoult nor Henri settled in the rue Pigalle, as they had planned. Marie found a house in the rue Neuve-des-Mathurins, where she made her *salon*, and Henri rented a studio in the rue Chausée d'Antin, so close that he could see the windows of Marie's house from his own window. Now at last the long years of troubled self-questioning and dedicated study began to bear fruit. In the *Salon* of 1840 he exhibited three pictures, the *St Catherine* to which Mme d'Agoult had referred in her letter from Pisa, a *Virgin with the Infant Jesus*, and a portrait of Liszt, perhaps one of the most remarkable works he ever executed. For these he was awarded a Gold Medal.

We know very little about the next few months in Paris, during which he was a privileged member of Mme d'Agoult's inner circle of friends and a familiar figure at her receptions, as, inevitably, no letters passed between them. But from some passing references in the letters which Liszt sent to Henri from his triumphant tour in Austria and Hungary during the winter, it would seem that there had been a new development in his life. There is very little surviving evidence from which we can tell whether Henri as a young man was ascetically or amorously inclined; but between December of 1839 and the summer of 1840 it seems fairly certain that he started an intimate relationship with a famous singer of the time, Caroline Ungher. She had had a passion for Liszt, and while he was in Trieste, soon after he and Marie had said good-bye to one another in Florence, he spent a great deal of time in her company. True to his promises to Marie, Franz sent her a full account of these meetings. It does not appear that they were lovers; Franz tells Marie that Caroline had decided that, though she had been in love with him in the past, she saw that Marie now came first and renounced her ambition to become his mistress. It is unlikely that Liszt was lying about this: it was not his way, however much he might attempt to justify himself when forced to any admission of guilt (and there were many such occasions). In any case, he soon left Trieste, and Caroline Ungher did not go with him. It chanced that, probably for professional reasons, she paid a visit to Rome in December 1839. She arrived with a letter for Henri, which Liszt had sent her from Vienna. "*Mon bon Lehmann*," he wrote, "Mlle Ungher will send you these lines as soon as she arrives in Rome. Go and see her straight away, it will be the best answer to make. I have told her at some length what I thought of your talent and your ideas. As for her,

I am sure you'll admire her and like her. Then, please, introduce Chevandier to her, as a Byron among landscape painters. You know I've got a weak spot for him. Good-bye, my dear Lehmann, again a million warm and sincere thanks for your marvellous drawing. I am entirely yours, and for always."

A little later, on New Year's eve, only a few days before his departure for Paris, Henri, writing to Marie d'Agoult, mentions in passing that among the few new people he has met is "Mlle Ungher, who is far less unsympathetic than I thought she would be." Meanwhile, Liszt was impatient to know what his friend thought of her. "Have you seen La Ungher?" he writes on the 8th of January. "What impression did she make on you?" Henri's answer is lost, but on February 17th Liszt writes again, from Budapest: "I am delighted that you have made friends with La Ungher. She's a charming and excellent woman. In any case, you know what I think of her: once more, I am enchanted that you have hit it off with her."

This is all we know, until the serio-comic sequel a few months later. Liszt arrived in Paris in April, and he and Mme d'Agoult seem to have forgotten their troubles for a while. At the beginning of May he left for his English tour, and in June Mme d'Agoult joined him there. "Sometimes I stay looking at the 'closed eyes' of your room for minutes together," Henri writes to her. "What made me so happy before now makes me unhappy. However . . . I know you had an excellent crossing. How did you find my uncle, who is enchanted with you – another victim? I imagine a caricature which would represent 'The Zyotic cult not subsidized by the State' in three *tableaux*. First chapel: Zy and her chief priest. Second chapel: Zy deprived of her chief priest and surrounded by minor priests, Clear, Ronchaud, Bulwer and Potocki. Third, grand chapel, where the people would be in various compartments: Alphonse as a beadle with halberd would drive back the infidels, the miscreants, George Sand, Chopin, Sainte-Beuve, etc. . . ."

Soon after, Henri returned to Italy; before he settled in Rome

1a. Henri Lehmann by Ingres

1b. Madame d'Agoult by
Henri Lehmann

2. Franz Liszt by Henri Lehmann (*Musée Carnavalet*)

again, he set off on a tour of Naples and the south with his fellow-artists Paul Chevandier and Théodore Chassériau. Meanwhile Mme d'Agoult followed Liszt on a tour of Germany. From Naples Henri wrote to her with the latest news about Carola Ungher: "Not having received my letters in Vienna, and thinking that I had stopped writing, she writes to me to say that we mustn't see one another again for a long time, and ends up wishing me happiness – a happiness she won't stand in the way of! A second, icy letter, in answer to mine begging her to let me hear her news, made me ask my brother to convey my profound respects to her. I must admit that I love her enough to want to see her again."

This news brought a torrent of scorn from Mme d'Agoult: as usual, when she suspected any form of rivalry in another woman, she was merciless. "I see that you're going to entangle yourself with La Carola again! You are really naïve to think that two letters addressed to Mlle Ungher in Vienna wouldn't reach her! It would really be a pity not to make a dupe of you, you submit so readily. This business of not receiving letters is her way of making a break with her lovers, it's not very original but it's useful. Dessauer,[1] whom I saw in Wiesbaden, told me that she had decidedly lost her voice; that she only had a *succés d'estime* in Vienna; that she'd got frighteningly fat, and that she always wanted to fast – which was becoming ridiculous. Someone else who was her lover told me it wasn't worth while, which of course doesn't prevent me wishing you all possible success; but you're going to abandon a clear, simple and honourable position to take up a probably ridiculous one, take care. In my opinion La Carola is a miserable, vain, cowardly, lying creature, whom you have had the silliness (forgive me) to take seriously and who is no longer pretty enough to consider in any other way."

To this tirade Henri made a gentle enough reply: "On the subject of La Carola, I think we could compose our differences if we were to talk together, although you go far too far in your execration, don't think I'm quite such a dupe as I like to appear

[1] Joseph Dessauer, Austrian song composer.

D   49

sometimes. I happen to have the proof that she didn't get my letters: a notice from the post office in Paris that letters addressed to her there are waiting for her to claim them!" The final word comes in a letter to Marie dated December 16th, 1840, from Rome: "Today is the anniversary of my first meeting with La Ungher, a date we had engraved on two rings, almost exactly identical, which we gave one another on parting. A matter for laughter – or sober reflection."

Meanwhile another, rather more serious shadow had fallen across their relationship, which shows up Henri's extreme sensitivity about the behaviour of friends and the rather ruthless egotism of which Mme d'Agoult was occasionally capable. Writing from Naples, he tells her that the trip has given him the chance to study his fellow travellers with some care. He is full of their praises: Chevandier is "marvellously gifted" and Liszt's prophecy about his future will soon come true; but Chassériau is a real genius, and he has absolute faith in him "as a man and as a painter". The third day after his arrival in Rome he drew a portrait of a woman whom Henri had coveted as the most desirable model for years. "The conception and the execution are both magnificent." Everything falls into his lap; but he deserves this good fortune because of "the beauty of his talent, the ardour of his youthful ambition, his sensibility, the nobility of his sentiments and his ideas which he expresses with an originality and brilliance equal to the charm and natural distinction of his manners". One could scarcely go further in hero-worship; Henri waxes indignant about those who criticise Chassériau for occasionally not having bothered to shave or put on a clean shirt; and he tells Marie that he is confident such trifles will not stand in the way of her appreciating him.

The greater the enthusiasm, the deeper the disillusionment. Henri was certainly right about Chassériau's promise of genius – he was perhaps the only pupil of Ingres who truly deserves that description – but wrong about him as a man. Chassériau, it seems, was as happy-go-lucky in his behaviour as he was in his dress.

A month later, after their return to Rome, Henri writes: "*A propos de Chassériau*, I don't retract anything I've said or written about him, but I must tell you about a little episode which I find absolutely inexplicable. You remember that Franz used always to urge me to make the acquaintance of the Abbé Lacordaire,[1] and paint his portrait. He spoke about it again when we met in Paris, and I had made up my mind to follow his advice when I set out. On the journey, while we were all discussing our future plans, I told Chassériau about this idea. In Naples we happened to talk about it again, and it was even arranged that Chevandier should take me to the Abbé. But in Rome Chevandier was deeply involved with a mistress someone was trying to get away from him – and so on and so on – and as according to Chassériau he was in an inflamed state of jealousy about her, even where his friends were concerned, I thought it wise not to trouble him. I left my card on them, they came to visit me, and it seemed to me proper to ask to see Chassériau's work as he had seen mine. He made excuses, and one fine day Fries[2] informs me that he is painting the portrait of the Abbé Lacordaire and that the Abbé himself had asked him to (which is a lie). I must admit that I was outraged at first, then I tried to find excuses for him, putting it down to forgetfulness, but his evasions, the embarrassment of Chevandier when I naïvely asked him for the Abbé's address,[3] prove to me that he knows what he's doing." Henri goes on bitterly to denounce the ingratitude of the two young painters he had admired so much, but tells Marie that he contented himself with refusing to dine at their table any more. To make matters worse, Chassériau sent him a note by one of his models containing a small sum which he owed him, and excused

[1] The Abbé Lacordaire was one of the outstanding Churchmen of the time, an advanced liberal and an extremely popular preacher during the July Monarchy. A portrait of him would have been bound to attract publicity.

[2] A fellow painter and neighbour of Henri's in the Palazetto Borghese.

[3] It is clear from the text that Henri wanted the Abbé's address in order to send him the letter quoted on p. 53.

himself for not coming himself because he was "obliged to take advantage of the absence of the Abbé from Rome to sketch in the background and the clothes of his portrait," thus pretending that Henri of course knew all about what he had obviously tried to hide from him. "I am so disgusted with my fellow men, that I live more alone than ever."

It is characteristic of Henri that even after this shock to his idealistic nature he should try to defend his double-crossing friend against the prejudices of their master, Ingres. It was as if Ingres sensed that his pupil was only to become great by transcending his teaching; Henri's intuition about this, too, was remarkable. "Monsieur Ingres is grotesquely wrong about Chassériau," he writes in the same letter, "I think he's really jealous of him – this between ourselves – because he runs down works which are truly admirable, and above all conceived in the spirit he tries to inculcate in his pupils, in an absolutely shocking way. He says he is false, timid, without wit or conversation, whereas he is in fact just the opposite . . . The confessions of these two men of genius, one of whom represents the past and the other the future, the perspicacity with which they recognize the impossibility of getting on with one another, which comes through, in the case of the younger man in spite of respect and admiration, in the case of the older man in spite of the gratification he ought to feel in having had such a pupil, interest me immensely. Far from having made capital out of the remarks they have let fall, I have tried on the contrary to bring them together, at least for the time being, by concealing their antipathy. All the same, I couldn't prevent myself mentioning the incident in question to M. Ingres, who drew far worse conclusions from it than I did; but, I repeat, his judgement is warped."

Henri must have felt the blow all the more keenly, because on his return to Italy he had been suffering from one of his periodic bouts of depression; perhaps brought on by the end of the affair with Carola Ungher. He tells Marie that his brother Rudolf had been deeply alarmed by the state he was in when he arrived in Rome. "I could feel neither joy nor peace, I was like a vegetable, I wasn't alive." Concealing the squalid intrigue about the portrait, he wrote to the Abbé Lacordaire for spiritual advice. He confessed his inner sufferings in a touching letter, which contains this anguished appeal for help: "I felt that I owe it to those who depend on me in this world to make one further effort to remain in it, and I thought that if there is a man who can bring peace to another man it can only be one who has known how to make a haven for himself in the rock of the eternal verities."

In these circumstances, Mme d'Agoult's sympathy was all important to him. But she appears only to have replied very briefly to his outburst, and as if not particularly interested. "I'm not surprised," she wrote to him from Fontainebleau at the beginning of October, "at the Chassériau-Chevandier affair, I am only surprised when I hear of something good in this world. I am sorry about the Lacordaire portrait, it would have been good publicity for you. I am even more sorry that you should have such illusions about friendships: luckily the Zy fortress is more impregnable than ever." At Fontainebleau Mme d'Agoult had found a new peace and happiness. She recovered from her illness; she had Blandine and Cosima with her, and Madame Liszt; in October Franz joined them for a few weeks, and something of the old intimacy seems to have returned to them. In fact she had little time for the miseries of others. Henri appears to have been hurt by her attitude, and returned to the attack in the months that followed. In January 1841 he wrote complaining that he had not heard from her for over two months. "Don't leave me in this uncertainty about your existence!" he begged her. "My life is monotonous, my days are filled with work, most of my evenings are spent in a sort of academy where costumes are designed, sometimes I pay a visit to two or three families I know, sometimes I make up a party of whist – for which I have a craze at the moment. As for benevolent illusions, I continue to learn. Little Chassériau is a new proof. He really is a despicable person, and in saying that, once more, I've not let myself be carried away by personal impressions. On the contrary, I've taken his part alone against every one else and right up to the last moment, but in the end I couldn't hold out any more, his behaviour has been too shocking and too unworthy on so many occasions. Don't encourage him in any way, I ought almost to say don't receive him, because, thinking in spite of everything that he might amuse you I wanted to give him a message for you; but his response was of such a nature that I wish to avoid at all costs the possibility of him boasting that he refused your invitations; far better that the contrary should be the case. M. Ingres had an extraordinary intuition about him: I opposed it with all my might, as a good friend, but I'm obliged to admit that it was correct."

The worst, however, was to come. At the beginning of February Marie wrote him a long, gossiping letter, in which she appeared to dismiss the subject of Chassériau: "I shall certainly not see him!" Unfortunately, before she sent the letter off Chassériau and she had met, and she added an ominous postscript: "Yesterday evening Chassériau came to my house, there was a crowd of people – it was one of my days. I received him politely. I thought it better if I knew absolutely nothing, and so I asked him about M. Ingres, about you, and about Chevandier. To the question: 'Have you brought some paintings back with you?' he replied, 'The portrait of M. Lacordaire' – 'Oh! Oh! but that was very well timed!' – 'But it was also by chance, because I have known M. Lacordaire for a long time, and he asked me to paint his portrait a long time ago.' Apart from that, he seemed to me neither timid nor boorish, as you suggested last spring, but very well behaved. He examined my portrait, praised and criticized it with great propriety. As he took his leave, he begged me to visit his *atelier*. I shall do so. If you were here and you found it disagreeable to meet him, I wouldn't invite him to my house, but as things are I must behave exactly as if I knew nothing special about him: neither over-solicitous, nor rude, neither standing up for him, nor hostile."

How convenient to be able to say that she must pretend she

knew nothing; but how cruel to give this as a reason for being ready to visit the rival *atelier*! The situation was comic, but the comedy was painful enough for Henri. If she had for a moment reflected, Marie must have realized that her postscript would give her friend, the elected "sharer of her sorrows", a disagreeable shock. She had implied that she would be on her guard, but seeing the budding genius of twenty-one boldly enter her salon, she allowed herself to be carried away at once by his effrontery, his charm and his flattery. And in her excitement she did not hesitate to let Henri know that she thought he was being absurd about Chassériau. Or was she perhaps unable, on a sudden impulse of malice, to resist repaying Henri for his advice about her quarrel with George Sand? Whatever the explanation, she succeeded in inflaming Henri's wounded feelings. His agitation, his bitterness are clear in his reply – which, curiously enough, was only sent a month later. "The way Chassériau introduced himself to you obliges me to come back to the whole disagreeable business, at greater length and more seriously than I intended. I simply asked you not to make any overtures to him, because when I said to him, in front of several other people, 'As you will no doubt see Mme d'Agoult,' he interrupted me with a very self-satisfied air, 'No, certainly not. I have no intention of going there.' So I said nothing, finding his remark as rude to you as it was to me. Since then, certain things have come to light which force me to revise my first opinion of him as altogether too hasty. During our voyage, he talked to me, with a naïveté I found rather charming, about all his remarkable qualities of heart and mind. I really was impressed by his gift for admiring himself, but at the same time I said to myself, 'Why shouldn't he share this feeling of his own worth with a friend?' I've seen him since, with his 'fine sensibility and noble sentiments' run after people he pretended to despise, when he had need of them, make false confidences to these people about his alleged friends, in order to do harm to the latter, and leave other people who had put themselves and their means – of which he had not failed to avail himself – entirely at his

55

disposal, for a week, ill in bed – and in the end offer them his little finger to bid them good-bye . . . He found a woman of the highest social position, who overwhelmed him with kindnesses and who is the sister of his most intimate friend, to say she would not have continued to receive him if she hadn't been afraid of upsetting her brother. She even said that on several occasions she'd invited the Abbé Lacordaire with M. Chassériau, in order to make him better known to the latter, although the invitation deprived her of the opportunity for intimate conversation with the Abbé *who would have been unwilling to talk freely in front of a young man whom he knew only slightly.* You see how that fits in with the supposed long and intimate association! I tell you all this, because it distresses me that in spite of your tact, your gift for reading people's characters in their faces and your great prudence, you have unfortunately allowed yourself to be involved with brazen liars and have trusted people who are scandalously indiscreet. You will say in reply: 'But I don't want to be closely associated with M. Chassériau, who as far as I am concerned is simply a young man of talent and intelligence whom I receive like anyone else.' He, however, seems to have other ambitions. Recently, some people were asking about you and Franz, and when I answered in what seemed to me a proper way, they looked as if they were falling out of the clouds: but M. Chassériau informed us that 'although Lehmann has been Mme d'Agoult's lover, he told me certain things that make me think that Liszt is not very well disposed towards him, and I would like . . .' And then with an outrageous conceit he declared his ridiculous pretensions towards you. Double treachery: to believe the opposite of what a man who has never lied to him tells him, and to try and make others believe that I actually spoke to him in a way that would support his infamous conclusions. Women having failed to make us quarrel, I don't think *gamins* are going to have any greater success. Believe me, telling you all this wearies me, disgusts me, and I would far rather have kept quiet about many of these details, but his abrupt arrival at your house, following on the pretensions he revealed here, and which I have only learnt since his departure, oblige me not to leave you in any doubt about the sly little humbug's inordinate ambitions."

Disastrously, this letter crossed one from Mme d'Agoult which can only have added fuel to the fire of Henri's distress. She seems, momentarily, to have completely lost her head about Chassériau. "You will see that my opinion of him is exactly the opposite of yours!" she cries, and goes on to describe how she immediately accepted the invitation to visit Chassériau's *atelier*, and went on the following Monday with Sainte-Beuve. His portraits she found superb, and Henri's criticism of one of them entirely unjust, adding with perhaps unconscious cruelty that the portrait of the Abbé Lacordaire had particularly impressed her. She invited him to dinner, on which occasion she reports that he captivated all her friends, including Henry Bulwer, Louis de Ronchaud and Alfred de Vigny; that he had asked to be allowed to draw something for her album, a crayon portrait of her and portraits of any of her friends she liked to propose as well. "In fact," she writes, "my impression is that he's a young man it would be difficult to think ill of without proof. I think he's full of self-confidence, but not to the point of absurdity; very clever, but does his cleverness go as far as intrigue and treachery? I find it impossible to believe. I remain on my guard, but I think you have been wrongly influenced and deceived about him." Wasn't the friendship of Chevandier, a person of the greatest probity, a proof of this? She even went so far as to have a long conversation with him about Henri, and read passages from Henri's letters in which he had expressed his admiration for him. She thought there were explanations for his apparent bad behaviour over the Lacordaire portrait, and that Ingres had made mischief. "In short, it seemed to me that you ought not to have quarrelled, and I tried to say everything that might make it possible, and necessary, for your relations with him to be restored to their old warmth."

Knowing that Mme d'Agoult had meanwhile received his earlier letter, Henri did not reply at once. When he did, it was with a calm it must have taken some effort to achieve. He begs her to think that his only object was to preserve her from the intrigues of someone he was convinced was a bad hat. He thanks her for trying to make peace between himself and Chassériau, but insists again, a little tartly, that no personal animosity entered into it on his side. "There remain two possibilities: one, that I was influenced by unfortunate coincidences, and therefore misunderstood what I saw and heard, and that all the people who spoke about him to me wanted to deceive me or were deceived themselves. In that case, time will teach me and I shall be only too glad to make honourable amends. Or you have been carried away by the crafty behaviour of someone who is very cold and very cunning, and who knows only too well how to adapt it to his own needs and desires: you know all about the latter now!"

It seems likely that Mme d'Agoult's Chassériau fever was considerably cooled when she eventually received Henri's first letter; or perhaps she suddenly realized that her friendship with Henri was in serious danger. In any case, her references to Chassériau after this are extremely cautious. "I assure you," she writes in April, "that I have no infatuation for Chassériau. I think you do him too great an honour in dressing him up as Mephistopheles; in any case don't be afraid of any indiscretion on my part, or – I believe I can say – any open hostility on his part towards you. He has made a drawing of me which I find good, and a good likeness, but it has not found favour because he has drawn me with my mouth open . . ." Perhaps Henri had the last word. Writing to her a few days later, he says: "You should know that Chassériau, whose friendship with Chevandier you thought such a great guarantee of good character has rewarded that friend for his generous behaviour and kindnesses by remarks and actions that I prefer not to describe, but which were such as to make all future relations between them impossible. It was Chevandier himself who told me the facts, and the result, and if you need the testimony of someone calmer and less suspect of bias or weakness of judgement, I suggest Father Lacordaire who has had the time to study the gentleman in question and is entirely of my opinion."

We do not know how deep a scar was left on the friendship between Marie and Henri by this affair. They do not appear to have exchanged many letters during the rest of 1841, but they may not have survived. More probably, the hiatus occurred because Mme d'Agoult felt that her position in Paris was increasingly secure, and her *salon* and circle of friends occupied more and more of her time. In addition there had been a new development in her life, which was to be of crucial importance to her when the long dreaded final separation from Liszt took place a few years later. During her early days in the Faubourg St Germain she had been introduced to a young poet, Delphine Gay, whose looks and talents had made her extremely popular. They became affectionate friends, from the very first time of meeting. Soon after Mme d'Agoult's return to Paris they met again one evening at the theatre, and their friendship was renewed with all the old warmth. Some years before, Delphine Gay had married Emile de Girardin, a well-known political journalist and editor of one of the most influential Paris papers, *La Presse*. Delphine invited Marie at once to one of her big literary dinners, and Marie in return invited the Girardins to her *salon*. They began to see a great deal of one another, and Delphine's husband gradually fell in love with her; thus joining the circle of devoted men friends, Henry Bulwer, Louis de Ronchaud, Sainte-Beuve and perhaps Henri himself, each of whom, it seems, entertained hopes at one time or another that when the inevitable end of her affair with Liszt arrived, he might be the lucky successor. Nothing, however, happened to disturb the friendly relations of the three of them; but Emile de Girardin's love gave him acute insight into Mme d'Agoult's powers of mind and imagination, and he began to believe that she could become a remarkable writer. Finally he persuaded her to write a piece of art criticism for *La Presse*, which appeared under the pseudonym of "Daniel Stern". It was a success. Slowly, a new Marie was born: critic, political commentator and novelist. Emile de Girardin had opened the way that was to save her when she found herself once more alone.

There are constant mentions of her new friends and allies in the letters to Henri. "The Girardins, and *La Presse*, at my command," she writes in October 1840. And a month later: "Delphine continues to be very good to me, her husband even better, he's a very interesting man." It seems that Mme d'Agoult began to think of her friendship with Delphine de Girardin as a kind of substitute for, or triumph over her ruined relationship with George Sand. "I haven't seen Mme Sand," she writes in January 1841, "she's written a novel which isn't selling – a fact which doesn't make her any the better humoured. Delphine is more radiant, more amusing, more triumphant than ever. Her husband, whom I see practically every day, has any amount of very zyotic qualities." She also begins to reveal her increasing interest in politics. In February 1841, after telling Henri that the Girardins are more and more attached to her and that she has entirely ceased to see George Sand, and adding maliciously that the Abbé de Lamennais "is supporting his prison sentence very well, he refuses to see any women, I think it's because he doesn't want to see Mme Sand", she observes that "political questions dominate everything else. We've got the fortifications now, it's a great triumph for Thiers and will bring him back to the centre of things. There's now a party all in favour of a Russian alliance. All in all, one is pretty well discouraged, and humiliated, very irritated with the King and one looks on all sides to find the great man who will lead us gloriously back to our salvation. But the great man doesn't appear to have been born yet ... Unless it's Daniel?"

The Abbé de Lamennais, whom Mme d'Agoult mentions in her letter, was one of the most extraordinary and fascinating figures of the time. A brilliant intellectual of the Church, a radical who had already quarrelled with the Pope and put his own interpretation on the scriptures to the scandal of his fellow-churchmen, he had been become an immensely influential journalist as editor, with Charles Didier, of *Le Monde*. His sentence of one year's imprisonment, when he was over sixty, was caused by an outspoken attack on the Government, in a famous polemic called *Le Pays et le Gouvernment*. But many years before, he had appeared in Mme d'Agoult's life in rather a dramatic way. Deeply interested in Liszt, he had somehow managed to extract from him a confession that he was in love with Marie and was about to elope with her. He hurried up from his estate in Brittany, and presented himself at Mme d'Agoult's house, insisting on seeing her. In a long and emotional interview he tried to persuade her to give up the project: to his surprise, he found her as obstinate and determined as he was himself. In spite of this, and his hostility towards her growing feminist ideas, and in curious contradiction to his general radicalism, "Monsieur Féli" remained good friends with her. In her *Mémoires* she described him vividly enough: "He was very small. His face was furrowed with frightening lines. His huge aquiline nose, the oblique, piercing glance of his eyes, gave him something of the look of a beast of prey . . . He had a bilious, violent temperament, at the same time suspicious and credulous. In his affections there was a lightning changeability which led him to behave with shocking injustice. Never any moderation, nothing temperate, very little attention to facts, very little reflection. Angel or demon: one was never in his eyes a simple human being."

Meanwhile Henri, in Rome, was devoting himself, with a kind of monastic fervour, almost exclusively to his artistic labours. One can guess that he was feeling more than usually doubtful of himself, unable to finish any picture that satisfied his acute sense of self-criticism, and not, apparently, lifted from his depression by his success in the Salon of 1840. Mme d'Agoult tried to encourage him to get down to hard work but at the same time to enjoy the simple pleasures of life, "don't be too virtuous, admire others a little less and respect yourself a little more." To which Henri replied: "Even before your excellent advice arrived, I'd begun to plunge myself into work, in fact I have five or six pictures in train. In the matter of innocent pleasures as recommended by you, I have allowed myself to paint the four most beautiful girls one can obtain as models in Rome, two heads and two heads and shoulders in costume . . . The best way for me not to admire others too much is not to see them at all, which is exactly what I am doing. I am at home to nobody, and I dine alone." The chief pictures on which he was at work were a portrait of the Comtesse de Perthuis, wife of King Louis-Philippe's A.D.C. (eventually exhibited at the Salon of 1842), a large composition of the *Flagellation* (also exhibited in 1842) and a group of female bathers inspired by Victor Hugo. In February 1841 he writes to Mme d'Agoult: "My four *baigneuses* after Victor Hugo were planned to be finished for the Carnival, but won't be ready before the end of the month. After that, during the serious days of Lent, I shall begin to occupy myself exclusively with the *Flagellation*. Apart from that, I go on making studies of heads, portraits of friends, and among other sketches one of the grand-daughter of the Duchess of Cambridge, an absolutely adorable child."

To Mme d'Agoult's words of encouragement, was added a heart-warming letter from Liszt to his "cher Clear": "I would envy you if I didn't love you so much, my very dear friend. You live according to the impulses of your mind and heart. What you imagine, what you dream, what you conceive, all goes on to your canvas, you express it with a candid splendour, alone, all-powerful in your retreat in the Borghese Palace. You escape contact with men in the mass, which is almost always degrading. The god of painting can live quietly within your soul; the discordant noises of the outside world do not come at every moment to disturb him and, miserably, to interrupt his grave, unhurried revelation. The approval or the disapproval of the multitude, the meaningless applause or the sottish absence of applause of the public do not affect you directly, immediately. And then, your work remains! It continues to exist through the years – through the centuries. How lucky is the painter of genius! How lucky you are, dear Clear. As for me, I can do little but resign myself to my role as public clown. Every day I find myself in a different city, a different country. Would you believe, for instance, that I've given more than fifty concerts during the last five weeks! So here I am absolutely exhausted, practically incapable of any further effort."

Henri's determination to try and exorcise his demons by rigorous concentration on his painting, was interrupted by appeals from his *cher maître*. Ingres had finished the famous *Antiochus et Stratonice*, commissioned by the Duc d'Orléans, early in 1840, and by September Mme d'Agoult reported that it was having a wild success in Paris, with all the critics praising it to the skies; adding, characteristically, that George Sand was against it simply because she thought that Marie and Ingres were close friends. Henri, in reply, told her that Ingres seemed profoundly pleased, and was emerging at last from the mood of sullen bitterness which had dominated him since his arrival in Rome. At the same time he confided to her that the master, aware perhaps of the short time that remained to him in Rome before his return to Paris, had called him in to help with the details of the paintings on which he was still at work. "I am working, too, for M. Ingres, but you must not mention this because he intends to pass off what I am doing for him as his own – though of course he will re-touch it." Some weeks later, he adds that he was obliged to drop his own painting in these circumstances. "I had to choose between not sending anything to the Salon, and refusing my old master a service and failing to fulfil a duty which piety demanded and which in any case could be very useful to me from the point of view of artistic education. So I promised to help, and I give him all the time he asks for, subordinating my own work to his needs. I shall not tell you what I'm doing for him, because he has asked me to be as discreet as possible. Enough, if I tell you that he allots me some of the most important parts of the work and that he's very pleased." According to Vicomte Delaborde, the chief pictures with which Henri helped at this time were the portraits of Cherubini and the *Virgin with the Host*. At the end of the work,

Ingres offered to pay Henri handsomely, but he refused to accept any money. As a farewell present, however, he gave Henri a study for his picture *The Martyrdom of St Symphorian*. "The way he apologized for only offering me that was quite adorable."

The celebrations prepared by the students for their master on his departure at the end of March had their faintly comic side. Henri was one of the committee of three charged with organizing a banquet, which was attended by sixty artists of almost every nationality. If they had hoped that an atmosphere of conviviality would develop, they were disappointed. The gloom that had enveloped the Villa Medici during the whole of Ingres's reign failed to disperse, and their hero remained as unsociable and St Bernard-like as ever. On the next day they accompanied him as far as the Ponte Milvio. Good-byes were exchanged with tears on both sides, after which Ingres, casting a last glance at the dome of St Peter's, pronounced, with sobs choking his voice, a few theatrical words of farewell to Raphael. When, however, the *vetturino* had disappeared into the distance and the students made their way back to the Villa Medici, according to one witness a curious thing happened: instead of a suitable sadness, a sudden mood of crazy relief and gaiety possessed them, they wanted to laugh and sing as if a great weight had been lifted from their shoulders, and the future appeared infinitely free and rich in possibilities of delicious adventure.

In Paris, Ingres entered at last into his own. He became the lion of the day, a gigantic banquet and a concert were given in his honour, and the King invited him to dinner at Neuilly. Mme d'Agoult sent reports to Henri. "As soon as I knew that M. Ingres had arrived I hurried to their address. They were out; two days later they were at my house. We were affectionate and charming to one another. He was delighted with my look of health in face and figure. Mme Ingres talked about Daniel, she was full of interest, in fact I was enchanted with them. As for you, you can imagine the praises they heaped upon you, noble spirit, devoted friend, etc. etc." The name of Chassériau was mentioned, where-

3a. Princess Christine
Trivulzio Belgiojoso
by Henri Lehmann

3b. Théodore Chassériau: a
self-portrait in early youth
(*Louvre*)

4a and b. Two drawings by Henri Lehmann from the Louis Bonnat Collection (Bayonne)

upon indignant complaints were poured out and comparisons were made between Henri and "a gentleman who behaved rather too conceitedly towards his master". Mme d'Agoult commented: "their enthusiasm for you has reached a tropical temperature." In a later letter she described the happy effect his triumphant return had had upon the master: "he is radiant, he finds Paris the first city in the world, Versailles magnificent, the King charming, all the women adorable, all the painters eminent, etc. etc. Delaroche was at the banquet, Delacroix was not. He and Mme Sand continue to talk of M. Ingres' *chinoiseries*. As for me, I also had my own little banquet for him, with Victor Hugo, Mrs. Mignet, Ampère, Duban and Balzac. At the famous public banquet M. Ingres embraced Chassériau, and the next day they had a long conversation together, which I fancy won't change the master's objections the least bit, especially as Mme Ingres is absolutely implacable, but at least decent appearances have been restored."

Henri's letters to Mme d'Agoult during the latter part of 1840 and 1841 are full of reports of "Prince" Daniel, whom he had brought back from Palestrina to Rome to keep him under his own eye. "I had your Danielesque letter this morning" she wrote to him in May. "What can I say to you? That you are the best of friends and that I daren't think of all the trouble and bother you've had on my behalf. The aforesaid Prince will be brought up in the fear of God and Henri Lehmann, I promise you. If the creature is not devoted to you, I shall strangle him with my own hands." In September she finally decided to bring him home to Paris, and sent Mme Belloni, the mother of Liszt's secretary, to fetch him. Soon after, Henri himself decided to leave Rome, feeling that he had absorbed everything that the city could give him, especially now that Ingres had gone, and growing impatient to resume his career in the centre of things. In addition, plans were on foot to give him a commission to decorate the Church of Saint-Merry; urged on by Mme d'Agoult Ingres was lending his powerful support. Henri returned to Paris, this time for good, in January 1842.

E

In the Spring of 1841 he had made an interesting friend. "I have recently met an Englishman called Handley," he tells Marie, "who is the most original and the most cultivated person you can imagine. He has read everything, and often comes out with remarkable ideas. He can understand all languages, speaks them all very badly, but knows their literature. If he ever crosses your line of vision, give him a place in your zyotic chapel, he will make an excellent part of its decor." Evidently they saw a great deal of one another, because a few months later Henri writes again: "With the Englishman I spoke to you about, I spent several days in the Sistine Chapel: he gave me his view as man of learning and poet, and in return I lent him my artistic eyes. I was happy to catch a glimpse of that side of art of which vanity, ignorance and laziness deprive most artists – the metaphysical side which we have so much difficulty in believing existed with the ancients because it exists so little with us, and because it didn't prevent them achieving, to a degree impossible for us to attain, the one thing we are able to appreciate: the beauty of means and execution ... This friend, with his cultivated and inquiring mind, his passionate devotion to it all, and his immense knowledge of the philosophers and poets of all literatures, helped me to admire, with far more understanding of what lay behind, to stand stupefied in fact before that colossus who remains silent and unknown in our artistically barren age, like the sphinx in the sands of the desert. You know I have always been deeply impressed by the vault and the *pendentifs*, but I can say that I did not grasp the full meaning of *The Last Judgement* until now. There is nothing else in my life worth talking about."

It must have been soon after this that the family home in Hamburg was burnt to the ground. Leo wrote to his son Rudolf that he could no longer support him in any way, as the younger brothers and sisters had first claim on his reduced resources. For a time Henri had to provide for him entirely; but in 1842 Rudolf had his first success with a picture exhibited in the Paris Salon of that year: the first step in a long and successful career.

IV

My great-uncle's friendship with Mme d'Agoult appears to have lasted another six or seven years. After the Revolution of 1848, for no precise reason that can now be discovered, they drifted apart. It is probable that as she turned more and more towards politics, and filled her *salon* with political notabilities, he felt that there was less and less place for him; but during the early years of his return to Paris they saw a great deal of one another. Marie desperately needed his loyalty and affection, for the great crisis of her life was approaching. With Louis de Ronchaud, and his friends the German poet Georg Herwegh and his wife Emma, whom he had introduced into Marie's *salon*, Henri was one of the small group of intimates on whom Marie leaned for support and consolation when the agony of the final break with Liszt began. Inevitably, as they were now neighbours in Paris, no letters exist; but there are many little scribbled notes from Marie which testify to her misery and confusion of spirit. "Think of me as a sick soul," she cries at one moment, and again, "If after your work you find the courage to come and distract me for a while, it would be an act of true charity. But I can neither think nor speak, so prepare yourself for a monologue."

During the winter of 1843–4 Liszt had been giving a series of fantastically successful concerts in the major cities of Germany, while his amorous adventures became more and more reckless, culminating in the flamboyant liaison with Lola Montez, acted out in full view of a maliciously amused public. At the same time he was still assuring Marie in his letters of his changeless devotion to her. But she seems to have been well aware of what was going on, and began to realize at last that their ways of life were incompatible. Her growing desperation is reflected in the little notes to Henri. "Your letter brought tears to my eyes," she wrote a few weeks before Christmas. "Sainte-Beuve is coming at four o'clock. I shall have my whole evening free. So come as soon as possible after your dinner. You know that mine is a kind of fiction, a pretence, a phantom that's gone before one has had time to see it. Love me very much so that you can always love me." And later: "I didn't say good-bye to you as I should have. I'm suffocating with misery; but I love you, and my apparent rudeness is nothing but an overwrought fear of collapsing into tears and emotional scenes." In spite of the fact that there were only nine years between them in age, and they were both in their thirties, Henri has now become the "*cher benjamin de ma vieillesse*", and is addressed from now on as "*mon fils*" or "*mon vieux fils*".

Liszt returned to Paris after many delays, in April. He tried at once to force his way back into Mme d'Agoult's life, but she had steeled herself to refuse to see him. He was shocked, and his vanity was wounded, but when he saw that it was hopeless the practical side of his nature took over, and he sent her several letters in which he coolly and sensibly discussed the future of their children. "It will not enter my mind ever to oppose the plan for their education on which you may decide," he wrote to her on May 7th. "You can be completely reassured as regards the financial arrangements I shall make."

As soon as this was settled, Marie decided to leave Paris and take a long rest with her mother in Touraine. But there was after all a dramatic, last-minute farewell meeting between the former lovers. On May 18th she wrote to Henri from the country: "Ronchaud will have told you, or will soon tell you about our journey. I spent several hours of the night before my departure at the Hotel Byron. Liszt was ill. We talked of you. Try to visit him. I left him without any scenes, and in a softened mood; while that lasts I want you to see him. I want you also to let me know exactly the state of his health. If the occasion arises, I want you to talk to him gently and seriously. Don't give him any advice, but don't admit that I haven't been absolutely right." She goes on to ask him to get in touch with the Abbé de Lamennais, as she believes that the latter has been talking to Liszt and may have considerable influence on him. "Tell Liszt again that I have never complained about anything. Write to me soon. Don't count on getting many letters from me. Solitude does me good, I shall be able to work well. That last scene in the Hotel Byron proved to me that I was very strong, but I need to be absolutely alone for a time."

Henri wrote back at once. "Ronchaud didn't turn up, but I knew of your nocturnal visit from Liszt himself. The evening of the day you left I heard of his illness. My first impulse was to go and see him at once, then I thought that such haste might appear a little affected, especially at such an hour (it was past eleven o'clock), so I put off my visit to the morning. He was sleeping when I arrived. When he woke up he asked me to come in, and seemed to me very much better. I spoke to him quietly and affectionately, and asked how he was. He said to me 'Mme d'Agoult has gone, I think. I saw her yesterday. It appears that I called out for her in my delirium, and my well-meaning devil of a servant thought that I was in earnest and went to look for her . . . She came, she stayed here for an hour.' After a few seconds of silence, I said: 'One always finds her when one needs her.' As I was completely ignorant about what had passed between you, I didn't dare say anything more, so the matter rested there . . . I left after having spent an hour with him."

The next day Henri wrote again: "I went back two days later. The improvement in his condition was even more striking. Nevertheless, he can't move without pain, and the concert's out of the question. I found Daniel there, saying good-bye, and Villers[1] . . . There was talk of Heine's article, which Franz had not read. 'What's more, I'd very much like to know – and those gentlemen would be very embarrassed to explain to me – what they mean by my absurdities.' Silence. 'In my public life, of course.' Another silence. 'In any case (referring to Heine's mean insinuations) it's not their fault, it's more or less the fault of their profession, almost everyone's the same.' I said that I didn't agree, and if it wasn't possible for everyone to follow their profession with distinction they could at least do so simply and honestly, it was a matter of the will . . ." After describing the endless rain in northern France, and

[1] Alexander de Villers, a diplomatist and friend of Liszt.

the impossibility of working at his mural decorations in the church of Saint-Merry owing to the dampness of the walls, he comes back to the theme of Liszt. "Your blindness was so great that I couldn't believe it. I deserve far less praise than you imagine for not having said anything about it, for I was convinced that you knew and had made up your mind about it, and that you preferred never to speak about it, in fact to pretend that you didn't know. In any case, I've had the great satisfaction of seeing my prophecy about the attitude of the world come true. The day before yesterday I found myself with Alfred de Vigny at Mme de X's house. She certainly doesn't adore you, but she condemned Liszt in the most severe and just way, accusing him of everything of which he is really guilty, and finding his behaviour inexcusable, even if – she added – you were the most impossible and exacting person in the world. Vigny was splendid, defending Franz a little, saying that unfortunately he belonged, body and soul, to a race that had no human feeling at all, the race of actors, and so on. As you can imagine, he was on your side. I was sorry that my memory is not so exactly retentive as it was once. Mme de X represents a part of society whose judgements carry some weight with you, that's why I repeat all this."

Mme d'Agoult replied: "Your letter gave me great pleasure. I still had a little bit of anxiety left for the Great Man. Now I am completely restored. The most difficult step has been taken, from now on nothing can shake me. I am very happy that your relations with him should have continued so naturally. Please go on giving me all the details you can." Henri commented with relief: "I needed to be reassured about the effect that nocturnal episode had had on you. You found that you were strong, you will remain strong for ever, because I fancy that the most tragic theatrical persuasions were used that night."

In a later letter Mme d'Agoult comes back to Henri's accusation that she had been blind about Liszt's behaviour: "I was blinded not about his acts, which were perfectly clear to me and filled me with bitterness, but about their deeper source which I refused to understand. I considered each one in isolation, they fell on my head like meteors which fall from heaven knows where. I kept on saying to myself 'another stone, but it will be the last' and now there's a permanent hail of them!"

There is no evidence that Henri ever saw Liszt again. Mme d'Agoult reported in this same summer of 1844 that he had said to a mutual friend: "If you like Mendelssohn, you will like Lehmann very much, because he's a kind of Mendelssohn", so it seems that his affectionate feelings for Henri were unchanged by the break with Mme d'Agoult. As far as we know, the last letter he ever sent him had been in the previous year, from St Petersburg, to thank him for a drawing of the portrait of Mme d'Agoult which he had particularly wanted to have. In this letter, he mentioned again how often he thought of the happy days they had spent together in Lucca and Rome, "there are some things which take root in one's memory, while others disappear altogether", and concluded: "Keep for me, my dear Lehmann, your 'clear and placid' friendship, and never fear that I shall lose mine for you, however troubled and buffeted by storms my poor life may be."

Of the letters that passed between Henri and Mme d'Agoult during that summer, many of Henri's appear to be lost. We see him in the early ones keeping up her spirits with lively descriptions of the gossip and goings-on in the circles they were both familiar with. "Mme Recamier doesn't appear in the least upset by the failure of Rancé[1]," he writes in May. "She made an appointment with me, and came up specially from the country to ask me to do a sort of idealized portrait of her for the daughter of Prince Augustus of Prussia, following the documents of the time, a portrait which should be at the same time a kind of reminiscence of Gérard's. Definitely, she finds herself to be a lady of infinite charm. If I succeed, she will accept a replica from me for Chateaubriand." Two years before, Henri had made a drawing of

[1] La Vie de Rancé by Chateaubriand, with whom Mme Recamier was now living.

Chateaubriand, and now did a portrait of Mme Recamier which was given to Chateaubriand. A little later he sends her a glowing account of the first night of *Antigone*, at the Théâtre-Français, particularly of the scenic effects; "a thousand times better than everything I've seen in modern drama, even where the effect of the scene had been achieved at great expense . . . Mme Sand was weeping in torrents, she said to Monsieur Léo that she'd pay another visit to the show, to see if it stood up to a second view, and, if it did, well, so much the worse for all the poetry that has been written since Sophocles!" In the same letter, he describes a visit to the Abbé de Lamennais: "He wasn't alone, but I shall return as soon as possible. I found Béranger there, and it was priceless to see those two old men, both so detached from the world, the one in his mood of bitter sadness, the other in his jovial *bonhomie*, discussing with such fine (and almost kindly) irony, so many people and things: Laffitte who was fading out, Chateaubriand who had outlived himself, Mlle Rachel, Walewski in Poland, Russia, everything was brought up. It was the oddest kind of contrast to go from them to the Princess Radziwill's, where the Count of Syracuse, brother of the King of Naples, and the Duke of Bauffremont were conversing, in rather less stimulating fashion, about the advantages and disadvantages of railways."

Mme d'Agoult does not seem to have remained shattered by the Liszt affair for very long. She was indeed, as she had discovered, very strong; and writing was the means by which she rebuilt her fallen house. At Monnaye she plunged herself into work on her novel *Nélida*,[1] a title which was an obvious anagram of her new *nom de plume*, Daniel (Stern). *Nélida* was eventually serialized in *La Revue Independante* early in 1846, against the advice of her friend Béranger who warned her that it would be a *succès de scandale*, but was not really good and would do her no good. She admitted afterwards that he had been right; but at the time she

[1] In her *Mémoires*, Mme d'Agoult says that she wrote the novel at the house she rented in Herblay in 1845–6 from her friend Hortense Allart; but she mentions it in a letter to Henri from Monnaye in 1844.

was possessed by what seems an almost demonic impulse to get the better, in art if she could not in life, of the man who had caused her such suffering. *Nélida* was her public revenge against Liszt; and like all such revenges it boomeranged. "*Vous aurez des ennuis sans fin,*" Béranger had said; and it seems likely that *Nélida* was one of the chief reasons why Liszt eventually turned against her and acted so cruelly in separating her from her children. At first, as he read the instalments, he was full of praise and refused to recognize himself in the character of Guermann Régnier, the artist. Even when it had come out as a two-volume novel, he is reported to have said to a friend who asked him, perhaps rather maliciously, what he thought of it, "*Pauvre Lehmann!*" Unfortunately, the rest of the world recognized that it was meant to be a portrait of him, and certainly not of Henri; and Liszt knew this, however unaffected he might pretend to be in public. There is a scene in the novel where Guermann, commissioned to paint the murals in a museum gallery, looks round the walls and suffers a horrible sensation. "His soul was filled with doubt; he felt himself unequal to the task; he was aware of the appalling discrepancy between his abilities and his ambition." Liszt was too quick-witted not to have sensed the injury intended in this passage.

Mme d'Agoult made matters worse by writing to Liszt herself when the hubbub began, saying she had intended no harm and hoped that he would forgive her if he had misinterpreted it. Perhaps she was frightened by what she had done; if so, his answer, cool, friendly, amused on the surface but quivering with bitterness to anyone who could read between the lines, can have given her no comfort. She even wrote to Henri, who appears to have reproached her: "You are certainly not fair to me, I haven't written a book against Liszt. I have nothing to gain (even looking at it from a purely selfish point of view) from doing harm to a man who has left such a mark on my life and who is the father of my three children. I had a hard task to free myself from his dominating personality and to show him what I was . . ."

It must be admitted that in publishing *Nélida* Mme d'Agoult was not only following a fashion of the time, but reacting to considerable literary provocation. In 1842 George Sand had published her novel *Horace* which was based on the affair between Marie and Franz, and had encouraged Balzac to publish the even crueller picture in *Béatrix*. Nevertheless, in the long run she did take Béranger's advice, in that she wrote – or rather published – no more fiction. He knew she wanted to excel in one way or another; he had told her frankly that as a novelist she would never be as good as George Sand, and suggested that she ought to write about public affairs. Emile de Girardin's advice was the same. Gradually, in her retreat at Herblay, the transformation took place by which the romantic poet of disappointed love became the radical bluestocking, militant feminist and shrewd commentator of the social and political scene; and eventually historian of the 1848 Revolution. It was at Herblay that she completed her *Essay on Liberty*. In June 1846 she wrote to Henri: "I've done some heroic work during all this time: I've rewritten, re-designed and harmonized all the first part of *Liberty*, the part you read. Your observations and criticisms have been followed, the whole thing's got more life and colour now. I'm amazed at my own perseverance."

Meanwhile, she seems to have conceived the idea of turning Henri into a writer as well. He was to become an art-critic; she would correct his prose, and she could absolutely guarantee his success. She suggested a series of articles under the general title of *Letters to a Young Painter*. She hinted that such articles would be a good weapon against the anti-Henri intrigues of Chassériau's supporters, which she believed were starting again. "I insist all the more that you should write the *Letters to a Young Painter* or *Letters on Painting*. If you do that, you will create for yourself a quite distinct place, and superior to anyone else. With very little trouble you will be able to produce an entirely new book, and, based as it will be on good paintings, it will live."

At the same time she seems to have had a slightly less disinterested motive in urging Henri to become a writer. When she finally returned from the country, she wanted her *salon* to be more brilliant and famous than before. It was important for her that it should be talked about not only in France, but abroad as well. Henri was to write articles in the German press, on the *Salon der Gräfin d'Agoult*. "You shouldn't talk about me personally," she wrote to him, "but describe the rooms, and make people see the most fascinating celebrities passing through them. I'll note several points for you, there's no hurry, but I think it could be useful for us. Say that it's a very modest *salon*, rather a circle of friends. Describe the Renaissance room and the violet room (the bust, the flowers, the *objets d'art*, etc., my album, the sketches by M. Ingres and his school). Say that it was there that [François Ponsard's] *Lucrèce*[1] was first read aloud, that young Filtich[1] was first heard playing in Paris, and other nonsense of that sort. The story of M. de Lamennais, who, when the mistress of the house reproached him one day, with a smile, with having written that women couldn't reason for more than a '*demi-quart d'heure*' and maintained that the '*demi*' was particularly offensive, replied – not without a touch of malice – 'I originally put "*quart d'heure*" but on re-reading what I'd written I thought that the addition of "*demi*" made a better phrase, and my writer's weakness won the day.' Then the custom of receiving friends for supper at midnight on New Year's Day. Count de Vigny coming to read his works there, etc. etc." She goes on with further details about the writers and politicians he was to mention as frequenting the *salon*: he was to make it clear that as far as politics went, the tone was neutral, celebrities of all parties frequenting it, though it was evident that she herself leaned towards the left.

The zealous care she shows in this letter for the propaganda she wanted Henri to make on her behalf, does not leave a very pleasant taste in the mouth. There are touches, such as "with a smile", that make one smile oneself. Nevertheless, one should in her defence remember that she was apprehensive about her return to Paris, and, with her former lover gone, saw in her *salon* her one secure way to acceptance, and triumph over her detractors.

[1] Carl Filtich was a pianist, an infant prodigy who died at the age of fourteen.

There does not appear to have been any weakening of the bonds of affection between her and Henri while she was at Herblay, though we only have her letters to go by. "I beg you, make of me a sort of ideal mother, and never imagine that you've got to use any diplomacy with me. I don't like your reticences, nor your '*allées tournantes*'. I love you much more than you think and what I love most passionately in the people I love are their weaknesses or their faults. Aren't you like that?" In the Spring of 1846 Henri had an exhibition of his work, and was collecting the notices of it to send to his family in Hamburg. "Let me see them before you send them off," she writes to him. "In anything to do with you I am sillier than any mother and more conceited than any sister." In the same letter she tells him: "I feel very happy about the coming summer. My work, in which I feel myself more than encouraged, the rides I take on horseback, and the mysterious presentiments which your beautiful angels of Saint-Merry awake from time to time in my soul, are enough for my calm and placid nature, and for that poetic philosophy which has triumphed in an existence which was for so long subject to evil influences. When the lilacs are in flower, and when you can let me have a few days with you, we will wander together through the '*allées tournantes*' (of the past), which your tender nature has relieved of so many thorns, and illuminated with so many gentle rays."

Of Henri's exhibition there is only one other mention in the correspondence. "I left your beautiful exhibition with joyous heart," she wrote, "and I keep on trying to repeat the movement of Ophelia's elbow." Two of the paintings in his exhibition had been hung in the Salon of 1846: one of *Ophelia*, and one of *Hamlet*. Apropos of the latter, he had received an enthusiastic letter from Alfred de Vigny: "It is not enough to tell everyone else, I want to tell you yourself how much I like your *Hamlet*. It's the man of the north, it's the man of doubt, it's the student of the University of Wittenberg, as he describes himself, it's the poor hesitating child, feeble, inadequate in character to the horrors and sufferings with which fate overwhelms him, it's the young prince elegant of habit and half mad in his disorder. I like the uncertain light which only illuminates the edge of his forehead and steeps his whole person in the same vague twilight which reigns in his thought. A sense of immense sadness overcame me when I saw it, and it comes back to me when I think of it – there are even tears in my eyes as I write to you. For the past week and more these thoughts have been in my mind, and I've only seen your picture once. I am amazed myself that the impression had remained in my mind as vivid as on the day I saw it. On Saturday I shall go again, but all alone, and dream in front of your *Hamlet* and so thank you in silence and from the bottom of my heart."

There are several references in the letters to the Princess Belgiojoso. Henri appears to have known her at least as early as 1840. In 1843 Mme d'Agoult jokingly reported to him that there was a story going the rounds in Paris that the Princess had stolen Henri from her and that she, Marie, had left Paris in a rage. Christine Trivulzio Belgiojoso was known as an ardent Italian patriot, and had been a friend of Liszt. This did not endear her to Marie, who thought her hypocritical and pretentious. In his references to her, Henri gives the impression of trying to defend her against Marie's insinuations; but little or nothing is known of their relations, except that in the Salon of 1844 Henri exhibited a picture of her, one of the most striking of his early portraits. During the events of 1848 she appeared in Naples, and took two hundred or so volunteers in her steamer to Lombardy, to join the revolution.[1]

The last letter written by Mme d'Agoult to Henri that survives is dated October 1st 1848. It is entirely concerned with political events, and is apparently a postscript to a previous one (now lost), keeping Henri up to date with the latest developments in the still revolutionary situation.

"This is an important postscript.

"They gave me your letter when I returned from the Chamber yesterday at six o'clock. Thinking that I should not have the time

[1] Sir Harold Acton: *The Last Bourbons of Naples.*

to answer this morning, I wrote at once and the letter was sent off by the *petite poste*. It contained my impressions and the information I had gathered, that is information from people who have no connection with the Bonapartist party. During the evening, by chance, I came into possession from a very good source of the party's plans, which seem to agree with what you were told. I quote: The Assemblée Nationale is to decide whether the President of the Republic shall be elected by universal suffrage or by itself. If it decides for universal suffrage, the party will wait peacefully for the inevitable result, the election of Louis Bonaparte.

"If it does not, it will carry out an '18th Brumaire', throw the Assemblée out and take power by force. The army will never fire against a Bonaparte.

"All this is going to happen in the immediate future.

"This news is serious. It doesn't in the least change my opinion, because I can't believe that such a ninny could carry through an '18th Brumaire' coup and that a man like Thiers could lend himself to it. But people who know Thiers say that nothing is less impossible, that he'll use any means to attain power, etc.

"Otherwise there's always the humiliating possibility of a referendum by universal suffrage which would probably, in fact, produce a majority for Napoleon.

"Consider whether this news is such that you prefer to postpone your return, in which case it will only be a question of waiting for the vote of the Assemblée, which, I believe, will decide for universal suffrage.

"Good-bye, I clasp your hand."

And soon after that, my great-uncle Henri, with his serious mind and sensitive heart, his "clear placid" charm, his self-doubt and his spiritual perturbations and the ironic wit with which he covered them up in public, his scrupulous loyalty to friends and dependants and his touchiness when he suspected even the slightest disloyalty on their part, his dandified habit and his blue eyes, gradually, as far as one can tell, slipped out of her life for good.

In the years to come, Marie d'Agoult's reputation as a courageous feminist, blue-stocking and ardent political liberal was steadily to increase. She was free from all conventional prejudice about the relations between the sexes, yet she remained essentially faithful to the dazzling, promiscuous, unsatisfactory genius with whom she had eloped in her thirtieth year. She was extremely ambitious, a schemer, and childishly jealous of any female rival who ever appeared to threaten her ambitions. She was always beautiful and brilliant, but I do not think she was a very nice character.

V

Henri himself had lived through some dramatic moments during the Revolution of 1848. He had joined the *Garde Nationale* during the February rising, and saw the mob tossing everything out of the Tuileries windows and firing salvos into the air for joy, while on the other side of the river a triumphant procession was conducting the Provisional Government to the Hôtel de Ville with cries of *Vive la République!* The next day he had an order to deliver to the General commanding the *Garde Nationale*, and so had a *laissez-passer* admitting him to the Tuileries. The fancy took him to visit the throne-room: where the great velvet canopy of the throne had hung only bare wall was to be seen, on which had been scrawled, in large letters, *Vive la République! Vive la Suisse! Vive l'Italie! Vive la Liberté pour la troisième fois reconquise, le 22, 23, 24 Février! Respect aux objets d'art!*

His brother Rudolf had joined him in Paris the previous year. He was ill in bed during the actual rising, but has left a description of Rachel singing the *Marseillaise* on the stage of the Théâtre Français, as the impersonation of the new Republic, immediately after: "Clad in an antique white tunic, a tricolour sash round her slender waist, and a red Phrygian bonnet on her head, and waving a huge tricolour flag, she half sang, half spoke, with very little voice; but the enthusiasm which her passionate delivery of those incendiary verses produced is indescribable. Her voice trembled with contained rage . . . The whole house rose and joined in chorus, the pit standing on the benches."

Rudolf also gives an account of a visit with Henri, at a later date, to Rachel's house (which had been given her by Count Walewski) in the Chaussée d'Antin. "We found a motley gathering of distinguished men of letters, artists, financiers, and politicians, and of elegant, rather *décolletées* ladies, many of both sexes smoking cigarettes in a separate room. Rachel did the honours with much dignity . . . In her bedroom, open for inspection after the French fashion, every inch of the walls was covered with trophies of her histrionic triumphs all over the civilized world. Wreaths, many of gold, illuminated addresses, costly presents, medals, caskets everywhere."

When the June rising occurred, Henri had again to go out with the *Garde Nationale*, and Rudolf, devoured by anxiety for his brother and finding it impossible to work, also volunteered. One extraordinary incident in his description of his experiences stands out: "Suddenly a tall girl, a well-known artists' model, who had recently sat to me for the *Ste Cécile*, made her appearance.[1] "*Bonjour, M. Lehmann*,' she said in the quietest of tones, as if she had met me in my studio. 'Shall I take you over the battlefield?' and as I readily accepted her offer, she added, 'You had better remove that piece of cardboard from your hat. The *Gardes Nationaux* are no favourites hereabout.' I did as she bade me, and followed her into the long, desolate rue du Faubourg St Antoine, which was intersected by numerous partly destroyed barricades, about fifty yards distant from each other. She had some incident to relate about the taking of each one of them, after a desperate struggle, by the troops. 'On this one Monsieur Affre, the Bishop of Paris, was shot just as he held up the crucifix, endeavouring to stop the firing and bring about an armistice. On that one my poor brother was shot, but he never relinquished his grasp on the red flag. What can you do against cannon?' she added with a sigh. 'But never

---

[1] In the *Place de la Bastille*. I have already quoted this description in *The Whispering Gallery*.

mind – our day will come! We women always sat knitting on the barricade next to the one that was being fought for, retiring gradually as the troops advanced.' I thought of the tricoteuses of 1793, of whom these were the grand-children."

In January of 1849 Henri received a visit from his younger brother Frederick, my grandfather, who had been settled by then for some years in Scotland. Henri showed him all the sights, and introduced him to his friends, including, it seems, Mme d'Agoult, much to Frederick's delight. He was twenty-three, and still unmarried.

The visit, however, had a special object in view. About a week before, Frederick had written to Henri to ask him to call at a certain address in the rue Richer, where a Miss Elizabeth W. was living, and if she needed money to give it to her on his behalf.

When he arrived in Paris, to his amazement Henri told him that Miss W. was not living there, but only a friend, a girl who seemed incapable of informing him where Miss W. was.

Frederick determined at once to try and solve the mystery, and set out for the rue Richer with his brother. On the way there, he told him the story.

"When I was in Hamburg last year, my good or evil genius, I scarcely know which to call it, led me to a well-known pouf run by the celebrated Madame R. It was in the middle of the day, and after a few minutes the swarms of ghastly women there so disgusted me that I was about to leave the place; when I was asked to stay because a wonderfully beautiful English girl was about to make her appearance. This intrigued me, I was curious to know what strange circumstances could bring one of the fair daughters of Albion from her island fastness to such a place.

"I didn't have long to wait, before an amazing beauty entered, lighting up the scene like the sun coming through the clouds. I stayed. She spoke fluent French, and her whole manner fascinated me. I immediately decided to try and win her. I succeeded. Two days later, when I said good-bye to her she told me that she also was going away in a few days' time, and would very shortly be back in England. This roused my curiosity so much that I pressed her to tell me more about herself. She came, she told me, from Kingston-on-Thames, and wanted to go back there. She had been in Turin, in Paris, in Brussels, and everywhere she had had serious and long-lasting liaisons. I felt an urgent need to keep in touch with her, and so gave her my real address in Edinburgh, but a false name; she in return told me her real name, Elizabeth W.

"In the following weeks, my business preoccupations, my journey to Holland, and so on, gradually pushed the recollection of this encounter out of my mind; until I suddenly received a letter from her, written in rather funny, stilted French, asking me to call on her in London at such and such an address.

"A few days later I came to London and determined to visit this mysterious creature. At last – at the end of the world – I found the address she had given me. It was evidently a suspicious sort of house. I was shown into a little parlour on the first floor, I called out her name several times, and before anyone understood me Lizzie appeared and flung herself into my arms, gasping for joy. She seemed to me more beautiful than ever; what followed was easy to foresee. After we had been together, she made me a total declaration of love, and told me that from the very first moment she had seen me she had taken a fancy to me. She then told me the extraordinary story of her life.

"She is the daughter of a Captain in the Royal Navy, therefore of a respectable family. She was born in London, but the family moved to Kingston when she was quite young. She has three brothers also in the Navy; the eldest is a Captain, is married, and lives in Kingston. She was the apple of her father's eye, and was spoilt by all her brothers: if her present looks are anything to go by, she must have looked like a young Venus.

"When she was fourteen years old – five years ago – an Italian Count C., chamberlain of His Majesty the King of Sardinia, came to London. He happened to see her in the house of her uncle, a ship builder, and, overcome with her beauty, conceived the diabolical plan of stealing the innocent child.

"One day, when everyone thought he had gone away, she saw his carriage coming up behind her as she was going to visit her aunt. He leaned out, asked her where she was going, and suggested he should take her to her aunt's house. She accepted his offer; the moment she was in the carriage, he set off at top speed for Dover, and forced her to cross with him to Boulogne, in spite of all her tears and resistance.

"Passing her off as his wife, Countess C., he then took her in short stages through Southern France to Turin. In Turin he surrounded her with every luxury, pandered to her every whim, and treated her exactly as if she were in fact legally married to him. The most distinguished figures in Turin society came to her *salon*, and she became the star of every brilliant social gathering. She had horses, coaches, servants, jewels, boxes at the Opera. She travelled with him throughout the whole of Italy, from Milan to Messina. She has been everywhere in Germany. He became her slave, and worshipped her; only one thing he forbade her, and that was ever to write home. As soon as she had grown old enough to understand what had happened to her, she longed to be able to do that more than anything else – but she assured me that even though she went down on her bare knees on the marble floor of his palace, he could not be moved on this point.

"Six times she had a miscarriage, and never succeeded in bearing him a living child.

"Three years later the disaster occurred. The Count sent her to take the waters, in a place not far from Genoa, while he himself set out for Russia. Suddenly, a thunderbolt out of a clear sky, she received a letter from him in which he announced that he was about to marry a Russian Princess, in order to shore up his tottering fortunes. The shock gave her convulsions, but she remained in his palace until he returned with his bride, when she packed her bags and retired to a hotel. He hurried after her on the very same day. A violent scene took place, when he made the scandalous proposal that she should live on his country estate, with all the servants she wanted and 10,000 francs, if she would only remain his mistress. She was so beside herself with rage, that he drew his sword to protect himself; whereupon she seized it and struck him across the face. Blood poured out of the wound, and he fell to the ground. Seeing this, she went off in a dead faint herself: he was carried back to his palace, and she to her bed.

"When the Count had recovered a few weeks later, he came to visit her again. She tried to prevent him getting into her room, but in vain. He then renewed all his former proposals, which she again refused to consider. Furious with resentment, he contrived to have her thrown out of the city by the police. She set out for Paris. Only a few miles out of Turin, a horseman galloping by threw a letter into the mailcoach, in which she was the only passenger. It was the Count: in the letter was a piece of paper with '*acceptez ceci*' written on it, and a cheque for 50,000 francs. She tore both into small pieces and flung them out of the window. The Count, seeing this act of defiance, shouted after her 'You will end on the guillotine! You will end on the guillotine!'

"After a few months in Paris, she left for Brussels, where she fell ill, was forced to pawn her jewels, and was soon overwhelmed with debts. Meanwhile, she had learnt that her parents had died; she wrote letter after letter to her brothers, to find out whether she had been left anything, but all of them were returned unopened.

"In this desperate situation, without any friends to advise or help her, at the suggestion of her nurse and without properly realizing what she was letting herself in for, she wrote to Madame R. in Hamburg. Madame R. immediately sent her enough money for the journey. She arrived in Hamburg in August 1848, only a few weeks, that is, before I saw her. She swore to me by all she held sacred that up to that moment no man except Count C. had touched her.

"Then followed the darkest weeks of her life. She made scheme after scheme to get away, but her debts were like chains of iron. Luckily, she fell into reasonably good hands. Count D., the French Ambassador in Hamburg, first of all; then Fontenilia,

French Ambassador in Hanover, claimed her favours. The latter paid half her debts, and she went to live with him for fourteen days in Hanover. They quarrelled; she then took up with Baron S., son of one of the most notorious Hanoverian ministers. He fell madly in love with her, paid the rest of her debts, and promised to have a lawsuit brought against her brothers, if they refused to pay up. Thereupon she left for England, alone, to find the brothers. I have seen Baron S.'s letters to her, written in the comic, half-educated way of an uncouth country squire, but full of kindness and love.

"As was only to be expected, her brothers refused to have anything to do with her, and the lawyer to whom Baron S. sent her appears to have cheated her right and left – and then to have disappeared. I was about to suggest a friend of mine, but she said that Baron S. wanted her to wait until he could make further arrangements himself. I therefore decided it would be more prudent to hold off for the moment. Apparently, she stayed in London at the Royal Hotel first of all, and then, for reasons I found difficult to understand, except that the Royal was very expensive, she went to the rather sinister house where I found her.

"We decided at once to look for lodgings where we could be with one another undisturbed. I spent the night with her at the house. She seemed to be full of love for me, and said: '*Vois tu, mon Frédéric, j'ai souvent aimé de caprice mais je te jure devant Dieu que je n'ai jamais aimé d'amour comme je t'aime.*'

"The following week-end I had to go to Cambridge, but just before I left she announced that she had found new lodgings, and would have moved in on my return. Meanwhile, some friends had taken a box at Covent Garden for Monday night, and invited me to bring Lizzie.

"As soon as my train from Cambridge got in, I hurried off to the new address, which struck me as being in a very undesirable quarter. Also, the rooms that I was to have myself were, I learnt, not free for several days. I was cast down by this; I was also dying of hunger, and as it was already late I refused to explore for some miserable restaurant in such a dreary, unknown district. 'Here I am,' I said to her, 'you must do something for me – I must have something – no matter what!' Thereupon she disappeared, and returned shortly after with a pint of stout and a mutton chop, which I devoured in no time at all. While I was eating, Lizzie dressed herself for the Opera, and we were able to arrive in good time.

"After another wonderful night with her, I told Lizzie how much I disliked the new lodgings, and thought it better to find a little house somewhere or other, where we could live until I went back to Scotland. She promised to make excuses to Baron S. meanwhile, to prevent him arriving in London until I had gone. She wept at the thought of our parting. By a lucky chance I met someone the same evening who told me of a house I could rent in Alpha Road.

"Two days later we were installed in a charming little house, furnished in excellent taste, with a neat walled garden, the very thing I had dreamed of. A couple were there to look after the cooking, and so on. You can have no idea of the charm of the sunny, cosy little sitting-room and the delicious comfort of the bedroom. Lizzie flung her arms round me and kissed me, when she saw it. We laughed and chattered together, as happy as children.

"The same evening we went out to Sadler's Wells Theatre, after an excellent dinner had been produced for us by the couple. The play was Shakespeare's *Coriolanus*. It was really a very bad performance, but I could think of nothing except Lizzie's dazzling beauty and the way all the lorgnettes in the theatre were turned on us.

"Alas, this idyll came to an end all too soon. I had to go back to Edinburgh, and Baron S., I suppose, arrived in London. At any rate I heard no word from Lizzie – she simply vanished out of my life until at the end of December – that is, scarcely ten days ago – I suddenly had a letter from Paris in which she told me that she was ill, would soon be going to Baron S. in Hanover, and would always cherish the same feelings for me. And that is why I sent you to the address in the rue Richer where we are going now."

When they reached their destination they found the girl Henri had told his brother about, lying in bed, alleging she was ill but looking very pretty all the same. To Frederick's astonishment she admitted at once, with the greatest frankness, that the letter Frederick had received as if from his Lizzie had in fact been written by her. She added that in any case Lizzie could neither read nor write; and that all the time she had been, not in Paris, but in London.

After which baffling piece of information, they withdrew. Frederick gloomily concluded that he was never going to see Lizzie again. Nevertheless, he went to the address again the next day, in the hopes of extracting her address in London from the friend; but a doctor was hovering round her all the time, and Frederick finally left without the information he wanted.

In March, Frederick was again in Paris. The political situation was boiling up once more. The left-wing press was baying recklessly for blood, and everyone seemed to be expecting riots, to which the intellectuals were – or so it seemed to the brothers – fatalistically resigned. On his first evening the inflammatory papers he bought on the Boulevard des Italiens so disturbed Frederick that he only slept fitfully that night, falling again and again into nightmares in which he heard the tocsin ringing all over the city. Henri had had enough, and decided to leave Paris with Frederick. While they were packing, Henri's *marchand de couleurs* arrived and announced that he had received orders to report to his company of the National Guard – that the trouble was going to start any moment. The brothers had one or two last chores to attend to, and when they went out found that most people pooh-poohed the idea of anything serious happening. A few minutes later, in the rue Lepelletier, they heard a shout "*les v'la – ils viennent!*' and hurrying to the Boulevard they saw an enormous procession of workers in their blue blouses, mixed with members of the

National Guard, advancing towards them and spreading across the street from one side to the other. They carried no weapons, only flags, and were shouting: "*Vive la constitution! Vive la republique romaine!*"

Henri had to get across the street somehow – time was short – in order to gain the rue Richelieu. With sinking heart he approached the procession, and asked if he could pass through their ranks. To his surprise, the men he spoke to replied with the utmost courtesy, "*Mais certainement, monsieur!*" Scarcely were they on the other side of the street, when the cavalry, which had been coolly waiting for the procession, made their charge. The demonstrators fled to right and to left into the side-streets, and the cry went up: "*Aux armes! Aux armes! Fermez!*" Whereupon all the shops closed down in a trice. In the middle of the scurrying tumult women could be seen wringing their hands, and exclaiming, "*Ah! Quel malheur!*"

Henri and Frederick made their way as fast as they could to the Gare du Nord. There, however, they found everything so quiet that Henri told Frederick to delay his departure for a few days, and he returned to take a room for the night in the Grand Hôtel de Castille in the rue Richelieu. From his window, looking out over the Boulevard des Italiens, he could see how tense the situation still was: National Guards and Dragoons patrolling the streets, all traffic controlled.

Before Henri left him, he was able to tell him the sequel and end to the story of Lizzie. Soon after leaving Paris in January, he had happened to be in Antwerp on business. Determined to see everything there was to see in the city, he allowed himself to be led one night to a dance hall, where an English girl suggested he should come upstairs. There he found an elegant room, with a buffet, full of French and German girls. The English girl who had first spoken to him disappeared, then came back, and asked him cautiously whether his name was Lehmann? Whether he lived in Edinburgh? And had recently set up house with a girl in London? . . . She disappeared again, and a little German girl appeared who, after a few words with him, made it clear that she knew Lizzie under the name of Sarah. She described her so exactly that Frederick could have no doubt about it. Then she suddenly said: "Would you like to see her tomorrow?" His heart beating fast, Frederick answered in complete confusion; the German girl gave him a wink and told him that Lizzie had arrived from London the day before, with only what she had on, and so many debts that *Madame* had refused to pay them.

Frederick was determined to bring matters to a conclusion at once, and refused to wait till the next day. The German girl therefore took him up to a room next to one where she said Lizzie was; she knocked on the door, and after a while it was opened – by Lizzie herself. The moment she saw Frederick she banged it to again. Frederick waited a little; and then without further ado walked into the room himself. He found Lizzie there, with two other girls and two men. She looked in the utmost distress – she introduced him as her brother from England – but he finally persuaded her to come into the next room with him. She was about to throw herself into his arms, when he said: "If you touch me, I will strike you!"

Lizzie then confessed that Baron S. had just arrived in Antwerp too, and was about to call for her. She seemed in a great state, fearing that Frederick was going to demand an explanation of the bills she had left in Alpha Road. She then said she *had* been in Paris when Henri had called – she could prove it by the stamps in her passport – but had been forced by Baron S. to leave at once to meet him in Antwerp.

At that moment, the Baron himself knocked on the door, which Lizzie had locked. Frederick let him wait for a good half hour, with a certain malicious satisfaction, while he tried to make sense of Lizzie's story, which seemed to him to become more and more confused the more she tried to explain her actions. One thing, however, became absolutely clear to him at last: that it was hopeless to go on with her.

The Baron, now thoroughly enraged, was banging on the door

with all his might and shouting; "*Madame, on vous attend!*" Frederick let her slip out. He went over to the window, and saw her get into a waiting cab with the Baron. They drove off; and that was the last he ever saw of her.

VI

Henri, it is clear, remained a devoted friend of his former master, Ingres, to the last. In July 1849 Mme Ingres, who had been ill for several months, died. Ingres was shattered by her death, and remained distraught for many months. His state of mind can be judged from the touching letter he sent to Henri at the beginning of September. "I am late in giving you news of my sad life since that day, of horrible memory, when I lost her, and lost her for ever. Alas, all alone, always without her! It is so frightful, I do not see how I am to escape from the despair that oppresses me every moment of my life. It is true that you, like all my friends, are an angel of consolation, if consolation in such a case as mine is conceivable. . . You must indeed miss her, because she loved you. So here I am, all alone, at the mercy of the future, full of sorrow for my own fate, inexpressible sorrow! The misfortune, at my age! Obliged to make myself a new home, and without her!

"I will see you again with pleasure, dear friend, and reunite you with my other children. Ah, who else could congratulate himself on having such worthy friends, such distinguished friends as you in this world? You will gather round your old friend, and, in time, I am told, she would like 'to see me more serene'. Those were her last words, words that echo at the bottom of my lacerated heart . . ."

It was eighteen years later, in January 1867, that his "children", his old pupils gathered round him for the last time at the burial service in the church of St Thomas Aquinas, and afterwards at his grave in Pére-Lachaise. Henri, by then Vice-President of the Académie des Beaux-Arts, was one of the four chosen to stand at each corner of the bier: with him was the architect Lefuel, President of the Académie, Vice-Admiral Count Bouët-Willaumez, a senator, and the Mayor of Montauban. A vast gathering of writers, artists and politicians attended the funeral. At Père-Lachaise he was laid to rest in the tomb which already contained the coffin of the first Madame Ingres. Orations were made by the Mayor, by Lefuel, one of the pupils of the Ecole des Beaux Arts, and then by Henri in the name of all the painter's ancient pupils. "Dear, revered master," he began. "Your disciples whom you liked to call your children, mourn you as if you were their father. Reunited around your tomb, they do not wish to see it close without having wished you, through me, a final farewell. We have lost your beloved person, your incomparable lessons, your reviving words of encouragement when our spirits were low. But your great example remains with us. It will teach us to love, in art as in life, only what is true, pure, noble and great."

In his art, Henri did indeed remain faithful to the ideals of Ingres; probably too faithful, for though his drawings continued to show remarkable vigour and freedom, and the finest of his portraits that uncanny power he had learnt from his master, the chilling hand of a misguided classicism seems to freeze all spontaneity out of his more elaborate compositions. Though he was too generous in spirit to keep up his master's absurd vendettas against contemporary artists who chose different paths from his own, and was in fact a friend of Delacroix, he appears to have been out of sympathy with both the realism of Daumier and Courbet and the Impressionism that was beginning to gain the day at the end of his life. His devotion to the ideals that Ingres expounded, gradually, one feels, led Henri himself to an academic dead end; and yet in the work of his greatest pupil Georges Seurat, it is surely that same classicism we see transformed and brought to new life.

Perhaps one should not make such a sweeping judgement, for all too little of the work of his maturity survives. Portait-painting remained his passion to the end: in his memorial exhibition held the year after he died, there were fifty-six portraits in oil in addition to a number of portrait sketches. Where are they all? He was dogged by misfortune. In the eyes of his contemporaries, his greatest work was the decoration of the *Galerie des Fêtes* in the Hôtel de Ville at Paris; a vast work which was begun on the orders of Louis Napoleon in January 1852 and completed in less than twelve months. The design contained fifty or sixty separate major figures, one hundred and eight figures in all, filling the various wall spaces and angles, and around each figure an allegorical scene represented an episode in the history of human endeavour, from the earliest times to the latest achievements of science. It is possible that the speed with which this gigantic commission had to be carried through was an advantage: Henri may have exhausted himself over it (in spite of employing seven or eight young assistants), but nearly all who saw the finished product agreed that it displayed a liveliness of imagination, a freedom and energy unusual in the "grandes machines" of the school of Ingres.

Eighteen years later the whole work was totally destroyed by fire during the disturbances of the Commune. When he heard of the disaster, Henri wrote an extraordinary and impressive letter to a friend: "I must admit that that ancient familiar, that other 'I' which watches and judges me, is a little surprised at the absolute calm – I will not say indifference, because on reflection there is evidently room for certain regrets – with which I view the purely personal side of the affair. I told *her*, and other friends, of my feelings with entire sincerity: I experience a kind of painful pleasure, a bitter satisfaction, in not emerging safe and sound, as it were completely untouched, from a catastrophe in which so much that was most excellent and beautiful of my generation, and of many others, was swallowed up. I would not, perhaps, have had the fortitude to *choose* such a destiny, but I readily accept the burden it obliges me to bear."

In the same upheavals, the paintings he had executed in the Palais de Justice a few years later were also destroyed by fire.

His misfortunes were not confined to his professional career. In his early forties he married the widow of a friend, whose maiden name had been Clémence Casadavant, and by whom he had two children, Louise and Léonie. Both these little girls died in childhood. In May of 1858 his brother Frederick came over to Paris from England, on an obscure mission which involved an interview with Heine. He took with him his eldest son, my father, though only in his third year, as Henri and Clémence wanted so much to see him. Louise was already dead; according to Frederick, Léonie was then "a tall thin child immensely intelligent and speaking rapidly, but . . . her skin is not clear and there is something sad about her. She somehow does not look as if she could live, and I tremble when I think that all poor Henri's hopes are on this one frail little bark. Beside Rudie she entirely disappears." A few months later she had died. Henri remained inconsolable for the death of his children. Even seventeen years later, when talking of Louise's death to Frederick, he burst into floods of tears.

He became a naturalized Frenchman, a Chevalier of the Legion d'Honneur in 1847 at the early age of thirty-three, and a Member of the Institut in 1864. When the Franco-Prussian War broke out, he decided never again to write in German, to make it quite clear, as he told his friends, that he now thought like a Frenchman and felt like a Frenchman. In 1875, when already suffering from a disease that overshadowed the last years of his life, he became Professor at the Ecole des Beaux Arts. He died in 1882. By then Mme d'Agoult had been dead for six years. Little Daniel, for whom he had made his journeys on horseback to Palestrina over forty years before, slowly succumbing to pernicious anaemia had only survived his twentieth birthday by a few months. The "Great Man", now the Abbé Liszt, was to live for another four years.

Henri appears to have remained to the end of his life the same introspective, fastidious, exactingly self-critical person who, in his youth in Rome, suffered from the long bouts of melancholy, approaching despair, from which Mme d'Agoult had tried to rescue him. It was clear that he was never so poor that, like some of his contemporaries, he did not know where the next meal was coming from; and in the happy early years of his marriage he appeared to those who came into contact with him to be rich as well as famous and respected. Nevertheless, his friend, Vicomte Henri Delaborde, who had known him intimately since his early days in Paris, said, in the speech which he delivered in his honour at the Académie des Beaux-Arts in October 1883, "In escaping poverty, he did not escape anxiety. But this very genuine anxiety was so little in evidence, it was concealed under an appearance so very much the contrary of the truth, that those who had neither the time nor the opportunity to look deeper, were tempted to believe that he was not above a certain worldly vanity . . . The trouble he constantly took to display to the world a deliberate good humour and what he himself called his '*gaieté de sang-froid*' – everything, in fact, including his seductive personal elegance, tended to conceal the secret difficulties of an existence the outward appearance of which was so smiling and fortunate."

PART TWO

No. 1 Doune Terrace

I

In the late forties and early fifties of the last century, one of the most distinguished, successful and generally admired men in the intellectual world of Edinburgh was Robert Chambers. He was known as the leading authority on the ancient lore and historical records of his native country, about which he had written a large number of books, beginning with *Traditions of Edinburgh* at the age of twenty-three; as an essayist of immense erudition and charm, responsible for the majority of the contributions to the popular weekly, *Chambers's Edinburgh Journal*, which he had founded with his brother William in 1832; and as a passionate student of the comparatively new science of geology, on one aspect of which he had just published a volume based on his own tireless explorations, *Ancient Sea Margins*.

It was not, however, known that he was also the author of another, far more ambitious book, *Vestiges of Creation*, perhaps the most important of pre-Darwinian works which adumbrated the theory of evolution. He was convinced that the commotion which it would (and did) cause in narrowly conventional religious circles, so powerful in Scotland at the time, could only do harm to his family, and he kept the secret until his death. Among the wilder contemporary guesses about the identity of the author were Prince Albert, Thackeray, and Byron's daughter, Lady Lovelace.

His house at No. 1 Doune Terrace was a lively centre of literary and artistic society, and visitors poured in to the many learned conversaziones and lighter musical parties which were held there: Robert Chambers was extremely fond of music and something of a performer on the flute himself, while his wife, as one of her daughters later recorded, "was born with music in her, and enchanted the literary world by her beauty and grace as she played the harp, or sang Scottish ballads to her own exquisite accompaniments on the piano". Among the guests at these evening parties were not only the notables in Edinburgh's university and professional life, but also an international mixture of well-known musicians, including the Hungarian refugee Remenyi, in whom Annie Chambers took an especial interest, Jenny Lind the famous singer, Lichtenstein, patron of many indigent musicians, and the composer Otto Goldschmidt, and many writers who had made or were beginning to make their names, including Thackeray, Edward Bulwer Lytton, Monckton Milnes, G. H. Lewes and the young Wilkie Collins. Eminent tourists from abroad were also constantly arriving with letters of introduction, in the hope of persuading the over-worked but all too kindly *savant* to provide them with a personally conducted tour of the antiquities of the city.

To this house my grandfather, Frederick Lehmann, was introduced some time in late 1850 or 1851. He had left his home in Hamburg six or seven years before when only just over eighteen, to make a career in commerce. He had started in Huddersfield, and had then gone up to Leith. He had fallen in love with Britain, whose way of life and development as a great world power excited his endless admiration, and in the late forties had taken out naturalization papers. He, too, was passionately fond of music, and owed his entry into the Chambers circle to his skill as a violin player. He rapidly became a favourite with the family, was engaged before long to the eldest daughter Nina, and married her in November 1852.

If there ever was a self-made man – if there ever was a thrifty, industrious Scot who starved and slaved until he had made his mark in the world and the hard-earned sixpences had turned into a comfortable balance at the bank – it was my great-grandfather. The Chambers family had been settled in Peebles for centuries: the earliest ancestor whose name is recorded was "William de la Chaumbre, Baili é Burgois de Pebles", in the list of those who signed bonds of allegiance to Edward I at Berwick-on-Tweed in 1296. In the eighteenth century Robert's ancestors had been wool-

len manufacturers, people of some substance, but living, as everyone in the quiet, respectable town of Peebles lived, in a very plain
and unostentatious style. His father James Chambers had gone to
Glasgow to study cotton manufacture when it was introduced
there, and at the time of Robert's birth had established nearly a
hundred looms in his house.

Robert was born in 1802 in a small, neat mansion, looking on to
the Eddleston Water, in which the family lived upstairs and the
weavers worked in the big room down below. He remembered
playing marbles with his brother William, two years his senior, on
the parlour floor, while the songs and gossip of the weavers
floated up to them; and then sometimes going downstairs to
watch the movements of the heddles and treadles and talk shyly
with the men, until recalled by their adored nurse and general
servant to the household, Jeanie Forbes, who could sing any
Scottish song they asked for. On one occasion, an especially vivid
recollection arising out of the mists of childhood, the two brothers
were taken to see a company of strolling players in George Col-
man's sentimental drama of love in the West Indies, *Inkle and
Yarico*. They were performing in the cramped upper room of a
public house, because the acting chief magistrate, an eccentric old
Calvinist known as Tammas, thought all dancing and theatrical
entertainments of any sort to be the works of the Devil and refused permission for the town hall to be used. "I'll oppose it with
all the means in my poo'er!" he had cried, waving his axe over his
head, when the manager of the troupe had come to him while he
was chopping logs in his garden.

Robert's lifelong interests in music and in general scientific
knowledge were clearly developed by the circumstances of his
childhood. His father had a rage for astronomy, and had bought a
telescope, which he shared with Mungo Park, the African explo-
rer, who had settled as a surgeon in Peebles. He also had a
German flute, and sitting at the open window of the parlour in the
summer twilights he would play an endless series of Scottish airs,
which could be heard all along Eddleston Water; then, as the

moon rose and the stars came out, the telescope was planted on the tea-table, and the boys were encouraged to have a peep and discuss what they saw with their father. He also possessed an edition of the *Encyclopedia Britannica*, which he had bought in a moment of extreme extravagance from the local bookseller, Sandy Elder, in whose shop a cow was generally to be seen chewing the cud quietly behind the bookshelves. Robert remembered discovering this treasure one day when he was about nine years old in a chest in the attic – there was no room in the parlour – and roaming through it like a bee going from flower to flower, for weeks and months on end. He also remembered that Sandy Elder ran a kind of circulating library, which his father patronized, and how he spent one whole morning reading a copy of Pope's translation of the Iliad which had been borrowed from Sandy's library, while outside the little room, in the High Street, an English regiment was parading recruits raised for Wellington's Peninsular campaign.

There seems little doubt that the most valuable part of the education the Chambers boys acquired, was provided by themselves: from the *Encyclopedia Britannica*, from Sandy Elder's circulating library, and from a pair of battered old school-globes which their father had bought at an auction for five shillings. At no single one of the schools in Peebles at that time was any history, geography or physical science taught; but at the grammar school an excellent grounding in Latin could be obtained, for a derisory fee – with the unstinted aid of the tawse. In after years, Robert was prepared to praise the headmaster, James Sloane, for his scholarship and the thoroughness of his methods, excusing the brutality on the grounds that there was scarcely any school in the country where it was not used, frequently and on the most trifling grounds, on the unfortunate children.

One revolting occasion haunted him. It was discovered one morning that two of the boarders had run away. A couple of town constables were promptly sent out to find them, caught them and brought them back in disgrace the same afternoon. The school was assembled to watch their punishment, while the constables in their scarlet coats guarded the doorway. Sloane then lectured the boys on their wickedness, and as soon as he had finished ordered them to strip for flogging. They resisted, in terror, were seized, stripped by the constables, and laid over a long table, when the tawse was mercilessly applied to their bottoms while they kicked and screamed. The school was then dismissed for the day, to meditate the awful consequences of childish rebellion. In those days, no parent would have dreamed of objecting.

Robert had not yet finished his time at this pleasant school, when disaster struck the family. The introduction of the power-loom a short while before was already beginning to wreck the primitive business of hand-loom weaving. James Chambers's commissions from the Glasgow merchants began to fall off, and he set himself up as a draper, in a more central part of the town.

Though not particularly well fitted for his new line of business, great-great-grandfather James might have done well enough, if his easy-going disposition had not led him to make a fatal mistake. I have related elsewhere[1] how at this time, in the middle of the Napoleonic wars, Peebles had been chosen as a suitable place for prisoners of war on parole to be housed. The first comers were Dutchmen, Walloons and Danes, sailors who had been captured in forays into coastal waters. They quickly settled into the life of the place as best they could, and no grudge seems to have been borne on either side; nor was any attempt made to break parole. A few years later, however, a very much larger contingent arrived, consisting mostly of naval and military officers who had been taken in the Peninsular War. They arrived in the town, batch by batch, without ceremony, and were received with enthusiasm by the people of Peebles, who not only hoped that their humdrum life would be considerably enlivened by these exotic guests, but also saw a chance of making some money out of them, small though their allowances were.

[1] In *The Whispering Gallery*. I apologize for covering a little of the same ground, though I hope more accurately, as in that book.

One of these hopeful tradesmen was James Chambers. He made friends with many of the officers, welcomed them to his house whenever they cared to drop in, and readily gave them credit for cloth and various items of drapery which they needed to repair the tattered uniforms in which they had arrived. Robert had a vivid recollection of afternoons in the parlour when he and his brother tried to pick up as much French as possible from the stories the officers told; and also of evenings at the theatre they had improvised in a disused ballroom, where one of the hand-weavers who happened to have a good knowledge of French, one William Hunter, interpreted for the Scottish part of the audience whenever they failed to grasp a witticism of Molière or a resounding line of Corneille. James Chamber's wife, Jean Gibson, was a little suspicious of all this easy-going intimacy, though she was perfectly happy to lend dresses and bonnets for the younger officers or midshipmen taking the female parts. She had reason; for a sudden order came from London that the prisoners were to be removed to Dumfriesshire to make way for a militia regiment. They departed, with many vows to my great-great-grandfather that they would pay their debts in full when peace came; but he never saw a penny.

James Chambers was, in fact, ruined; and very soon after the family decided to make a fresh start, in whatever humble way was necessary, in Edinburgh. They left in December 1813, having arranged for Robert to stay on for a few months to complete his schooling under Sloane. The boys afterwards called this period: The Dark Ages.

II

When Robert eventually followed the rest of the family to Edinburgh, enough money was scraped together to send him, the promising scholar, to Mr Benjamin Mackay's classical academy in West Register Street. The idea was that he should go from there to the university, and in due course enter the Church. This plan was, in fact, far beyond the means of his parents at that time, but a distant relation had vaguely promised to help.

A second blow, however, fell very soon after. James Chambers had found a rather squalid job as manager of a salt works in Joppa Pans, a smelly and smoky little place on the seashore half-way between Portobello and Musselburgh. He was not long in discovering that by far the most profitable part of the trade consisted in smuggling salt across the border into England. His respectable soul was shocked, and he made no bones about expressing his disapproval. He was, therefore, already far from popular with his employers, when he was set upon one night and robbed of a large sum of money he had been collecting from clients. Not only was he disabled for a long time by the injuries he received, but the opportunity was taken to get rid of him. This misfortune finally broke his spirit, and it was left to his wife Jean to restore the family fortunes as best she could. The immediate result for Robert was that he had to leave Mackay's academy, abandon for good the idea of going to university, and start fending for himself. He was fourteen years old.

Meanwhile, his brother William had been taken in as an apprentice by a bookseller in Calton Street, opposite the Black Bull inn. His duties seem to have consisted mainly in acting as general dogsbody, sweeping and dusting, running all the errands, and delivering vast quantities of circulars advertising the advantages of buying a ticket in the State Lottery, for which the bookseller was an agent, all over the town. For all this he received the sum of four shillings a week precisely: he was warned that he could not expect more until the five years of his apprenticeship were over. He made up his mind that somehow or other he would make the money do. Luckily – in his eyes – he found lodgings at the top of a building in the West Port, where a widow from Peebles lived with her two sons. She provided him with a bed in a closet with a narrow window looking out on one of the poorest and most crowded streets in the city, cooked for him, and allowed him to sit by her fire when the cold was unendurable in the unheated bedroom; and she charged him eighteen pence a week. His daily expenditure on food came, on the average, to threepence halfpenny: in the three meals which this princely sum provided, porridge and broth (or *kail*) were the chief ingredients, very occasionally varied by a little salt fish. Tea, coffee and sugar were out. Ladling out the same broth night after night, his landlady would sagely remark that "eating is just a use", by which she meant that however much the palate might revolt, it was all the same when the food went down. A more frugal existence can scarcely be imagined. Strangely enough, his health does not seem to have suffered.

Soon after he left Peebles, Robert came to join William in these lodgings. Later in his life, he observed that he could not understand how he had ever lived through it. He could not even afford a candle, and used to sit as close as possible to the embers of the fire in his landlady's room, in order to be able to read his Horace or his Virgil and look up the words he didn't understand in his dictionary. The remarkable thing is that even in these circumstances, and even on this abominable diet, he managed to find time and energy to indulge his immense curiosity about the antiquities of the city. At that time, the older part of Edinburgh, as his brother William observed in his *Memoirs,* "remained a dense cluster of tall dark buildings, lining the central street and diverging lanes, or closes, with comparatively little change in exterior aspect. However altered as regards the quality of the dwellers on the different floors, the tenements still exhibited innumerable artistic and heraldic tokens of the past; nor were the environs of the town less illustrative of the moving incidents of the older times. To this huge antiquarian preserve, with its varied legends, my brother immediately attached himself with the fervour of a first love . . . Patiently ranging up one close, and down another, ascending stairs and poking into obscure courts, he took note of carvings over doorways, pondered on the structure of old gables and windows, examined *risps* – the antique mechanisms which had answered the purpose of doorknockers; and extending the scope of his researches, left scarcely a bit of Arthur's Seat or the Braid of Hills unexplored."

One of the more curious places he became intimately acquainted with was the Old Tolbooth. This tall and gloomy building in the High Street had become, at the beginning of the nineteenth century, a combined prison for debtors and criminals. It was run in an easy-going way that seems extraordinary to us today, and the young William had no difficulty in making visits there as often as he liked, in order to sell his lottery tickets to the prisoners. Perhaps even more extraordinary was the fact that Robert would often go there to get warm, when his landlady's fire was particularly low, treating the prison as a kind of friendly inn. In fact the part known as the West End, where the debtors and other civil prisoners were confined, was a very much safer and friendlier place for them in most cases than the circumstances they had left: many were small shopkeepers who had struggled for years in deepening poverty to cope with ill luck, mounting debts and taxes. The East End, where the criminals were locked up, was separate, but you had to go through the great Hall to reach both divisions, and those who were condemned to death were led across this Hall to the place of execution, which was the flat roof of a lower building on the Western side.

Robert and his brother would move freely among the throng in the Hall, staying as long as they pleased and chatting with those with whom they had made friends. There was one young man there who had failed in business, and who had previously been known to the family: through him they learned a great deal about the other prisoners and their way of life. The Governor in these last years of the prison's existence (it was pulled down in 1817) was Captain Sibbald, described by William as a "benevolently disposed little man, with a merry twinkle in his eye, dressed in a sober pepper-and-salt coloured suit". He had a great reputation for kindness and for the help he contrived to give to prisoners in the most desperate plight, men with large families to support and destitute youths who had come a cropper before they had really started in life. He even tolerated the existence in the prison of an erratic genius known to all as Davie, who had lost all his money and his friends in the outer world, and found the Tolbooth a happy haven. An elaborate pretence was kept up of concealing him from Captain Sibbald's eye during his last rounds at night, the Governor obligingly jingling his keys particularly noisily as he approached the room where he knew Davie would be sleeping. During the day, of course, there was no restriction on his activities: he acted as general messenger and shopper for the West Enders, posted their letters, smuggled in spirits, ordered dinners for special celebrations to be brought in from Mrs Ferguson's tavern near by, regaled them with songs, and joined them whenever invited in a game of whist. The brothers remembered him moving busily and contentedly about the Hall, with a woollen cap on his bald head, taking his instructions for the morning from the prisoners and their visitors, relations, friends, down-at-heel lawyers and doctors who had lost their regular practices through drink or neglect, or hanging round the tables in the prison's own cosy little kitchen-tavern where beef steaks, ale and porter could be ordered when money permitted, in the hope of being given the leavings.

All these strange sights, comic, pathetic and sometimes horrifying, all the strange stories he heard, were stored up in Robert's memory, to be discussed and laughed over in later life, and often used in his literary works.

When Robert found himself flung on the world to make his own way, at the age of fourteen, he felt for a long time numbed with grief and near despair, and was filled with bitterness that none of his family's relations on either side appeared ready to lift a finger to help him or his brother. At first he managed to get a little private teaching at Portobello; after which he took various jobs which were ridiculously badly paid and which he finally gave up. He had failed to complete his education, in which he had shown such promise, and he had learned no profession. All he had was his sturdy health, his passion for learning, and his obstinate Scottish determination to win through.

One Sunday evening he and William went for a walk along the slopes overlooking the Firth and the shores of Fife beyond. They began to talk about their rather cheerless prospects; and William suddenly came out with an idea that had been in his mind for some time. He proposed to Robert that he should abandon his desperate efforts to find work as a teacher or a clerk, and start up in business on his own. He must become a bookseller, said William; and when Robert, scarcely sixteen, looked bewildered at the thought, and asked where on earth he was going to get his capital and stock-in-trade, William told him that he had thought of that, and reminded him that their parents still had a mass of old books that they had dragged about from home to home and had no real use or place for. Why shouldn't Robert put them up for sale on a stall somewhere in the town? They might not be many, and not worth much, but even if he only got a couple of pounds for them he could reinvest the money in more books, and so – with luck – expand further and further. They could go regularly to the evening book auctions, particularly those of an odd character called Peter Cairns, whose premises were in the Agency Office opposite the University, and which they had already frequented for the pleasure of reading, in a warm, well-lighted room, the books displayed in advance of auction, and of listening to Cairn's sarcastic witticisms as he cajoled his audience into making bids. A small profit on a steady turnover, William cannily persuaded Robert, if kept up for a sufficient number of years, could be the foundation of something big.

To Robert's surprise, he found his parents willing to part with the tattered library, all except the *Encyclopedia Britannica* and the family Bible; to which, rather sadly, he added his own school editions of the classics. He decided to look for a shop with room for a stall in front in Leith Walk, the broad street joining Edinburgh to its seaport. The situation was useful, as the Walk was constantly used as a thoroughfare by merchants, sailors, and other visitors who came by sea. In addition, according to William's account, a swarm of beggars could be seen there every day, "old blind fiddlers seated by the wayside; sailors deficient in a leg or an arm, with long queues hanging down their backs, who were always singing ballads about sea-fights; and cripples of various sorts, who contrived to move along in wooden bowls, or in low-wheeled vehicles drawn by dogs". Most of the houses were rather mean and jerry-built, and many were occupied on the street-level by small shops for the sale of shells, corals and other curiosities brought in by the seafarers. Robert found one that was vacant, rented it for the large sum of six pounds a year, and moved in upstairs with William. They had about ten shillings worth of furniture between them at the start, and the first night lay on the floor with only a rug to cover them and a pile of books for pillow. They were suddenly full of hope and a sense of adventure, and thought it all very amusing.

The broad highway of Leith Walk made it easy to set up stalls without obstructing the traffic. When Robert started in business, there were two other bookstalls, and all three were on the shady side of the street, not too close and not too far from one another, so that potential purchasers were apt to drift from one to the next, their interest gradually more and more aroused and their appetite whetted. For this reason there was no sense of rivalry between the three traders: the other two showed a very friendly spirit to Robert, and helped him to distinguish between the habitual browsers and nibblers who had no intention of buying, and those who could be counted upon, if left in peace, or persuaded eventually to make a purchase. Whenever they had new books, or new-looking remainders to sell, they deliberately made the outsides dirty or cut up some of the pages, knowing that most of the stall frequenters refused to believe that they could get a clean book as cheaply as an old one.

Within a year, Robert had converted his original two pounds' worth of old family books into stock worth more than twenty pounds, and had managed somehow or other to live off his trade at the same time. The united daily housekeeping expenses of the brothers was about a shilling, and they rarely spent more than six-pence beyond that. When William had finished his apprentice-ship, he decided to set up on his own in the same line of business, so they separated. He did well, but having invested in a ramshackle printing outfit he gradually became more and more absorbed in developing the opportunities it presented. "I think there was a degree of infatuation," he wrote in his *Memoirs*, "in my attach-ment to that jangling, creaking, wheezing little press. Placed at the only window in my apartment, within a few feet of my bed, I could see its outlines in the silvery moonlight when I awoke . . . when daylight came fully in, it was impossible to resist the desire to rise and have an hour or two of exercise at the little machine." Displaying his usual shrewdness and capacity for endless hard work, he prospered. Robert had meanwhile begun to write – "it came upon him like an inspiration at nineteen years of age." William also had an inspiration. Why shouldn't they start a little magazine together? He would print and produce it, and Robert would edit and write most of it. So it was that their first joint literary venture, the *Kaleidoscope, or Edinburgh Literary Amusement* was born. It was to appear once a fortnight, and the first number was ready one Saturday in October, 1821.

The *Kaleidoscope* did not last very long, and did not do much more than cover its expenses. It folded in January 1822; but it had at least given the brothers a taste of the pleasures to be derived from running a literary magazine together; a pleasure which was to be fully, and profitably, realised ten years later when the first number of *Chambers's Edinburgh Journal* came out.

III

At about this time a lucky chance brought Robert into contact with Sir Walter Scott. Sometimes copies of well-known books, which he had for sale, lacked a few pages. It was Robert's practise to write these pages out in his own hand, and bind them in. His penmanship began to be much admired, and through an old friend of his mother's, who came to his stall one morning, specimens of his penmanship were brought to the notice of Archibald Constable, the most powerful of booksellers and publishers in Edinburgh at the time.

One of these specimens happened to consist of extracts from Sir Walter Scott's poems. Constable was interested, and wanted to give the struggling young bookseller-author a helping hand. He suggested that Robert should write out as a volume the songs in the *Lady of the Lake*, which he, Constable, would bind in elegant fashion; he would then give Robert a letter of introduction which he could take with the gift to the poet.

A few months later the volume was ready, and Robert set off in some trepidation for Castle Street. Scott received him in his study with great kindness, praised the penmanship, and promised to put the volume in his library at Abbotsford. He showed great interest in his trade in old books, and asked him particularly to let him know if he came across any of especial value or rarity. Robert left treading on air: he felt as if he had talked with one of the gods on Olympus. Some weeks later he called on Scott again, with some books he thought might appeal to him, and a catalogue with other special items marked. Scott bought the books on the spot, and asked Robert to bring several items from the catalogue the next morning. "He seems confused", Robert wrote later, "in speaking, and forgets by the end of the topic what he said at the beginning; as if he were fretting with impatience to get people away, and to sit down to his eternal task again."

However, the ardent young bookseller had made a good impression, and in the course of the next few years Scott became very attached and saw a great deal of him. One of the first results, immensely valuable and exciting for the two brothers, was that when, in the autumn of the same year, George IV made his state visit to Edinburgh, Scott used his vast influence to obtain commissions for Robert to write out the official addresses of a number of public bodies, while William worked day and night at his press, printing off all kinds of broadsheets, popular songs, and programmes of the processions, all of which sold in thousands.

Following on this lucky windfall, Robert decided to produce a volume of sketches of various country characters, known to him personally or by description of his friends, who were popularly believed to have been the originals of characters in Scott's earlier novels. He called it *Illustrations of the Author of Waverley*: William printed and bound a first impression of a thousand copies, which sold out at once.

This success emboldened Robert to set to work on his *Traditions of Edinburgh*, in which he gathered together all the results of his roamings through the old parts of the city, and all that he had heard about famous characters of the recent past. One of his chief sources of the latter was Charles Kirkpatrick Sharpe, an eccentric Edinburgh personality who was roped in by Scott to be one of the original contributors to the *Quarterly Review*. His rather effeminate figure, dressed in a long blue frock-coat, black trousers over white stockings and neat shoes, his brown wig coming down to his eyebrows, was a familiar sight on Princes Street. He was renowned for his rather feline wit, and aristocratic temper. In his high, shrill voice he would complain of the degeneracy of the times, asking why people of good birth no longer committed any interesting crimes. Robert went to call on him at No. 93 Princes Street, and was shown into a small room, stuffed full of family trinkets and curiosities, including a calling card of the famous beauty, Lady Charlotte Campbell, stuck into a picture frame. Like so many others of an older generation, he took a liking to Robert at once, and talked freely and wittily to him, drawing on his vast store of gossip and personal experience to answer Robert's questions.

When the first volume of the *Traditions* came out, Scott was said to have been amazed at where "the boy got all the information". One day he called at the stall with Lockhart: Robert was so overcome, that he remained absolutely tongue-tied. "While I stood silent," wrote Robert, "I heard him tell his companion that Charles Sharpe was a writer in the *Traditions*, and taking up the volume he read aloud what he called one of his *quaint bits*. 'The ninth Earl of Eglintoune was one of those patriarchal peers who live to an advanced age – indefatigible in the frequency of their marriages and the number of their children – who linger on and on, with an unfailing succession of young countesses, and die at last leaving a progeny interspersed throughout the whole of Douglas's *Peerage*, two volumes, folio, re-edited by Wood.' And then both gentlemen went on laughing for perhaps two minutes with interjections; 'How like Charlie!' – 'What a strange being he is!' – 'Two volumes, folio, *re-edited by Wood* – ha, ha, ha! There you have him past all doubt!' – and so on. I was too much abashed to tell Sir Walter that it was only an impudent little bit of writing of my own, part of the solution into which I had diffused the actual notes of Sharpe. But, having occasion next day to write to Mr Lockhart, I mentioned Sir Walter's mistake; and he was soon after good enough to inform me that he had set his friend right as to the authorship, and that they had had a *second* hearty laugh on the subject."

In the years that followed, Robert, still in his twenties, produced more and more books about Scottish lore; and in all of them he had the sympathy, and often the assistance of Scott. Soon after the publication of his complete *Traditions of Edinburgh,* Scott sent him a packet of manuscripts, which contained all that he could remember of "old persons and things" in Edinburgh. When, later, Robert was preparing his work on *The Popular Rhymes of Scotland,* Scott again sent him all that he could remember, all that had come his way, on the subject. For some years after, until his health began to fail, he would walk home with Robert from the Parliament House, day after day, pouring out his reminiscences and his comments on the historical subjects on which Robert was at work. After 1826, Robert saw him less and less. When Scott died in the late summer of 1832, Robert and William were among the chief mourners from Edinburgh. In a carriage they had hired, they followed the long funeral procession from Abbotsford, through the villages of Darnick and Melrose, to Dryburgh. All along the route the farmers and villagers treated the event as a day of national mourning. "The spectacle presented at the final solemnity," wrote William, "the large concourse of mourners clustered under the trees and near the ruins of the abbey, the sonorous reading of the funeral service amidst the silent crowd, and the gloomy atmosphere overhead, is one never to be forgotten. Few amongst those present felt more acutely than my brother; and when the coffin was lowered into the tomb, his heart swelled with uncontrollable emotion."

By this time Robert had a wide circle of friends and acquaintances in Edinburgh. One of the most original and fascinating was James Hogg, the Ettrick Shepherd, who used to come up from his farm in Selkirk once or twice a year to pay a round of visits. In the *Traditions,* describing life in the capital in the previous century, Robert says that "Tavern dissipation formerly prevailed to an incredible extent, and engrossed the leisure hours of all professional men, scarcely excepting the most stern and dignified. No rank class, or profession, indeed, formed an exception to this rule. Nothing was so common in the morning, as to meet a nobleman or two reeling home from a close in the High Street, where they had spent the whole night in drinking. Nor was it unusual to find the half of his Majesty's most honourable Lords of Council and Session mounting the Bench, in the forenoon, in a state little removed from absolute civilation . . . The entertainments of an oyster cellar were such as would make a modern fine lady faint at the bare recital." In spite of this last observation, it would seem that the convivial habits of the lowland Scots had by no means died out; James Hogg, in any case, managed to revive them during the fortnight or so of his visits. According to Robert, he spent almost the whole of this time breakfasting, dining and supping with his friends, from Sir Walter Scott to the humblest aspiring poets and booksellers' assistants, keeping them in a roar with his droll stories and witticisms, singing his own songs with ever greater pantomime as the applause warmed his spirits up, and leaving his hosts in a state not far from "absolute civilation".

At the end of each visit the Shepherd was accustomed to throw a gigantic farewell party at his inn in Candlemaker Row. Robert has left a description of one of these extraordinary feasts which he attended. In the morning Hogg would go round saying to each friend he visited that he was inviting *twae-three lads* to sup with him, that the friend would be very welcome and could bring any of *his* friends he liked with him. The result was that "something like a Highland host" arrived at the inn, and could hardly be accommodated at the table that crowded the largest room. "What a strangely miscellaneous company is found to have been gathered together! Meal-dealers are there from the Grassmarket, genteel and slender young men from the Parliament House, printers from the Cowgate and booksellers from the New Town. Between a couple of young advocates sits a decent grocer from Bristo Street; and amidst a host of shop-lads from the Luckenbooths is perched a stiffish young probationer, who scarcely knows whether he should be here or not, and has much dread that the company will sit late. Jolly, honest-like bakers, in pepper-and-salt coats, give great uneasiness to squads of black-coats in juxtaposition with them; and several dainty-looking youths, in white neck-cloths and black silk eye-glass ribbons, are evidently much discomposed by a rough tyke of a horse-dealer who has got in amongst them, and keeps calling out all kinds of coarse jokes to a crony about thirteen men off on the same side of the table. Many of Mr Hogg's Selkirkshire store-farming friends are there, with their well-oxygenated complexions and Dandie Dinmont-like bulk of figure." In addition, Mr Taylor, the commissioner of police for the ward in which the inn was situated, and a number of other local officials, had been invited in order to give the occasion an air of respectability, Mr Taylor taking the chair.

According to Robert, at the end of the meal Mr Taylor proposed the "loyal and patriotic" toasts, and then, after a long and pompous speech, "the toast of the evening, Mr James Hogg".

As soon as Hogg had made his usual reply, "Gentlemen, I was ever proud to be called a poet, but I never was so proud as I am this nicht", and a great deal more in the same vein, the local dignitaries got down to the serious business of making congratulatory speeches to one another. "The commissioners, bailies and moderators have the ball at their foot, and not another man can get in a word. Every imaginable public body in the city, from the University to the Potterow Friendly Society, is toasted, most of them with the honours." This went on for about two hours, a storm of civic toasts during which "it is all in vain for Mr Hogg's literary or professional friends to raise their voices".

At last, about two o'clock in the morning, the bill was called for a second time and paid by general contribution, and Mr Taylor left the chair. Then the really convivial part of the evening began. "As the company diminishes in number, it increases in mirth, and at last the extremities of the table are abandoned, and the thinned host gathers in one cluster of intense fun and good fellowship around the chair. Hogg now shines out for the first time in all his lustre, tells stories, sings, and makes all life and glee. *The Laird o' Lamington,* the *Women Folk,* and *Paddy O'Rafferty,* his three most comic ditties, are given with a force and fire that carries all before it."

My great-grandfather had a great admiration for the Ettrick Shepherd, and thought him more of a prodigy than Burns, because he had had no education to speak of. He did not, of course, rate him as high as a poet, but he had a special fondness for original untaught, salty characters, and like many other literary folk he had been surprised by *The Queen's Wake.* "Wha wad hae thought there was as muckle in that sheep's head o' yours?" one of his cronies is supposed to have said when the volume came out. But James Hogg conquered Edinburgh not so much by his poetic gifts as by his unique, dionysiac joy in life. In writing of his own life, he said: "One may think on reading over this memoir, that I have worn out a life of misery and wretchedness; but the case has been quite the reverse. I never knew either man or woman who has been so universally happy as I have been." He always treated Robert as "an unaccountable sort of person", and never could be persuaded to believe that he hadn't invented the whole of the *Traditions of Edinburgh* out of his own head.

IV

The "Dark Ages" were at last over, and by 1825 both the brothers were established, William as a successful business man and Robert as a man of letters. They had even survived a further family disaster. Their father, James Chambers, had returned to live in Edinburgh, and feeling that the tide of family fortune had at last turned, made a foolish attempt to regain possession of a property that had once belonged to the family. He lost his suit, as everyone told him he would, and William and Robert had to find money to pay the costs. They had not got so far in their careers that this was easy: Robert had to make the painful decision to sell the copyright of his *Traditions of Edinburgh*. Very soon after, James died, totally broken in health and spirits.

Robert's early successes had been due largely to the fact that he was peculiarly gifted to satisfy the appetite that had awakened in Scotland at this time for anything to do with its recent past. There was a consciousness that an old Scotland of legend and ballad was rapidly disappearing: Robert's passion, and his historic task, was to collect from living people stories, songs, traditions that might otherwise have been totally lost at their deaths, and to describe the face of an ancient Edinburgh that was vanishing in great schemes of rebuilding. But what was eventually to give him a far greater title to fame was his perception that as industrialization developed a vast popular need was growing up for information and instruction in as cheap a form as possible; and the shrewd, skilful and responsible way in which he, with the aid of his brother, set out to supply this need of a new age, an adventure whose consequences spread far beyond Scotland.

What has been described as the "cheap literature movement" had in fact begun before the end of the eighteenth century, but the Napoleonic wars postponed its expansion. In 1820, in order to stop the flood of polemical and scurrilous pamphlets of a political nature that had begun to appear very soon after 1815, a stamp duty was imposed on any pamphlet or regular paper that was not purely literary or concerned with general information. One of the first of the new class of periodical that this ordinance favoured was the *Kaleidoscope*, which the brothers had brought out in 1821; and another was the *Mirror,* which was started in London in 1822. Soon after, the Society for the Diffusion of Useful Knowledge was founded, and devoted itself to producing a series of low-priced treatises on scientific subjects. In 1827, their friend the bookseller-publisher Archibald Constable started his *Miscellany,* a series of popular volumes containing information of an instructive or entertaining kind. Gradually the number of such publications grew, on both sides of the border. In Edinburgh, the best and most successful was George Mudie's *Cornucopia*: it contained four pages, and as it was sold for threepence at a time when most newspapers cost sevenpence, it was thought to be wonderfully cheap.

Both Robert and William were intensely interested in this new literature, and in their bookselling days had studied it carefully as it passed through their hands. They noticed that one of the reasons for the failure of most of the projects to reach the success they became convinced they could have, was the irregularity of their appearance: they were generally run by erratic and eccentric people with a greater fondness for reading than business sense, who seemed unable to keep to a precise time-table. Their contents were also extremely miscellaneous, and collected in a very haphazard way, as one might put a scrapbook together. The two brothers came to believe that a similar paper, but of a much less trivial character, which aimed to have a serious educational purpose but at the same time was well and attractively written, might gain a great success. Robert was a little daunted at first by the risks involved in such a venture, but he had faith in William's business ability and energy and could not in the end resist the opportunity of going in with him as chief contributor.

So it was that the first number of *Chambers's Edinburgh Journal* appeared on Saturday 4th February 1832, with an introductory explanation by William, in which he described their aim, in rather sententious-pathetic terms, as being that "every Saturday, when the poorest labourer in the country draws his humble earnings, he shall have it in his power to purchase with an insignificant portion of even that humble sum, a meal of healthful, useful, and agreeable mental instruction". The *Journal* was to come out once a week, and cost three-halfpence.

There was no doubt about the popularity of the meal. In a few days thirty thousand copies were sold in Scotland alone; a far higher circulation than they had dared to expect, and extraordinary by the standards of the day. Soon after, they managed to find an agent for London, and sold another twenty thousand there. What was even more satisfactory, this was no mere curiosity sale: the circulation remained around 50,000 for some years, and then gradually climbed to 80,000 and over.

A couple of months later, the Society for the Diffusion of Useful Knowledge produced its *Penny Magazine*. Whether this venture was influenced by the success of *Chambers's Journal* we do not know, but it certainly did not affect their sales. The *Penny Magazine* lasted, with what appears to have been considerable success, till 1845. Robert and William attributed its eventual failure to its being a little too technical and abstruse for the mass public it was intended to appeal to. In any case, it is clear that it was Robert's genius for charming his readers in the form of essay which he perfected for the *Journal*, in providing food for the imagination as well as food for the intellect, that was decisive in its success among country folk and working-class people in the towns as well as men of education. He hit just the right note from the start. In October of 1832 the Scottish poet Allan Cunningham wrote to Robert: "I am truly glad of your great circulation; your work is by a thousand degrees the best of all the latter progeny of the press. It is an original work, and while it continues so must keep the lead of the paste and scissors productions. My wife, who has just returned from Scotland, says that your *Journal* is very popular among her native hills of Galloway. The shepherds, who are scattered there at the rate of one to every four miles square, read it constantly, and they circulate it in this way : the first shepherd who gets it reads it, and at an understood hour places it under a stone under a certain hill-top; then shepherd the second in his own time finds it, reads it, and carries it to another hill, where it is found like Ossian's chief under its own grey stone by shepherd the third, and so it passes on its way, scattering information over the land."

Another friend of theirs told them that at a country town near Edinburgh where he lived, a group of eager young readers used regularly to walk two or three miles out on the road in order to intercept the carrier bringing the new numbers from Edinburgh, and so obtain their copies a few hours earlier.

In the light of these fascinating glimpses of the way in which the *Journal* was passed from hand to hand even in the countryside, it seems probable that its actual readership was something in the neighbourhood of a quarter of a million.

The popularity of *Chambers's Journal* certainly influenced Leigh Hunt when he started *The London Journal* two years later, as he acknowledged in his opening editorial. Robert wrote to congratulate him, making it generously clear that so far from fearing *The London Journal* as a rival, he believed that the more such publications were started the better they would all do. Leigh Hunt promptly published this letter (characteristically without permission) and only a little while afterwards wrote to thank Robert. "I forgot to say one thing in my public remarks on your letter, to express my hearty agreement with you as to the opinion that publications of this kind do no injury to one another. But this was implied in my address to the public in the first number, and I hope was self-evident. Most unaffectedly do I rejoice at hearing your own words confirm, and in so pleasant and touching a manner, the report of the great success of you and your brother in your speculation . . . Any kind of a bit of a nest of retreat, with powers to send forth my young comfortably into the world, and keep up my note of cheerfulness and encouragement to all ears while I still have a voice left, is all that I desire for myself, or ever did."

This success transformed the lives of the two brothers. They moved to new business premises, and the general publishing firm of W. & R. Chambers was founded. So close was the sympathy and collaboration between them, that for over twenty years no memorandum of agreement existed in the new firm. They had nothing except their own small and hard-won capital to start with, asked for no loans, and took in no other partners; but so assured did the future of the *Journal* seem after only a few numbers had been published, that they were able to extract themselves from the cramped position of relying on hand-presses, "even" – as William recorded – "with relays of men toiling night and day", bought proper printing machinery (worked by steam), and were soon sending a set of stereotype plates for each number to London, for the English impression to be printed there, while they used another set in Edinburgh for the main Scottish impression.

One curious result of the brothers' determination to steer clear of religious as well as party political allegiances, was that they began to be attacked by bigots of the Kirk for not giving the *Journal* the character of a "religious publication". They were even denounced from the pulpit. This persecution went on for twenty years or so; Robert and William treated it as a joke.

A few years later Thomas Hood, on a visit to Edinburgh, asked if they would let him see the *Journal* being printed. He was surprised to notice that the sheets that were coming out of the presses were dated more than a fortnight in advance. They explained that in order to get the parcels out to even the remotest districts on time, each number was made up, stereotyped and put to press three weeks ahead. Hood observed that to have to organize things in that way would drive him mad; but it is evident that it was

precisely attention to such details, entirely foreign to most of the
papers that had come out before, that brought the brothers their
triumph.

V

In 1829 Robert married Anne Kirkwood, and settled into a contented domestic life, with a large family growing up round him
which eventually consisted of eight daughters and three sons. For
the next twelve years or so he was deeply absorbed in his literary
work, and in his regular articles for *Chambers' Journal*. He seems
to have had a remarkably happy and genial disposition, and in
spite of his "plodding industry", rarely if ever to have suffered
from explosions of exasperation or moods of discouragement.
Writing to a friend in 1835, he said: "Men, it is allowed, are apt
to speak of things as they find them; and, for my part, I would say
that it is possible to lead the life of a literary man without any of
those grievances and evil passions which others picture as insepar-
able from the profession. I envy none, despise none, but, on the
contrary, yield due respect to all, whether above or beneath me . . .
The result is, that hardly such a thing as an annoyance ever breaks
the calm tenor of my life, and that there is not one person with
whom I was ever acquainted whom I cannot meet as a friend."

His books continued to pour out, the *Popular Rhymes of Scotland*, the *Picture of Scotland*, the material for both of which he collected as much by long wanderings by coach and on foot all over
his native country as from old documents; and perhaps most interesting of all, his *History of the Rebellion of 1745*. Though he took
the view that the Hanoverian succession should have been
accepted, and thought that it was a crime to plunge the Kingdom
into civil war, it is clear that Robert had strong, sentimental
Jacobite sympathies. A reviewer in the *Quarterly* went so far as to
say that his "Jacobitism seems that of a rampart Highlander"
though the chief evidence for this judgement appears to have

been his belief, about which he made no bones, that the Pretender's followers were sincere men, heroically devoted to an ideal for which they suffered cruelly.

As in the case of so many of Robert's most popular works, the *History of the Rebellion* owed a great deal to his zeal for collecting material from living sources: he got into touch with as many decendants as possible of the most prominent figures in the rebellion, who supplied him with stories and traditions handed down in their families. In addition, he followed Prince Charlie's wanderings over the Highlands, in and out of caves and huts, using, as no railways had yet penetrated there, country carts and whatever miserable boats were available. He found that the country folk in these remote places were still Roman Catholics, and passionately enthusiastic about the Prince's cause.

The book went through edition after edition; but the seventh edition was enormously enlarged because Robert had been allowed to use the still unpublished records in the famous manuscript, the *Lyon in Mourning*. This precious document had been compiled by Bishop Forbes, a Jacobite who was imprisoned – as a kind of "protective custody" – during the rebellion in Edinburgh Castle, where he had formed the plan of writing down all the eyewitness accounts and background stories that could still be obtained from survivors of the catastrophe. The ten volumes, bound in black, came into the possession of Sir Henry Steuart of Allanton after the Bishop's death, and one day Robert, on a visit to Allanton House, was told of their existence and managed to persuade Sir Henry to let him use them for a revision of his *History*. In addition, he published a more elaborate study of the *Lyon* in his *Jacobite Memoirs of the Rebellion of 1745*.

In 1840 Robert received his first mark of public recognition, and was elected a member of the Royal Society of Edinburgh. Extraordinary though it may sound, he had already published thirty books of one sort and another. During these years he was more and more preoccupied with scientific investigations, and carried on an extensive correspondence with the scientists of the day, often visiting London for meetings and discussions. His great work was beginning to take shape in his mind; and in order to be able to devote himself to it, away from the social distractions of Edinburgh, and also in order to be able to keep the secret more effectively, he moved to St Andrew's for two or three years. At that time St Andrews had not yet become a fashionable golfing resort, and, with its University life, was ideal for Robert's purpose. Existence was still very primitive in many ways: the town bellman or crier brought the news every day, and Mrs Chambers, clasping a tiny linen book in which she had written down the words of ballads she knew she would be expected to sing, was carried out to dinner on a sedan chair accompanied by a host of small runners. Robert took elaborate precautions to prevent rumours about the author's identity from getting around. He arranged with his friend Alexander Ireland that he should act as intermediary. The manuscript was first of all written out by his wife, then sent to Ireland in Manchester, and forwarded by him to the publishers in London. The proofs took the same circuitous course in reverse. This secret service stuff had the added advantage of concealing the fact that the author was a Scot.

Vestiges of Creation was published in October 1844, fifteen years before *The Origin of Species*. It was not until 1884 that Ireland, after both Robert and William were dead, revealed the authorship in his introduction to the twelfth edition; though by then the assumption was fairly widespread that it was Robert's book. Immediately on its publication, it became the topic of the day, and a friend of Robert's, who did not know that he was the author, wrote to him from London that nothing like it had happened since the publication of *Waverley,* and little else was talked about in scientific circles. It was reviewed at length everywhere, generally with rage and indignation, and very soon "answers" began to appear, challenging or ridiculing the "theory of development" it put forward, in tracts, pamphlets, magazine articles, sermons and lectures. Within seven months four editions had to be printed. Many scientists were among the most hostile critics. In June the following year Robert himself was present at a scientific meeting in London, at which Sir John Herschel delivered an address condemning it, much to the satisfaction of those in the audience who could hear his feeble voice. A professor of physiology, who had a strong suspicion that Robert had written it, came up to him afterwards and said, slyly, "The poor author of the *Vestiges* has got it in all directions tonight." But Robert refused to be drawn, and only replied: "Yes, it would be curious if he had been present and heard it all. I wonder how he would have felt."

Darwin was among those who remained calmer, criticizing the accuracy of a great deal of the geological and zoological data, but recognizing the importance of the work and its literary skill. In a letter to William Darwin Fox in February 1845, he wrote: "Have you read that strange, unphilosophical, but capitally written book, the *Vestiges*? It has made more talk than any work of late, and has been by some atrributed to me – at which I ought to be much flattered and unflattered." Later in his life, as he told one of Robert's daughters, he felt he had not done full justice to it; and in the fourth edition of *The Origin of Species* (in 1868) he added a brief appreciation: "The work, from its powerful and brilliant style, though displaying in the earlier editions little accurate knowledge, and a great want of scientific caution, immediately had a very wide circulation. In my opinion it had done excellent service in this country in calling attention to the subject, in removing prejudice, in thus preparing the ground for the reception of analogous views."

Robert took the hostility of the scientists in his usual phlegmatic and good-humoured way. "It is no discredit to them," he wrote, "that they are, almost without exception, engaged each in his own little department of science, and able to give little or no attention to other parts of that vast field. From year to year, and from age to age, we see them at work, adding no doubt much to the known, and advancing many important interests, but, at the same time, doing little for the establishment of comprehensive views of nature. Experiments in however narrow a walk, facts of whatever minuteness, make reputations in scientific societies; all beyond is regarded with suspicion and distrust."

An amusing incident took place at Robert's own dinner-table, one evening not long after *Vestiges* had been published. One of the noisier guests, who had been dominating the conversation, started talking about the book and asking who could possibly be the author. Various guesses were promptly made and a lively discussion developed, during which Robert, his wife, and Alexander Ireland who happened to be present, kept as quiet as they could, furtively exchanging glances and doing their best to keep straight faces. Among the guests was a middle-aged lady novelist, an eccentric creature who had a reputation for dabbling in science as well as pouring out a stream of mediocre fiction. The guest who had started the discussion suddenly looked at her and said: "I have a strong suspicion that the lady opposite is the author of that naughty book. Is it not so? Come now, confess. You cannot deny it." Instead of denying it, the novelist hesitated, looked embarrassed and said nothing, shaking her head and laughing in a coy, significant way, as if to say "Of course I can't *admit* it, but . . ."

Once the book was through the press, Robert and his family returned to Edinburgh and took up residence at a new house, No. I Doune Terrace. At about the same time there was published, under his own name, the *Cyclopedia of English Literature,* the first work of its kind ever to be compiled. Revised editions are still issued.

VI

Robert Chambers's house at No. I Doune Terrace was famous for its musical evenings, in which the children took an active part. Early on, Nina, the eldest, showed a gift for the piano even more remarkable than her mother's. All the girls appear to have had pleasing voices, in particular Amelia, known in the family as "Tuckie", who also composed songs. Sometimes Nina played the piano, while her mother played the harp; sometimes one or other of them would accompany ballads and songs which the twins, Jenny and Lizzie, would dance for the guests, while Mary, whom Robert called "The Andalusian Maid" for her beautiful hazel eyes, would be drawing in a corner.

Robert radiated good humour and affection, and all those who knew the family agree that the atmosphere of their home was especially happy and free. Unless he was out on his geological and antiquarian explorations, Robert would work in his study most of the day, and again for a while after dinner (dinner was generally at five). Then, when the guests began to arrive, he would come out and join in the conversation, the singing and the playing; or often, when no guests were expected, would read to his assembled children; or watch them practise the dances they had learned that morning from their dancing master, who wore old-fashioned tights, played the fiddle as he showed them the steps, and sported a green wig, which was a source of endless amazement to his young pupils.

Sometimes the evenings assumed a stranger aspect. Sir Edward Bulwer Lytton (brother of Henri's friend) whose fame as a novelist had steadily increased in the previous decade, appears at this time to have been interested in mesmerism, which was all the rage, and tried experiments on the girls. One or two of them were particularly susceptible, and he succeeded in making them try to climb up a bell pull, or believe that they could not remove their hands from a wall against which he had placed them, until he made a few passes over their heads. On several memorable occasions Bulwer Lytton arrived with the famous Edinburgh physician, Professor Simpson (afterwards Sir James Simpson) who was described by a wag as having "the body of Bacchus with the wit of Jove". He was making experiments with chloroform at the time. Robert would come in to find several of his children hypnotized into trance-like attitudes about the room, or half way up the curtains, while others were lying unconscious on the floor with handkerchiefs soaked in chloroform over their mouths. None of

this seemed to have worried Mrs Chambers, who took the view
that it was only too fortunate if her children could help in the advancement of science.

Two of the guests who were especially popular with the children were G. H. Lewes, and Dicky Doyle. Lewes had not yet met
George Eliot, but was already well known as an outstanding
writer on philosophical and scientific problems. Excitement
among the children grew steadily on the evenings when Lewes
was expected. Soon after he appeared, he would collect them
round him, some on his knees, others sitting on the floor, and
start telling them stories, on one evening weird and macabre, on
another fairy-tale romances with happy endings. But they were
puzzled, and a little frightened, when they were taken to see him
act Shylock in *The Merchant of Venice*: it all seemed so very
different from their story-telling evenings, which would end in
hilarious singsongs. Richard Doyle, who had already made a
name by his drawings in *Punch*, for which he had designed the
cover, used to play a game of "five dots" with the girls: someone
would put them down at random on a piece of paper and the
problem was to draw a human form within the area so defined.
Needless to say, Dicky Doyle himself was the fastest, the most
ingenious and amusing at this game, closely followed by the
Andalusian Maid.

Occasionally they would be joined in the game by Noel
Paton, a close friend of the family, and an artist who was afterwards made limner to the Queen in Scotland. Though a very good
looking young man at the time, he was known for some odd
reason as "Grandpapa". He used to help them in designing
scenery and costumes for their amateur theatricals. One night, a
few years later, Annie Chambers had a vivid dream. She was at an
evening party and was asked to accompany a guest who was going
to sing. When she sat down at the piano she found in front of her
a piece of music on which had been drawn the picture of a young
man lying on a couch with what looked like an angel hovering
over his head. Hardly had she begun to play when she awoke to

find herself in the darkness of her bedroom with my great-grand-father sleeping peacefully beside her. So vivid, however, were the words of the song and the accompanying music, that she woke him up, and persuaded him to go with her to the piano in the drawing-room next door, before they faded. Then, while she sang out of her dream, Robert, in his dressing-gown and cotton nightcap with a tassel on the top, took down the words:

> With thy genius bending o'er thee,
> With thy great and noble Art,
> With thy rich and glorious fancy,
> And thy loving tender heart;
>
> Death cannot come nigh thee,
> Still aside must turn his dart,
> Before thee lies a glorious pathway,
> On, for thou must play thy part.

The next morning Annie sent a letter off to the Patons describing the extraordinary dream and enclosing these words of the song. Noel Paton's sister answered at once, saying that her brother had in fact been ill at the time, but as soon as he read the letter felt very much better and determined to set to work again.

Also very popular with the children were the two pseudo-Jacobite Princes, John Sobieski Stuart and his brother who had taken the title Prince Charles Edward adopted on his return to France, the Comte d'Albany. They looked magnificent in the Royal Stuart tartan, with glengarries and eagle plumes, Highland chieftains to the life; but it seems more likely that they had nothing to do with the Stuarts, but were the sons of a certain Lieutenant Thomas Allen in the Royal Navy. They had introduced themselves to Robert after the publication of his *History of the Rebellion*. Whether he believed in their pretensions we do not know; but at least he found them excellent company, and the children were seduced by the stumpy packets of sweets they always brought with them to the musical evenings.

One visitor to the house, who would appear for a few days and then vanish again as if pursued by the Furies, was Thomas de Quincey; a tragic figure in dishevelled clothes, with lined and careworn face ("a face like death in life" one witness who saw him at this time has said) that would nevertheless light up with extraordinary imaginative fire when the conversation caught his fancy. For some years, during the eighteen thirties, he had been in the habit of taking refuge in the Sanctuary of Holyrood to escape imprisonment for his ever mounting debts. Eventually, however, his debts even there grew so heavy that he lost the right of sanctuary, and was forced to live a kind of *maquis* existence in Edinburgh, changing and multiplying his lodgings continually. He was caught, and imprisoned, and released on the intervention of the publisher Adam Black. He then took his almost starving family to Lasswade, just outside Edinburgh, but continued to reappear in the city without warning, living the same hunted life from landlady to landlady while he searched desperately for work. It was not till his mother died in 1846 and his two eldest children had taken his affairs in hand that he began to escape from this nightmare.

Just before the family moved to St Andrews, Robert had received a letter from him, in which he alleged that he had heard that Robert was "weary of the labour connected with the essays" he wrote for the *Journal*, and offering to stand in for him. "I should be happy to furnish a series of essays on Life, Manners, Literature and other subjects. And as I know experimentally that the discovery and shaping of subjects is in itself a laborious thing, I should be happy to make that a part of my undertaking. All this, I repeat, is meant only upon the assumption that the report I have heard is accurate. I am at present, and for three or four months to come, condemned to fight off creditors with one hand, whilst with the other I furnish support to nine persons daily. Still, I am obliged to count all literary labours within my reach."

Robert was by no means "weary of the labour" and nothing seems to have come of this offer, except that they became friends.

As he loved both music and children, De Quincey must have found Doune Terrace very sympathetic. He used often to spend Sunday evenings there, and kept a pair of wellington boots in the house so that he should always have a change, in case he was obliged to leave his belongings at his latest lodgings without daring to return. These boots were still at Doune Terrace when he died. A vivid glimpse of the harassed confusion in which he lived is given in one of his letters to Mrs Chambers, dated (at the beginning) March 4th, without any year. It was in answer to one of hers, for he begins by apologizing for his delay in writing, without being able to find out exactly how remiss he had been, for the date on her letter "if date your note ever had (a point on which it is lawful to be sceptical with regard to all notes emanating from ladies), had perished on that upper right-hand corner of the first page, which in my awkwardness I tore off in the act of opening it". He describes his struggle to correct for the press "papers written originally with so much carelessness that they do not allow themselves to be righted", and an attack of influenza which had been followed by partial blindness, but from which he had now fully recovered. He felt, in fact, better than he had for years; but with this statement the letter broke off, and was only resumed ten days later. He apologized again, complaining that "the letter had *lost itself*" among a pile of manuscripts and other letters; he explained that he had been about to write again, when "the absconding individual" emerged from the chaos, but to his surprise without a signature. Such a lapse would never have occurred he concluded, if his daughters who generally kept things straight for him had not been absent. The letter was full of erasures and interjections and qualifications squeezed in between the lines.

If happy-go-lucky disorder reigned in De Quincey's household, it was not unknown in Doune Terrace. A few years later, after her marriage, Nina, on a visit to her parents, wrote: "The Chambers family are the same delightful vague people they have always been. . . . This is a most dangerous house to let anything out of your sight for a minute. Things make mysterious disappearances.

If you lay them down for a minute, they get shunted on to a side rail and are lost to sight for ever so long. In an unwary moment I took my match box out of my desk and left it. I looked in vain for days, missing it a good deal. At last, one evening, where do you think I found it? Suspended to a string from the ceiling of the back drawing-room. I seize it, sombody cries out: 'Oh don't take that away, it is to weigh down the ventilator and keep it shut.' I take it away nevertheless, and now I see somebody's bunch of keys supplies its place, and I have no doubt is in its turn being looked for in vain."

Annie Chambers kept a hospitable table, and no one was likely to leave her dinners with a feeling of inadequate nourishment. One of the most celebrated was given in honour of George Outram, poet and brother of Sir James, the famous "Bayard of India". It started at five, and the guests did not leave till long after ten, by which time songs and improvizations on the harp were in full swing. The menu began with Hotch Potch, which was followed by Cockie Leekie, Crabbit Heads (stuffed haddock), Salmon, Scallops, Haggis, Poor man o'mutton, and a large variety of sweets including, as the main attraction, strawberries and cream in soup plates. A truly Scottish feast.

One of the most welcome and appreciative guests at her table was the young James Payn, who had been a regular contributor to the *Journal* long before he became Assistant Editor in the late fifties. He wrote in his *Recollections* that Robert, at first meeting, gave the impression of being rather dry and unforthcoming; it was not till later that he recognized how much humour sparkled in his eye. "His nature was essentially 'good'; from the pleasure he took in the popularity of his friends, I used to call him 'the Well-Wisher' – nor did he confine himself, as so many benevolent folks do, to wishing . . . His manner however, on first acquaintance, was somewhat solid and unsympathetic. He had a very striking face and figure, as well-known in Edinburgh as St Gile's Cathedral, but a stranger would have taken him for a divine, possibly even for one of the 'unco' guid'. In London his white tie, and grave demeanour, caused him to be always taken for a clergyman; a very great mistake, which used to tickle him exceedingly. 'When I don't give a beggar the penny he solicits,' he used to say, 'he generally tells me after a few cursory remarks, that the ministers are always the hardest.'"

It is clear from Payn's account that Robert was too modest and gentle to have any conceit about having reached his fame and fortune the hard way. In this he was a contrast to his brother William, who, according to Payn, "was always talking of the poverty of his youth, and hinting – very broadly – at the genius which had raised him to eminence. He was fond of holding forth upon the miseries of a poor lad, who had to 'thole' and toil for his livelihood, and had afterwards, by diligence and merit, made a great figure in the world; and the peroration – for which everybody was quite prepared (i.e. with their handkerchiefs, not at their eyes, but stuffed in their mouths) – used to be always '*I was that Boy*'. All this was hateful to Robert, and gave him, as well it might, extreme annoyance."

On one occasion, an American magazine asked Payn to write an article on the early life of the two brothers. Robert refused to help, saying that he was absolutely sick of the "two-hundred-times-told story", and advised Payn to apply to William, who would "be delighted to tell you the whole truth about it – and more. He will be sure to say that we came bare-footed into Edinburgh; whereas, as a matter of facts we came in the 'Flea'" – the Flea being the name of the coach that ran between Peebles and Edinburgh.

VII

Among the more interesting Edinburgh friends of the Chambers family were the Murrays. Lord Murray was a popular Whig lawyer who had been elected Member of Parliament for Leith Burghs in 1832, was knighted as Lord Advocate, and afterwards promoted to the bench. "Few persons," wrote William in his *Story of a Long and Busy Life*, "connected with art, science or literature in Edinburgh, escaped being acquainted with this marvellously genial person. His qualities were good nature, love of humour, and particularly a love of pleasant society in his new home, a large and splendid dwelling in Great Stuart Street, with an outlook behind to the picturesque dell of the Water of Leith." Here Lord Murray gave large but select dinner parties, which were famous for the excellence of the food and the rarity of the wines that were served. Even more famous were the weekly evening parties, to which a far greater company was invited. Lady Murray presided, performing on the piano, for which she had a fanatical love, and persuading whatever other distinguished players she could find, to perform on the flute, harp or violin.

Owing to his outstanding gift as a violinist, which soon became widely known, Frederick Lehmann was often invited to these parties after he had settled in Leith; and it seems likely that he first met Robert Chambers and his eldest daughter Nina at one of them. On the other hand, it is possible that he was first introduced to them by a younger member of the Murray family, Oswald, an artist who appears to have been a pupil or protégé of Henri's in Paris, and who struck up an intimate friendship with Frederick when he returned to Edinburgh towards the beginning of 1850.

In any case, within the year Frederick was a regular visitor at No. 1 Doune Terrace. In his reminiscences, he writes: "Robert Chambers himself played the flute very fairly, and his wife and some of his daughters were not only excellent pianists, but were endowed with musical faculties to a very unusual degree. I remember a little dance for which Mrs Chambers and one of the girls played the music on a piano and a harmonium. Musicians will understand my surprise when I heard the daughter interrupt her mother, saying: 'Not in G, mamma, let us play it in A'; whereupon they resumed in the altered key, as if such transposition, instead of being a difficult and intricate feat, was the simplest and most natural attribute of the performance . . . What innocent evenings of mirth and frolic we used to have, and when Robert Chambers, the most industrious of mortals, emerged late from his study, Jove-like, and with a little of the dampness of his Olympian clouds clinging to him, how the whole mad company would immediately be on its best behaviour, all the girls flocking to the feet of their father and trying to be fit company for him."

It seems, however, that there were times when Robert's fondness for reading out of some philosophical work tried the patience of his adoring children. Nina's sister, Mary, ("The Andalusian Maid") related in a letter to Frederick that they invented an imaginary lover called Charles, and used to pretend, when their father came in from his study, that Charles had hurriedly to be hidden behind the curtains or smuggled out of the room. One evening "he came in as usual to read us some philosophical work or other; and Tuckey, who cannot endure when he begins to read, and who generally acts as Charles in an emergency, went out of the room. Presently there is the sound of a guitar heard outside in the garden, and we all look at each other and whisper: 'Oh, there's Charles at last. Good gracious! I hope Papa won't hear him. Oh heavens! I wish he would be quiet until Papa goes out of the room. Annie, go to the window and sign to him to go away just now.' Then papa, who had heard it all, of course, looks up quite angry and says: 'Dear bless me, what's the use of my reading to you if you all go on making signs to each other in that way?' However, he goes on again. Presently the door hastily opens and a head pops in, but the moment after disappears again on seeing papa, leaving nothing but a general impression of tremendous black moustache, a hat, and cane; then, of course, we are all in fits of laughing . . ."

As far as one can make out from my grand-parents' letters that have survived, as late as July 1852 Frederick was still "Sir" or "Mr Lehmann" and Nina "Miss Chambers". The first begins:

"Dear Sir, I received the music you have so kindly sent me, about an hour ago. What a quantity there is! It struck terror into my heart.

"There is plenty to choose from and it will be pleasant occupation to do so. You asked for a promissory note. Well, I think I may safely promise to play the whole of the three books fifty years hence; the 2, 3, 5, etc., I know already almost by heart and will play them say twenty years after this, or longer if you like. I must beg you not to send the 'Berceuse'. I did not understand somehow or other (I told you how stupid I was) that it was Madame [Pauline] Viardot who wrote it for you. I see how precious it must be, and fear to receive it. If you can name any night next week when you are disengaged, not at Queensferry, and musically inclined, we shall be very happy indeed to see you. Yours truly, Nina Chambers."

Frederick refused to take no for an answer, and wrote back the next day:

"Dear Miss Chambers, I send you the 'Berceuse' in spite of your protestations. You will like it very much and the oftener you play it the better. It is an airy, twilight music, and ought to be played very gently, very piano, never above a whisper. Remembering that

> 'All that's bright must fade
> The brightest, still the fleetest.'

"I will not trust to the chance nor enlarge on the charms of playing with you fifty years hence, to an admiring circle of our respective grandchildren, nor with all due deference to your memory would I tax it to remember the music I sent you for twenty years, but as a happy medium I would rather propose to come on Tuesday next, fiddler, fiddle and all. Tell me if that will meet your views, and believe me, dear Miss Chambers, Yours sincerely Frederick Lehmann."

Very soon after, the intimacy which these and other letters show as dawning had turned into love, Frederick had proposed and been accepted, and Nina's letters begin "My own beloved". It seems that at first Robert Chambers was not altogether enthusiastic about his daughter's engagement, or her determination to take things into her own hands. "O Frederick," she cries, "I would not mind this so much if Papa would only speak to me as if I were a rational human being with a comprehending intellect like him. He does not admire women with minds. I assure you solemnly of this. He would have us all after one pattern, mild unoffending creatures of property, sitting quite straight up in our chairs (he cannot bear to see a woman leaning back on her chair or lounging on a sofa), making a small observation of assent now and then, waltzing slowly and stiffly across a room, writing a small delicate female hand, and expressing little thoughts in the most strictly proper and polite terms. Why am I not like this? I am no true woman in his eyes, this I am persuaded of. None of us are, I fear. Why am I born with reason, and with power to comprehend readily and to argue? I wish I were a toy, a pretty little toy, but then you would not have bought me."

By September, they were more deeply in love than ever. Frederick had to go to Germany on business, and Nina wrote to him from Allenheads in Northumberland: "What have we done, Frederick? The more I think of it the more terrible it appears. Is there no escape? 'None' answers this uncompromising little ring looking fiercely at me with its bright eye. I am beginning to think, or rather to resume my old thoughts, that marriage is a great mistake. To love is beautiful, but – it is like eating gooseberries after grapes, a proceeding which I know from experience you disapprove of, marriage after love . . . Do you remember when I used to say: 'Well, why don't you marry, Mr Lehmann, then we could be friends?' And you replied: 'But supposing you did not like my wife?' Whereat I outwardly smiled politely, but inwardly thought I should detest her; and when that scheme fell through, I actually thought of marrying myself, and visions of a professor, and a severe room very high up somewhere filled with telescopes and mathematical apparatuses and hung around with funeral pictures of eclipses and ornamented here and there with minerals and fossil remains and dried up things of all sorts which would make one *wither* to look at, rose sternly before me, and all this was to be the price of meeting my *friend* Mr Lehmann at Lady Murray's now and then and being permitted to talk to him and sit beside him without remark, there being no danger to be apprehended from a married flirtation. *Vergebens, ach vergebens.* I could fall in love a little with philosophy, but I could not marry it. . . . *Je t'embrace.* Oh yes, a million times, until you are tired."

The marriage was finally fixed for the end of November. Both Nina and Frederick fell ill with severe chills a fortnight before, and it was therefore decided not to risk a Church ceremony: the Bishop agreed to come to the Chambers house.

"How gorgeous I was," wrote Frederick fourteen years later, "and how many times I felt nervously in the right hand pocket of an embroidered cashmere waistcoat which I still possess, whether I had not forgotten the little ring. There comes a vision of you radiant in a cloud of tulle and lace, followed by a host of faithful satellites sweeping through No. I Doune Terrace like the milky way through the sky."

All their friends in Edinburgh came to the wedding breakfast, nearly sixty guests in all. When they put on their going-away clothes, Mrs Chambers, who had miraculously restrained her tears, pressed Frederick to her bosom and cried: "Oh my dearest Frederick how am I to bear your loss, I love you like my own son!" Everyone kissed them as they left the house, handfuls of coppers were thrown to the gaping crowd, and old shoes attached to "Uncle William's musty, carriage", which carried them off in the direction of Currie, from where they were to catch a train to Carlisle, and so to London, to the St James' Hotel in Jermyn Street.

PART THREE

The Enchanted Cottager

I

My grandfather died before any of my generation in the family could know him; but from all accounts he seems to have been a man of outstanding energy, resolution and intelligence. His charm was great: one of Nina's Scottish Aunts exclaimed soon after his marriage that he was a "Prince of good fellows", an "Emperor of men", and would always uphold him as A 1, as lover, husband and friend. He was, however, born with a divided nature. His early diaries are full of introspective self-questioning and sensitive, expert appreciation of music he had recently heard, Bach, Beethoven, Mozart and the masters of his time. He had an almost hero-worshipping interest in his brother Henri's career as a painter, and all his life he read voraciously in English, German, French and Italian. And yet he chose for himself a commercial career, and appears, quite early on, to have made up his mind to be a rich man at all costs. He did not fail; nevertheless throughout his life one feels that the tension remained, between the pull of money-making and the pull of the artistic world of music, literature and painting. I cannot help thinking that the restless, goading business genius of his brother-in-law, Ernst Benzon, who had married his sister Elizabeth or "Lizbeth" and brought him into partnership with the Vickers family in the engineering firm of Naylor Vickers at about the time of his marriage, had something to do with the iron set of his will towards business success. Benzon, who was at that time managing the firm's American affairs with brilliant effect, persuaded Frederick to take Nina for a long part-honey-moon, part-business trip to America at the beginning of 1853. On their return, he decided that he wanted Frederick with him in Liverpool; though this at first caused trouble with the Vickers and Naylor families, who thought that Benzon's ultimate aim was to push them out, all difficulties were eventually resolved and suspicions allayed, and to Liverpool Frederick and Nina went for the first years of their marriage. A few years later, under a new arrangement with the Vickers family, they moved to Sheffield, and took a house called Fieldhead on the outskirts, where my father was born, and then my uncle Freddy.

Frederick took Nina on many of his business trips to the continent during these years, to Hamburg where she was introduced to his family, and to Paris where she met Henri, his wife Clémence, and their first child Louise. Her health, however, never very robust, seems to have been especially delicate in the early years after she had been transplanted from Edinburgh, and she was often left at home for long periods. She minded this – she seems rarely to have been happy when Frederick was away – and to console her he wrote her long, almost daily letters from his various points of call.

One journey especially she minded. In the Autumn of 1855 Elizabeth had been unwell, and her doctor recommended a winter in Rome; Ernst, her husband, was kept by pressing affairs in England, while Rudolf was prepared to look after her when she got to Rome, but not to come and fetch her; so Frederick agreed to accompany her, and to settle some business in Germany on the way back. It was little wonder that Nina was not happy about this, as she was expecting the birth of her first child within eight or nine weeks; but Frederick felt there was nothing for it but to do his duty by his sister. He kept on reminding her in his letters that the journey was in many ways exhausting and tiresome for him too; but he sent her some fascinating descriptions of sights and incidents on the way.

He made a detour on his return, through Venice, Vienna and Berlin. His account of the journey between Trieste and Vienna brings vividly before our eyes some of the hazards and adventures to be encountered on such an expedition in those days before the European railway network had been completed. "I was up at $\frac{1}{2}$ past 4 and left for Trieste at 6 a.m.," he writes from Vienna on the 18th November, "As we neared the town and again as we left

Trieste I continually thought of your enthusiastic remembrance of first getting a view of this beautifully situated place, and as, on leaving, we slowly toiled up the steep winding road I imagined you with your Papa and Mama rolling down rapidly and coming nearer and nearer to the beautiful panorama which I left behind me. I was only about 3 hours in Trieste, which were almost taken up by passing my luggage at the Dogana, recovering that eternal and ever to be confounded passport for the 20th time from the police, taking my place by the *Schnell Post* and so on. We were to have been in time at Laibach for the quick train and thus would have reached Vienna last night. . . . We were four in the carriage. A German, an Italian and an Irishwoman beside myself. Each of the others understood and talked only his or her language, but all wanted to talk to each other and particularly to understand what each said. I was appointed interpreter by acclamation, and you may imagine that my office was no sinecure.

"The German was a *Gutsbesitzer* from near Dresden and had not much to say, the Italian was a Sea Captain who had never made a journey by land but was now on his way to Vienna to go down the Danube and take command of a vessel at Galatz. He did not like the journey, and said: '*Non mi piace questa maniera di navigazione. E la prime, ma sera anche l'ultima volta.*'

"The Irishwoman did not say 'An if I would I could a tale of woe unfold', but she did unfold it with a vengeance. She had landed that morning from Corfu, where her husband was with an artillery regiment. So far he has, by protection and intercession of friends, been kept on the island, but he is liable to be sent to the Crimea at any moment and she is in one continual tremble at the idea. She seemed to have taken over a kind of store or shop to supply the soldiers with haberdashery, and she was now on her way to London to make some purchases. She had left 5 children – one a baby of only 4 months old – on Corfu and wanted to go by the quickest route to get back in no time. The poor soul talked of nothing but the horrors of the war and how the cholera was raging among the militiamen on the island. She depicted the

143

cholera cases so minutely and horribly that I thought I felt gripes at the mere recital, and begged her to drop that subject. She did not speak a word of anything but English (or rather Irish) and had no idea how to get to London. She only knew she was to go to Vienna, and thence to London by Ostend. I pitied the poor forlorn woman, and drew her up her route in English, also wrote her out in German a letter to all the railway authorities saying where she wanted to go and requesting them to give her dispatch and assistance. . . .

"The road was horrid to Laibach and the *Schnell Post* so slow that we missed the quick train and did not get here until 5.30 this morning. I did not go to bed for I knew I would have slept the whole day if I once gave way. So at 8 I strolled out and heard high mass at St Stephen's. . . . Do not forget, love, that almost ever since I left you I have been thrown quite off my feet and have been in one constant ferment. The journey from Rome is the most fatiguing I ever made in my life."

Nina never found Liverpool to her liking, she hated the life they had to live there, and she worried about Frederick overtaxing his strength. On one occasion, when she had gone back to Doune Terrace to recuperate after illness, and heard that Frederick too had been unwell, she burst out in a letter to him: "Now listen to me. You work too hard. Why do you work so hard? It is to get as much money as you possibly can, in a short space of time. Men sacrifice their brightest, most enjoyable years, nay their length of days, for this longed for end . . . Oh Frederick, it is not worth this terrible sacrifice. This hard work kills you. Let us not be so ambitious, let us content ourselves with less and live more humbly. Ah, I bitterly regret you gave up your business in Edinburgh. With that we should have had enough, quite enough, and you would have not only had to work just the reasonable number of hours a day, but you would have lived in a healthful climate, in a lovely town, surrounded with kind, intimate and attached friends. It was *ambition* which made us give up readily and eagerly this moderate lot to seize upon a lucky chance of a far wealthier one. Since then, we have gone through much change and excitement. But what does it come to? We seem to have so many cares, we live in a place we dislike. We have, it is true, a beautiful house, within which is every comfort and almost luxury, but . . . we live in a sort of lonely splendour . . . I have learnt a lesson now, and my only ambition is to be *happy* – not *rich*. With our intellectual capacities, artistic affinities and sympathetic *hearts,* we could be happy with far less than we have now, or aspire for in the future."

The next day she was sorry she had spoken so frankly, and wrote: "I fear after all I may only be disturbing your mind and unsettling your resolution by my letters." Nevertheless, these thoughts always persisted in the back of her mind. She visited London several times, generally staying with her Aunt Janet; and it seemed to her that if they could only get to London, she could persuade Frederick to indulge the other, the artistic side of his nature, far more easily and with far more beneficent results for both of them. It was, therefore, with joy that she heard at the end of 1858 that Frederick and Benzon had taken the plunge, and had decided to move south to develop the firm's City office. "Oh Fred," she cried, "can I, do I, shall I, must I believe it? It seems too, too blessed news . . . How happy the Wills's will be. How much more we shall see of Papa, Mama, everybody we care for. Ah, the great centre is the place to live in, where everyone and everything gathers. No Mrs Willis Dickson to come patronizing me in a vulgar rural way and bringing subscriptions in her muff. O, it is too, too, too jolly. O, what music we'll make in London."

Frederick at last found a house at 139 Westbourne Terrace, and they moved in at the beginning of 1859. They had hardly got the place straight, however, when Nina, who was expecting her third child, was advised to spend the summer months in the Isle of Wight; so beginning the long love-affair, still persisting, between my family and that delectable island.

Frederick went over to prospect, and chose a little cottage in Shanklin, by the Chine. Towards the end of July Nina moved in, with Rudie and Freddy, and two servants, Baillie and Susan. She wrote to my grandfather almost every day, and her letters shed a wonderfully vivid light not only on her own moods, feelings and tastes, but also on seaside life in the island at that period. On the 26th she writes to him in Westbourne Terrace: "This is a day of beauty, perfectly heavenly. I get beautiful potatoes now from our own little garden here, so mealy and nice, and oh *such* eggs since you left; great big snowy things, warm out of the nests. Two ladies came wanting our cottage this morning and saying they had never seen anything so exquisite, and telling Susan that Rudolph was the most beautiful child they had ever seen. We live in the most patriarchal way. It was cool last night, so I took my supper of a boiled egg and glass of beer in the kitchen and was regaled by personal experiences of the slowest kind from my two domestics. They are both simple-hearted creatures and we get on swimmingly. It is *so* easy, *so* simple, *so* charming. No dressing, no people, only the glorious sea, the firm yellow sands glittering with pebbles, the ships in the distance with the sun gilding their sails, and then the repose and shade and peace of the cottage. Never have I, since I was a child, enjoyed anything like it. It is just the innocent simplicity and happiness I remember to have enjoyed at the seaside places of my childhood and which I thought never to see, never to feel again. Last evening I sat, the one solitary being at our side of the shore, our *bay* I may call it. The sun was setting behind me, but I saw it lighting up all the little sails. The tide was high and the little waves came sparkling up close to my feet as I sat there, alone with them and with no other sound near. After that I walked home to my shady lovely nest, where, as I told you, I took my egg in the kitchen."

As the days went by, Nina's enthusiasm for her idyllic existence at Chine Cottage steadily grew. "Again a delicious day," she wrote a few days later. "I have remarked that when it is very hot on the sands it is cool and breezy at our cot and when it is cool on the sands it is warm and comfy with us. What a fortunate circumstance this is. My fruit and vegetable woman has just been here and the poultry man and I have made my purchases. It is quite like Hamburg, all the baskets full of things coming to the door, letting one choose so comfortably. I have bought 12 apples for stewing, 2 marrows, a cucumber and a lettuce for 1/– and such a tender pair of chicks for 4/6." And in the next letter: "Baillie is cutting beans in the little kitchen for our dinner, and Susan putting on the plums to stew. The doors are all open and we talk to each other continually. It is so delightfully patriarchal, this dwelling in tents in the cultivated wilderness. I dare say these two girls will get to know me better and feel more attached to me in this short time than in years of conventional servant life. The fact is we all work together, somewhat in the old-fashioned mistress and hand-maiden style, only they won't let me do anything either for the children or anything else they can help."

There seemed to be only one snag, and that was that the trippers were continually coming into the garden to ask the way down the chine. "I found a ticket lying among the trees," she writes in the same letter, "with 'To the Chine Gate' and a hand pointing down, which I instantly stuck on the paling, and still, when I was at dinner yesterday, a lady and gentleman coolly walked up to the very windows and asked me the way. Every-body stops and looks in and raves about the Hortensia and the Fuchsia." When the weather changed, however, a more serious looking snag loomed up. "It is now 11 o'clock," she writes to Frederick who had gone to Sheffield on business, "and I have just come in from a two hours ramble on the shore with my boys. The sea drove us home by coming up to the stones. It has been raining again this morning and the sea is stormy, but the weather is beautiful again. Do you know, I fear, I fear the cot will not be agreeable next month as it has been in the very hot weather. It gets damp-looking in the evenings and will be worse when the days are shorter . . . I can smell from the beds that there is damp-ness, and I almost think of going up to the top of the cliff, and leaving the cot, in a fortnight, but I do nothing till you come and give your opinion. It somehow struck me rather forcibly last evening. I left the cot, looking dark and dankish, to go to the village, and up on the top of the cliff it seemed so light and sunny still, and such a glorious sea view from those houses, that I felt perhaps in a week or two our cot might not be quite the thing for the health of the children. There is no hurry, however. The cot has great charms still, but *rheumatiz* frightens me."

As soon as the rain stopped, everything was delightful again. "This is a delicious day, so breezy and bright," she writes at the beginning of August. "Rudie and I have just come in from a field ramble on the top of the cliffs, the sea being up to the very rocks just now, and no walking on the shore possible. He and Fred have had their sea-bath today and are as fresh as early rose-buds. We are very hungry for our dinner, which consists of roast chicken for Rudie and me, but tea for Freddy and cold sirloin for the hand-maidens. Tell Lizbeth she may imagine what a charming place Shanklin is for me where the cucumbers are only a penny each. You see they grow in the open air, no frame or hothouse needed in this delicious southern climate. I saw a cottage yesterday covered with a vine and the grapes clustered all over the rustic chimney pot." In her next letter, even the shadow of the damp bedding had lifted: "I get more and more contented here. The life suits me deliciously for a time. I see so much of the children. I am in fact not the 'Missus' unapproachable of an establishment here, but rather one of the three who take charge of the little house and the little boys, and every evening you would be amused to see me sitting by the kitchen fire for a warm, while the four take their tea, all of us chatting together, boys, mother and servants indiscriminately. . . Our rheumatics seems to have gone and the very mattresses seem to have dried at last, so my only *shadow* is gone, and the cot is in as great favour as ever. These pretty villas on the cliff are very dear, a guinea each room, and in some of them 20 lodgers. They belong mostly to Proutens. It is like Heligoland here: they are all related and intermarried . . . It was tremendously blowy yesterday. We walked along the sands towards Sandown, and then ascended by a path in the cliff to the top and walked home by the delicious meadows, along which I think you may go all the way to Sandown. But wasn't it windy? Rudie said in a tone of rage, as he held on his hat, 'I don't like this windy place. I like our own cot best.' And certainly it was as peaceful and lovely at 'our own cot' when we came down to it as if there was no wind at all."

She decided to have some photographs taken of the boys, and discovered a local photographer only a short way from the cottage: "You never saw anything so wild and picturesque as this photograph place. It is a little tumbledown cottage overlooking the chine, with a great passion-flower completely covering the porch, a peach-tree loaded with fruit all over one side, the wildest of gardens sloping down chinewards, one mass of fuchsias, hortensias, verbenas, geraniums, ferns, heliotropes and so on, and a kind of amateur theatre-looking place peeping out of this luxuriant wilderness of flowers, where the portraits are taken."

As usual, Frederick was anxious to visualize their life in as much detail as possible, and Nina gives him a description of the pattern of their daily round: "Every morning after our breakfast, S. and B. take the boys down to the sands, give them their baths (a good hour after their breakfast) and let them play about. Meanwhile I write my letter to you and receive the visits of my butcher, vegetable woman, and so on. Then in they come. Susan cooks the dinner, Freddy goes to bed and I take Rudie out myself till one. After dinner I lie down and S. and B. go out to the sands till teatime, I joining them generally after an hour's rest. After tea the boys play about our own little garden till seven when they both gather all the toys into the wheelbarrow, wheel it into the room, and trot off to bed. Then I have a game of romps with them and by 8 they are sound asleep. Then our candles are lighted, I take my work, they sit at theirs and a domestic conversation ensues, at much of which I have several good laughs in my sleeve. At 9.30 all take a bit of 'bread and cheese' and I add a glass of beer to myself and then they both attend me, as if I were a grand lady, to my chamber, and in a short while we are all asleep."

Frederick kept her supplied with books and papers. "I have got both *Athenaeum* and *Sat. Review* today, a great treat," she writes a week after their arrival, and again: "Those novels of Anthony Trollope are excellent, so well written. You must read them in an idle hour some day. They are quite out of the common, a great advance on his blessed mother's vulgar trash." *The Times*, irregularly sent on from Westbourne Terrace, arrived two or three days late. "Do you know, I think I should go mad if I were to read *The Times* regularly. I no sooner get one impression delightfully fixed into my mind than behold I have to cast it entirely off and take an entirely opposite one. That Serpentine discussion is more likely to send people to early graves than the smell I should think. It is a perfectly awful system that of everybody writing his own particular opinion in a letter to *The Times*, and everybody's particular opinion is always somehow so exactly the opposite of everybody else's particular opinion. It is maddening, and so it is with every subject ever discussed in that torment of a paper."

A visit from Frederick was planned for the first week-end in August, and he was to bring *The Virginians* and the first part of *Once a Week* with him, as well as the coffee-pot and the old cook from Westbourne Terrace. Nina's object was to give the "old goose" as she called the cook, a holiday, as "we hear this morning from Mrs Taplin the old goose has been so 'upset' with the workmen in the 'ouse and the 'ouse is so dirty, etc. etc., and cook very poorly. One of her fits no doubt. She is always upset when men are in the house, and doubtless she imagines no end of stewpans and kitchen forks are missing. It is very hard if the O.G. can't keep her own kitchen, passage, and stairs clean when she has nothing else to do." Frederick's mother had come over from Hamburg to stay with him, and had been very difficult (as she generally was with all her children, quarrelling on the slightest provocation, so that on one occasion Mme d'Agoult had even had to intercede for Henri); she had demanded to be escorted back to Hamburg and it was touch and go whether Frederick would not have to postpone his visit to the island; but in the end brother Rudolf nobly agreed to see the old lady home, and even take her to a *Kurort* first. Nina, rejoicing at the reprieve, adds as a final appetizer, "The weather is really superb. People who live always in Yorkshire don't know what an English climate really is. How much it adds to happiness, this unfailing mildness, blueness and sunshine. The sea is one dazzling mass of sapphire blue with diamonds sparkling upon it."

The visit was a great success. "That weather we had on Saturday," Nina writes to him after his return, "how often we will look back to it in after days! And how nice that I never felt the least bad effects. It was a pleasure without alloy. 'We have much to be thankful for,' as old Aunt Betty would say, and I do think we *are* thankful. I am sure I feel my heart brimfull, nay overflowing sometimes with gratitude for our present and past happinesses. . . . I am the enchanted cottager."

The O.G. had come too, and scattered disorder, and returned to do the same at Westbourne Terrace. "I am glad you found the house clean," Nina writes to Frederick who had got home before the O.G. "The mere absence of the ancientest of mariners would have that effect. Susan says our little cot was never so dirty after not having been cleaned for a week, as after she had been one day in it. Every dish, every saucepan out and dirtied, and the floor and fireplace ditto."

The children clamoured for their father's return, and he came again the next week-end. He brought three brace of grouse, and another two brace arrived from Tom Vickers in the north a couple of days later, the first of the season. They decided that Frederick's visits were to be a regular Friday event, and they even planned to move to a larger cottage at the top of the cliff and spend a fortnight all together later in the month. But all their plans fell through: Frederick had to hurry off to Sweden on business. As Nina's time was growing near, it was arranged that "Hopey" Walker, her sister Mary's sister-in-law, of whom she was very fond, should join her at the cottage.

"You say you will never forget this sweet cot," she writes to him in Sweden, "nor the short happy visits you have made to it – nor I indeed. I am happy still, dearest, but there is the smallest shade over it now. No more Fridays to look forward to, you see. That last delightful Sunday will be a memory for life." She describes an expedition she had made with Rudie, to Sandown: "Rudie and I got quite safely home last night. Our driver took a footman on the box to Sandown, and they both stopped at the Brading Inn and imbibed something a little stronger than water, I expect, as the driver got communicative and enquired the distance in a general point of view of Sweden now from Shanklin. "I said Sweden was somewhere near the North Pole, and he thought that must be a good length away and must be reached in ships he supposed, to which I assented. He then went on, impressed and in silence."

Frederick responded by describing his epic dash across Europe with George Vickers to catch the steamer *Bore*, which apparently only sailed at rare intervals, from Lübeck to Scandinavia. "We are here," he wrote from on board, "as by a miracle and after no end of trouble. The dance began with George losing his portmanteau between London and Calais, altho' it was registered with my luggage for Cologne. Altho' it was a slight consolation, he did not feel quite reconciled to the loss by the fact that the Duke of Cambridge, a very portly good-natured looking man, travelled with his Equerry in the same train with us to Cologne *en route* for Frankfurt, where his mistress or morganatic wife Mrs FitzGeorge has preceded him. It was satisfactory to see him quite as dusty and sleepy, quite as unshaven, and eating the same hurried lunch of hard veal cutlets at Malines, also having to wait 3 hours at Lille, from four to seven, same as ourselves." As soon as they crossed the German border a telegram arrived announcing that the *Bore* would sail from Lübeck without fail at one o'clock the next day. "After maddening consultations with Bradshaw," they discovered that no scheduled train would get them to Lübeck before four o'clock. What were they to do? The *Bore* would not sail again for several days, and the "overland" journey via Kiel and Copenhagen would take five days. Speed was essential: they decided on a special train. "We at once composed telegrams to Lübeck telling the Railway to send a train for us to Lanenburg, and another message to Lüneburg, where we left the train this morning, to order posthorses to Lanenburg, as there is no railway. As we were in a quick train stopping almost nowhere it took the greatest dodging to get our telegrams sent off without being left behind. Having finally managed one at Hanover and another at Minden, we resigned ourselves to what sleep we could get, but waking up in Hanover we found ourselves minus George's handbag (all that remained to him of his luggage), and a pair of boots I had taken off to sleep." Their first despairing impulse was to give them up for lost; then George Vickers decided to comb through the train, and found them in an empty carriage where the thief had dumped them until he could jump off. They reached Lüneburg at 7.30 a.m., to find no telegram from Lübeck about the special train awaiting them. "Still we determined to make for it. We chartered a carriage and pair and after two hours and a half of horrid roads crossed the Elbe at Lanenburg. Here was our fate. To be or not to be. To get off, or to retrace our steps to Hamburg after all our efforts. Imagine our joy as we searched the station to be met by the words: '*Ihr Zug ist gang fertig meine Herren!*' In we jumped, tearing away through slow Germany, whistling, signalling, the telegraph ringing bells at each station and the astonished natives endeavouring to get a peep of the travelling princes. At half past eleven we were in Lübeck in time to secure the last two berths in the *Bore*, to telegraph to Sheffield that we had caught the boat, to telegraph to Hamburg to send George's trunk to Stockholm whenever it turned up, to telegraph to Stockholm to George's tailor to have some clothes ready against his arrival, to buy some sponges which I found I had forgotten to pack, to walk on board and then to have such a wash and shave as only people in our condition can appreciate." He adds the astonishing information that the special train cost them about thirteen pounds.

In Nina's next letter she describes some exotic visitors who had appeared in Shanklin. "I pictured you going about and seeing a little of the gay Northern capital yesterday . . . Today, when we were sitting on the beach, a very handsome young couple, dressed in the most *distingué* way, came down (looking in the face like aristocratic Jews). The husband, who was a Prince Yusuf or some such name, conducted his wife, who was all embroidery and feathers, to a bathing machine and grandly handed her in, where her maid already awaited her – the same maid I saw arrive when waiting for you and Hopey. Miss Sampson had to go in and bathe her, while her maid held towels inside all ready. The hood was let down and we just caught a glimpse of Miss Sampson ducking her like a child, while her handsome husband stood anxiously gazing, *watch in hand*. It was so comical to see this Princess treated like a baby, so helpless and so handsome, and so fearfully well taken care of. It was quite a glimpse of a new life to me . . ."

There was also another visitor: "A poor Italian, who can't speak a word of English, is in the 'garden' just now, playing the French organ to the delight of the boys. He came when they were out, and I told him to go away and come back at *mezzo giorno* when the children would be here, and I said it in Italian and the man cried and said he hadn't heard his own language here before."

Nina filled her letters with descriptions of the children and their doings, as she knew how much pleasure it gave Frederick. They were both bursting with health after their seaside holiday : "Rudie is so much too big for their little room and even Freddy is growing out of it. They are both off to the meadows in their fresh clean frocks and jackets, quite radiant and happy. Rudolph was much interested in your letter and description of your journey . . . Last night, as I was toasting his feet at the fire before taking him to bed, he begged me to sing to him, so I began Flora MacDonald's Lament. As I went on, his lip began to tremble, his eyes filled with tears, and at last when I came to the lines, 'Farewell to the lad I shall ne'er see again,' he flung his head down on my breast, burst into tears and said, 'Oh Mama, don't say that, don't say she ne'er saw him again. Oh say that she saw him, Mama – cruel, cruel men to take him away,' and I could hardly console him, and had to invent an appendix of my own wherein I proved that Flora found her bonnie prince Charlie at last and they both sailed away in a little boat together to a beautiful country where the oranges grow . . . You see, he is a Jacobite before he is 4! Accordingly as I was the 8th he is the 9th. I must write and tell Papa that."

The days went on as before, as the summer drew to an end. "Hopey is such a comfort and makes us such delicious Scotch dinners and bakes all kinds of cakes for tea." She and Nina explored new houses, but in the end again decided not to move. "I am getting more and more attached to Shanklin and this cot," and "The Proutens say if I return next year they'll have the cottage redone up and some new furniture put in, which would really be tempting. Hopey and I are more madly in love with it than ever, I think." "The moon is full now and the sea like a golden bath every night. I never wish or care to go anywhere else than to this favourite spot of Nature and Russians." There was, however, one villa that strongly attracted them. "Today I am going to look well over Sea Villa with an eye to next year. Hopey and I looked at every house on the beach yesterday, and found Mrs Colenutt's out and out the neatest, freshest and cleanest besides having the prettiest verandah, and she is such a nice, clean, obliging woman. She told us her family would be away to Carisbrook today and she'd show me the whole house: two sitting rooms and six bed-rooms, which I could have for 5 guineas a week." It was in Sea Villa that she established herself on her next but one recorded visit, in 1862.

In one of her last letters to Frederick in Sweden, she writes: "This is a shining spot to look back to, and it has cheered me up and borne me clear of many little household vexations which troubled me, and in short given me new spirit for another town career. Won't I have the house looking its Sunday best when my beloved comes home, and oh what a welcome will be his." But on the 14th September they hurried back to London, a few days before Frederick was due, and in the early morning of the 15th Nina's third child, my uncle Ernest, was born.

PART FOUR
A Circle of Friends in the Sixties

I

Since they had settled at 139 Westbourne Terrace at the beginning
of 1859, my grandparents had rapidly drawn a large circle of
friends around them, musical, literary and artistic. My father, in
his *Memories of Half a Century*, itself published more than half a
century ago and long out of print, drew a tantalisingly incomplete
picture of their circle, all the members of which were known to
him in his boyhood. When, at my mother's death, I came into
possession of the family papers, I found that they included not
only all my grandmother's letters to my grandfather and many of
his to her, but also Frederick's incomplete diaries and reminiscences and a large body of letters from their friends. From these
it has been possible to fill in many fascinating details which my
father left obscure. These papers throw an extraordinarily vivid
light on middle-class life of the time, where money was plentiful
and the arts were cherished.

Looked at from the point of view of our own over-taxed and
almost servant-less age, this social life in Victorian London a
hundred years ago seems quite extraordinarily intense, glamorous
– and exhausting. My grandparents and their middle-class contemporaries lived in big houses not only because they could
afford to, but because they could staff them in adequate fashion
very cheaply; and the big houses and the big staffs, and the cheapness of good food and drink made entertaining possible on a scale
and in a rhythm that only the very rich could allow themselves
today. It seems to have been nothing remarkable in my grandparents' house to sit down twelve or even twenty to dinner
several times a week, and to invite twenty or thirty more people
in afterwards. And at these after-dinner gatherings there was
nearly always music in which a number of those present often
took part, singing, playing the piano or the violin, or joining in

quartets. Nina's health, as I have said, was never very secure, and soon after they reached London my grandfather took a house on the heights of Highgate called "Woodlands". To Highgate Nina could slip away for rest and recuperation, though even there, it seems, the parties were apt, sooner or later, to start up again.

These dinners and musical evenings and parties to the opera and theatre – and of course to Dickens's readings – were the arteries through which social life so vigorously ran. And when the conversation and the music-making and the drinking had to pause because one took a rest in the country or went abroad for holidays or health, there were long, long letters to feed the fires of friendship and love. Nina's letters, my grandfather's and my father's reminiscences, extend far beyond the sixties; but I have limited myself here more or less to that decade because I think that Dickens's death in 1870 did in a sense close a chapter. Though the parties went on, perhaps on an even grander scale when Frederick and Nina moved to Berkeley Square in the seventies, I have somehow the impression that a certain note of gaiety and intimate enjoyment, of discovery, that characterizes the early years in London was absent – or was at any rate fading. What is more, I think the strenuous round progressively took its toll of Nina's strength and spirits. It was not only a matter of physical health; though her enjoyment of her role as hostess and patroness is clear, she seems throughout her married life to have suffered sudden revulsions against the elaborate, extravagant parade of entertaining and being entertained. She wondered, sometimes – as I have already quoted from her letters to show – what use it was Frederick wearing his best powers out in the money-making grind; she was ready for quite a different, modest life such as some of her aunts and cousins lived, it seemed so happily, in Scotland.

In Liverpool there were moments almost of despair; but when she was able to gather new friends around her in London – especially with Woodlands in the background – these revulsions came more rarely. London was not Edinburgh; but how many compensations there were, how exciting it was all the same.

5a. Robert Chambers

5b. Frederick and
Nina Lehmann at the
time of their marriage

6a. Alphonse de Lamartine: a drawing by Rudolf Lehmann

6b. Joseph Joachim: a drawing by Rudolf Lehmann

Before his marriage, Frederick was often in London on business, and made many friends in the musical world, especially among the visiting celebrities from Germany and Paris. There was the great violinist Joseph Joachim, infant prodigy of the forties and in a few years' time to be the favourite of the "Monday Pops"; there was Joachim's patroness, the famous singer Pauline Viardot-Garcia, who played such an important part in Turgenev's life; Carl Hallé, pianist and conductor, driven to England by the 1848 Revolution in France, who first formed his celebrated orchestra for the Exhibition of 1851; and Madame Norman-Neruda, another distinguished violinist of the time, one of the circle of devotees who surrounded Hallé, and who later, in the eighties, married him when her husband and his wife were both dead and he had become Sir Charles Hallé; the ageing composer Meyerbeer, Clara Schumann and many others. To this new circle in London, then, Frederick contributed a great deal on the musical side, all the more fortunate because Nina was exceptionally gifted as a pianist – Wilkie Collins once said that *after* Nina Lehmann Hallé was the best pianist in England – and her sister Tuckie a very pleasing singer. Frederick himself never lost his love of the violin; he became a member of the well-known amateur musical society. The Wandering Minstrels, and when in Leipzig during the autumn of 1864 took the opportunity to have a series of refresher lessons with the famous violinist Ferdinand David, leader of the orchestra at the Oewandhaus.

From Nina's side came many of the literary friends. Her aunt Janet, Robert Chambers' sister, had married W. H. Wills, who became assistant editor to Dickens on the *Daily News*, and then on Dickens' own popular weekly *Household Words* and its successor *All The Year Round* from 1850 to his retirement in 1869. Wills was immensely capable, energetic and reliable: Thackeray is reported to have said, when looking for an assistant editor for the *Cornhill*, "If only there were another Wills my fortune would be made!" It was through Uncle Harry Wills, known Dickensianly as "The Dodger" in the family for some reason now lost, that Nina got to know Wilkie Collins, and then Dickens himself a little later when she and Frederick were living near Sheffield. From Edinburgh days she already knew Bulwer Lytton, James Payn and G. H. Lewes – and through Lewes was soon to come to know George Eliot. And through the *Household Words* circle the friendships spread out, to "stentorian" John Forster and Lord Houghton and Charles Reade; to the Proctors, "Barry Cornwall" who provided a link with the already misty world of Wordsworth and Byron and Charles Lamb, and his wife Anne Proctor who became a close and lifelong friend of Nina's; and many others. On the artistic side their friends included brother Rudolf's growing circle of painter colleagues, and those three great pillars of the Victorian artistic establishment, Leighton, Landseer and Millais; Nina had known Millais at her father's house, in fact on one occasion he remarked that they had known one another so long that they had "rocked one another's cradles".

II

On a Tuesday morning in July 1860, my grandfather overslept – a rare enough event in the life of someone so methodical and reliable. Nina was again in the Isle of Wight, and after a visit alone to the French play *Pattes de Mouches* he went home to find that his manservant, Spaul, had gone to bed. This was unfortunate, because he had forgotten to tell him that he wanted to be called at seven the next morning, to catch a special train from London Bridge to Higham in Kent: he had been invited to attend the wedding of Dickens's daughter Katie to Wilkie Collins's brother Charles, at which Nina's sister Amelia – "Tuckie" – was to be a bridesmaid.

He did not wake up till quarter to nine, and missed the train. When he eventually reached Higham Station just before midday, the stationmaster told him that the wedding would be nearly over and he'd better make straight for Gad's Hill. On the way, he wrote to Nina, he was overtaken "by the whole party coming in ever so many carriages from Church. First Charlie and Katie, and didn't I give them a cheer. Then Wilkie, Holman Hunt, Tuck and Miss Crawford who insisted on picking me up. When the others joined us at the house, the astonishment at my presence was general, as I had been given up, but Mamie just flew into my arms before everybody and kissing me over and over again, said, "You dear, you darling I am *so* glad you've come." The wedding breakfast, he told Nina, "was a gorgeous affair and looked so pretty. Everything on the table in the way of decoration was white, none but white flowers." The newly weds only sat down at the table for a moment, then disappeared while the guests played games on the lawn. When they reappeared for the going away, Katie was "crying bitterly on her father's shoulder, Mamie dissolved in tears, Charlie as white as snow. No end of God Bless yous, King John Forster adding in his d—d stentorian voice, 'Take care of her, Charlie, you have got a most precious treasure.' Shaking of hands, a vision of a postilion in red, a shower of old shoes and excunt Mr and Mrs Charles Collins." After their departure there was an expedition to Rochester Castle and to Chatham, where they listened to a military band, and then back to Gad's Hill about half past six, where they "had time to get warm by a game of croquet, saw the children of the neighbouring people get tea and cake, and went in to dinner at seven. I sat next to old Forster, a most unmanageable wild beast, which I am happy to say I tamed successfully for the evening at least . . . Dinner over at nine, a cigar in the garden, Tuck sings to everybody's enthusiastic delight, a country dance and we all fly at eleven to our special train waiting our return at Higham."

As Frederick's description of the wedding at Gad's Hill shows, Dickens had already become an intimate friend by 1860. The first reference I can find to him in my grandparents' correspondence is in a letter from Frederick to Nina in July 1859: "I must tell you about Dickens's reading on Thursday evening. The story of Captain Doubledick from *The Poor Traveller*, the Boots at the Holly Tree Inn and Mrs Gamp. The Boots story of the Children's elopement was a perfect masterpiece as a reading and certainly that charming little tale 'se prête admirablement' to such a performance. It was curious tho' to hear him wind up with the very significant moral that it were much better if many of the grown up couples were separated and brought back before the fatal knot was tied. Mrs Gamp does not make so nice a whole, being taken out here and there from *Martin Chuzzlewit*, but I wished for you to hear that immortal woman pronounce her wonderful sentiments. The whole room was in a continual roar. But the audience was the queerest assemblage of odd ugly never-before-seen people you ever beheld. The women's toilettes were something to be remembered or rather forgotten for their hideousness."

During the whole decade of the sixties Dickens was a frequent guest at my grandparents' house, and they as often visited or dined with him. As their friendship ripened, Frederick would sometimes join Dickens on a jaunt to Paris, where they would indulge in what can only be described as a gigantic restaurant crawl together. It was the last phase of Dickens' life: at the height of his fame and success, he was nevertheless the prey of sometimes almost unendurable internal tensions, which made him extremely restless. *Great Expectations* was published in 1861, and *Our Mutual Friend* in 1864–5; but after these two masterpieces, apart from the unfinished *Edwin Drood*, he wrote no more novels, and more and more of his energies were devoted to his public activities as journalist, actor and reader-impersonator of his own works. One thing my grandfather and Dickens had in common was a fondness for walking: they took regular long walks together of a Sunday while Dickens was at Hyde Park Gate, and on one occasion walked back together from the Star and Garter at Richmond after a dinner celebration with Forster and other cronies.

My father had one very vivid memory of Dickens. "I cannot have been more than six or seven years old when my father and mother took me to one of his readings at, I think, St James's Hall. First he read the death of Paul Dombey, which left me in floods of tears, and next came the trial scene from *Pickwick*. I shall never forget my amazement when he assumed the character of Mr Justice Stareleigh. The face and figure that I knew, that I had seen on the stage a moment before, seemed to vanish as if by magic, and there appeared instead a fat, pompous, pursy little man, with a plump imbecile face, from which every vestige of good temper and cheerfulness – everything in fact except an expression of self-sufficient stupidity – had been removed. The upper lip had become long, the corners of the mouth drooped, the nose was short and podgy, all the angles of the chin had gone, the chin itself had receded into the throat, and the eyes, lately so humorous and human, had become as malicious and obstinate as those of a pig. It was a marvellous effort in transformation. When the reading was over my father and mother took me round with them to the room behind. As soon as Dickens caught sight of me he seized me up in his arms and gave me a sounding kiss."

It was after the Gad's Hill wedding and the departure of Charlie and Katie that Mamie Dickens discovered her father in Katie's room, his face buried in her wedding dress, murmuring brokenly, "But for me Kate would never have left home." But if Katie's departure from the broken home distressed Dickens, he seems to have been only too anxious to send his sons away to the ends of the earth as soon as they were grown up. He has been defended as a devoted father, whose care for his children's welfare is only more clearly revealed by this propensity. All the same, it is possible to look at it in a different light, and see the workings of guilt, perhaps even a fear that the boys might learn something discreditable about his relations with Ellen Ternan. It is also possible – as Katie many years later hinted – that Georgina Hogarth was the prime mover in this matter. Charley had been sent to China, Walter to India; and in 1863 Dickens consulted Frederick, in a series of letters which my father carefully kept from publication during his lifetime, about the possibility of getting his next son, Alfred, a business post abroad. At first he thought of Ceylon; then it occurred to him that Frederick might be able to find him some apprenticeship at once, in Hamburg or elsewhere in Germany. "I have a horror of him being idle!" he exclaims in one letter; and in another, "I am afraid to keep my boys about London. You see Frank is already here and I am afraid of their spoiling one another." A few weeks later he writes from Paris, where he had gone to give readings at the British Embassy: "I still hanker after India or some such distant field, for the reasons I suggested to you when I last saw you." In the end these mysterious negotiations, which must have been decidedly uncomfortable for my grandfather, were cut short by his departure for a long business tour in America, and Dickens's decision to make Alfred learn the silk trade in order to earn a living in China. The wretched boy was, however, eventually sent to Australia.

The only piece of advice Dickens ever gave Frederick in return, as far as I can discover, was on how to prepare a big dog's dinner: "The recipe for one dog's allowance is this: 2 pints oatmeal, 1 pint barley meal, 1 pound mangel wurzel, boiled together, and then mixed with pot-liquor which is poured over it. If there be no pot-liquor in the house, a sheep's head will make it very well. Any bones that happen to be about may be put into the mixture for the exercise of the dog's teeth. Its effect on the body and spirits of the creature is quite surprising. I have my dogs fed once a day, always at the same hour."

Dickens was an enthusiastic dog-lover, but the occasion for this zestful prescription is obscure, as my grandparents do not appear to have kept any big dogs until later.

In February 1860 my grandmother describes "a very nice evening with the Dickens's, but such a queer dinner. We were 12. Albany Fonblanque,[1] an old man with his wife, Mr and Mrs Forster, Charlie and Wilkie, young C. Dickens and myself. Dinner consisted of potato soup, soles, stewed kidneys and pork

[1] Born in 1793, Fonblanque, a Benthamite radical, made his name as editor of The Daily Examiner in the second quarter of the century.

cutlets, roast mutton and veal and a pudding. No games – nothing but a Chopin and a Mendelssohn from me with Dickens and Wilkie as attentive auditors, and a piece alarmingly played by Mamie herself." Nina seems to have grown especially fond of Mamie Dickens. There are constant references to her in the letters, from which it emerges that Mamie not only often came to visit but also to stay with her, in London, at Woodlands, and at the seaside. "I walked nearly all the way to Mamie," she writes in 1860 from Westbourne Terrace, "and I was received as a lover might be by a loving and beloved mistress." And a little later, "I have a letter from Mamie again begging me to go to Gad's Hill, but I won't. She says she *will* come uninvited, and camp here, with 'Tit' and a bundle." While Frederick was in America, Mamie seems to have attached herself to Nina particularly closely, stayed several times at Westbourne Terrace, and went with Nina to some of her father's readings – "awfully affecting" as Nina described them. "I sat next to Dickens at dinner," writes Nina during one of Mamie's visits, "and he and I *roared* as we usually do when we get together. Mamie had a bad cold and was awfully quiet and sombre . . . After dinner she clung to me like a leech and never let me away from her side, though Madame Hallé wanted me beside her."

In 1864 they went down to stay at the Sea House Hotel in Worthing together. "Mamie and I are most agreeably surprised with Worthing," Nina writes. "It is a dear little place, quiet, simple, with a glorious sea, bright, *very very* clean, and altogether the very thing I require. . . . Mamie has a little room opening out of mine, and both look straight out on a sea sparkling with diamonds at this very minute. There is a neat little Pier right opposite our window, but nobody is ever on it except a man with a telescope under his arm." Nina's health improved so much that they began to go for long walks every day, often for ten miles or so along the coast towards Lancing and Shoreham, "trotting along the road at the real Dickens pace" as Nina describes it, "on and on we went, with the sea lying fast asleep and looking oh so lazy on our right, behind the glittering white shores of the beach, and on our left equally lazy fields with still lazier cattle browsing about, and too sleepy to look at us . . . Then back, like two Trampers, and off to our warm salt bath as a refresher." Sleepy as the cattle after these excursions, at half-past nine Nina "felt fatigue getting too much for me, so I marched off to bed, Mamie as usual attending me, folding up all my clothes, tucking me in, and I was asleep in a moment".

In one of her letters Nina describes a visit she made with Mamie to an exhibition of photographs at the French Gallery in Pall Mall. "Mamie and I came home in a cab, very tired, and just as we got into the house the bell rang, and looking from the stairs I heard Mr Browning saying, 'Well, is Mrs Lehmann at home *today*?' I ran down and brought him in triumphantly . . . Is it not kind of him to come so often?" My grandparents had got to know Browning after Elizabeth Barrett's death, when he settled in Warwick Crescent – not far away from them – and he soon became one of their most faithful friends and constant guests, right up to the end of his life. During the last two or three years of his widower's life in London, he had hardly seen anyone except his relations and the Proctors, while working away at his *Dramatis Personae*, and *The Ring and the Book*; then suddenly, in 1863, he decided that his seclusion was a mistake, and began to accept all the invitations that came to him. My father, who was only five or six when Browning came into their lives, has left a description of him as seen through the hero-worshipping eyes of a boy who has been told that he is in the presence of a great poet: "He had the happy knack of making even a small boy feel that it gave him real pleasure to shake that small boy by the hand or to pat him on the back and talk to him about the little interests of his life . . . His dress was simple, his manner was genial, and his appearance, though he was by no means a tall man, was in the highest degree manly and impressive. His massive, noble head was splendidly set on a strong neck; his shoulders were solid, and his chest was deep, a fit generator for the resonant voice with which he held you in conversation . . . I can still feel the grip of his hand and see the kind light in his eyes as he looked into mine." Browning had evidently a special fondness for my father as a small boy, and wanted at one time to give him a pony which had belonged to Pen, his own son. It seems to have been a muddle, for when Frederick saw the animal he decided it was far too large and too temperamental for a boy of only seven. "I don't know by what stupid misconception," wrote Browning, "I had got into my head that your boy was some four years older. I would not have had an accident spoil Rudie's pleasure for the world." I have, nevertheless, a lingering suspicion that the offer was not entirely disinterested, and that Pen had got bored with trying to manage a rather violent animal – "abundantly spirited" is Browning's own description.

My grandfather became, in Browning's words, "Pen's very earliest patron," by buying an enormous picture he had painted at the beginning of his artistic career, of an elderly French *curé* sitting, with evident worldly enjoyment, beside a table on which stood an assortment of liqueurs and coffee, and reading a French novel. This rather ghastly and lurid canvas hung in our house by the Thames until my father's death, when it departed to its final resting place in the Browning Institute at Waco, Texas. When he bought it, Frederick received an enthusiastic letter from Browning: "With this note you will receive the picture. What can I say in sending it that you do not perfectly understand? Really, I doubt if anything ever made me more happy than such a prodigious incitement to Pen's industry, and, what he has always wanted, a confidence in his own power of doing good and original work. We can't but believe (all of us here) that your personal kindness had more to do with the purchase than you would desire us to think. Still, it is hard not to fancy that you find sufficient pleasure in being the first to bring forward a young fellow who may – and ought – to justify such a distinction by future success. It is simply the truth to say that your approval of the picture would have been preferable immeasurably to its purchase by almost anybody else; you must know why well enough. There, I shall say no more, but remember this circumstance so long as 'this machine is to him'."

That Nina, with her gift for charming and attaching people to herself had made a conquest of Browning is clear from many letters he addressed to her. There is one dated July 1869, in which he writes: "You should not bid me be 'like my old self' – because my last self is always the most affectionately disposed to you of all the selves; and I can do myself (honestly to speak) no greater pleasure than to go to you on Monday week. I always think my heart is on my sleeve and that who likes may see it, and know whether it means kindly or otherwise to them - for all one's excuses, referrings, and misleading stupidity; and unless it plays one false indeed, it must beat very gratefully whenever your name is mentioned; with such recollections of long kindliness unvaried by a minutest touch of anything like the contrary." And yet, curiously enough, it is not playful and intimate letters such as these, or any of the other many Browning records that survived in my family, that have made me *feel* the living presence of Browning in my grandparent's circle of friends; but a trifle of no importance in itself, a chance discovery; as I was looking through the volumes of Browning's poems in our family library after my mother's death, a visiting card fell out of one of them. It was addressed to Nina, and on it was simply written, in Browning's handwriting, "Thanks and good-bye."

Frederick was introduced to G. H. Lewes for the first time at the house Robert Chambers had taken in London in the early fifties. Through Lewes, of course, both he and Nina came to know George Eliot well. Of her my grandfather writes in his reminiscences: "She had a large head and most striking and somewhat Dante-esque features. She was distinctly plain, but her voice was soft and melodious and always exercised a spell on me." He goes on to describe how, a few years later when he was alone in London, he used to go to their house in Regent's Park - The Priory, to which they had moved in 1863 - every Monday evening for many months, for musical practice: "George Eliot was a very fair pianist. Not gifted, but enthusiastic and painstaking. We played together every piano and violin sonata of Mozart and Beethoven. I knew the traditions of the best players and was able to give her some hints, which she always received eagerly and thankfully. Our audience consisted of Lewes only, and he used to groan with delight whenever we were rather successful." I have a picture of him inscribed to my grandmother, in which he looks exactly as if he were in the middle of a deep, prolonged groan.

Like many other visitors, Frederick sometimes found the atmosphere in the Lewes home rather daunting. In a letter of the time (to Nina) he wrote: "Saturday I dined at the Lewes's and had a quiet, somewhat subdued dinner. She speaks always in a very low voice and somehow everybody is on his best behaviour and tries for his best mental posture in the presence of these two extraordinary mortals." On another occasion he reports that the subject of conversation was "*Geist*, the second part of Faust, and Swinburne's poetry" (*Poems and Ballads* had come out a few months earlier).

The novelist, with her early, triumphant successes behind her, was on the threshold of her greatest achievement. She had just published *Felix Holt*, and *Middlemarch* was germinating; but in between was to come *The Spanish Gypsy*, the long planned but not altogether fortunate excursion into poetry. Some few months after the dinner, she and Lewes set out for Spain and made a special visit to Nina who was wintering in Pau for her health. "We look upon you as a sort of heroine," George Eliot told Nina, "parted so long from your husband and your home, and take a deep interest in you." This delighted Nina, who remarked in a letter to Frederick: "If people would only say such things and smooth my fur the right way, instead of lecturing me as they do, I would take a more cheerful view of my position . . . Please understand for the future I am a sort of heroine." The Leweses persuaded Nina to play them her "arrangement" of *Adelaide*, told her that Rudolf's portrait of her, which they had recently seen in London, did not make her look nearly pretty enough, spoiled the children, praised the Maltese terrier, Chang, and altogether ingratiated themselves with the invalid in every way possible. At one point Lewes was sent away to visit another lonely Briton in Pau, while George Eliot made Nina tell her the whole story of her courtship and marriage as they walked in the gardens. While they were there the sirocco was blowing; Nina comments that it was "like going into a hot-house when you go out. The valley was full of a seething mist over which the mountains towered clear and serene. George Eliot in looking at this mist said, 'I love to see that mist – it is beautiful – it looks as if creation were going on underneath'." At the end of the visit Nina wrote, "the Leweses are gone after two delightful cosy days. I have got to know her as I should never have done in years in London, and I think she loves me – we are sworn friends . . . When she went away last night I said something of hoping she would like me and we should be friends. She said, 'I do. I love you better every hour.' She said it so sweetly with her soft penetrating voice, it did not sound as such a compliment would from any other lips." Their mutual vows were kept, and George Eliot remained an intimate friend of my grandmother's to the end.

A year or two after their meeting in Pau, they were invited to the Priory to hear Tennyson read his poetry. Frederick had some difficulty, at first, in accustoming himself to Tennyson's "very marked northern dialect". He remembered that the poet "used to interrupt himself to say quite naïvely: 'We now come to one of my best things. This has been tried before now, but not successfully,' and so on, making his own Greek chorus. He read the *Northern Farmer* and almost the whole of *Maud*. We were spellbound and he seemed to enjoy it so much that his son had had at last to make him stop, by reminding him of the lateness of the hour."

III

Of all that circle of friends, it was, I think, Wilkie Collins who became the most attached, the most closely enmeshed in my grandparents' own lives, who poured himself out most spontaneously to them – to judge at any rate from the letters – and who appeared the most frequently at the dinner parties and musical evenings, though his taste in music was indifferent. He once wrote to them, "In *one* respect only, I have been far worse for the delightful party at Hallé's, the 'Great Kreutzer' Sonata has upset me about classical music. I'm afraid I don't like classical music after all – I am afraid I am not the Amateur I once thought myself."

The earliest actual reference to Wilkie I can find in the family papers, is in a letter of 1855 from Janet Wills, in which she describes attending a performance of *The Lighthouse* in Colonel Waugh's private theatre at Campden House in Church Street. "Last night Florence and I were at the dress rehearsal of the play at the pretty little theatre attached to Campden House, Kensington, where it is played tonight for the benefit of the consumption hospital with the original cast. Mrs Collins sat next to me and got every now and then so excited applauding her son Wilkie that I thought the respectable, comely old woman would explode, he all the time looking and acting most muffishly. Nothing could be better than the drama as drama, but oh, he makes a most unloving and unlovable lover. Dickens and Mark (Lemon) do *not* act, it is the perfection of *real* nature."

As Wilkie grew into the Westbourne Terrace household, he quickly made himself a favourite with my father and his brothers. He took them to the Pantomime, gave them presents, helped them with their homework, and told them stories they always remembered. "He took our young imaginations captive," my father wrote, "with stories of Tom Sayers, the prizefighter, with whom he had often conversed, whose face-destroying hand he had shaken, whose awful arm he had felt . . . I can see him now as I used to see him in those early, unforgotten days: a neat figure of a cheerful plumpness, very small feet and hands, a full brown beard, a high and rounded forehead, a small nose not naturally intended to support a pair of large spectacles behind which his eyes shone with humour and friendship; not by any means the sort of man imagination would have pictured as the creator of Count Fosco and the inventor of the terrors of *Armadale* and the absorbing mystery of *The Moonstone*." My father also remembered that he had certain old-fashioned peculiarities of speech, pronouncing "really" and "real" as if they had been spelt "railly" and "rail", and "obliged" as "obleeged".

Wilkie used to stay in Highgate with my grandparents, and in fact wrote a great deal of *Man and Wife* at Woodlands in a succession of visits in 1869 and 1870, and eventually dedicated the book to them. He invited Frederick to a small stag party, with Holman Hunt and Augustus Egg, to celebrate the publication of *The Woman in White*; he hauled him off to Paris, he joined him on a trip to the Tyrol and Switzerland, where on one occasion when Wilkie was in great pain my grandfather had to go to four chemists in order to get enough laudanum legally for the dose he needed; and he told him all his secrets. "Work, walk, visit to my morganatic family – such is life," he once wrote to Frederick. It is clear from this that his closest friends knew all about Martha Rudd and his children by her, though it was very well concealed from everyone else. The true facts about Wilkie Collins's mistresses, Caroline Graves and Martha Rudd, only began to emerge into the light, and be pieced together, just before the last war, when the reminiscences of Katie Collins (at the end of her life Mrs Perugini) were published by her friend Gladys Storey. One wonders whether Nina, who was no prude in such matters, ever went to visit Martha Rudd – Mrs Dawson as she came to be known; and whether the letter Wilkie wrote to Frederick in 1869 about a mysterious "catastrophe", in which my grandfather had clearly offered financial help – "No man, whatever his disappointments may be, can consider himself other than a fortunate man, when he has got such a friend as you are" – was connected with her appearance in his life at about that time. In any case the existence of Caroline Graves[1] was no secret to either of them, for in September 1866 Frederick writes to Nina in Pau: "I had invited Wilkie from Paris to dine with me today at the Reform, and found his acceptance on my return. I rushed to tell him it was no go, as the club was shut up. He was still in bed at 11.30. Mrs Graves and Wilkie insisted on Rudolf and me dining at 9 Melcombe Place, which we have just done and a capital dinner she gave us. She had cooked most of it herself I am sure, but you would not have guessed it from her very *décolleté* white silk gown. She seemed immensely taken with Rudolf. Wilkie was delightful as usual, and sends you no end of love." And when some years later, during his American tour, Wilkie wrote to Frederick, "I hear you have called like a good fellow at Gloucester Place, and have heard something of me there from time to time," it is clear that Caroline Graves was the person who gave Frederick the news.

Wilkie, it seems, contracted the habit of taking laudanum to deaden the pain of the acute gout from which he began to suffer comparatively early in life. In 1863 he had a peculiarly violent attack, and on Dickens's advice he decided to try a cure at a foreign spa. He settled on Aix-la-Chapelle, and soon after his arrival he wrote to Nina: "Under any circumstances I should have written to tell you all my news, and to ask for all your news in return. But a letter from my brother telling me that you too have been ill, puts the pen at once into my hands."

He insists on a long letter from her as soon as she is well enough to write it, and goes on: "As for me, I am all over sulphur, inside

[1] In his admirable biography of Wilkie Collins, Mr Kenneth Robinson gives us the curious information that, in spite of the conventional secrecy which veiled the liaison, Caroline Graves's name appeared in the London Post Office Directory as resident at the successive houses where W. Collins himself lived.

and out; and if ever a man felt fit for the infernal regions already, I (in respect to the sulphurous part of the satanic climate) am that man. The invalid custom here is to rise at seven in the morning, to go out and drink the water hot from the spring, and to be entertained between the gulps with a band of music on an empty stomach. You who know me will acquit me of sanctioning by my presence any such uncomfortable proceeding as this." He describes how he sends his servant out for the water, like "the worst London egg you ever had for breakfast in your life," and drinks it in bed. "The next curative proceeding discloses me, towards the afternoon, in a private stone-pit, up to my middle in the hot sulphur spring; more of this hot water is pouring down on me from a pipe in the ceiling; a worthy German stands by my side, directing the water in a continuous shower on all my weak points with one hand and shampooing me with the other. We exchange cheerful remarks in French (English being all Greek to him and German all Hebrew to me); and, oh, don't we massacre the language of our lively neighbours! This great creature has made an entirely new discovery in the science of language – he does without verbs. '*Trop fort? Bon pour vous fort. Trop chaud? Bon pour vous chaud. Promenade aujourd'hui? Aha! Bon pour vous promenade. Encore la jambe – encore le dos – frottement, ah, oui, oui, frottement excellent pour vous. Repos bon pour vous – à votre service, monsieur – bon jour!*' What an excellent method! Do think of it for your boys – I would practice it myself if I had my time to begin over again."

It is probable that Wilkie's gout was made more acute by his passion for good food and wine. He concludes this letter: "The hotel provides me with a delightful open carriage to dine out in, contains a cellar of the best Hock and Moselle wines I ever tasted, and possesses a Parisian cook who encourages my natural gluttony by a continuous succession of entrées which are to be eaten but not described." In his trips abroad with Frederick, the *cuisine* always came first when he was choosing an hotel. In a later letter to Nina, he says: "I look on meat simply as a material for sauces." When

7a. Nina Lehmann with Mamie Dickens and her dog 'Tit' at Worthing, 1864

7b. The boys at 'Woodlands' in the sixties (the author's father on the right, seated)

8a. 'Woodlands' (Highgate) in the early sixties

8b. Conversation Piece at Cannes in the eighties: the author's grand-parents with their daughter Nina (*standing*)

Frederick was off to America, he sent Wilkie some bottles of Stoughton bitters. Wilkie replied, saying: "I suspended an immortal work of fiction, by going downstairs and tasting a second bottle properly combined with gin. Result delicious! Thank you a thousand times!" Many years afterwards he wrote to Nina, who had sent him some butter: "Your delicious butter came on the very day when I was thinking of keeping a private cow in the back yard, and presiding myself over the pastoral churn . . . Oh! I was foolish enough to eat slices of plain joints two days following. The bilious miseries that followed proved obstinate until I most fortunately ate some *pâté de foie gras*. The cure was instantaneous – and lasting."

Wilkie's letters to my grandparents are full of vivid details about his work on whatever the current novel or play might be. In the late autumn of 1866 he was on a trip to Italy, and wrote at length to Nina, who by that time had become his "Dear Padrona", about the coming production of *The Frozen Deep* at the Olympic Theatre in London, and the plans for putting a French stage version of *Armadale* on in Paris. "How pleasant it would be," he exclaimed at the end, "if we could all meet in the Forum!" Nina was in Pau, and suggested that as she couldn't come to Rome he might come to her on his way back. It was all arranged; and then the total failure of *The Frozen Deep* sent him hurrying back to London. In a letter of apology to Nina – "injured and admirable Padrona" – he writes: "Is my tail put down? No – a thousand times, no! I am at work on the dramatic *Armadale*, and I will take John Bull by the scruff of the neck, and force him into the theatre to see it – before or after it has been played in French, I don't know which – but into the theatre John Bull shall go. I have some idea of advertising next time that will make the public hair stand on end. And so enough, and more than enough of theatrical matters. Oh, I wanted you so at Rome – in the Protestant cemetery – don't start! No ghosts – only a cat. I went to show my friend Pigott the grave of the illustrious Shelley. Approaching the resting place of the divine poet in a bright sunlight, the finest black Tom you ever saw discovered at an incredible distance that a catanthropist had entered the cemetery – rushed up at a gallop, with his tail at right angles to his spine, turned over on his back with his four paws in the air, and said in the language of cats, 'Shelley be hanged! Come and tickle me!' I stooped and tickled him. We were both profoundly affected ... Is this all I have to tell you about Rome? By no means. Then why don't I go on and tell it? Because it is five o'clock – the British muffin-bell is ringing – the dismal British Sunday is closing in. I have promised to dine with the Benzons (where I shall meet Fred) and to take Charlie and Katie (who is in the doctor's hands again) on my way. I must walk to keep my horrid corpulence down, and the time is slipping away; and though I want to go on talking to you, I must submit to another disappointment and give it up."

When Nina sent these letters to London for Frederick to read, she spoke with emotion of his friendship that had continued "for nearly twenty years, always the same, always kind, always interested, always true, always loving and faithful – *that* is worthy the name of friendship indeed".

A comic footnote to the disaster that had brought Wilkie hurrying back to London is found in a letter from Frederick to Nina, of December 1866: "I had a glass with dear Wilkie last night at the Albion. He was very shiny about the nose, but charming as usual. He did not wonder at *The Frozen Deep* being a failure now that he had seen how badly it was played. My dear he told me that Mamie who is staying with the Forsters has *dyed* her hair the fashionable colour yellow with a dash of auburn red. What do you say to that?"

Wilkie's irrepressible spirits bubble up as constantly in his letters to Frederick as to the Padrona. When Frederick was on his voyage round the world in 1869 he wrote to him with news of her. "I am to meet the Padrona at Proctor's on Thursday. And I *did* meet her at Payn's last week – looking very well, and beautifully dressed. But two events occurred worth mentioning. The Padrona – assisting the force of a few sensible remarks by appropriate gesticulation – knocked over her tumbler of champagne, and flooded the table. Shortly afterwards I assisted a few sensible remarks, on my part, by appropriate gesticulation, and knocked over *my* tumbler, and flooded the table. And Mrs Payn seeing her cloth ruined kept her temper like an angel, and smiled upon me while rivulets of champagne were flowing over *my* dress trousers and *her* morocco leather chair. Excellent woman!"

Another glimpse of Nina's relations with Wilkie and his brother Charles, is given in her letter, dated April 1864, from Hastings where Charles and his wife Katie Dickens were staying in lodgings near her: "Wilkie turned up for a couple of hours from Tunbridge Wells, and has just gone back. We agreed we should take a snack together at their lodgings at 3, so over I went with my contribution of a lemon tart and 3 sponge cakes (the former turned out to be deceptive and aged, and was bestowed upon the maid of all work subsequently, in company with a Madeira cake provided by Charlie). They had ham in slices, which also proved fallacious, but it didn't matter as Wilkie had lost the train and didn't appear till 4.15. Then I carried them over to the hotel where I got a charming refection of cold beef and pickles for the Wilkie of my old affections washed down by brandy and water. That proved a success. He looks so well, and is delightful as ever . . . Charlie and Kitty and I agreed not to separate the whole day, and as they had chops for dinner and I a joint of lamb (at the hotel) we agreed to stick to the hotel. Do come back my darling, soon soon. Katie and Charlie miss you as much as I do, we know now what you were. You kept us all up. You are one of the youth of England who have already burst into your vigour and energy."

Wilkie's letters are full of painful references to the illnesses which tormented him and against which he struggled so bravely to keep on writing. "I am all over pain today – obliged to shift the pen from my right hand to my left to get a dip of ink" – "I am so weak I can hardly write even a note" – "My knees tremble on the stairs and my back aches after half an hour's walking – no, *tottering* – on the sunny side of the street" – and so to the end of his life.

IV

Though Bulwer Lytton had been at one time a visitor to Doune Terrace, it was through Dickens that my grandfather and he were brought together. Frederick has left an amusing account of some of his visits to Knebworth, both in his letters to Nina and in his reminiscences. The first visit took place in the spring of 1861, a few years before Lytton was raised to the peerage. *Pelham* had been written more than thirty years before, but the old Regency dandy was still at work: *A Strange Story* was due to start serialization in *All The Year Round* a few months later, and according to Dickens "seemed to succeed capitally!" Though only in his late fifties, he already behaved like an old man; "In a dirty shirt and frayed trousers and stooping much," wrote Frederick, "he looked 70 at least." In the evenings, however, he became rejuvenated, though Frederick suspected that the transformation was not due entirely to natural causes: "Before dinner he apparently took a pick-me-up, which infused new life into him. He came down in evening dress, as spruce as possible and seemingly twenty years younger than when he left us to dress . . . About 11 the power of the elixir, or whatever it was, seemed to wane. Lytton became again a bent old man, his talk flagged, and he faded away from us to work, for he was the most industrious of mortals and was said often to work half the night."

Frederick found Knebworth an enchanted castle, though of a slightly comic sort: "It is a wonderful place, a perfect old Curiosity Shop. Everything that Wardour Street ever had in it for the last three centuries" had found its way there, including every kind of "heraldic monstrosity". Old leather, carved wood, tapestries, silk hangings, old armour and "stained glass enough to make an antiquarian stark mad. The Dining Room is a gorgeous banqueting hall the whole height of the house, a gallery at one end, banners, devices, a blaze of plate, and, I am sorry to add, an Arctic climate in spite of an enormous fire." Every room was so full of extraordinary treasures that no one, thought Frederick, could be dull for an instant. If his bibliomaniac friends could have but a peep into the library, their peace of mind would be gone for ever. "The Drawing Room is a fine long old gallery full of the most interesting portraits, about every one of which he has some story which he tells *con gusto*." Frederick's own room was called the Hampden Chamber, and the paper consisted of stripes of griffins alternating with stripes of the Lytton motto "*Hoc Virtutis Opus*". "I wish I could draw it for you," he wrote to Nina, "how it would drive one mad in an illness."

While the effect of the elixir lasted, during dinner and after, Lytton would be animated and extremely interesting on every kind of topic. Frederick noticed that he only drank claret and that only from a bottle placed at his side, and having quickly found out that this was the only "liquor at table fit to drink", made Lytton share it with him. After dinner, lighting a large *chibouk*, he drew his chair up to the fire and invited his guests to do like-wise. On these occasions, Frederick observes, "his conversation was most bewitching. For a large part, his deafness prevented him from joining freely in the conversation, but with a few friends round him willing and eager to listen, I remember no talk like his. He was essentially a monologist, but Dickens – the only man who could perhaps have disputed the palm with him – used to call him the greatest conversationalist of the age."

Lytton's conversation ranged over literature, politics, art and agriculture – in which he prided himself that he was an expert. In turn he would hold forth about the politicians of the day, Derby, Bright, Gladstone, Disraeli. He held strong (and prescient) views about the last named. "You mark my words," he said to Frederick in 1866 or 67, "nothing will satisfy him until he is Prime Minister and an Earl." He laid down the law about Louis Napoleon,

Richard Owen, Fourierism, told stories of Madame de Stäel, and described his encounter with Lord Brougham at Cannes, which, according to Frederick, "would have made you die of laughing". He thought *The Woman in White* "great trash" and *Great Expectations* Dickens' best novel, and said that he couldn't read Tennyson at all. He told Frederick he admired the "wonderful universality" of the Germans, was amazed at Schiller's knowledge of history, philosophy and all manner of other studies, compared him unfavourably with Byron in this respect, and said that coming to Goethe after a course of Emerson, he felt "like a man escaping from a black hole into pure air". The monologist's performance might include sudden bursts into recitation, Scott's "Young Lochinvar", or similar poems. Then, falling silent for a moment, he would invite Frederick's sister Elisabeth to sing, and, though he couldn't hear a note, expressed himself delighted with her efforts.

Frederick noted that Lytton had a curious drawling way of talking, interspersing his remarks with frequent "erras" to help him out when he was waiting for the proper word; and would sometimes emphasize a sentence or even a single word by loudly raising his voice to give added dramatic effect. "I remember," he wrote, "dining with him *en petit comité*, when conversation somehow drifted towards the universality of belief in a Divine Creator, and while I write I can hear him saying: 'When – erra – I had the honour – erra – of becoming Her Majesty's Secretary of State for the Colonies, I made it my first business – erra - to instruct my agents all over the habitable globe – erra – to report to me if they knew of any nation, tribe or community – erra –' (thus far he had spoken in a low melodious voice, when suddenly he changed his register and shot out the following words as from a catapult and like the blast of a trumpet) – '*who did not believe in a God!*'"

Lytton was not without a pretty wit. Frederick once found himself a fellow-guest at a house-warming party of the Lord Chief Justice, Sir Alexander Cockburn, at 40 Hertford Street.

The house appeared to be entirely bare of pictures or ornaments of any sort, and Frederick, knowing that "the Chief" had taste and a lively interest in contemporary art, expressed to Lytton his surprise at this bareness. Lytton looked quietly round the walls, and replied: "Just the kind of house – erra – for him to start from after breakfast – erra – *to hang a man!*"

During his first visit to Knebworth Frederick found among his fellow-guests a certain Miss Mattie Griffith from Kentucky. She was a poet, and had written an enthusiastic ode to Lytton, overflowing with adulation. But her real claim to fame was that she had inherited a large number of negroes and had set them all free, for which liberal act she was ostracized in Kentucky and forced to retire to Boston. "Although a strong abolitionist," writes my grandfather, "she was fire and flames for the preservation of the Union, and deeply felt the terrors of war between the North and the South. When, therefore, Lytton spread out a map of the United States, and declared in his most didactic way that if any lesson was taught by history, 'such unwieldy empires must fall to pieces and split up into a number of States', I was amused to see Miss Griffith dancing a wild Indian war dance behind his back, and shaking her little fist at him."

Mattie Griffith came to visit my grandparents in London, and they made great friends with her. She booked her passage back to America in the ill-starred *Great Eastern*. In the middle of September I find Nina writing from "Woodlands": "Well what do you think of poor Mattie being nearly wrecked in that horrid *Gt. Eastern*, that leviathan of misfortune, and back again in England. What an awful time they had, lying like a log for 3 days, ploughing up and down, all praying, and expecting every moment to go down! Thank GOD we were not there. Never let us tempt the gods by going in the *G.E.*"

Lytton was not alone among Frederick's friends in doubting the capacity of the Union to survive. "I stick to my prediction," wrote Dickens to Uncle Harry Wills in August 1861, "that the people of the North will neither gain the money nor the men required by the Government; and that an ignoble and contempt-ible compromise will be made soon." And on the eve of his departure for America in 1862, Wilkie Collins wrote to Frederick: "The one chance for that miserable country on the other side of the Atlantic is that those two blatant impostors, Lincoln and McClellan, will fail to get the 300,000 new men they ask for. If I thought it would be the least use, I would go down on both my knees and pray with all my might for the total failure of the new enlistment scheme. But the Devil being the ruling power in American affairs and I not being (I venture to hope) on par-ticularly good terms with him, it seems hopeless on this occasion to put any trust in the efficacy of fervent aspirations and cramped knees." Frederick, however – and presumably his partners in Naylor Vickers – remained convinced that the cause of the North was not only just but would prosper, and he set forth undaunted to conclude his business deals with what Wilkie called "your customers for light steel and my customers for light reading".

My grandfather records that Lytton became very much attached to my aunt Nina (later Lady Campbell), when she was a small girl of five or six, the youngest of the family, and persuaded my grandmother to bring her along on one of the visits to Kneb-worth. "It was touching," Frederick remarked, "to see our frail bent old host in his usual toilet of an old Clo'man wander hand in hand with his small friend thro' the gardens, wasting I fear much wisdom and good counsel varied by wonderful stories." To Frederick, Lytton seemed a lonely and unhappy man, whose gloom was increased by the gloom of Knebworth. "You cannot imagine the desolation and melancholy of this place under the present leaden sky," he wrote to Nina. "I was much touched by coming suddenly upon a little monument in the gardens all embowered in ivy and bearing the following inscription:

Alas, poor Beau!
Died Feb. 28, 1852,

It is but to a dog that this
     stone is inscribed,
Yet what now is left within the Home of
Thy fathers, O Solitary Master,
That will grieve for thy departure
Or rejoice at thy return? – E.B.L."

V

In addition to their many friends, new and old, Frederick and Nina saw a great deal of their relations, in particular of Nina's who seem to have congregated in London in some numbers at this time. The great enterprise of *Chambers's Encyclopaedia* had been launched in 1859, and for this reason and in order to be near the British Museum and the library of the Athenaeum for his work on *The Book of Days*, Robert Chambers moved to London in 1861. He took a house in St John's Wood called Verulam House, which he described as providing "a large garden, lawn, hot-houses, and in short the whole paraphernalia of a gentleman's country house, with a fine conservatory adjoining the drawing-room, and containing a fountain surrounded with flowers".

His daughter Annie, who had married James Dowie, recollected that "beside plenty of space for the beloved books, and spare room for guests, there was no end of scope for the romping of grandchildren. On the lawn, adjoining a rustic summer house, there were some fine trees, one of them a splendid spreading oak, beneath which my mother often took breakfast, at which she usually held a levee of cats. Her fondness for these animals was extraordinary, and she always maintained that they were a misunderstood and ill-used people. Her more special favourites were two beautiful white cats, known as Mr and Mrs Archie, and one of their kittens was generally perched on her shoulder when she was seated under the tree."

Mrs Chambers died in London only two years later. A rather

touching and amusing picture of the eccentric old lady is given in a letter of Nina's from Shanklin in September 1862. Mrs Chambers had suddenly arrived on the island with her youngest daughter Alice, who was only a few years older than my father though she was technically his aunt. "Mama and Alice took a bedroom near and lived with me till yesterday, when they took a parlour and bedroom next door; but of course we are always together, and Alice's cheerful voice rings about the house all day, pitched at such a height that one would think it *must* fall. It was a *fuite* of Mama's of course, but she enjoys the place in her own pottering way immensely, and has already sniffed out all the drains and condemned them, particularly the Chine one by Sampsons'. The Sampsons (the owners of the bathing-machines) are greatly impressed by her presence and dignity. She goes about in her white dressing-gown, regardless of crinolines and all existing fashions, spends small competencies on shrimps, never takes a meal at the time we have it, and returns to her couch at about 6.45, leaving Alice to spend her evenings and sup with Hopie and me (rather a bore). Yesterday she announced with an air of the deepest mystery and importance that she was going to give a concert. Alice, *prima donna* - admission by ticket, one half-penny. She intended giving it in her own rooms, but came round and asked if she might give it in *my* room, as the fact was the upper notes of her piano were slightly defective, and most of the lower ones wouldn't sound at all. So I gave my consent. Alice wrote ten tickets and we were all obliged to purchase. The boys came clamouring for half-pennies – the free list was suspended – Lisa (the parlour maid), Julie (the German nurse), and Matilda (the German governess) were commanded to disburse ... Then Mama said in a grand voice, 'Let Mrs Colenutt (the landlady) know of this. I desire she may come too!' 'Free list?' I whispered. 'By no means. She must pay for her ticket.' So poor Mrs C. had to buy her ticket; and finally, when we were all seated, she knocked at the door, held her ticket out timidly, and stood without a smile at the back of the door the whole time. Mama had got

Matilda to make a wreath for Alice, who looked like a midge
in the sunshine with it on, and all the boys had sprigs in their hats
and sat with the greatest solemnity the whole time. The concert
consisted of Mama and Alice playing three duets, and before each
she always turned to Mrs Colenutt – who was ready to sink with
awe – as being the principal feature in the audience, and said
impressively: 'Scotch – Lowland.' 'English – very old.' 'Favourite
air of Sir Walter Scott's – supposed to be Highland.' When it
was over Mrs Colenutt curtsied and said it was, 'beautiful, and
well worth the money'. Hopie and I retired after the whole thing,
and actually danced with laughter. Mama was on the contrary as
serious as a judge, and Alice subsequently confided to Hopie on
the sands that she had made fourpence-halfpenny by the affair,
having disposed of nine tickets. Ah, Fred, it is too funny. Mama
said afterwards to Hopie and me, 'Now, that is a thing Mrs
Walnut will never forget. She was deeply impressed'."

Robert Chambers was devoted to Nina's children, and they
often visited Verulam House and disported themselves on the
lawn that provided such "scope for the romping of grand-
children". Two or three years after Nina's mother's death, unable
to bear the rigours of living alone, he married a widow, Mrs
Frith, and returned to St Andrews. His brother William, who
had lived much in retirement after the deaths of all his children
in infancy, had just been appointed Lord Provost of Edinburgh,
a post that Robert had declined in 1848. He was still hale; but
Robert's health was failing. He had overtaxed his strength with
his labour on *The Book of Days*, an enormous work taken on in a
rash moment, which was scarcely worthy of his intellectual
powers, and for which he certainly did not need the money as
the *Encyclopaedia* was proving a great financial success; and when
his second wife also died, in 1870, he declined rapidly. He just
managed to finish his last book, *The Life of Smollett*, and died in
March 1871, murmuring: "Quite happy – quite comfortable –
nothing more."

The rival Chambers establishment was the home of Uncle

Harry Wills and Aunt Janet, first at 39 Belsize Road, and later in Regent's Park Terrace. Before they came to live in London, my grandparents used to stay in Belsize Road; and during Frederick's journey to Rome in the Autumn of 1855, Aunt Janet insisted on Nina, who was expecting her first child, being under her eye in London. In those days the district was still half-rural. "I could take you such lovely walks here," wrote Nina, "that even Aunt Janet does not know, but, alas, the glory of nature is gone and the golden leaves all lie trampled under mud." She describes to Frederick one particular "glorious old avenue" where she walked, absolutely solitary, thinking of him and longing for his return. "If it is possible I will take you there. It is the avenue which belonged to a religious house, now pulled down, and it is called Belsize Park. In summer it must be glorious, but soon these fine noble trees will be cut to the ground, rooted from their ancient home, and those detestable modern villa eyesores will be ranged in stucco primness in their stead."

Nina and Harry Wills were very fond of one another. "Uncle Harry told me this morning," she wrote during the same Autumn visit, "that the fact of the matter was he would miss me dreadfully when I went away, and wouldn't know what to do without me. We agree so beautifully, and there is a charm of simplicity and goodness about him which quite endears him to me. He has the heart of a child with the mind of a man, and is altogether so fresh and genial."

The Wills's were in London until 1867, when Uncle Harry decided to move to Hertfordshire, where he could indulge his passion for riding to hounds. *Household Words* had come to an end in the Spring of 1859, owing to Dickens's row with the publishers, Bradbury and Evans, and Wills came over with him to the new venture *All The Year Round*, as co-proprietor, sub-editor and commercial manager. During the next eight years he was kept extremely busy at the office in Wellington Street, as Dickens was constantly on the move, giving his readings all over the country, making expeditions to Paris, and finally in 1867 touring the United States for the last time. The letters they exchanged prove that Dickens, wherever he was, kept the most careful eye on the progress of the journal, read all the manuscripts and made precise suggestions for make-up; nevertheless if Dickens was out of town, the final responsibility lay with Wills, and it is a tribute to his character and ability that Dickens always had complete trust in him, and that no shadow of a quarrel ever seems to have fallen over their relationship. It was certainly profitable to Uncle Harry; as early as 1860 he appears, from family records, to have been making the (by contemporary standards) very large sum of £2,000 a year.

Wills tried to dissuade Dickens from the fatal last trip to America, and Dickens wrote back, on June 6, 1867, "I cannot tell you how warmly I feel your letter, or how deeply I appreciate the affection and regard in which it originates. I thank you for it with all my heart. You will not suppose that I make light of any of your misgivings if I present the other side of the question. Every objection that you make strongly impresses me, and will be revolved in my mind again and again." However, the lure of the triumphal applause – perhaps more than of the monetary gain (which he estimated at £10,000) – was too strong for him, and he believed that he had unusual powers of recuperation: "I always seem to myself to have rested far more than I have worked, and I do really believe that I have some exceptional faculty of accumulating young feelings in short pauses, which obliterates a quantity of wear and tear."

In October 1862 Dickens went to Paris with Georgina Hogarth and Mamie, and a few weeks later Uncle Harry, who wanted to arrange the Christmas number of *All The Year Round* with him, and had at the same time been charged by Baroness Burdett Coutts (then Miss Burdett Coutts) to deliver a "boxful of flowers" to the Empress Eugenie, joined him. My grandparents arrived in Paris at the same time. After Wills had fulfilled his mission, "the omnibus brought me to the room Dickens had ordered for me; a capital one with a good fire, and I went over the way. I found Mamie and Georgina, Dick being out (it was half-past four). Very glad to see me; inquired after you very cordially; didn't know that Nina and Fred were on their way. Dick, when he came in, very cheery. We had a capital dinner at 6 p.m." This dinner took place at the Café Voisin, and my grand-parents added their signatures on a copy of the menu to those of Dickens, Georgina Hogarth, Mamie and Uncle Harry, and sent it to Aunt Janet to placate her for not having been with them.

My father remembered Uncle Harry in his country days as "an absolutely fearless rider", and his preference was for large and powerful horses, to the control of which his muscular strength – for he was very thin and slightly built – was not always quite adequate. His thinness, indeed, was the constant object of his friends' chaff. One story related how someone, noticing his absence from a gathering and asking where he was, had been advised to look for him in the flute-case and had found him snugly tucked up there. Another told how an absent-minded old lady, sitting next to him at dinner, had mistaken his leg for the leg of her chair and had curled her own leg comfortably round it. A year after Dickens's American tour he had a bad accident in the hunting field and in 1869, at the age of sixty, he decided to retire. He had first come to London in the legendary past, when Robert Cham-bers was engaged in the last struggles to overcome poverty and obscurity in Edinburgh, and remembered, on the way up from the West Country, "the hasty dinners at the great inns we stayed at on the road, all alike – the long tables, the big joints, the invariable pigeon pie, the selfish scrambling of the passengers to get their full three-and-sixpence worth tucked in in time for the warning notes of the guard's horn; the tin, thin tripod plate-warmer at the fire, the nimble waiters in white cotton stockings and pumps, who were constantly wiping plates with napkins whipped in and out of side-pockets of their natty striped jackets." His first impressions, as a small boy of eleven, of London, were of "the number and perseverance of hawkers of pale, sour, cold-looking oranges – and of the endless succession of old-clothes men." "The sound of 'Ole Clo! Old Clo! Old Clo!' never left the ear an instant's respite: an endless procession of Jews with empty black bags under their arms, walking rapidly, uttering the same sound, but on different notes . . . the prodigious number of these candidates for cast clothing is not so wonderful when we remember that the poor could get at that time nothing else to wear."

Aunt Janet seems to have been thoroughly Scottish, very decided in her opinions, strict in her outlook and neat in her person; but gifted with a sharp wit and capable of holding an after-dinner audience enthralled with her unaccompanied rendering of old Scottish songs, such as "Our gudeman came hame at e'en". She had taken the part of the weird prophetess, Nurse Esther, in the performance of *The Frozen Deep* at Tavistock House in January 1857. Sixty or seventy stayed to supper every night after the emotional orgy of this drama, during which, according to Douglas Jerrold, "the men were sobbing, and Mark Lemon on the stage was crying every night, although he had seen and played in it so often". In spite of her wit and dramatic capabilities, she does not seem to have been very easy to get on with, and Frederick never to have quite hit it off with her.

Among those present at the first night of *The Frozen Deep* was Nina's sister Eliza, or Ella, who had married a brilliantly promising doctor, William (afterwards Sir William) Priestley, the year before. They prospered, and moved into Hertford Street, Mayfair, in 1863, where later many family parties took place. But in the year they moved, and in the week when Princess Alexandra passed through a festive London to her marriage with the future King Edward VII, he fell ill with diphtheria, caught from a patient, and it was many months before he was out of danger. "We are in awful anxiety about Prie," wrote Nina in the middle of March. "I wish I had a better account of him to send you. I sent this morning, and he is not better. I shall send once more before closing this letter, to give you the last news. We are preparing ourselves for the worst – oh what shall we do. You will have to be a protector to Ella, in case of the worst. Papa and Mama are prostrate with dismay." A week later, however, she exclaims: "Prie is *safe – safe – safe* – Hurrah! I am quite ill and kept up on sal volatile with the excitement."

Very slowly, he recovered, to become one of the famous gynaecologists of the day. He was made when, in the following year, he was commanded by Queen Victoria to go out to Darmstadt to attend her daughter, Princess Louis of Hesse in her confinement. "Prie is enjoying himself at Darmstadt," wrote Nina, "and rapidly losing his heart to his Royal patient. She fascinates him on sofas and in lovely dressing-gowns. The Princess Royal is expected there, and Prie's patient said to him: 'She is coming far more to see you than to see me, Dr Priestley, which is not sisterly of her.' Poor Prie has to write long letters to the Queen beginning 'Madam', at the Queen's express desire." The child that was born on this occasion became Grand Duchess Sergius of Russia.

Nina's other sister, Tuckie, after many years of indecision, finally married Frederick's brother Rudolf in 1861. He carried her off to Rome, and they did not finally return to settle in London until 1866, when they took a house on Campden Hill that had belonged to John Philips, a popular painter of Spanish scenes. Directly after the marriage, Nina described to Frederick (on his way to Spain) the letter she had just received: "I got a charming graphic letter from Tuckie yesterday. They were in Antwerp at the Memorial Fête. She seems in a dream of happiness. They have found Joachim and a hundred other old friends of Rudolf's there. Tuckie's descriptions are so bright and clear. Rudolf's 'overflowing love and tenderness' she can't attempt to describe, so she just says 'O Nina, *that man*!'"

In his next letter Frederick, who had stopped in St Jean de Luz to pass a few hours with his brother Henri and Clemence, sent Nina rather a woeful description of the household. They were staying "in the best house in the place, having their own menage, bathing and drinking, talking torrents, splitting hairs, but otherwise tranquilly vegetating . . . With them is a brother artist,

Amaury Duval, whom you met once, I believe, fifty-four, a bachelor, disappointed and full of ailments. The three talk continually of their health . . . Poor Henri was made for better things, but he cannot get over the loss of his children." Nina replied: "What you say of Henri and Clemence interests me much though it makes me sad. *What* a different life Rudolf has given himself. He is young again with even more to make him young and energetic than he had when he really *was* young."

Great-uncle Rudolf had had a number of successes in his Roman days, the chief being a vast and elaborate representation of Pope Sixtus V blessing the Pontine Marshes after the completion of the irrigation works, which was bought by the French Government for the Lille museum; and a half-length female figure of a grape-gatherer, which was awarded a gold medal in the Paris Salon, bought by the Duc de Montpensier (King Louis-Philippe's brother), and made dubiously famous by being reproduced on blinds and curtain material, manufactured in Birmingham. He painted a quantity of Italian genre pictures, for which he made long expeditions out into the Abruzzi and the Volscan mountains; a Madonna for which his model was the afterwards world famous actress Adelaide Ristori, then a member of a company of strolling players, and according to Rudolf one of the most beautiful women he had ever seen, with blue eyes, chestnut hair and a deep melodious voice;[1] and a picture called "Graziella" which had a curious history, very characteristic of the times. The subject had been taken from Lamartine's *Confidences,* and showed Lamartine himself reading his poems to a fisher-girl who died of love when he left her; Frederick Leighton, then still in his student years, had sat for the poet. The picture was exhibited in the Salon of 1855, when Lamartine himself saw it. He immediately wrote to Rudolf, "I owe you the greatest service an artist with the pen can receive from an artist with the brush; that you

[1] The great crux of the Ristori's career was when she appeared in Paris, in 1855, and challenged Rachel, then at the height of her fame. She had a resounding success.

have understood, felt, appreciated one of his early inspirations, and have illustrated it, giving it the colour and life of another art. Graziella was but a dream – you have made her a reality. When I say dream I speak metaphorically, for nothing in that episode of my life is imaginary but the names . . . I return this morning to the Salon exclusively for your sake. Your brother will have told you that the impression, natural in myself, has been shared by a select and feeling public. An old connoisseur, very hard to please, said to me yesterday that in those rooms you were the Petrarch of the brush. Your fame will spread . . ."

Rudolf was already well known for his portrait sketches. In those days artists' studios were one of the "sights" of Rome, and the rich and famous visitors who flocked to Rome for the winter were regularly taken round them by special guides. These constant interruptions were sometimes rather distracting to the artists, but they did their best to exploit them. One contemporary of Rudolf's lived entirely off copies he made for visitors of a picture which was always hanging prominently in his *atelier*, showing an Italian peasant girl riding on a donkey – contrived exactly to suit the sentimental taste of the day. Rudolf himself had a gift for dashing off a pleasant likeness in pencil, and used to persuade many of the visitors to stay for the necessary half hour, while he charmed them with his talk, as his sketch book reveals; these visitors ranged from King Edward VII (then Prince of Wales) and the Emperor Frederick III (also as a young Prince), to the Brownings.

As time went on, Rudolf devoted himself more and more to portraits, especially after he settled in England. His heyday appears to have been during the seventies and eighties, when he painted elaborately finished oil portraits, agreeable, life-like, but not very penetrating, nor very exciting from the artistic point of view, of almost everybody who was anybody. Soon after he had settled on Campden Hill in the sixties, however, commissions began to come in, and some of his most vigorous portraits date from this decade.

The circle of the inter-related Lehmann and Chambers families living in London and dining out with one another at this time was completed by the Benzons, who conducted a grand establishment at No. 10 Kensington Palace Gardens, now one of the mansions belonging to the Soviet Russian diplomatic mission. Though his sister Lisbeth became, one gathers, rather a strained and discontented person, Frederick himself got on capitally with them, particularly as they were deeply attached to his children. Ernst Benzon was a genial fellow, and as Frederick reported in 1866, "as round as a ball all over, quite fat and enormous – or abnormous", who retained to the end of his life a strong German accent and way of speech. Though deeply absorbed in his business affairs, he took a keen interest in the arts – perhaps not wanting to be left behind by Frederick – even if his appreciation was not always very profound. Nina's observations about him were sometimes rather tart. Describing an unsuccessful musical party in 1863 at Kensington Palace Gardens, she writes to Frederick: "B. always said it was *schön* when it wasn't, and looked like a fish out of water, gasping for the ocean of iron and steel again."

A more successful, almost entirely family occasion, figures in a letter of Frederick's in November 1866: "Well, Lisbeth's dinner on Sunday went off very nicely. The Pries, the Rudolfs, the Wills, Deutsch, Mr Boxall, de Mussy and I, twelve in all. Boxall, the dear sweet old man, kept us in a continual roar with the stupidest of stories, Aunt Janet was brilliant and Ella her worthy pupil, more so if possible. The ball went back and forward like a flash of lightning and no family party with only three strangers as policemen ever behaved better." This Boxall must, I think, have been William Boxall, Director of the National Gallery, who was knighted the following year. After dinner, one of Benzon's American associates, Sebastian Schlesinger, who was staying in England at the time, looked in and a friend who arrived with him accompanied him in "a tremendous ballad of Schumann, and then Lis and Tuck sang. Duet as usual. As for Tuckie, no power on earth could prevail on her to sing a note by herself. Everybody went down on his knees, but no use, and it is on account of Lisbeth for Sebastian tells me that on Monday they all dined again at 10 K.P.G. and at 11 she suddenly began to sing like an inspired angel. Caprice, nothing else."

Tuckie's unusual musical gifts were inherited by several of her children, outstandingly by her daughter, Liza Lehmann, composer as well as singer, who made her début at a Monday "Pop" in 1885.

The Benzons liked to invite my grandparents' literary and artistic friends to their luxurious table, and it was at 10 Kensington Palace Gardens that a celebrated row took place between John Forster and Browning. My grandfather, after describing Forster's passion for having a finger in the pie of all his literary friends' work, particularly in that of Browning, writes in his reminiscences: "However valuable such aid (or interference) may have been to Browning while he was living in Florence, it may have become irksome when Browning took up his domicile in London. Forster exercised a kind of patent-right or ownership over Browning. It was an understood thing that on Sundays Browning had to dine with F. or that anyone wanting Browning to dinner on Sundays could only secure him after some diplomatic negotiations of which one of the fundamental conditions was that Mr and Mrs F. were to be invited together with B. Forster was kind but ponderous, Browning nervous and sensitive and probably unable to tolerate their kind of literary bear-leading." At this particular dinner, Browning and Forster had already been nagging at one another, when Browning was unlucky enough to mention what he considered the scandal of conditions at Marlborough House, where the Princess of Wales had suddenly been taken violently ill and no carriage could be found to fetch a doctor. "Forster at once ridiculed the story as a foolish invention. Browning gave chapter and verse, adding that he had it from Lady William Russell. Forster retorted that he did not believe it a whit more on account of that authority. Suddenly Browning got very fierce and said, 'Dare to say one word in disparagement of that lady' – seizing a decanter while he spoke – 'and I will pitch this bottle of claret at your head!' Forster seemed as much taken aback as the other guests, and Benzon who had gone out of the room for a moment with Sir Edwin Landseer and on returning with him found Browning standing up in a kind of frenzy with a decanter in his hand ready for action, had the greatest difficulty in realizing the situation."

A revealing and slightly absurd glimpse of Benzon emerges from a letter of my father's, written some years later when he was a schoolboy at Highgate, to his brother Freddy. A children's party had been held at the Schlesingers' house. After the children had been packed off, "dinner was to have taken place at 7.30, but owing to the late arrival of Mr and Mrs Benzon did not come off till 8.15. Old Benzon returned from Sheffield at 6.15 and I think it did the old chap a good deal of credit to be able to put in an appearance as early as he did. He was in a tremendous state of excitement when he came. Something in the way of business had succeeded. The dinner was grand." Apart from the Benzons, great-uncle Rudolf had been invited, and Pen Browning who was "in one of his mad humours", and "performed a fling or a reel *solus* in the middle of the room" after dinner. "Old Benzon was very fine. He began to tell me the story of an accident which happened to him 12 years ago in Sheffield. It seems that he and Mr Vickers were making some experiments and a bit of iron flew up and caught him on the jaw. It cut his lip and took out a tooth. He said: 'I could do nothing but bleed like a pig. I staggered about and when dey took me home I vondered vether it was cot broadways or longways . . .' He went on at this story for about half an hour and described every detail of it. Mrs Benzon was very jolly as in fact she always is to us. She was joking away, in her usual strain without any intermission."

The Dr de Mussy who appears in Frederick's letter as being a fellow-guest at 10 Kensington Palace Gardens became, through the Priestleys, very intimate with the family in the course of the sixties, and in fact was credited with having an affair with

Lisbeth. He was a rather enigmatic figure: a physician to the French Royal family, he appears to have followed the Orleanists to England after the Revolution of 1848, and to have stayed until the ban on the family was removed after the fall of Napoleon III. He never felt himself entirely at home in England. He was accused of rapacity in his fees by some of his English patients, including the Proctors, but Nina asserted that she knew for a fact that he treated many poor artists for nothing. In December 1869 Nina writes to Frederick: "What do you think I did? I went *uninvited* to pass the evening with the de Mussys, just to see whether they *meant* what they say, when they give you general invitations . . . My dear, their surprise when I walked into the room! The Dr, his wife Odette, and the Belgian belle-mère all sitting round a lamp. He reading with an awful old coat and slippers on, and a tashed head – they all neat and working. I don't think they ever got over the surprise till I went away, when I imagine they would all wake from a dream. As the Dr put my shawl on for me downstairs, he said, 'Excuse me, my dear, but I am so confused I have not got over it yet, *c'est la première fois qu'une pareille chose m'arrive depuis que je suis en Angleterre, et si vous ferez ce coup de génie souvent, je commencerai a croire que j'habite encore mon cher pays'*."

Nina, however, did not think much of their taste in music. "I stayed two hours – had my knitting – played to them on their new Broadwood. They sat and gazed at my fingers, which made me nervous, and were perfectly frozen and unsympathetic about the music. After the *Dialogue* of Schubert, he said '*Est-ce de Sullivan, ce morceau?*' I said, with real scorn, 'If Sullivan had written that, he might quietly retire into his grave.' 'Oh, *le pauvre petit homme, pourquoi?*'"

In the same letter, she describes an episode at a dinner party of her own, at which she placed Dr de Mussy on her right, and Lisbeth on the other side of the table. "Poor Lis was therefore not beside her love but right opposite him. She was in a boiling rage with him for something, and after the unlucky man came up from dinner she took him right away to the corner ottoman and laid into him right and left. He kept rubbing his nose with a puzzled air, and never answered!"

Before her father and mother settled in London, Nina used to make periodical visits to Doune Terrace with her children, especially when Frederick was abroad. There is a very lively description of a minor railway accident in which they were involved on one of these expeditions, in a letter to Frederick, who was in Sweden, in 1860. It reveals all Nina's gaiety of spirits, common sense and courage in emergencies. "I was in a perfect ferment of anxiety as our journey approached and got up at 5 on Friday morning to be ready. At last all was ready, roped and down in the hall, Marian and I standing there waiting. The procession came down in this wise. First Matilda with Rudie in one hand and her bandbox in the other. Two steps above, Spaul with Freddy on his back. Two steps above that Baillie with Babe in one arm and a bloated bag bursting with bottles and napkins in the other. One step above, Susan with a very stiff neck and a large basket of provisions, followed by the mild Elizabeth, partially concealed by two railway rugs and one large fur. They all happened to be together on the one flight of steps and made me roar and forget all my anxiety. Marian bade us good-bye and off we set in a fly and a cab, Spaul looking like death with a fearfully swollen jaw, ready to bury us all in a respectable but *not* economical manner at the shortest notice and to retire subsequently into a separate but adjacent grave (being attached to the family, but too respectful to be *too* near). As our train was to start at 9.20, and I remembered your principles with regard to time of waiting at stations, you will not be surprised to hear I was not much more than an hour too soon.

"It was fortunate, as Matilda's box, of a baskety and German nature and seemingly ballasted with stones, had been quietly left behind in the smoking room (where of course it had been put to be at hand and easily found). The misery of Spaul was touching; back he had to go though, and back he came with it in time, the unconscious Matilda thinking – if she thought at all – it was safely tarpaulined on the top of the carriage all the time. This also put me into fits, her unconscious face and the idea of Spaul thinking that the bandbox had been her entire luggage. He handed in *The Times* with a funereal smile and eventually retired, leaving behind him an undertaker's blessing and a grave-digger's hope that we should all reach our long home safely in time. At the station was Auntie (Janet), inclined to pathos but disregarded, the Dodger, very spry, Jack, heavy, Prie, paternal and bearing outward signs of having sat up all night to be ready in the morning. Last came Hopie, bright and kind. We got packed into a centre carriage. The Dodger, I believe, tipped the guard, the bell rang, the door was shut, the window let down, more last words and at last we were off.

"Well, I must cut the journey short. . . . Very near Edinburgh, all the milk done – there in half an hour say we. Baillie preparing all our things, stands emptying Babe's bottle into an article better understood than expressed - we run into a goods train - we all clash for a moment. Rudie's head is bumped, he howls – Freddy howls – baby howls. I call out for orange jelly – howls stop. I let the carriage window down. Guard loquitur: 'Anybody hurt here, Mum?' 'No, what's up?' 'Run into a goods train.' 'Oh, is that all - very well.' Sit down again and wait. Passenger from Berwick of a reassuring nature walks up and down. 'It's a mewhrcy we werwhnet all smashed - the goods train is in wribands – etc. etc.' Suddenly I think I should like to see a railway accident. Ask Berwick passenger to take me out and show me. Roofs of vans, splinters, smashes, intoxicated wheels and crazy engine strewn promiscuous. Invalid lady in carriage by herself: 'For God's sake let me out of here and take me where there is another lady.' 'I am that other lady,' I say. 'Don't be frightened. We're all right now. It's being telegraphed both ways. No danger. I'll take you in, if you don't mind the children.' 'Thank you, thank you. How kind and composed you are.' 'Ah, you see, I'm strong, and you're not.' Wait an hour; engine hastens to our rescue, back to Dunbar, very slow and stopping often. Then shunt on to the 'up line', and go down cautiously on that, past all the débris, lighted now by the torches of 50 navvies or whatever they are. Reach Edinburgh quite jolly at 11. Find Molly bathed in tears at the station and Papa cool and kindly. . . .

"Mind you, it *was* a shock and I am so glad you were not there, as your face would have turned white I know and frightened me. I felt I was the head there to whom all looked and I was as unconcerned as possible with my heart very nearly fainting within me once or twice. I had Babe in my arms in a centre seat luckily at the time, and Freddy sat opposite me by himself – also lucky. The passengers farther in front were the worst used, but only the poor engine drivers were severely hurt. Molly saw them in the train with their heads all bandaged. Our carriage and the forward ones were uncoupled from the rest of the train which bounded back fifty yards from us. But why should I bother you with what is over. The facts I suppose are that a goods train (as they usually do – particularly when they know an Express to be behind – is it because they get paralysed with fear?) had stopped. They had not hoisted a danger signal in time. Still we had time, barely, to slacken a little over 40 miles speed, else I won't answer for consequences. Our engine leapt on the back of the goods van, and so and so and so – it was done; but it was well and neatly done and really a most successful collision and I'm not a grain the worse – indeed much the better. So there's my description."

The children seem to have been fortunate in their upbringing. They were never kept at a distance from their parents, as so often happened in Victorian families, discipline was light and they were encouraged to express themselves naturally, to learn to read good books, appreciate music and painting and to act as well if the spirit took them.

In November 1864, when she got back to Westbourne Terrace from Worthing, Nina found that the new footman, John, was causing great excitement among the children. She had brought presents for them, and "the things were soon unpacked, and gave great satisfaction. All this time I vaguely heard Rudolph dinning some long story about John, our new man, and when at last I had time to listen, it simply made me roar. I can't tell it with Rudie's earnest belief and simplicity. No, I *must* try it in Rudie's own words. 'Oh, Mama – I think we have succeeded at last with a man. He's *such* an actor. Oh Mama, he's given me the whole suit of Richard the 3rd to my own self. It's crimson velvet and satin knickerbockers and a velvet cap with plumes and lots of gold lace and all to myself. It's beautiful. And he can act Lord Dund*rary* and Hamlet, he can do all the parts in Hamlet quite by himself. Would you ever believe it of a footman?' He went on breathless, but oh, my dear, that's not the best. When they were all gone upstairs, Julie, who is also deeply impressed by the dramatic genius of John, said, 'Oh, Madame Lehmann, you should see Nina pointing to Ernie and saying "Off mit his hett – so much for Bockingham!"' This was the clinch, and I nearly rolled off the sofa. It seems John has frequented the Re-unions of the *great* (basements) in Belgravia, where they are much given to acting. . . .

"After I had written this on Saturday, Rudie and Freddy burst into my room as Richard 3rd and Catesby, that gentleman (the latter) was attired in the Pyrenees costume and looked the character completely. He said his speech with a solemnity and composure which might well be imitated, and was utterly un-moved when the ranting Rudie ordered him to decapitate Buckingham. Rudie acted in the fine old-fashioned *barn-style*, and would have taken a provincial audience by storm. He flourished his dagger when he had nothing else to do, and soon finished Nina and Ernie, who, having been trained evidently, stretched themselves dead in easy positions on my bedroom floor and were severely put down when they sniggered. At last I also was neatly finished off with one well-directed thrust of the sanguinary Richard, whereupon he and Catesby strutted out of the room, perfectly satisfied with themselves. *You* would have died on the spot without the help of a dagger. In the midst of the most tragic and awful bits, Richard couldn't help every now and then holding up his cape to me and saying, 'It's real velvet, Mama, it really is, and look at the nice black tails on the fur.' These children are too much. . . ."

A vivid picture of the warmth and happiness of the children's relationship with their mother is given in a letter of Nina's from Pau, in March 1867, just after she had returned from St Jean de Luz: "At last we got to Pau, and the snow was falling fast and thick and everybody shivering; but soon I was home, and the sight of Ernie and Nina, beautiful and radiant at the door, would have warmed up a much colder person than I was. I thought they were positively grown, and I am *sure* Rudie has. Poor Freddy was laid up with a bilious cold, but nothing of importance, and Pau is very sickly just now, I hear. He looks quite nice and well and pretty, and I dare say will be up today. Rudolph looked magnificent as he burst in from school, and clasped me tight in his rough schoolboy arms, bless him! He seemed to purr over me with contentment, and quite thinks himself the protector of his *petite mère* now. Your books (thanks, my dear) came shortly after his return from school, and, till he has finished it, I mayn't hope for a look. Did I tell you what awful questions he asks me when he is reading sometimes? 'Ma, what is an illicit passion?' is one of the mildest of them. Only fancy, he is turning out *decidedly* musical. The proof is that during my absence he has found out on the piano all the tunes (popular English, you know, *à la* Christy Minstrels) he knows or has heard for himself, and plays them *perfectly* correctly. This shows his ear is good. Ernie goes on beautifully, and will be a dainty little performer some day – a delicate touch, I think, he will have. Our Nina looked superbly beautiful, I can't help saying it. I should say it whoever's child she was, and you know I never *quite* believe I made her myself. Indeed, I *can't* believe it, when I look at my plain, almost ugly self sometimes. Rudie *adores* his school. He implores me always to stay here, never to go away. He says the boys are so much nicer in France – never tease, never chaff; such delightful boys, he says.

Isn't this amusing? I must say I have always particularly detested that chaffing, so-called *manly* system of behaviour in English schools. It is unknown here, at all events, where a fellow 'can wear what he likes, you know, Ma, and the other fellows never notice it a bit'. He not only learns French, but I was amused to hear him fondling Chang this morning in the purest Béarnais."

A few weeks later, she writes: "My glory is that the boys are now my attentive and almost appreciative audience. I have to play one Chopin after another, and they are riveted. Rudie sits trying to keep the tears in sometimes, and they beg me to go on and on and on. Is it not delicious? And no sympathy, no admiration, has ever given me such thrills of pleasure as their innocent satisfaction in their mother's playing. It seems to me as if for the rest of my life I should care for nothing else in the whole world but pleasing you and these children. Still, I don't know. I suppose I shall like well enough to show my pretty dresses at parties when I come home, and see other people's pretty (not quite so pretty, you know) dresses, and see old faces and hear old sagas of all kinds."

In after years Rudie, my father, was to write of his mother's piano playing: "Her ear was faultless, and not less so was the instinctive sympathy with which she gave life and symmetry and charm to any piece she played. Tenderness or rapture, yearning or passion – all the emotions that the musician strives to express were within the range of those frail but wonder-working fingers moving over the keyboard with a quickness, a precision, and an ease that would have been astonishing had the movements not seemed so perfectly natural and inevitable. The praise may seem high, but there are many still living who can testify to its simple truth."

VI

Some of the most revealing light on the social life and values of
my grandparents' circle is shed by the accounts they left of many
incidents in their friendship with the eccentric Henry Fothergill
Chorley, a well-known literary and musical figure of the time.
Chorley was the author of a great many novels, plays and
operatic *libretti*, but his real contemporary fame and influence
came from the fact that he was music critic on *The Athenaeum*.
My grandfather in his reminiscences wrote that in the middle
years of the century "music in London really meant Italian opera
or Handel's oratorios"; for anything else there was an extremely
limited public. . . . No single critic could now make or mar a
reputation, but in those antediluvian days Chorley, as the mouth-
piece of *The Athenaeum*, was master of the situation and ruled
supreme. He took the most violent likes and dislikes; he was
passionately fond of Mendelssohn, but for years conducted a
bitter campaign against Schumann's music and Madame Schumann (whom he called "the old Shoe-woman") as the living
representative of it. My grandfather, while deploring these
excesses, took the view that Chorley was neither dishonest nor
petty, but simply lacked the appropriate gifts and education for
his job. He had made Chorley's acquaintance in London before
his marriage, and they often used to go travelling together. Few
details of these travels survive; and I find it rather maddening, for
instance, to come upon such entries as these in my grandfather's
diary of 1864: "Went with Mme (Pauline) Viardot, Tourgenieff
and Chorley to Carlsruhe," and a few days later, "dined at
the Villa Viardot with Tourgenieff and Chorley" – nothing
more.

According to my father, on whom as a boy he made a very
vivid impression, Chorley "was tall and thin. His eyes blinked
and twinkled as he spoke; and his quaint picking gestures and
high staccato voice made an impression which caused one of his

friends to describe him as the missing link between the chimpanzee and the cockatoo." In a letter of 1859, while Nina was in Shanklin, Frederick writes to her: "Chorley dined with me at the Club last night and was exceedingly amusing. He never loses a chance of showing you his immense importance, his in fact being the '*unglückseliger Atlas*' on whom the world rests, the fountain of knowledge and advice to which all throng. He took occasion to tell me during the sitting, that he had just finished a political novel called *Roccabella*, begun in 1849. He has deposited in it his experience of Refugee life and I suppose his ultra Tory ideas. It will come out immediately. He has to go to Paris to translate Gounod's *Faust*. His translation of Dinorah nearly ready. The publishers pay him his own price. Meyerbeer wants him to write an opera to be done here but he won't. For he is to arrange *The Tempest*[1] into an opera 'Hermione & Perdita' to be composed by Gounod. Madame Viardot is to do Hermione and sing English. Fancy her lovely Greek features as the statue. He is just finishing an article for the *Edinburgh Review* on some of Horace Walpole's correspondence lately found. He has got the forcing of Government to give an annual grant for music on his back, etc. etc. Fancy all this jerked out with a snout at each climax."

Chorley seems to have been rather a lonely man, always looking for affection which he could rarely inspire – he was deeply in love with "Tuckie" before her marriage – who found his chief consolations in dining out and giving rather grand dinner parties at his house in Eaton Place; and in the bottle. In a letter of 1860, describing a great musical party at the Hallés, Frederick writes: "Among the devotees was Chorley, transparent with rosy skin and yellow hair. He had drunk the elixir of life in just the right quantity last night, and was wonderfully youthful and frisky."

Frederick's whole picture of their party is somewhat irreverent: "Prince Galatzin was going as I came. His wife's English maid had that day died at her feet in a fit of apoplexy, so they were

[1] Evidently a slip for *The Winter's Tale*.

greatly disturbed and he will take his wife away a little to get over it. He asked: '*Où diable êtes vous donc, j'ai été deux fois chez vous?*' As I entered the sacred temple the well-known priests and priestesses were there officiating or performing their devotions. At the altar, were Hallé, Santley,[1] Belletti and Mlle Artot.[2] The last-named sang a pretty lullaby by Gounod, but may on the whole, for my part, vanish into infinite space as Carlyle has it. Hallé played old Chopins and Bachs, and one suite which I had not heard before – which was quite enchanting. His nose was more powerful than ever, and paled the ineffectual lights of lamps and candles. I noticed that a young lady's dress (close to Hallé) appeared pink, while (away from him) it was white, and can only account for this effect by the powerful reflection of his nose ... The tribe of Prinseps with the Murillo daughter were attended by their henchmen Holman Hunt and Dick Doyle, Miss Schwabe who *would* speak to me made ineffectual attempts to get rid of her two brothers who loved her too well to leave her for a moment. Manuel Garcia told me the same story of Ernst's playing a sonata of Bach's one evening many years ago which I have patiently listened to twice before ... Round this camp of gipsies a thin line of respectable and heavy outsiders sat frigid, trying to overcome the turbulent mass, not without a certain effect. Lady Molesworth bestowed some of her fat on each of the two parties and still had plenty to spare. Madame Hallé gave me her hand to kiss, but I regret to say it was covered by a washed glove which smelt strongly of turpentine. *Everybody* enquired after you and Tuck. Chorley was *sweet*, and we walked down together as far as the corner of Park Lane ... He had only made H. Hunt's acquaintance at Gad's Hill and was very much struck by his appearance, with the notion that he paints Christ from his own face. In the 'Light of the World' there is certainly some similarity.

[1] Charles Santley (later Sir Charles), born 1834, baritone, was one of the famous English singers of the time.

[2] Desirée Artot, born 1835, soprano, was a pupil of Pauline Viardot. Tchaikovsky imagined himself, for a time, to be in love with her.

He quite hugged this discovery as you know he does anything he thinks he has found out."

Lady Molesworth appears constantly in the parties which Frederick and Nina describe to one another. She was the widow of Sir William Molesworth, radical politician and editor of Hobbes, and after her husband's death in 1855 became a familiar figure in London society. She tried to flirt with Frederick, but, as one can see, with little effect.

Chorley's dinners were prepared with enormous care, a great while ahead, and were certainly first class, even when there was only one guest. When my grandfather made a long projected journey to Spain in the summer of 1861, Chorley went with him. He had invited himself. "I did not know until later," Frederick writes in his reminiscences, "that Chorley had a curious habit of joining on to any proposed excursion or journey that smiled to him." He had happened one day to mention his forthcoming trip, and Chorley "listened and said: 'That sounds very nice. I don't mind if I go with you'." Frederick was in fact rather pleased, as Nina did not feel up to it, and he was rewarded with a feast on the eve of departure. "The dear old Chorl had quite a wonderful little dinner waiting for me. One chef d'oeuvre followed another. Little fried packets of hashed salmon, same outside as those wonderful soles you wot of. Thin veal cutlets alternating with slices of ham with boiled cucumber in the middle and green peas and potatoes handed round in that famous tripartite dish. After that, half a grouse for each and French beans boiled in cream. Champagne on ice, claret, etc. etc. A marvellous pudding wound up the feast but it is beyond my powers of description."

They took different routes through France as my grandfather had business to attend to, and were to meet in Bayonne, Chorley arriving a few days ahead though starting later. When, however Frederick got to Bayonne at last, there was no sign of Chorley. He took the omnibus to Biarritz, spent most of the day there, and was relieved when he got back to find "dear old Chorley, just arrived, tottering down the High Street – the Dickens' had insisted on keeping him at Gad's Hill, and he was full of their great kindness to him". Dickens himself refers to this in a letter to Harry Wills: "Chorley was here before starting for Spain, and walked – with me, at my pace – two and twenty miles, without appearing in the least the worse for it. At which I stood amazed, and have ever since remained in that attitude." Chorley had already decided that in return he would invite the Dickens family to a sumptuous dinner in November, got Frederick to agree to join them, and spent a great deal of the trip brooding, as was his wont, about the menu.

From Madrid Frederick wrote: "A Spanish barber made a lovely transformation yesterday of dear Chorley, cropping his whiskers close: he has left him only a long tuft at the chin and has twirled his moustaches into fine ends at each side à la Louis Napoleon. The effect is striking, and rather improves the characteristic face by dividing its great length. He is as pleased as Punch, there is no tiring him, and he goes twirling the moustaches up and down the streets as if he were in Burlington Arcade. We get on famously." On their first evening Frederick proposed that they should go to a garden near the town where a well-known band was playing. Chorley was too tired, and retired to bed, so Frederick went alone, and found that the band was as good as they had been told, and "discoursed the most delightful Spanish music. Knowing Chorley's passion for *couleur locale* and National Music, I felt it criminal to enjoy the treat without him and dispatched my *valet de place* post-haste to the hotel to fetch him. After a while he came. The band, however, had ceased to play Spanish airs, and as Chorley entered the garden commenced the well-worn Miserere from *Il Trovatore* – the stock piece of every London hurdy-gurdy. Tableau. For this poor Chorley had left his bed, but he put it down in a long account with fate and bore it like a man."

There is a description of one of Chorley's parties, and Nina's success at it, in a letter to Frederick in the Spring of 1863. "On

Sunday evening Chorley's great party came off. I wish you had seen what a pretty dress I had on. White silk with scarlet geraniums and scarlet velvet. I never had such a becoming attire. The men came crowding round and completely hedged me away, thank Heaven, from the row of Olympian goddesses who sat in awful majesty in an inner room, surveying me with a sort of amazed insolence, through their absurd eyeglasses. Leighton did me the honour to stick by me, and pay me his exclusive attention the whole night. As for Chorley he chuckled himself pink over me . . . Hallé played charmingly as usual. Banks and Parepa sang the Tempest. The latter could have held 4 outside passengers on her back and breast with ease, but really her face is pleasant . . ."

Another description of a party of Chorley's in my grandfather's letters, throws some curious light on the behaviour of the Dickens daughters in the middle sixties. The marriage between Katie and Charles Collins appears to have been dogged by misfortune. The charming, attractive, feckless Charlie, onetime painter in the pre-Raphaelite manner and author of many humorous sketches and a travel book, *A Cruise upon Wheels*, that found great favour at the time, had always been delicate and his health steadily deteriorated after the marriage. He died in 1873, but already in 1864 Dickens had come to the conclusion that Katie was likely to be left a young widow. Perhaps it was this shadow of disaster that made Katie so discontented, and so intensely eager – so it seems from many passages in the letters – to find other lovers. Frederick, however, had hinted darkly that Charlie was guilty of an "infamy" in marrying at all. In 1866 he wrote: "On Monday Chorley's dinner came off. My dear, anything more demented and awful I never witnessed. We were fourteen, ten at one table and four at a side table. Chorley, Mamie, Mrs Vivian and Mr Underwood at the side table, from which Mamie kept darting distressed and furious glances and shaping her mouth all the time for the word 'beast' whenever Chorley looked away from her. At the big table we sat as follows: Captain Vivian, Lady Molesworth, Charlie C., Prinsep, Kitty C., ego, Lady Tiernan, Marcus Stone, Costa, Hon. Mrs Stonor. Kitty looked a spectacle of woe and between Prinsep and me was quite distracted. She told me that Mamie, who looked round and matronlike, was to be pitied and she could not lead such a life, but added mysteriously, 'she takes her happiness when she can, and a few visits to town lately have given her all she cares for'. She added, 'Of course, it will come out. Sure to.' My dear, these two girls are going to the devil as fast as can be. From what I hear from third parties who don't know how intimate we are with them, society is beginning to fight very shy of them, especially of Kitty C . . . Mamie may blaze up in a firework any day. Kitty is burning away both character and I fear health slowly but steadily. When she smiled something of her former pretty self reappeared, only to make the pained and woebegone expression that would follow more distressing. While these two girls, for both of whom I have an old kind of affection, gave me to think, the old haridans Molesworth and Tiernan and the young stupid owls Stonor and Vivian and the men that did not assimilate and Chorley who wore the costume of his fancy ball and was, if sober, still quite imbecile, behaved like a set of maniacs, especially the society women and Chorley. They made fun of him and he liked it, and the Dickens and Collins faction was at one end of the drawing-room and Society at the other and when I came up Mamie said the Society women were beasts and the little rooms were suffocating and I was not at all sure I wasn't in Bedlam."

As he grew older, Chorley grew more feeble, more cantankerous, and more bibulous. Already, at the first night of a play with which he was associated in the Autumn of 1864, my grandmother, who heard the full story from Mamie Dickens, records him as having been "*dead drunk*" from the very start. She describes the evening in a letter to Frederick: "He was to dine with the Dickens's at the office first. When he entered the room, they saw in an instant he was gone. He was long past speech, and it is Dickens's idea that he has been in this state all the time he has been alone at Biarritz. That is his *idea* you know. At dinner he couldn't speak, so the three Dickens's talked to each other without minding him. I need not write all the misadventures. He got to the theatre alone somehow, went into Mr Oxenford's box and fell on the floor. The box-keeper picked him up, and was going to take him away, when Mr O. said, 'Oh, never mind, he's an old friend of mine, leave him.' During the evening he made his way half asleep to Dr de Mussy's box, and gradually recovered *slightly*."

Nobody seems to have been excessively embarrassed by these performances. Sometimes he would arrive at a friend's house for dinner in a very confused state, assume that he was in his own house and start ordering the servants about. There was one notable occasion when Chorley was staying with my grandparents in Highgate. Nina gives a graphic picture of the first evening: "He seemed well when he came - drank two glasses of sherry at one gulp, and (the sherry could *not* have done it) got queer. At last he didn't in the very least know where he was, and asked me confidentially if I could tell him. I said he was at Woodlands. He said: 'Where's that?' Well, dinner came . . . He had settled in his own mind that he was at home. Consequently he kept on ringing the bell, giving Martin all sorts of orders, and calling him Drury - his own man's name. He got huffy at me for ringing once and giving an order myself! At the end of dinner, he tottered up, held on for a moment as if the chair was a mast and he was crossing the Channel, asked me if I would be good enough to take care of his guests for him, and particularly to see that Mr Collins got what wine he liked, feebly said, 'Drury!' whereat Martin took his arm, and so vanished to bed. Afterwards when I went up, I took a peep at him through the door, and saw him asleep in a large highly coloured turban."

Worse was to come the next morning, when my grandmother gave a dinner party especially in his honour. To this she had invited Charles Reade, her sister Tuckie, Wilkie Collins, Anne Proctor and among others a certain Mr Bockett. When dinner had started, Chorley's delusion that he was at home came on him again. Nina continues her hilarious account: "We were all known to him except Bockett. I saw him now and then puzzling over Bockett, unable to account for Bockett – but in his old-fashioned chivalrous way with the greatest stranger, sending all the dishes round to Bockett, pressing things on Bockett - 'Take the champagne to Mr Bockett, please,' and so on. During the evening afterwards, in the music-room, he said: 'I shall certainly ask Mr Bockett again. He's ver-ry nice.' 'But,' said Kitty, 'have you ever seen him before?' 'Well,' said Chorley, meditating, 'No – but then (with a little important snigger) this little dinner of mine has been a complete –' perhaps he meant a complete surprise to him, but he waved off the end of the sentence. Every now and then he quite recovered himself, and told us how confused he had been. During one of these intervals, he went up to Wilkie and most touchingly apologized to him." The background to this apology seems to have been that Chorley had refused to allow Wilkie to light his cigar, saying that he never allowed smoking in *his* dining-room.

In 1869, writing to Nina, Dickens gave rather a cruel picture of Chorley in his loneliness: "I saw Chorley yesterday in his own room. A sad and solitary sight. The widowed Drake, with a certain gincoherence of manner, presented a blooming countenance and buxom form in the passage; so buxom indeed that she was obliged to retire before me like a modest stopper before I could get into the dining decanter where poor Chorley reposed like the dregs of last season's wine."

Awkward though the old fellow might sometimes be, Nina developed a great fondness for him, to which he touchingly responded. When, in the early months of 1865, she had fallen seriously ill, he wrote to Frederick: "I cannot tell you how sorry I am that you should have any anxiety now; but I *can* tell you that should you by any mischance (which may God avert!) want a relief, I am ready. I can sit up in any lower storey, without wanting to go to sleep, I can take directions and I make no noise. I earnestly hope and believe that I shall not be wanted; *but* you would do me an unkindness if, supposing I could be of any good, you did not remember now how I am your obliged and faithful – H. F. Chorley."

Chorley was not the only person who sometimes caused trouble at these dinner parties. One of my grandparents' most frequent visitors was Sir Alexander Cockburn, who had been made Lord Chief Justice in 1859, "The Chief" as he was known among his friends. He was, apparently, a very remarkable conversationalist, but suffered from an extremely uncertain temper. Sir John Millais once said to Frederick, "you should never have that man on the premises without having the fire engines ready". Frederick had cause to remember this on two disastrous occasions. The *cause cèlebre* of the time was the trial of the Tichborne claimant, and Cockburn was in the habit of expressing himself at any party he attended with considerable violence against the claimant – rather curious behaviour, one might think, in the Judge who was trying the case. One night, at my grandfather's table, Cockburn was, as usual, inveighing against the claimant, when Lord Houghton, a fellow-guest, tried to put a word in for him, saying that many people thought he had strong arguments on his side. Cockburn immediately cut him short, remarking angrily: "I should have thought that impossible from anyone with the meanest intellect." Poor Lord Houghton paused for a moment, and then replied as gently as possible: "But surely that was very rude." Cockburn glared at him and boorishly added: "I mean it to be so."

Naturally enough, this was never forgiven by Lord Houghton, nor was another of Cockburn's insults forgiven by Sir Edwin Landseer. The dinner party on this occasion was at Woodlands. Cockburn and Landseer arrived together in an open phaeton with Cockburn driving, to all appearances the best of friends. At the end of the dinner the conversation came round to the subject of Shakespeare, and Landseer, in an expansive mood, remarked that even Shakespeare could make mistakes, because in

As You Like It he made a stag shed "big, round tears". "I have made stags my special study," said Landseer with some truth, "and I know for a fact that it is quite impossible for them to shed tears." Whereupon Cockburn rounded upon Landseer, and said in a loud and angry voice: "And don't you think you are committing a most unwarrantable impertinence in criticizing Shakespeare?" Landseer turned pale, and all my grandfather could do was to hustle the famous artist and most of the other guests into the garden while Cockburn joined the ladies. My grandfather saw that, apart from the catastrophe to his dinner party, he was faced with the awkward problem of getting Landseer home: Woodlands was far out of town, it was a Sunday evening, and no cabs were to be had for love or money. He therefore, with a slyness that I must admit surprises me, went up to Landseer and said, "Remember, Sir Edwin, that long after he has joined all the other Lord Chief Justices and is forgotten, your name will remain as that of the greatest English painter of this or any other age." Landseer was, of course, much mollified by this diplomatic speech. "That's true," he replied with satisfaction, "and I am willing to make it up and ride home with him; but, begad sir, he had better know that if he begins again, I am the man to get down, take off my coat, and fight him in the lanes." This contest, however, between the Lord Chief Justice and the champion of the Monarch of the Glen never took place, because Cockburn refused to be placated, and Landseer was given a lift home by other guests of the evening. Later, my grandfather discovered that the whole row was due not to Cockburn's excessive worship of the Bard, but to the fact that on the drive to Woodlands Landseer had refused an important favour to an illegitimate son of Cockburn's.

Chorley reappears again in a letter of Sir George Grove's to Nina. My grandparents had, I think, got to know Grove in the early years of their London life. In his biography of Grove, Charles Graves writes that in 1863 "he was already *persona gratissima* at the pleasant gatherings organized by Frederick

Lehmann and his wife, whose house in Westbourne Terrace was a focus of artistic, literary and musical activity". In the early summer of that year Grove wrote to his friend Miss von Glehn, giving a description of a Sunday spent with my grandparents. After hearing a "very dull sermon" in a church near Victoria, "a very pusey place indeed", he walked across the Park to Westbourne Terrace, where he found a company had already assembled. After lunch he "started with the Lehmanns and their boys, some in a carriage and some on horses, for their country house at Muswell Hill. A very pretty neighbourhood and a very pretty new house – everything regardless of expense, but in very good taste." After the expedition to Woodlands they all returned to Westbourne Terrace for dinner, at which Browning, Felix Moscheles, the Benzons and a debutante singer called Miss Enequist joined them. A few days later he was again a visitor for "a great dinner party, followed by a musical 'at home'. At dinner were Dickens and his sister-in-law, Robert Browning, Robert Chambers, Miss Gabriel and ourselves. It was very pleasant. Dickens was very amusing, but not the least forced, and Browning was also interesting. Dickens was full of a ship of Mormon immigrants which he had been seeing: 1200 of the cleanest, best-conducted, most excellent looking people he ever saw. No doubt there will be an account of it in *All The Year Round*. After dinner came a host. Sullivan with Dannreuther and Taylor and Lotto, a new violinist. Ward R.A. and his wife, Holman Hunt, Deichman, Miss Enequist – besides others whom I did not know. Chorley, Rathbone, Deutsch, etc. etc."

Frederick and Nina became very attached to Grove. Nina, in particular, he made the confidante of all his sorrows and amours. On one occasion, she writes to Frederick: "I come to town from Woodlands tonight, because George Grove takes a chop with me and pours out his woes at 1.30." My father loved him. "The mere thought of him," he writes, "brings a burst of sunshine into the mind. There never was a man of more delightful humour or of a more abounding gaiety and amiability. Cheerfulness entered the room with him and stayed even after he had left, so infectious were his spirits. He was all his life a very hard worker, but his enthusiasms remained fresh and unimpaired to the end." In the summer of 1867, in spite of her long winter rest in Pau, Nina appears to have fallen ill again, and Chorley again to have distressed himself extremely about her state. "Thanks, dear friend, for your account of yourself," Grove writes. "It is bad enough, but, thank God, not so bad as I had heard, last of all from old Chorley, who came trembling and crying to our gate yesterday morning, quite a wreck of a wreck. Can't you keep yourself quiet, and recollect that you are a very weak fragile creature, and also awfully valuable to all your friends, and put yourself in a big jewel-box and be looked at and aired only occasionally? . . . Write to me again, and the sooner the better. I am going to dine with Arthur tonight, and shall drink your health (to myself) with my first glass of claret."

The Arthur mentioned in this letter was Arthur Sullivan, introduced into my grandparents' circle by Chorley when he was scarcely twenty but already a brilliant young hope of English music. He sent Nina an excited description of the first performance of his music to *The Tempest* in Manchester in January 1863 under the aegis of Hallé: "Well, it is all over, and loud applause follows. The band applauds at me. Hallé leans over and applauds at me. The audience see that something is up, and continue. At last Hallé beckons to me to come up. I wink, I nod, I interrogate with my eyebrows, and at last rush madly from my seat and up the platform. When I show myself my breath is literally taken away by the noise . . . One gentleman sitting near Mrs Hallé, seeing me rush away, said, 'What! Is *that* Sullivan, that boy?' (Oh, that I had a dagger!) 'I thought he was a relation of yours.' Others thought I was a contemporary of Beethoven, or at least his immediate successor."

From that time Sullivan pops in and out of Nina's letters, as a guest at dinner or at musical evenings, and there are constant references, not always enthusiastic, to concerts where his music

217

was being played. "On Saturday," she writes in December 1869, "I took Mrs Millais to the Palace to hear Sullivan's *Prodigal Son*. First his overture *In Memoriam* was done. Not much tune in that. He conducted himself - but alas, Sims Reeves[1] failed him, and at the last moment a feeble being called Perren kindly undertook the part. The Soprano was nothing at all – horrid in fact, a Miss Vanzini (hired name). Therefore one can hardly judge, but I didn't care for it. Mrs Millais thought as I did. We rushed away directly it was done, as we all dreaded seeing the gifted and now risen young composer. Sullivan told me he had broken off his engagement as he felt he could make no woman happy as his wife! The fact is he doesn't care a straw for her, as I saw all along."

By far the best loved and most intimate of my grandparents' musical circle was the violinist Joachim, who was so uninterruptedly in demand to play at musical evenings, at my grandparents', at the Benzons' in Kensington Palace Gardens, at the Hallés', in fact all over musical London, that one wonders how he ever found time for his own professional life. A letter of Frederick's to Nina in 1867 describes a party, given by Leighton at the famous house he had had built for himself ten years before in Holland Park Road, at which Hallé and Joachim were the star performers, and Adelaide Sartoris, Charles Kemble's younger daughter, a famous singer of the time who had originally made her name in the part of Norma at the Fenice in Venice, and was now in semi-retirement and dabbling in literature, a star attraction – for some.

"All the faithful assembled to the call. At 11 you could have seen the idol with the flashing nostrils, Sartoria the Fat, on her throne, her court around her." His sister Lisbeth was there, Rudolf and Tuckie, Val Prinsep, the young painter who had started as a follower of the Pre-Raphaelites but now was falling under the influence of Leighton, the Barings, Dicky Doyle,

---

[1] John Sims Reeves, born 1818, was held to be the first English tenor of his day.

Dr de Mussy, Chorley "very wrong[1] and tottery", and Kitty Collins in one of her bad moods: "the little hussy could hardly get herself to bow to me and to exchange a few words, but sidled up at once to Sartoris and remained stationed in the cool and refreshing shadow of the idol for the rest of the evening . . . Leighton's studio looked lovely. Lamps all round and a sunlight from above lighted up his pictures, finished and unfinished. Hallé played a charming suite of Bach and Joe a Romance of Beethoven, but beside these solos they played two whole sonatas of Beethoven – the two that follow each other in our book in A and C minor. The latter they began only after 12: it was quite too much music and not the kind of music I care to hear with a lot of men and women knowing about as much of music as my hat. I think they ought to play small salon pieces and give people a chance of talking. O, it was slow, my dear, and the court never mixed for a moment with those who had not the entrée. The thing is quite too farcical for an observant spectator who does not care a rap for either the fat idol or any of her imbecile attendants."

At that time Joachim was very excited about a new Bach discovery. "I dined with the divine Joe," wrote Frederick, describing a family party which was attended by Browning and Wilkie Collins, at 11 Orme Square, at which Tuckie, as usual, refused to sing alone. "Joachim was more gracious and played a new thing, *l'Eclair*, and a Siciliana and my own particular *Bach* which you have heard once or twice from me. Just think, Rietz the concert director in Dresden, in mooning about the Hofkirche noticed an old 'Schrank' of which the key had been lost for years. He got permission to force it open and found in it a whole set of manuscript Violin Sonatas of Bach. Undoubtedly genuine, and have never seen the light of day. Joachim has just got copies and is going to play them immediately."

Mrs. Sartoris ("Sartoria the Fat") appears again in a letter of Frederick's written not long after, when describing a party of Sir Alexander Cockburn's, at which Tuckie did at last agree to sing

[1] When Chorley was sober his friends used to say he was "right".

alone. "The dinner at the Chief's was a great success. I did not know to the last whether the Rudolfs would go, because they were afraid of trusting to only a verbal invitation. Fortunately she had written the Chief to ask whether she had understood him right and had of course a reply in the affirmative . . . There were besides the 3 Lehmanns, Mrs and Miss Sartoris, Leighton, of course as faithful shadow. I do not see so much difference between French and English society. An *amant* seems a recognized social status, and some women get asked to parties with their *amants*, just as others with their husbands. All right. It's none of my business and does Leighton the greatest credit, for anything more repulsive than this mountain of rolling fat with those spitfire eyes I never saw . . . The judges and lawyers kept the table in a roar with legal stories, our Chief keeping the lead as usual. Tuckie had told me before dinner that she had had such a letter from you that she must sing, dead or alive, but she was nearly dead and the teeth were chattering in her head partly with cold and partly with nervousness. So Rudolf and I did not know till the last minute whether she *would* sing but she did, five songs, one after another with tremendous success, the Chief in a state of transport and everybody enchanted, Mrs Sartoris and Leighton keeping up the enthusiasm and asking for more. She sang one by Cherubini, two by Schumann, one by Beethoven, and finished off with Gossip Joan."

Some idea of the stamina of the mid-Victorian diner-out is given by the fact that Frederick went straight on from the Chief's to a party given by the Proctors in Weymouth Street "where that fashionable person 'everybody' was disporting himself. Again the Sartoris and Leighton. She (old hag) came up to me to say how enchanted she had been with Tuck's singing altho' she did not seem in voice, etc. etc., so artistic, so this so that." Only a few days before the aged Proctor couple had given a party, where eighty people had turned up, including Dante Gabriel Rossetti and Matthew Arnold, and "Lady Molesworth in a *red velvet* jacket". Frederick had failed to be present, and Anne Proctor had particularly lamented that she had therefore been unable to introduce him to Matthew Arnold. However, on this occasion Arnold again appeared, and Frederick "had a long talk with him".

A few weeks after Sullivan's concert in 1869, Sir Alexander Cockburn gave a party for Joachim – though apparently without telling him that it was to be a grand social gathering. "Loads of swells asked to hear Joachim," writes Nina. "His bow was newly haired, and he wouldn't play for ever so long. At last he and I played an Andante of Mozart's, but after that he locked up his violin. Gladstone was there with his wife and daughter. Goschen was there and all the 'click' of course. The Chief was in such a state because Joachim would not play any more. Came to me like a raving maniac. So I went to dear old Jo (who had been playing with me for an hour and a half before dinner) and implored him to play. He was adamant. He had not expected a party – he was angry. No, no, no – he would *not* play. At last, seeing the Chief in one of his furies, I whispered to Joachim, '*do it for the sake of poor old Fred in Japan* !' My dear, his face softened in a moment, and he got up, unlocked the case, took out the violin, said to me, '*Tell Fred when you write that I was a good boy,*' and played (accompanied by Sullivan) the Mendelssohn Concerto, all through ! It was touch and go – and all owing to *you*, darling, that he did this."

Meanwhile, "poor old Fred in Japan" was exploring scenes curiously different from those that Nina described from the West End of Victorian London.

Wilkie Collins had written to him in October, in a strain typical of the anxieties of his friends when he was off on his travels : "Where will you be when this reaches you ? I am told you have got to San Francisco. That will do. Come back. Leave well alone, and come back. I will describe Japan to you, and take you to see the manufacturers afterwards at the Baker Street Bazaars." Frederick, however, could not resist the opportunity of travelling home East-West, via Japan and India. He arrived in

Yokohama on the eve of the Japanese New Year's Day (February 1st), noting, as they sailed in, that they passed "no end of sail and rowboats and many villages on each side of the bay", and that the first vessels he saw in the roadstead "were flying the new flag of the North German Confederation and belonged to Hamburg and Bremen; English, American and Russian men-of-war crowded the port." He was too exhausted to take in much that evening, but the next day he set out on a voyage of discovery. "As this is Japanese New Year's Day," he wrote, "most offices and many shops are closed. After tiffin, we went into the so-called Yoshiwara or lower quarter of the town. One street contains nothing but houses of ill-fame, which are here a Government undertaking. Girls are brought up in these houses, and often marry out of them. The Japanese do not seem to look down upon or despise them in any way. Those I saw were mostly very ugly, here and there a passable face. They were playing battledore and shuttlecock in the street. If one of the players misses the shuttlecock the other playfully slaps her posterior with the battledore. I saw men play the game with paint brushes stuck thro' their hair, and the moment one made a miss, the other out with his brush and made a black mark on his opponent's face. I passed innumerable stalls of eatables with little rolls of rice rolled up in pancake or in fresh fish or salt fish. Confectioners without end, all selling among other things all sizes of p——s made of sugar, some painted flesh colour, some gilt. The p——s being a subject of adoration in Japan meets you continually in all kinds of shapes. Men went about with sticks to which a number of toys and emblems hung attached, and generally there was a p——s among them.

"Here a juggler gathered a large crowd and assured them he would begin the performance the moment they paid in the requisite amount. There peeps were to be had thro' six holes into a small camera, and the paintings were explained in a lugubrious chant. The temples were much frequented. Those I saw had a flight of stairs leading up to a platform on which an altar was raised and some candles lit. As the pious came to the steps, they pulled a long rope attached to a big lamp-shaped gong, made a great noise, threw some coins wrapped in paper on to the platform, clapped their hands as if to ask the deity to attend well, said a short prayer and walked off.

"We called on a number of merchants and were received with deep salaams. They put their hands to their feet and bow nearly to the ground. All receive and make presents today. Foreign merchants often send champagne, and we saw many Japanese drinking champagne and a few very tight. Some gave us little presents of paper and knicknacks. Everything meant for a present is tied with a red and white string, to which often a paper bag containing a piece of fish is attached. . . .

"I went into three bath houses. One of them was only railed off by open lattice-work from the street, from which you could see all the bathers. All had only a very low open railing to divide men and women. In all a great number of both sexes sat cowering on their heels or in other sitting postures on a wooden floor. Each bather had a small tub of hot water before him and was scrubbing him or herself *con gusto*. I saw women of all ages with mere children. . . . Among a crowd of women, I saw one of the male attendants scrub a young girl of very handsome form; neither he nor she smiled. All went on in the gravest and most business-like manner. One man, after boiling himself the colour of a lobster, only put on a loose jacket covering him to a little below the waist and carried his leggings and other belongings in his hand, to let his naked body grow cool gradually as he stalked home along the crowded street. Nobody paid the slightest attention. The thing is quite amazing, and proves more decisively than anything that all ideas of morality or propriety are simply questions of latitude."

VII

By that time my grandparents had moved from Westbourne Terrace to Bolton Street, off Piccadilly. While Frederick was away on his endless business trips, all over the world, Nina continued to entertain and join in the social whirl of her circle with what seems like an ever increasing zeal; perhaps there was even something a little feverish about it, for she must have felt at times rather daunted, in spite of the presence of the children and her Chambers relations. She overdid it; she dazzled, and then she collapsed. In the midst of her successes as a London hostess, she longed for quiet and the simple life. "Oh dear, how conventional town life is after all," she cries, "with one's servants and one's unapproachable kitchen and all the 'below stairs' immutable laws and privileges which one never dreams of daring to interfere with, but silently submits to."

The discovery of the way some of these "immutable laws and privileges" worked in London homes had shocked her a few years before. Writing to Frederick about their cook, Johns, she revealed: "I have found that Johns demanded and *got* money from the tradespeople here *every* time I paid the books. Innocent I, paying up to the last penny, never thinking of deceit! The butcher's man says they (the cooks) do it in all large establishments, so you see Johns has put us on the footing of a large establishment while we should just be a young couple yet, trying to be economical. This system is a worm at the root of all economy, for of course it is a cook's interest to make the books large that she may be better paid, and so on, but it is a disagreeable subject, and I mean to ask Mrs Proctor's advice." However, Johns was forgiven soon after, because she "worked like a horse" when 139 Westbourne Terrace had to be prepared for Frederick's homecoming. "I forgive Johns a very great deal for this as what cook of her standing will clean a whole house down, and insist on my keeping the kitchen-maid to help *me*. It is the ways she saw at Lady Molesworth's, and such people, that she imitates as to perquisites, and it is more the system than the individual that is to blame – and the tradesmen beyond all." In spite of the irritation and dismay that "below stairs" problems caused her, Nina's sense of humour was never long in reasserting itself. One day, in the same summer at Woodlands, the "Old Goose", her original cook when she first came to London, unexpectedly paid her a visit. "All of a sudden the Witch of Endor, my little old cook, appeared on the scene, gorgeously got up; a white crepe bonnet with a pink rose flopped down on the very top of it, a French barège silk shawl with every colour that has or has not been invented since rainbows began, and a light silk dress – a mauve parasol, and green kids completed the costume. She looked 90 at the least. She says she is with an old Indian Judge in Gloucester Terrace, but she don't like the place, m'm, 'cos he always 'ollers out so in the night, and she thinks he's deranged. (What a dangerous couple of lunatics to be together.) And she don't like the butcher at all, m'm – he's bad 'ee is; there was 11 ounces short on that shoulder o' mutton, m'm – ye-e-es m'm there was – and she don't like their ways. She broke out about the foul things '*Spole* used to say of you and all your sisters, m'm – oh, it was hoffle to 'ear that man a calling you and your family, m'm,' and so on. Mama would like to have her in the event of *her* cook being lawfully united to the policeman, but my impression is the cook and the policeman have got on so nicely without the interference of the church, and find it so much more convenient and economical to board and lodge and 'do for the family' at Verulam, that there will be no chance of her leaving."

As her letters from the Isle of Wight show, Nina had always been attracted by a simple, patriarchal way of life. When she was at Biarritz in February 1867, one day she hired a *petite voiture* for a drive over to St Jean de Luz, with her maid, Martha. "I fell in love again with the quiet, quaint, deserted old place. I looked over great barracks, *maisons à louer*, for the fun of the thing; went through Moorish-looking courts and halls and up staircases with old carved wood balustrades, up which Noah's immediate relatives must have walked when the Ark anchored at St Jean de Luz, as I am positively prepared to assert it did. One lodging struck me from the outside. Above a pottery shop, where an old grey-headed, spotlessly linened man was sitting with his cat beside him, I saw two open windows with snowy-white curtains waving in the breeze. 'Martha, I want to live there. Let's go in directly and see about it.' The polite old man took me up into the cleanest of rooms, with a large alcove with a bed in it. 'Martha, I see myself at that window with my worsted work on that table, don't you?' 'Oh my, good gracious me, yes'm.' At the other end of the clean little passage was the cleanest, the most old-fashioned kitchen in the world; a large old-fashioned casement window, deep in, with a seat looking on to a little garden; an alcove with a bed at one side. 'Martha, do you see yourself under that flowered coverlet?' 'Oh my, good gracious me, yes'm, I think I do.' I very nearly settled with the old man on the spot, but I didn't, and just took his name in writing. It was the most deliciously antique-looking place, just after my heart, with a squint of the sea if taken with the left eye, and not a soul to be seen in the street." A few days later she made up her mind, and moved in, writing a rhap-sodic letter to Frederick: "If you could see my spotless old landlord, who lives alone here with his servant. His servant, did I say? She is no other than Noah's grandmother, whom he must have left behind when he sailed from this port. She is much too old, much too withered, much too bony, much too brown, much too tough *ever* to die . . . It is impossible to convey to you any idea at all of this old old wifie, and this old old mannie and the queer, queer kitchen, where just now I went inside the great chimney, and looking up it, saw a *star* quivering in the sky! I take my meals in that chimney, Martha cooking them before my eyes."

Above all, Nina rejoiced to get away to her "dear, dear, dearest Woodlands" when she felt done up by the London season. When they first rented it from its owner, Mr Cameron, it was a newish, three-storied house with attics, standing in ample grounds with a coachhouse and dove-cot to one side. It had a pretty, lattice-work veranda, on to which french windows gave, running most of the length of the ground floor on the lawn side, with a balcony above. The view from the window was a continual delight to Nina. "This morning when I got up," she writes in August 1861, "I couldn't see the lawn for the densest mist I ever saw. All of a sudden it cleared off, leaving the flowers and grass sparkling with dew and the spiders' webs like fair garments of diamonds hung out to dry. A delicious sparkling morning, with all the peculiar scents of Autumn strong in the healthy air." There was a pond under the trees, where they found they could catch small perch to cook for dinner, an oleander that was "a mass of gorgeous blushing roses", and the beds were filled with late summer flowers. "Lisbeth went off," she writes at the end of September, "with a bouquet much bigger than herself, of gorgeous dahlias, asters, the last and still lovely roses, canariensis, nasturtium wreaths." Above all she exulted in the contrast with town air. "The difference of the air," she writes, "was so tremendous that I began to tremble at the chances of my ever being able to live contentedly in town again. I just opened my mouth and drank in the delicious invigorating purity, as if I had been dying with thirst and somebody had brought me a sparkling glass of pure water." Her parents came up for dinner, and "we sat out in the garden till 9 o'clock, Padre pointing out all the various stars and constellations to Jan and me, as they came shining out one after another into the glorious night sky."

They became so attached to Woodlands, that the next year they decided to buy it from Mr Cameron, and Nina's letters are filled with descriptions of repainting and re-furnishing, the chintzes and carpets she was choosing, and the furniture she was picking up in odd shops and sales. "You see, I daresay," she wrote to Frederick, "that I am full of Woodlands, that Woodlands is my theme, my delight, and I can hardly talk of anything else. Our bedroom will be so fairylike, it will be disgraceful that man should ever enter it! There – sir. The bed as I told you is to be painted like the wardrobes and will be *perfect*. It will be hung in pink watered chintz (a new thing that looks like watered silk) covered with light white muslin. The window hung in the same. Then the furniture covered with a lovely pink chintz, ascertained to stand the ordeal of washing to the greatest advantage." In early October she announced the first visitor to see the changes in progress: "Hopie came at last today and was amazed, *lost* in the house. She had no idea of it – none – and sat in mute speechless enthusiasm in the small drawing-room, gazing rapturously at the chimney-piece-window which I had filled up with flowers, and china." And in the next letter: "If I could only give you a picture that could convey an idea of the brilliant beauty in which Woodlands bathes this morning! The atmosphere is so clear that we see to the Essex hills, over the terraces of trees, the ivy covered tower of Hornsey, the lines of delicious green fields dotted with white houses – sheep – horses - cattle. In the front our own delicious lawn, with its graceful Deodars waving slightly in the crisp yet mild morning breeze, the warm sun shining over all - shining into the open window of my little drawing-room where I sit writing to my Beloved, shining on the flowers with which my windows are all alive, shining on my children who are sparkling about the lawn followed fast by their long shadows." She felt revived at once by this crisp air, "quite a new woman already, when I think of the white wan feeble thing I was a few days ago."

A typical sequence is recorded during Frederick's world tour in 1869–70. The winter season had been fast and furious for her, every week crowded with dinners, concerts and visits. There had been Sullivan's concert with Mrs Millais; and Joachim's evening at the Chief's; continual dinner parties with her in-laws, the Benzons, at 10 Kensington Palace Gardens; and regular visits to the "Pops", in which Madame Neruda was figuring prominently at the time. "Neruda played splendidly on Monday," writes Nina in November. "She is not to be compared with Joachim as a quartette leader. She plays deliciously, finely with exquisite purity and neatness, *but* she has not the grand thrilling power and force of Jupiter. Juno she is, but not Jupiter – and she fails where a woman must fail." A week or two later she writes: "Neruda played the Schubert Pathetic quartette in A minor like an angel, and his grand Trio in B flat (which I once played). I had sent her in some flowers and she gave me a charming bow and smile. In fact she looks often towards me as if for sympathy, and she gets it." Soon after, she invited Hallé and Neruda to dinner with the Chief, who had begged to be invited, Mamie and Katie Collins and other friends. "The dinner was entirely in French, and I got on better than I expected," she wrote. "After dinner Hallé good-naturedly sat down and played a Chopin, and that lovely thing of Schubert's he often plays. Then I had to beg Neruda. She had brought her violin, but I thought she looked cross. However, she did do it. The Andante of Air and Variations of Mozart's Sonata, and then *your* Spohr Andante of which I am a good deal blazed. She played beautifully. I never asked for more. After that talk buzzed louder and louder, faster and faster, then we went for refreshments, which consisted of tea, cakes, ices, sandwiches, claret and champagne. They *did* so enjoy that. The Chief took down Neruda. After all were gone, the Collins's, Mamie and the Stones remained as usual to finish every scrap and drain every drop, and I must say it was great fun."

The climax is described in her last letter to Frederick before he sailed for home. "Friday 4th, I went in the evening to the Benzons where, to my awe, I found Madame Schumann and Marie – but no music." On Sunday she went again to the Benzons, this time for dinner, where she found herself among a large company which included the Hallés, Leighton, Browning, the Joachim family, and the "Chief" later in the evening. On Monday Sir George Grove and Joachim lunched with her. On Tuesday she dined with the Forsters to meet Carlyle, who spoke flatteringly to her about her father's work, said that his life of

Smollett was "vastly superior to anything that has iver been said about him before", and when she played some Scotch tunes to him, remarked, "I niver haard a sweeter finger on the pianyforty in all my life." A couple of days later she gave a great party herself, with twelve to dinner, including Mamie and Katie Dickens and her husband, Browning, the Leslie Stephens, and the Joachims; and after dinner invited "only twenty" for a musical evening. On the following Monday she dined again with Mamie and Katie Dickens, and the next night (March 15th) she took the Joachims to Dickens's "*last* Farewell Reading" – "he made a little good-bye speech, in which his voice became broken with emotion, very sweet and touching it was". And so it went on for the next two or three weeks, until she found herelf "running down the hill on such an alarmingly thin pair of shoulder blades" that she cancelled all her engagements and fled to Woodlands. "I saw that town-life (and I was asked out every night) was too much for me," she confessed to Frederick. "I have never put my nose into town since!"

Very soon after Frederick's return from his world tour, Dickens had his mortal stroke. My grandparents were summoned down to Gad's Hill to pay their last respects to the friend who had changed so much in their lives. Katie, and particularly Mamie, remained among their most intimate circle; but I don't think it was ever the same again.

It is often said that the great age of letter writing is past: the telephone, the speed and ease of travel in this age of fast motor-cars and aeroplanes have destroyed the *need* for letters as a means of communication between friends; they have become short, scrappy, briefly allusive, bread-and-butter notes or hurried expressions of congratulations and condolence. I believe this to be largely, though maybe not entirely, true; but certainly I can think of no one in my lifetime, except perhaps Virginia Woolf, who could, or would bother regularly to write letters so fresh, so vivid, so full of news and observation, and so self-revealing as my grandmother wrote all her life to her family and friends. From them one has an extraordinarily complete picture of her, far more complete than any of the surviving portraits present: essentially Victorian in her wifely devotion, her doting delight in the sweet ways of her children, her attitude towards the "lower classes"; and yet in so many ways unconventional and unexpected in her comments on what she felt and what she saw, often indeed tartly critical, never in the least stuffy or priggish. At the time when everyone was talking about the imminent separation between Dickens and his wife, she received a letter from her Aunt Janet, full of shocked condemnation for poor Mrs Dickens, because Wills had been down to Brighton to see her and found her – reading a novel on the pier. She enclosed this letter in one of her own to Frederick, and commented: "Discontent lurks under every line somehow. She is getting morbidly sensitive . . . I don't see the harm of Mrs Dickens reading a novel on the pier. Is she to bury herself within four walls and weep her lost lord all day? She must live and do something. She must sit on the pier I suppose for the sake of the sea air, and she must read something, having nothing else to do."

Her description of the English residents in Pau, in 1866, is full of delightfully mocking humour: "Somehow the English people here all look mad – quite mad, to me. Why do they stick, for instance, things on their heads that they would never dream of, even in nightmares, in England? Old grey-haired gentlemen walking in round hats made of white calico, with grey veils hanging from them. Old ladies in the oddest black mushrooms with feathers rampant – all on end somehow, and *all moulting* – and long drabbled skirts and cloaks that must have been fashioned *before* the ark. But they all look quite happy, quite satisfied with themselves and their attire. Matilda and I can't help bursting into fits of laughter, though, at some of them and, O heavens, their French! And these polite French people, who never smile even, but pretend to understand it all!"

Again, it is surely the daughter of Robert Chambers who speaks in this surprisingly modern-sounding comment, made nearly a century ago, on middle-class Victorian English education: "In these days it seems to me dreadful that boys grow up knowing literally nothing of Geology, Astronomy, I may add Chemistry. For it's all very well being fond of the pretty experiments, but that's the outside of the science after all. Don't you agree with me? Latin verses may teach a boy elegance of expression (not at the time, Heaven knows) but the study of science teaches him to think. To my mind there is no question as to the immense superiority of foreign training to English – and the cheapness too! It is a sin and a shame!"

Perhaps more delightful than anything is the spontaneous feeling for nature that runs all through her letters. For instance, writing from St Jean de Luz to my grandfather in 1867, she says: "I never saw such waves as there are here. They come rolling in slowly and majestically, and when near the beach grow an immense height; then they curl over, and you seem to look into a great deep, clear, green cavern, when over they go, tumbling into a magnificent mass of white spray. Oh, how I long to have you here sometimes; how you would enjoy it – but most of all you would enjoy the downs, away at the end of the beach, high up on the rocks that suddenly pile themselves up. Oh, what a walk that is – miles and miles – all along the cliff – undulating beautiful downs covered with primroses and (scentless) violets . . ."

My grandmother kept her circle together above all, I believe, because she had a quite unusual gift for friendship. I have already described how Chorley was ready to watch by her bedside when she was ill. Wilkie Collins became more and more devoted to her, and wrote her his freest, most amusing and most affectionate letters. Towards the end of his life, when he was utterly broken in health, my grandparents were among the very small circle of friends he still cared to see. In one of the very last of his letters, written to my grandfather only two or three weeks before his death, he concluded with the words: "My grateful love to the best and dearest of Padronas." Anne Proctor was another among her intimate friends whose affection seemed to grow greater as the years went by. They kept up a long and intimate correspondence until Anne Proctor's death, as a very old woman, in 1886. I have a letter from her to Nina, written a few years before, in which she says: "I have many faults, but I am not ungrateful. I do not forget all you have done for me – kind welcomes, happy days, beautiful gifts – the most precious things I have I owe to you." To Sir George Grove at the end of his life she became his "dearest old friend", and when my grandfather died in 1891 Pauline Viardot wrote to her from France: "My darling Nina, is it not dreadful to lose one's true and only real companion of life? Oh, I know that so well, I have felt it, and feel it still so keenly . . . I send you all the love and sympathy of a faithful heart."

Before that, when the news of Wilkie Collins's death came to Nina at St Andrews, she had written to my father at Cambridge: "And so our poor dear genial delightful *matchless* old Wilkie is gone. It made one very sad but he could never have enjoyed life again if he had recovered . . . Wilkie was almost the very last link left that bound us to the glory of departed days. Dickens, Lytton, Houghton, Wilkie, Charles Collins, poor old Chorley – it seems like a former life, not on this earth at all."

PART FIVE

Frederick in America

I

My grandfather's acquaintance with America, and his business relations with the great and expanding manufacturing interests of
the North, began early in his career. As I have already related,
directly after his marriage he took my grandmother out on a
combined business and honeymoon trip, in December 1852. After
he had dealt with his affairs in New York and Boston, they both
went down south to Washington, Richmond and Charleston.
His experiences there, of a slave society in action, were, I think,
decisive in directing his sympathies entirely towards the North in
the Civil War that broke out a decade later.

During the whole of their first visit Frederick kept a diary,
which seems in the main to have been formed out of copies of
letters to his brother Emil in Hamburg, from which the extracts
which follow are taken. The diary begins, however, with a page
and a half in my grandmother's handwriting, written in Washington on the 1st of February 1853:

"Arrived at the seat of American government after decidedly
the most pleasant railway journey I have yet experienced in this
great country of equality. Equality is very noble, but not comfortable after all. All grades of society meet in travelling here in the
one, long, many-seated car, and I, not being republican, cannot
help sighing as remembrances of the luxurious, exclusive, softly-
cushioned, carpeted English railway carriage rise within me and
excite a little impatience at the contrast with the American car.
The crush, too, owing to this universal scheme, is very annoying,
and one has to go before the time in order to secure a seat, a proceeding which the traveller of every grade in England would
smile at, I think. However, it is absurd for one little woman
stuffed with British prejudices, as her husband declares her to be
(though she solemnly declares the calumny to be perfectly

237

unfounded and entirely false), to make lamentations over a system which so evidently is an admirable one for a community. After all, it is not the liberty, equality and brotherly love I complain of, not at all, but oh! if the liberty, equality and brotherly love would only give up the habit of spitting; far from that, Washington in particular has little monuments to this filthy custom dotted everywhere, in the shape, I need not add, of spittoons. This it is which makes the huge ugly car to me an abomination . . ."

After a few lines about Philadelphia, from where they had just come and which made "a very favourable impression" upon them, Nina gives way to Frederick in whose hand all the rest of the diary is written. My grandfather begins with further eulogy of Philadelphia, and then writes a paragraph about Baltimore, "a nice, cosy, dirty town". Here he had his first sight of the slaves. "Being in the capital of Maryland, where slavery is the law of the land, we were for the first time waited on by slaves. I am no sentimentalist, but I can never overcome a silent terror creeping over me when I see one of these wretched, listless, vacant, shining black statues behind my chair." After which, he goes into his description of Washington:

"A most dreary, uncomfortable town this Washington. Such bragging great designs for a metropolis with such desolate results are quite distressing. Imagine the Capitol, a fine striking building on a commanding rising ground, at one end of the city, and the President's house, a large, two-storeyed mansion of no great pretensions from an architectural point of view, at the other, with an interval of two miles of howling wilderness – that is, several huge barrack-looking townships of hovels and lots of poor little shops bordering a dirty broad road, at both sides of which poor thin trees try to make avenues but can't. Then there is the Patent Office and the Post Office, *et plus rien*. I never saw anything more dreary and desolate. As I have more leisure here than I had in any other town through which I have passed, the hideousness of this hotel life becomes more apparent and depressing.

"Here is, for instance, the National Hotel. Imagine a house with some 300 rooms with white walls and as little furniture as can be, viz. bed, table, chairs, washstand and looking glass. No wardrobe, no pegs, in fact going little beyond the furniture of which my Boston friend complained – a small bed and a large Bible . . . The floor of the hotel is generally occupied by lounging smokers, for whose convenience easy chairs are ranged along the walls. Here the republican spitting habit keeps up a perpetual fire, or rather water. The floor is inundated with it, notwithstanding an array of spittoons. Round this parterre are bathrooms, the hairdresser's shop, the bar, the reading rooms, and even the telegraph office. A constant round of eating and drinking is kept up. Your board is charged so much, and for that each person may do his or her worst at breakfast, lunch, dinner, tea and supper. And they do it too. You see delicate females have a beefsteak, eggs, buckwheat cakes and hot corn-bread, with tea and coffee, for their breakfasts, and dispatch it all in a bewilderingly short time . . . Everything is done wholesale and badly, and you get almost every dish cold. You try beef, mutton, ducks and geese in succession, and give it up in despair. Turkeys and cranberries are most to be relied upon, and I have taken to make my dinner of these items. So much for the dinner, but the company – ugh ! There they sit, solemn, grave and devouring, and the moment they find their stomach refuses to admit any further bolt into it, off they rush. The only amusing feature at dinner is the army of waiters putting down the dessert. They are regularly drilled, and march at a given signal in military order two abreast to their different stations. Arrived at his post, each waiter stands motionless with dish in hand until the commander-in-chief, alias head-waiter, gives them the signal, when down go some fifty or sixty dishes with a noise like a peal of distant thunder."

On February 5th they set off for Richmond, and on board the *Mount Vernon*, as they steamed along the Potomac, he added some observations on slavery :

"Amongst the lions of Washington I forgot to mention the

Patent Office, a building in which models of all American pa-
tented inventions or improvements are kept. Not having a very
practical turn of mind, I was less interested by these professed contents of the building than by a sort of Museum upstairs in which
one large glass case particularly invited my attention. It contains
the original 'Declaration of Independence', this talisman of the
American Republic. I could not overcome an involuntary
shudder as I read in it, set forth in the most glorious language, that
all men are born equal, and that man has certain inalienable rights,
amongst which first and foremost is the pursuit of liberty, health
and happiness – and the avenging spirit of slavery rose before me.
Ugh! Going into the barber's shop on board just now, I enquired
of the barber, himself a free coloured man, whether a female servant on board, who struck me by her transparent white colour
and as woolly a head of hair as that of any negro woman, was slave
or free, coloured or white.

"'Certainly she is a mulatto woman, but she is free.' He went on
telling me in reply to my enquiries, that Mrs Stowe's tale was by
no means overcoloured; indeed the reverse, and rightly so, because if she told the whole truth nobody would believe her. 'I
know it from experience, sir, because I have passed my whole life
in the South, and on this very river we daily see those scenes she
describes. And yesterday we had a gang of slaves on board, and
any man might see the degradation of women, the separation of
families and the examination of people like so many cattle. If you
go to Richmond you have but to go into the slave market and you
will see it all. You can buy a woman there as you buy a cabbage in
other markets. Today a trial comes off against a woman for teaching slaves to write and read. That is a penitentiary crime and
punished by ten years' imprisonment.'

"These things certainly strike you with a sort of ghastly un-
natural terror as they come upon you there in shape and form, and
the impression on a rational mind must be stronger than 10,000
Uncle Tom novels. One remains struck with a silent bewilder-
ment at the incongruity of a free enlightened republic forbidding

to men, who are born their equals by their own gospel, the light of knowledge."

As their journey continued, Frederick's thoughts became increasingly darkened by what he was witnessing of the American slave-system. "Mrs Stowe's tale", *Uncle Tom's Cabin*, had been published as a book the year before, and had given an enormous impetus to the antislavery cause, increasing the dangerous rift between North and South that the quarrel about whether the newly-incorporated territories should be slave or free had already created. The South was on the defensive. Frederick recorded a conversation on board the *Mount Vernon*, as they chugged along the foggy river, with a fellow-traveller who "wore a white cravat and a white beaver hat, and might have been a clergyman". "Believe me, sir," said the traveller, "there is not a man in his senses here that does not see the bane of slavery. It is acknowledged by everyone to be the curse of this country. The land we travel through just now is literally accursed by slavery, for it has been worked till it will produce nothing, and had to be given up and lie waste; it's a curse to business, a curse and bar to all improvements, and a curse to society in every fiber and relation." On Frederick asking what, if that was in fact the situation, the remedy could be, the traveller continued: "No doubt the negroes could be improved and might be educated to be useful citizens, but 200 years of slavery have so debased and degraded the race that it will take more than 200 years to raise them up to civilization again. The Abolition cry in the North is only a party cry and those same people that are writing so furiously against slavery would not give a black man 50 cents to help him in his escape to Canada. You must not forget that it is a question of property." The traveller went on to say that there was a growing feeling in the South against any form of cruel and unjust treatment of slaves, that no families were separated now in the auctions (a declaration that Frederick's own observation was soon to prove false), and that "slavery must inevitably perish, however long it may take".

When they reached the capital of Virginia, they were taken to the Exchange Hotel, which seemed to them a decided improvement on Washington. "The public rooms are large and well furnished, the bedrooms comfortable, the food palatable, and the servants attentive," noted Frederick. "Amongst them is a man as white as myself, and the only remarkable feature about him is a crop of long and somewhat woolly fair hair. He is a slave and was bought by the proprietor of this hotel some months ago. One of his fellow slaves told me his history. 'I know all about his family,' he said. 'His father was a very rich merchant up the river, his mother a very bright but coloured woman. The father hated them and sold him and his mother south.' It may appear an unpardonable weakness to a philosopher that wherever a slave is found almost like ourselves, we feel a keener sense of the injustice, a more savage horror and disgust at the institution, than at the sight of a very black man, but still I think the feeling is but human. I cannot look at that man with his blue eyes, fair hair and European features without feeling painfully bewildered and awestruck. When I think that his master can sell him tomorrow to pick cotton on a plantation, can beat him almost to death, can prostitute his wife, can sell his children without any man having the right to interfere, my hair stands on end."

They had arrived in Richmond on Saturday, and on the following Tuesday Frederick put down his horrified impressions of the slave-market, after a second visit. "I went first yesterday morning," he wrote, "and the scene so utterly unhinged my mind that I found it impossible to write just then.

"Eli, the black head waiter, showed me to the place. He seems to have taken a special fancy to Nina and myself, and told me that he belongs to a speculator here, who hires him out at so much a month... The slave-market was but a few steps below the hotel. It was a wooden sort of low-roofed ware-room. On the door was a sign-board with 'R. Dickinson and Brother, Auctioneers', and somewhat below hung the usual red flag to intimate that a sale was going on.

"On a platform, raised a few steps above the floor, stood a

negro and the auctioneer, surrounded by the motley group of
buyers. The negro did not show the least sign of resistance, nor
did he, nor any one of the many others that I saw sold after, show
the least sense of his situation. He answered every question put to
him, and seemed anxious to bring as high a price as possible, as the
greater their value, I suppose, the better their treatment.

"'Now gentlemen,' called out the auctioneer, who looked
quite a mild and gentlemanly man, 'who will give me a bid for
this boy? He is warranted perfectly sound. No mark on him.'
Here his attendant tucked up the slave's drawers above the knee
and made him take off his shoes. 'A good foot and leg, you see,
gentlemen, fit for anything.' Then several gentlemen came up to
him, felt his feet and legs, felt his throat, and asked him if he was
quite healthy. The slave said, 'yes.' 'Grin, my boy,' said another,
upon which the negro showed a set of the most magnificent
teeth. 'Here is ivory for you, gentlemen,' shouted the auctioneer,
and the buyers, having touched him all over, looked down his
throat and asked him what work he had done, to which the slave
replied, 'I have worked on a farm, but I can drive a waggon and
do almost anything.' The bidding then began, and soon got very
spirited ... The man was sold for $1,150.

"Then came another ... 'Here's a boy, gentlemen, who has a
mark on his forehead, he says from a rock he got thrown at him,
and moreover his left leg is bad from the kick of a horse. He is
whipped some on the back and I don't warrant him sound.' They
made him walk, they made him strip, and at last he was knocked
down for $750 to a Mr Thomas.

"Then came a girl. 'Gentlemen, that girl has got a scar on her
leg, please to take notice. Jim, show that girl.' The poor girl was
stripped to show the scar. 'Now then, my pretty girl, look alive.
Quite healthy, I guess?' 'Yes, sir.' 'Let's see your feet.' They
touched her all over just as farmers do a cow; asked her if she had
any children. She said, 'No.' 'Are you with child now?' 'No,
sir.' He felt her body doubtfully. Then some other men asked her
questions too revolting to be repeated. It was whispered that she

had run off several times, and this sign of nerve and smartness seemed to increase the will to own her. She could work, and, as the saying is here, do most any work. She was sold for $850.

"So it went on, lame and sound, the defects being generally pointed out in a tone conveying the wish to deal fair. I could not stay any longer and felt both times a sort of nausea coming over me, and had to compel myself to stay and be a spectator that I might really see what I had read about, and what conveyed only a sort of dreamy meaning to me before. There were little boys and girls from five to ten and upwards. Their teeth were looked at, their ribs felt. They were made to count, which but one could do up to ten, upon which he was declared to be a likely boy. When the men and women were asked their ages they generally replied, 'My master says I am twenty or thirty.' One said to a question whether he was twenty, 'Well, I don't think I am, for a few years ago I was very young.' Men built like giants, who could break any of their buyers to pieces, submit like lambs to inspections and questions. They seem utterly used to it, and only with some poor fellows I thought I remarked their restless eyes following the bids and trying to find out who was really bidding (this is generally done by a nod of the head) and who would be their owner.

"I would not live in a Slave State for anything in the world. Their dark, shining, plaintive, subdued faces were haunting me the whole of last night ...

"There is a young and beautiful lady in this hotel. She is very imperious to the black waiters, and I have noticed that every time she speaks to them thus, she looks up at me with a half ashamed air and guilty eye. Her husband, a canal contractor and a mild, jolly sort of man, went with me this morning to secure seats at the theatre. On the way there he said, 'I don't like the Northerners. I am a Southern man to the backbone and I like the people here. The Northerners have interfered with our institutions and by God we'll maintain them. I would fight for them any day.' I said to him that I had been told they had only been made stubborn by the interference of the Abolitionists, but that in the South they wanted themselves to get rid of slavery if they only knew how.

"'Well,' said he, 'I'll just tell you what it is. These black people are a doomed race, and will be so until it shall please the Almighty God to change their lot. You see, that's just the whole thing, and no more's to be said about it.'

"I'm almost sorry to say I did not hold my tongue, as the stupidity and enormity of the speech was so evident, but I could not help asking him, 'Well, suppose your forefathers had said we are just doomed to be a dependent colony of Britain and bear our lot till it shall please Almighty God to change it, where would you be now?' 'Oho,' said he, 'that's another thing altogether.' So I just changed the conversation."

A week later, they had arrived in Charleston. "Today I address you from the sunny South," wrote Frederick, "the change of climate is so palpable and overwhelming that is has come upon me as if by enchantment. Perhaps the more so as we spent yesterday on the Atlantic." He described his last impressions of Richmond. "On Wednesday I walked out some distance from Richmond up to the brow of a hill that overlooks the town and the valley of the river ... As I turned, beautiful little Richmond was before me in all her glory, her capitol crowning the whole, with the American banner fluttering gallantly in the breeze. It was a splendid sight, but one old negro, passing me and taking off his hat to me in listless humility, was sufficient to mar the effect of the whole, for it conjured up the hideous phantom of slavery stalking like pestilence through this fair land, and I returned home dejected in spite of what ought to have been an exhilarating walk.

"In the afternoon we saw a large tobacco manufactory belonging to a Mr Grant. He manufactures only chewing tobacco, and we followed the leaf through its various processes of immersion, drying, cutting, priming, etc., till it comes out at last in the veritable round package from which the almighty Yankee cuts his plugs and sucks his inspiration. All the men and children in the factory, to the number of upwards of 200, are coloured people, and, of course, slaves. A certain amount of work, or as it is called, task, is required of them in virtue of their slavery, and for whatever more they do they get paid. This explained the astonishing celerity of their movements, and I was glad to learn that most of them earn $1 per day and some more. They are all well clothed and fed by Mr Grant, and look ten times as strong and healthy as a Manchester or Glasgow factory hand. So much for the honour of truth. Wherever slavery is not abused, it gets very much the aspect of the regular relation between employer and employed, but the curse of the idea that all these people are utterly at the mercy of one man remains the same, and it will never do as an argument that in a great many cases, perhaps in most, slaves are treated kindly, and are as well off as the working classes in England. The possibility and the fact of the exceptions damns the institution all the same."

The aspect of Charleston itself delighted him, and he could not imagine anything "more delicious than to inhale here the pure and gentle breeze from the sea . . . I am told that it is one of the most exclusive and aristocratic old towns of the Union. The South Carolinians pride themselves upon being the lineal descendants of the Cavaliers, just as the New England people boast of the Puritans as their ancestors. Everybody that can afford it has a private carriage; it seems to be the stamp of gentility, which must be had here at any cost, and no matter how it looks . . . But you see the funniest turnouts that ever were got up. Immense rumbling family coaches of the last century, with the most miserable horses to match."

Nevertheless, what he saw of the slave-market at Charleston horrified him even more deeply than Richmond, and finally convinced him that the whole system was utterly wicked and should be abolished. "The Post Office stands in the principal business street. At each side of it is a sort of open square, and the one to the left of the P.O. is employed for slave auctions. Here, while the ordinary business of life is pursued all around, while people read their letters as they come from the P.O. with a large thoroughfare before it, men, women and children are sold like so many beasts of burden to the highest bidder.

"I saw scenes of misery that made my hair stand on end. Stout men, crying like children at being parted from their wives, and children clinging in vain to their mother; and more agonies than I have a mind to recapitulate. They sold amongst others an old coloured woman of above sixty. She was palsied, and had a continual shaking in all her limbs. What anybody could have wanted with her I could not imagine, for she repeatedly declared she could do no manner of work. Still the bidding went on slowly. A brute of a fellow shouted: 'Sixty-five. Now knock her down to me, I want her, old age and all.' Then he went to her and said: 'How old are you, my pretty girl?' knocked her in the ribs and pulled her about. Just as the auctioneer had almost finished, a man drove up with a cart right to where the crowd had collected round the old negro woman, and cried with a stentorian voice: 'Now, gentlemen, I'll sell this horse and cart as it is here. Who will give me a bid?' Thereupon ensued an altercation between him and the auctioneer, but he kept his post, and the two biddings went on simultaneously, the one for the horse and cart, the other for the old woman.

"I could stand it no longer, and ran away very sick. When you speak to benevolent Southerners about such a scene as this, they shrug their shoulders and say that that is the evil attending the institution; at the same time they maintain that the Bible proves that the whole race is accursed on account of Ham ridiculing father Noah in his cups.

"One feels quite astounded at the wicked idea of imputing to the all-merciful Supreme Being an unquenchable search for revenge. Were it not better that the Bible had never been printed than that the code of love and brotherhood should be turned into the service of this vile and horrible institution?

"I have seen enough of slavery, Not all the happiness of negroes in the plantations, not all the kindness and benevolence of their masters, will make me change my feelings with regard to the enormity of the laws that give man power to buy a fellow creature."

II

My grandfather paid another hurried visit to New York and Boston in 1855, this time without Nina. The business of Naylor Vickers in America was clearly expanding, and in 1862, a year after the outbreak of the civil war, he was obliged to make a longer visit, as I have already mentioned, being away from mid-August to early November, and returning to America early in the following March. He was arranging large and important contracts, though not of arms as there is no evidence that Vickers at that time was manufacturing arms.

The war had begun in April of the previous year, with the Confederate bombardment of Fort Sumter in Charleston harbour. Lincoln, inaugurated President of the United States in March, had refused to recognize the secession of the Southern States declared in February, though he had appealed for a recognition of all that bound the North and South together before it was too late. Each side had high hopes for victory; the industrial superiority of the North was as great as its superiority in man-power, but the South was a compact territory with great defensive advantages. The chief weakness of the South was at sea; if the North could reorganize its naval forces – as it eventually did – the blockade of the Southern ports and the ruin of their vital trade with Europe was inevitable. That, however, was in the future. When Frederick arrived in the late summer of 1862, though the Federal General Ulysses Grant had had a series of outstanding successes in the Mississipi valley, the Union had fared badly in Virginia, their General McClellan having been outmanoeuvred by the Confederates under Robert E. Lee and "Stonewall" Jackson. Everything was in confusion, and the issue dangerously in doubt.

The second battle of Bull Run was fought on August 29th, and on September 5th Frederick wrote to Nina from Washington: "I wrote you a hurried note on Saturday last, August 30th, from New York to say that, as the news from Washington was threatening, I would defer my visit. On Sunday morning the papers published a despatch from that disgraceful liar Pope, claiming a great victory over the rebels at Bull Run. The despatch was dated Friday night and people thought the danger over. Early on Monday I left New York and got here same night. Ever since, I have been in the midst of the intensest and most painful excitement. Instead of a victory for the Federals (Union) they had been most shamefully and fearfully beaten. Rumours flew thick and fast, and by Wednesday morning it oozed out that the whole army was back in and coming back to the old camps around Washington. The army is utterly disorganized and wants rest, drill and reinforcements. Washington is a camp. This hotel contains Sigel, Banks and endless minor lights. Generals and Colonels all over the place, orderlies flying, troops moving night and day. Artillery rumbling, cavalry marching quickly, infantry slowly. In the midst of all this I have to attend to the most important interests of the firm, and think I have been very successful. Whenever I wanted to write to you, somebody called, a telegram came or had to be sent, I had to dance attendance at the War Office or with pressing letters. I meant to go back to New York yesterday, but business kept me and I shall not get off this evening . . .

"Washington is now considered safe, and if the rebels cross into Maryland people think they can be checked. However, all is conjecture. They are probably too clever to risk themselves so far from home."

It is clear that the state of chaos and the alarm in Government circles at Washington which he had witnessed, was having the effect of weakening his faith in the power of the North to succeed as he wished.

A few days later he wrote from New York:

"Here I sit sweltering, with nothing on but a shirt and a pair of trousers. The heat has been maddening today, and it is 80 degrees now by the glass which hangs by the open door of the hotel. And in spite of all this terrific heat, which almost unfits one for anything but rest of mind and body in a darkened room, one has to be up and doing. The devil is loose. The Confederates are in Maryland threatening Baltimore and Philadelphia and scaring the North from its propriety. The poor bewildered Government at Washington is at a discount, and perhaps before many days are over will be among the things that were . . .

"Possibly they may weather the storm yet and retrieve their fortunes by a defeat of the bold Southerners who are playing a dangerous game. *Nous verrons.* In the meantime, let us be joyful that I am safe back in New York and have not to throw myself upon the protection of the British Ambassador or take ignominious flight on a Federal gunboat . . .

"The humiliation of the people is not a pleasant sight to behold. They may have deserved their fate, but the wailing and impotent gnashing of teeths of a quondam great nation is a deplorable spectacle. I have written over 40 pages of letter-paper today, and in spite of the heat have to keep my head cool to steer the old ship safely thro' the breakers. No fear of it, but I am thankful I am here, and only now and then when the picture of you and those dear boys and that lovely angel baby and the fresh greensward at Woodlands will mix itself up with ever such incongrous and anomalous circumstances and surroundings, my head grows weary and my heart sickens for home sweet home."

In the midst of the turmoil of America at war and his grave business problems, Frederick continued to be sustained by the thought of his family at home. When he wrote to Nina on September 14th, he had just heard of their removal to Shanklin, and exclaimed that it was "real balm of Gilead" to think of them all there, "enjoying the dear old sea and the pebbles, the diamonds and the little crabs, the roses and our old friend the hydrangea at the Lovers' cottage, the breezy cliff and the waving cornfields, the shady woods, the rich green fields, and the toothless Sampson."

He told her that he was reefing sails against the hurricane that seemed to threaten so imminently:

"All my large past transactions are wound up and paid for . . . on Friday I decided to remove all our property from Baltimore and Philadelphia and sent somebody down to superintend the prompt execution of my orders. We have no reliable news here, and while one set of rumours makes the Confederates retreat in all haste to Virginia, the other reports a steady advance towards Pennsylvania. Chaos seems to have come again. No one man commands general confidence, hence recrimination, apathy, hesitation."

He continued the next morning: "Tonight we have news of a great Union victory. I really hope it is true, for unless they can score a peg now and then, their situation will become so absurd as to be quite painful to the visitor. To hear them speak in deep humiliation of the imbecility of their Government and the incapacity of their Generals, when one has been so used to brag and defiance, makes one feel that resentment and sarcasm are quite out of place, and you have to tone yourself down to respectful pity."

He also reported that he had been seeing something of Mattie Griffith, with whom he had made friends the previous year at Knebworth. "I was to meet Horace Greeley, the Editor of the *Tribune* at Mat. Griffith's by appointment. I went and saw this curious nondescript of an imperturbable fanatic, who thinks that with some more reverses all will come right, abolition of slavery will be proclaimed and the South will collapse as if by magic. I also met Mr Dale Owen there, Papa and Janet's friend and a very pleasant man, with whom last night and on several previous occasions I have had some very interesting conversations. There are generally 3 or 4 young ladies at Miss Griffith's who sit in sackcloth and ashes at the feet of whatever Gamaliel may be holding forth and do the chorus of wailing and lamentation."

A few days later he left New York for Boston: "I said goodbye to Mr Owen and Miss Griffith on Friday evening. I told her you sent your love to her and that you loved all who *liked* me, whereupon she quietly replied: 'I not only *love* you, but I love your wife dearly.' Poor thing, she is in sore tribulation about the course of events in this country. Monday last we had a victory announced by McClellan. Then nothing was officially allowed to transpire from him until Friday, when at last we heard: 'The Rebels are retiring to Virginia, and Maryland and Pennsylvania are safe.' Thousands of lives and millions of money sacrificed in order that the North may be 'safe' and 'as we were' and all to begin again *ab ovo*. I had hoped and still hope that now some compromise will be attempted. Both North and South have failed at invasion and might now come to terms, 'sadder and wiser men', but nobody seems to think that there is the remotest chance of peace. It is awful. Such carnage has never been known. There seems to be no generalship, no manoeuvering, but just a butchery that lasts a week. Whoever gets most reinforcements and holds out longest kills most and keeps the field. The victor buries his own and the enemy's dead, and nothing further happens. No victor has ever followed up one of these great holocausts to any great success. This is now the third within three months. The week's battle of the Chickahominy, the week's battles at Manassas and Centerville, and now again a whole week's carnage at Sharpsburg.

"On the boat last night, a Philadelphia clergyman on his way to do duty for a brother clergyman in Boston, opened his heart to me. 'The country is mad and the Government is hurrying us on to ruin with ever increasing speed. I have only one wish and that is to go away for ever and live in England, where you have peace and liberty.'"

Before sending the letter off, he added a postscript in some excitement: "At last we have great news in the President's proclaiming all slaves of people in rebellion on the 1st January next free for ever. There is no going behind this, and slavery is now doomed in the United States, whatever that may be at the end of the war. As the South will certainly not submit before the end of

the year, the proclamation amounts to virtual abolition where-
ever the North may succeed in planting its flag. I am delighted,
but I see no peace. On the contrary, the war will probably only
begin in earnest now, and get more inveterate and savage as it
proceeds."

Nina's reactions to these letters were mixed. She did not like to
think of Frederick so near to the fighting when he was in Washington; and though she shared his detestation of slavery, she
could not fail to be influenced by the general English sympathy
for the Southern cause, particularly in her own circle, at that
time. When she got his first letter from Washington, she wrote
back: "So you are at Washington, young man, smelling gun-
powder and hearing the booming of distant (but not half distant
enough) cannon! Is that the conduct of a sedate and careful father
of an absent family?" And when he got back to New York, she
wrote rather reproachfully: "Don't, dear, call them the 'Rebels'
always. There are other names for them. How my interests and
my wishes tear different ways, but none of this." The news about
Lincoln's Proclamation provoked exclamations of bewildered
dismay from her: "I wish I knew you were at this moment in the
good *Scotia*. I believe I would kiss the Captain if he brought you
over. Perhaps you don't like me to say such silly things? That
Proclamation of the President's is awful. One passage made my
blood run cold as I read it, that one which so suggestively says that
the negroes will not be interfered with in their attempts at gaining
liberty. This is merely bidding the negroes 'go in' to murder their
masters if they can, or, still worse, their helpless mistresses and the
little ones left at home. So it seemed to me as I read it, but I daresay it is of no use after all . . . I wish, I wish we had nothing to do
with it."

All her life Nina had a horror of violence and she wrote on one
occasion to Frederick: "We are still part-savages. You may say
that war – fighting – quarrelling – struggling, are part of our
human nature, and as such will soon be got rid of – not now being
intended by our creator to be got rid of – but then why do all our

finest and higher instincts rebel in horror against war and its abominations?"

Frederick tried to console her for his long absence and her anxieties by suggesting that they should take a holiday in Paris together as soon as he got back. "I have had no rest whatever so far, not a shadow of a holiday, and I think that a month in Paris is due to us. I hope to be home 3rd November, and after a fortnight of the children I hope you will be ready for a regular good prowl and frolic in Paris just by our two selves." To which Nina replied: "You certainly shall have a holiday, my own darling, and it shall be *whenever* and *wherever* you like. We could get a nice little *appartement* like Ghemar's, I daresay, or a wee suite of rooms near the Dickens's; that is if you still wish Paris, We could pick up lovely things for Woodlands there, couldn't we? Everybody says Naylor Vickers are making a fortune."

There is no doubt that the Proclamation about slavery was crucial in turning the tide of Frederick's ebbing faith in the cause of the North, though it was some time before it was fully restored. He was far-sighted enough to realize that, however exhausting and horrible the struggles the Americans might still have to go through, Lincoln had given the Union millions of new allies by this step, and started a great movement that could only gather force. Hitherto, the war had been essentially about secession. Now it was about slavery. And Frederick was also shrewd enough to see that, however high tempers might rise on either side from time to time, the blockade of the Southern ports was not likely now to lead to war between the North and England.

III

Once in Boston, Frederick was able to vary the exhausting business scramble with visits to some of the notable intellectual figures of New England at that time, and, incidentally, to hear their views about the war.

He had already met Nathaniel Hawthorne when he was Consul at Liverpool, nearly ten years before. In his reminiscences he writes as follows: "Hawthorne was sent as United States Consul to Liverpool in 1854, he being one of the many instances of the American Government's constant practice of doing honour to their eminent literary men by appointing them to posts of emolument. I was invited by an American friend of mine in Liverpool to meet Hawthorne soon after his arrival. His appearance was very striking, his face handsome and intellectual and the large liquid eyes full of latent fire and poetical imagination. He was not only reticent, but almost taciturn, and when he did speak was apt to pause and then jerk out the rest of the sentence. Americans have, as a rule, a very remarkable facility of expression. Here was a curious exception. I remember condoling with him for having exchanged Boston, the 'hub of creation', for uncongenial Liverpool, when he replied: 'Oh, Liverpool is a very pleasant place' – (then a pause sufficiently long for me to look surprised, and then suddenly the end of the sentence) – 'to get away from.'

"After Hawthorne left Liverpool, we did not meet again until my visit to America in the autumn of 1862, under the following circumstances. Robert Chambers had given me a letter for Ralph Waldo Emerson, which made him ask me to spend a day with him at Concord. He seemed to me the beau ideal of a contented and virtuous sage. Placidity and serenity were to my mind the chief characteristics of his face and manner. His conversation flowed without the slightest effort, copiously and harmoniously. He took me all over Concord, pointing out all the lions of the war of independence. He seemed proud of the wealth of his New England orchard, the apple trees having done specially well that year. All his surroundings, not only his family but his house and furniture seemed to fit Emerson, and left upon me the very pleasant impression of my having come in contact with a master mind living in refined frugality. Among others, Emerson had asked Hawthorne to meet me. As usual, he hardly ever spoke, and I only remember him breaking his apparent vow of silence when appealed to by a Mr Bradford, who, after a fiery denunciation of the South and having come to the end of his peroration, passionately turned to his silent listener with the words: 'Don't you agree with me?' Then Hawthorne astonished him by uttering the monosyllable 'No', after which he again relapsed into silence.

"Emerson told me that Hawthorne's increased taciturnity caused much anxiety to his family. My recollection of him is of one gloomy and much troubled, while I shall always think of Emerson as pellucid and at peace."

Between his time at Liverpool and my grandfather's second meeting with him, Hawthorne had visited Rome and Florence and written *The Marble Faun*. This was his last novel; on his return to Concord the gloom which struck Frederick so forcibly and which appears to have been to a large extent caused by the war, prevented him from writing much more than occasional papers. He died two years later.

The Mr Bradford mentioned by Frederick had retired to Concord after some years of preaching and schoolmastering, to live the simple life on Emersonian principles, in the magic circle that Emerson, Thoreau and his friend Ellery Channing had created there.

This visit to Concord is more fully described by my grandfather in a long letter written on September 27th to my grandmother. On receiving Frederick's letter with Robert Chamber's introduction, Emerson wrote back: "I am very happy to hear from Mr Chambers, and it will give me great pleasure to see one so nearly allied to him as yourself. I am at this moment confined at home by a sprained foot, or I should go into the city today to fetch you. Meantime, my house is but an hour's ride from Boston by the Fitchburg Railroad, and if you will take the eleven o'clock a.m. train on Saturday we will show you our little village, give you a country dinner, thank you heartily for all the good news you shall bring us of Mr Chambers; and, if you cannot face a Sunday in the country, there is an evening train to the city at 6.30 p.m. Pray let me expect you."

Frederick took the train recommended, and "found Mr Emerson waiting for me at the station in his buggy, and recognized him at once by portraits I knew of him. A charming old sage, with the kindest and most refined manner. He speaks well, and likes to speak about all manner of interesting men and things. From his writings I had expected a sort of oracular Carlyle, but a total absence of affection or mannerism put me at once at my ease. The day was bright, pure and serene beyond description. He drove me about thro' the dreamy, quiet village of Concord, pointing me out its lions. A small grey obelisk records the spot where the first blood was shed between the Colonials and the English in the revolutionary war. The clergyman of the place asked all his congregation one Sunday to join him next day, each with a young tree to be planted near the monument. It was done, and now they have grown up to a pretty grove and avenue. Near it stands the Manse about which Hawthorne has written so charmingly. On we drove to a slight eminence, where Emerson pointed out the different villages; one was said to be built on shoes, another upon peach-stones and a third upon milk, according to their respective trades.

"We got to his place about two. Nothing could be simpler and more unpretending. He had asked Hawthorne, William Ellery Channing, a poet, and a Mr Bradford, a literary man, to meet me at dinner, at which his wife and daughter completed the party. Hawthorne remembered me and you quite well . . . He is just the same shy, monosyllabic man, apparently with oceans of thoughts and talk if he could only turn on the stream.

"Emerson asked much after Papa, and everybody seems always most anxious to make sure of his being the author of *Vestiges of Creation*. The conversation was so pleasantly animated that the six hours and a half had slipped away before I was aware of it. Hawthorne pressed me twice to come and see him. All except him thought the South would soon give in. Fight them with abolition of slavery, and they had no chance . . . It is quite marvellous to see men like Emerson quietly ignore the stern logic of facts, persist in drawing on the future and declare their unshaken faith in the triumph of the North and the restoration of the Union."

Apart from Hawthorne, the only person Frederick met at this time who shared his persisting doubts about the immediate and overwhelming victory of the North, was James T. Fields, the Boston bookseller and publisher, friend of Dickens and Wilkie Collins. "Fields thinks differently," writes Frederick after describing the party at Concord, "probably from the English wind that blows fresh into his bookstore, but he tells me that it would be hopeless to try and make his wife share his views. I have breakfasted twice with them, each morning at 8 at my request. Their house is a perfect gem of brightness and cleanliness. They have a charming view over the blue Charles river. Each room is full of books and engravings, everywhere portraits of English authors, everywhere autographs and letters from eminent men; an atmosphere of literature and refinement pervading the whole. We had a long walk yesterday, and tomorrow he will take me a walk of 25 miles to the Blue Hills to show me the country about Boston. We are drawn together by our common great affection for dear Dickens, whom he worships. I was glad to be able to give him one of Dicken's good *cartes de visites*, and have promised more from England. Fields took me to poor Longfellow, who received me very kindly and was glad to hear my news of his literary friends in England. He lives in a little paradise, and I cannot imagine why the Benzons never took us there. Since the frightful loss of his wife, Longfellow is completely crushed and just barely vegetates. He had fame, money, and perfect domestic happiness, a loving wife and charming children. One little match, which she ignited by treading upon it, did all the mischief."

Frederick then goes on to describe the way the war was striking home, even into peaceful New England: "Russell Lowell lost two nephews, fine young fellows, in the last battle. Wendell Holmes, the life of Cambridge, had started off to the battlefield to find and tend his wounded son, shot in the neck. To day I hear he has found him and is bringing him home with every hope of his recovery, at which there is great rejoicing.[1] Fields took me to Lowell, but he was not at home, and considering the loss he has just had I was scarcely sorry. You see the war is spreading death and desolation through all these bright homes, and still none of them think of giving in. They scorn the idea."

In the same letter, he enclosed two communications he had received from Mattie Griffith in New York. "I find that everybody here knows and esteems her. The Fields and Emersons talked with great regard of her." Frederick could not resist writing her a letter of congratulation when Lincoln's Proclamation was published, and she in replying sent him a letter of introduction to Wendell Phillips, the great abolitionist agitator and orator. "I daresay you have so many friends in Boston that an additional acquaintance will only prove an annoyance. If, however, curiosity prompts you to call on Mr P., my only direction is for you to walk down that narrow, dirty Essex Street, and stop at the smallest, shabbiest house you find, ring and ask for Mr Phillips. I think that advice will safely land you in the august presence, and when you have seen the man you will not remember the house . . .

"Do you not see the account of McClellan's (doubtful) great victories? I hope he may follow them up. What you told me of the letter in the *Post* relative to the treatment of the negroes by the Union soldiers has been terribly confirmed by additional public statements. Is it not frightful? Poor negroes, they have not deserved to be '*les miserables*', the Pariahs which the insolent American men have doomed them to be. I confess to you my heart sinks when I reflect upon all this horrid state of affairs. I am neither cheerful, nor strong, nor brave enough to bear this fearful process of regeneration through which the country is now passing. I am afraid we are to be ground to powder for our sins, so long persisted in, before we can be reconstructed, for I cannot yet doubt that the glorious ideal of this nation will be fulfilled both as idea and fact. But much I fear that the great battle between the child of the free and the bondman has not only to be fought in the two

---

[1] He recovered, and eventually became a Judge of the Supreme Court.

great divisions of the land, but in every community, almost every heart, before the terrible Ishmael, slavery, shall be banished to the blank wilderness of 'nowhere and nevermore'.

"I need not, however, weary you by 'carrying coals to Newcastle'. Shall you not be glad to get beyond the dismal sound of this war, and land once more on the peaceful, green shores of Old England? I am sure you will."

Mattie Griffith's remarks about the battle of slavery needing to be fought, not merely between North and South but in almost every heart in America, received a grim confirmation from a demonstration Frederick had just witnessed in Boston. "Do you know *Train*?" he wrote to Nina. "The humbug has come back, and is addressing enthusiastic audiences of 2000 people *against* abolition. The fellow reviled Boston's best men, Tremont, Sumner and Phillips, and the ruffians cheered him to the top of their bent. When you cite the fact to people as a curious phenomenon and an evidence of division, they merely shrug their shoulders and say it means nothing. In fact, there are two stereotyped phrases: 1. You do not understand the Americans, and 2. I guess we shall come out all right in the end."

In the second letter, Mattie Griffith referred to the international implications of the new turn of events. "Ah, yes! The war will be more bloody and grim after this. The South will afford no quarter anywhere. Yet I am afraid Jeff Davis will be shrewd enough to propose gradual emancipation to France as the price of recognition and intervention. Then, our 1st of January Jubilee will be destroyed. How do you think France and England would treat such an overture? Surely Anti-Slavery England will not cheat us of this glory. I cannot believe it possible, If she does, I hope you will do all you can to set Exeter Hall eloquence into a blaze. We had, last night, quite a fusillade on the occasion. The poor blacks in Broadway wore happier countenances, and appeared to walk with a more cheerful, elate step."

By that time, Frederick was finding himself near the end of his tether. He had to go back to New York, where he saw Mattie

Griffith again and then make one last visit to "beastly Washington". "Oh Lord, if you only knew how frightfully tired I am of America, and how often I have to battle with the blues when pictures of you and the children rise up before me in the grim, relentless distance. Weel, a weel. I must just go through with it, and won't we have a jolly winter, my worrrrrd ... If there is anybody with you when I come home, *anybody* except Hopie, Mamie or Jan, I shall just quietly murder him or her. So I have given you fair warning."

IV

In the early Spring of 1863 Frederick had again to make an urgent dash to America, on official business with the War Department of the Union Government. He was only away just over two months in all, and apart from short notes, only two long letters to Nina survive from the visit. They are, nevertheless, of considerable interest, dealing with the international situation mentioned by Mattie Griffith as Frederick saw it from the vantage point of Washington, and with the hardening will of the North to subdue the South – at all costs. The war itself had not gone well for the North in the interval; the turning point, in which their superior manpower and weight of arms was finally to tilt the balance, was still to come.

In his first letter from Washington Frederick tells Nina that immediately on arrival he had dined with General McClellan, still the chief soldier under the President in command of the Union Forces, and directly after that with Lord Lyons, the British Minister, and was about to dine with Monsieur Mercier, the French Minister. The General, he wrote, was "a small, quiet, unassuming man, without the faintest outward attributes of a hero. A poor, dull face with a small forehead and lack-lustre eyes. If he ever saves this Republic, physiology and phrenology are not worth a red cent. On Thursday morning I left New York, and arrived here about ten o'clock at night. This hotel or boarding house (Wormley's) is principally patronized by U.S. Senators during Congress, and by respectable people who want to be quiet and hate the rush and gilt of Willard's. Consequently Wormley's was hard to find, and when found at last had gone to bed. Thomas, an old negro factotum, received us half asleep, and to my expression of hope that altho' the house seemed empty they would come up to the good reputation I had heard of them, merely answered: 'Never you fear, Mas'r, we'll treat you *nicely*.' And so they are doing, all things considered. I have a nice quiet sitting room and ditto bedroom. The food is fair, the guests only two or three, and the attendance black and kindly . . .

"This is Easter Sunday, 5th April, and we have a foot of snow in the streets fallen overnight. A furious gale is blowing, and Washington is a howling wilderness. On Friday I sent my letters to Lord Lyons, M. Mercier and their two Secretaries, Mr Clay and M. Treilhard. Lord Lyons at once sent me an invitation to dinner last night. He received me very kindly, and said: 'You have brought me a letter from my dear friend Browning. You must tell me all about him, for we spent such happy days together in Rome.' (Pray thank dear Browning for his letter of introduction and tell him how promptly Lord L. *a fait honneur à sa signature*.) He is tall, looks forty-five to fifty, and is the very personification of good breeding. Undemonstrative, perhaps cold, but suave, polished and easy. He told me that a good many of the Legation had gone to Baltimore for the Sunday. There was only one stranger, whose name I did not catch, and two attachés – or rather one and the Secretary Mr Clay. The latter is much better looking than his brother, but has the usual intolerable air of *suffisance* of English attachés about him . . . Our dinner was very fair, the attendance admirable, and the whole thing was over in less than an hour. Scarcely any wine was taken after dinner, and there being no ladies Lord L. gave the signal to rise. Having been told that he says very little, I was agreeably surprised to find him pleasantly communicative. He seems to believe that in the course of 3 or 4 years, if the conscription is not resisted, the North will get a good army, immediately under the control of the Washington authorities and detached from local ties, that they will then get some good generals, and will finally overcome all organized resistance of the South. We had a long chat, and once he said: 'My position here is one of constant worry and irritation, and upon my word, I believe I am the only impartial Englishman left, unless, begging your pardon, you should happen to be the other one.'"

Lord Lyons, almost immediately after, sent him another invitation to dinner, but Frederick had to refuse as he was dining with M. Mercier. Lyons seems to have taken an immediate liking to Frederick, because Clay informed him that he had said to Lyons after dinner that he had never seen him so open and talkative before. "You have undoubtedly touched the secret spring to draw him out."

Before the dinner at the French Legation took place, M. Mercier called on Frederick one afternoon, "and sat for an hour talking politics by the yard and nonsense by the mile. He explained to me that during the entire late mediation scheme he had been on the best terms with Seward and is so now; that Seward had first shown him the text of his message to Congress (which was thought in England to give Mercier the lie direct), and that he had given his assent to every line of it. There was at the time an intrigue against Seward to which he (Mercier) would not lend himself, and so on. This is only another instance of unruffled peace between the diplomatists while the newspapers cry fire and sword, and the gullible public get frightened into fits. Mercier is satisfied that this war can only be ended by European intervention, and that if England had joined France and both had said: 'Unless you settle your differences by a given time, we recognize the Confederacy and open the ports,' the North would have given in at once, 'mais l'Angleterre n'a pas voulu. Elle a peur d'une guerre avec le Nord, mais elle aura cette guerre, elle l'aura, qu'elle fasse tout ce qu'elle voudra. J'aime beaucoup l'alliance Anglaise qui est après tout pour la

France le seul moyen de garder l'equilibre et la paix en Europe, mais j'avoue que les Anglais sont des amis très difficiles et bien des fois très désagréables. Ce sont eux qui de leur côté apportent les difficultiés et les obstacles dans l'alliance, etc.'"

"I dined with Mercier," Frederick continues later, "there was only Madame Mercier and an attaché. He talked for four and sometimes very well. I had put on a white cravat as at Lord Lyons' where I found them all dressed up to their eyes. Mercier was in his shooting jacket, and on seeing me said: '*Comment, avec une cravate blanche? Mais nous n'aurons qu'un dîner tout à fait sans cérémonie.*' I told him that it seemed *de rigeur* at Lord Lyon's, altho' there was no party. '*O, les Anglais,*' he replied, '*je crois que Lord Lyons dînerait en cravate blanche tout seul vis-à-vis de lui-même.*' In the evening I asked Mme to play, and she did play a few of Chopin's Nocturnes, not without a certain taste and a good deal of execution. . . ." Whether Mercier was speaking with the voice of his master, the Emperor, or not, it is clear from the rest of these letters that Frederick knew that he was living in a world of illusions.

Back in New York a few days later, he wrote: "Yesterday we had a great mass meeting in Union Square, called a Sumter Meeting, to celebrate the rising of the North after the taking of Sumter by the Confeds, 2 years ago yesterday. There were 6 stands, and from each some hoarse patriot was stirring up the people and defying the universe. Tremont, Sigel and *hoc genus omne* blazed away, but the acoustics of the open air were much against them. While they were talking the Confederates *down* in Union Square, gold went *up* in the city in consequence of news of a repulse at Charleston. Tell Papa, and who else may care, that in my opinion the talk of war between England and America will remain *talk only*; it is not the *interest* of the North to have a war with England. They would like it dearly if they could afford it. But what Europe has taken for granted from the first – i.e. the impossibility of conquering and subjugating the South – has not yet even distantly dawned upon the Northern mind. They are perfectly, and almost unanimously convinced of the possibility of success, and it will take years and years before they will give up trying. No party that advocates anything but war, until they shall have recovered every inch of the former Union, has the remotest chance of influence, or even existence. The ambition to be a mighty nation, equal to or greater than any in Europe, is the idea which holds possession of the Northern mind, to the exclusion and disregard of every other. All reverses will be put down to the Administration or bad generals, but nothing will make them give up but utter and hopeless exhaustion. In my opinion the war is only beginning, and will last more years than I dare to think of. This, however, is England's safety, for as a war with England would mean an alliance between the South and England against the North, the latter cannot afford to fight the South *and* England. Reluctantly but steadily they will abandon the delights of war with England for the hope of subduing the South.

"On the other hand, England is so well convinced that the evil of war with the North would immeasurably outweigh any benefit we might derive from opening the Southern ports, that I am satisfied that England will do all consistent with her honour and dignity to prevent war. Hence I believe in endless palaver and angry correspondence between the two countries, but in nothing more."

After declaring these unpopular and disturbing (to European ears) but prophetic views, Frederick put his affairs in order and returned to his beloved family and "the green sward at Woodlands". "I shall be with you three weeks after this letter," he wrote to Nina. "I therefore give you the earliest possible notice, that you may set your house in order and disband your army corps of lovers. Rudie writes me that he believes you are melancholy and think of your husband in America, *altho'* you have 3 men who are quarrelling every night which of them shall share your bed. Dangerous as it sounds I don't mind *these* 3 men, and only think of the general detachment of lifeguards that seem to be on duty with great zeal and regularity . . ."

He adds as an afterthought, "I read *Orley Farm* with great interest, and advise you to get it if you have not read it yet."

Frederick was not to visit America again, until some years after the war had ended as he foresaw (though more swiftly), when he set out on his trip round the world in 1869.

PART SIX

The Earthquake at Cannes

I

After Frederick's trip round the world in 1869–70, the letters between him and Nina grow rarer, more spasmodic, though never less affectionate. There are no records for the years after 1870 so full as for the earlier years. They made their final move, to 15 Berkeley Square, at the end of 1870: there their musical parties continued in the season with at least equal brilliance, Brahms being added to the musical notables who frequented them. Both Frederick and Nina became increasingly absorbed in the activities of their children; and both of them, for reasons mainly of health, were continually on the move from one spa or seaside resort to another. Nina's longings began to turn back more and more to her ancestral Scotland, while Frederick took frequent trips all over Europe, sometimes accompanied by one of the children. Both began to grow very fond of Cannes as a winter resort.

Let us move forward to the year 1886. Frederick is taking a great deal less active interest in his business; he is only sixty years old, he is rich, but the tireless exertions of his life are beginning to tell on him, he is often oppressed by bouts of melancholy, and he is soon to retire. Of his children, my father, Rudie, has been called to the Bar, is planning a political career in the Liberal interest – he has already stood for Cheltenham (and lost) – and has been passionately interested in rowing ever since his undergraduate days at Trinity College, Cambridge. Freddy, the indolent charmer, whom even in his childhood his grandfather Robert Chambers called "Major Jollyboy" and "Frederico Jocoso", followed Rudie to Highgate School and has gone through Sandhurst to join the Army. Neither is yet married. Ernie, who went to Eton, has passed his examinations for the Diplomatic service and has been posted to Washington; he has matrimonial troubles, arousing the ire of his father which Nina tries to calm. The youngest, Nina, has married Sir Guy Campbell, has a son, Guy Colin, who is two years old, and has just lost her baby, Pamela, in a "choleraic epidemic" at Sandgate.

In the late spring of 1886 Frederick started on one of his wanderings in search of a cure. He went from Algiers to Monte Carlo, from there to Evian, to St Moritz, and finally to Aix-les-Bains. He was in such a state of depression, that Nina decided to join him in Evian for a while. She sent him a letter from Paris *en route*: "You wrote me in lowest spirits which grieves me, but I quite understand it under the circumstances. The 'nothing-to-do' and such heaps of time not to do it in must be awfully trying to you. Don't fret as to *me*. I am not coming to Evian in search of wild amusement, the Lord save the mark. I am simply and entirely and solely coming to be with *you* for a time, and where you happen to be is all the same to me though I am glad it isn't on the top of some uncomfortable and ugly Swiss mountain, but on the shore of a lovely lake where nature must be the all satisfying joy, and I am sure will be to me."

After she got back from Evian, Nina went to St Andrews in July; and then in November she set forth to spend the winter in Cannes. In the first week of December, she wrote from the Hotel Montfleuri, "My dearest, I was right glad of your more than welcome letter – welcome as roses in December, young peas in January, green trees and blue seas at Christmas, and all the other upside down delights of this marvellous place. I feel this time, after two trying winters spent in dark London, as if I must *always* come back here in November for the rest of my life." She was expecting the arrival of her daughter, Nina, her husband and the boy Guy Colin, who planned to spend the winter with her. "Our rooms are all en suite," she wrote, "facing south with a marble balcony, then there is the big beautiful garden and the (enclosed by wire work I am glad to say) pond with heaps of ducks and hens and chickens, and a monkey up a tree, and the great mild mastiff Ectorre, whom I always remember here, and who attends and wags his tail at all the arrivals as they alight."

When they first went to Cannes, in the seventies, Wilkie Collins had written to "The Padrona": "I am charmed to hear that the Cannes climate has done you so much good. Thirty years ago, I remember it as a delightfully snug, small, cheap place, with two English people only established in it – Lord Brougham and another Britisher whose name I forget. It is plain that I should not know Cannes again if I saw it now." He was right: it had become a prosperous, smart winter resort, full above all of English sun-seekers. On this visit Nina found many old friends, including Dr de Mussy and his wife, the latter looking like "a feather bed tied in the middle", and there were "callers" every day, among them "that delightful Dutch-looking Miss Cavendish Bentinck" who was staying with "Chatty" Dempster; Lady Bolsover "who is at our hotel and has such a nice dear girl of a daughter called Lady Ottoline",[1] and who "talked with deep interest of the marriage of Guy's cousin George Wyndham, as the bride, poor dear, has just been staying with them at Welbeck"; the "large family of Actons"[2]; Captain Nugent retired from the Guards, his delicate refined-looking wife and grown-up twin sons, one just entering the Guards and looking as if he would vanish if you blew at him, the other at Oxford; Sir Edward and Lady Ward, the former longing for Frederick to come out and join him at whist; Mrs Schenley who regaled them at a "superb luncheon", the table being covered with roses "of every hue and shape – one lovelier than another, and in thousands I think – quite 50 or 60 glasses full of them on the table and a large vase of them in the centre, all of them out of the open garden"; The Duchesse de Luynes, who was much taken with young Nina; Baron Louis La Grange and "his charming American wife, the Baron asking much after Rudie"; Countess Kilmansegg, and the Countess of Caserta.[3] "The whole

---

[1] The future Bloomsbury hostess, Lady Ottoline Morrell.

[2] Lord Acton, the historian, and his family.

[3] Wife and first cousin of Alfonso, pretender to the throne of the Two Sicilies after the death of Francis II in 1894.

swelldom of Cannes has now called, worse luck, as the calls must be returned, but people are generally out."

Soon after Nina Campbell and her family arrived they had an alarming experience. They hired a *voiture*, "a little open Victoria", to go up to visit their friend Mrs Taylor "at the very top of the high hills at Montbrillant", and on their way back the coachman lost control of his horse. "In vain the frightened idiot tried to pull the reins – the *mécanique* had either snapped or would not act – in short we were off!" Sir Guy jumped out in order to get at the reins, failed, the coachman also jumped out, was dragged along by the reins as he struggled and then thrown clear, and Nina and her daughter found themselves alone in the driverless *voiture*, careering downhill at ever increasing speed. "When all was as we thought over, and we knew we must in another moment be either killed or frightfully wounded in all likelihood, to my amazement I saw Guy with his elbows pinned into his side, reminding me in a flash of race-runners, and his face deadly white, set, and his mouth clenched, dashed up to us, and as I waited as it were in agony of hope and despair, he flew past us and caught hold of the horse. In my life I shall not forget Guy's face."

A worse experience, however, was to come. A week or two later, Nina and her daughter made an expedition to Antibes, "and had the most delicious day together. We set off at 10.30 (with our own safe man with whom we are making an *arrangement* – and hang expense, as Uncle Harry used to say) and took our bit lunchie with us. Fowl and tongue and German sausage and rolls and butter and fresh lemonade and oranges. When we got to the Cap we found a lovely spot on the sands, with a big flat stone that did for a table. The coachman gave us the cushions of the carriage, and then we two arranged our little meal with the sea rippling up in its shining blueness at our feet, the pines and eucalyptus trees in their greenness at our back, with squares and rounds of blue sky darting through them, *and* the Mediterranean fleet in front, no doubt gazing through their glasses now and then at this small English peek-meek. Our coachman partook of *his* little bite near us, our horse – a decent beast – had its nose buried in its bag, and all was peace, sunshine, beauty. We spoke of you, and said, 'Oh, how Papa would enjoy this.' After our innocent meal, we drove into the quaint old town and walked about the narrow shady streets, through the little market place with its gourds and oranges and dried figs and stout rosy women sitting with still stouter rosier babies, to every one of whom Nina made up, winning every stout rosy mother's heart on the instant, and eliciting wobbly smiles from the babies themselves." They were restored; the incident of the runaway *voiture* was forgotten, the coachmen of Cannes forgiven, and in the perfect weather in which the sun was so overpowering at midday that "the outside shutters have to be nearly shut" a further source of happiness was promised by the arrival of Freddy at Monte Carlo. A "delicious letter" had arrived from "our dear Wilkie, just like his old self", and "we are both looking forward to your coming whenever business claims allow you to think of it". Then, a few days later, the earthquake occurred.

On the 23rd February 1887 Nina wrote to Frederick: "This morning at a little before 6 the whole hotel was woken up by a shock of earthquake which lasted – it *seemed* an age – about a minute. It was the most horrible sensation and sound I ever heard . . . In one minute, almost before the vibration ceased doors were flung open everywhere and a terrified and shocked population in nightgowns, caps, shawls, blankets, *anything*, was, crowding to the staircase . . . First, as I woke, I thought it was people over my head dashing their beds and other furniture all across the room, and shaking walls and floors to bits! But as it went on with an awful rumble and clatter like great furniture vans being driven past, or a luggage train shock, shock, shocking into a noisy station, I felt in a moment it could not be that." Nina and her daughter flung on shawls, tried to put on some clothes, but as they did so another slight shock came. Their first thought was for the small boy, Guy Colin, who had been in bed with a bronchial attack: his nurse, Lydia, was found to be in a demoralized state of terror. "Then Nina said she would fly down to the delightful Dr Müller, who has been attending little Guy in his attack, and ask what we were to do. Everybody by this time was downstairs, many in the garden, in all sorts of undress." The comforting Dr Müller, who was to make a series of godlike pronouncements during the night of horror, said, "Yes, we had better bring the child down." Down he was brought, to the *salon* on the ground floor, "by that time crowded with frightened and *most* queerly costumed people, all extremely friendly not to say clinging to each other – and the proud south-aspect ones who had hitherto looked down upon their north-room fellow creatures, hobnobbing with the north-room ones and hanging upon their lips if perchance one of them had ever experienced such a thing before or knew anything of earthquakes.

"A lady from Chile, or some such place, rose I can't say how many centigrade, because she had scarcely ever known anything *but* earthquakes. When she used, after a friendly party at her house, to take her friends to the door to say goodnight, they would all look up at the sky and say, 'Oh, the stars look like an earthquake tonight', or simply, 'It's earthquaky', whereupon the lady would calmly move all her furniture to a side, so as to form a nice gangway for the children to escape without breaking their shins. This lady became an oracle.

"Well, we all stopped down in their ground-floor *salon* for a good while, till at last no other shock coming we got calmed down. I need not tell you Nina and I were *perfectly* ourselves all through, having run too many dangers together not to know by now how to behave, and up we went again – half the hotel, however, remaining down, and *many* talking of running away at once to other places. We got some coffee upstairs and had put little Guy to bed again, when bang went another saxpence and the horrible and awe-inspiring, for it is nothing else, rattle and rumble came again – about half past 8 this time, or rather sooner. This was the finishing stroke. Everybody whose confidence by this time had been partly restored, now flew out for good, and Dr Müller, whom we again consulted and who was perfectly quiet and calm, still said, 'Take the child down' . . . More frightened people than ever, but better clothed this time – fringes looming again, curls budding out of curl paper, petticoats and gowns instead of night-dresses and shawls. But the *fright* much greater, intensified by this new shock so long after, slighter though it was. Our terrible anx-iety was for the boy, but I think it has not hurt him. Dr Müller said it might retard a little the recovery but would not, he thought, harm him as we had been so careful. We kept him there till about 2 p.m., but brought him back to our rooms then, where we are ourselves. We are all rather afraid of the great marble staircase, as at the best of time it gives us pause, not seemingly having any-thing to *rest* upon; but there is a back one, more solid looking, at the far end of the passage. The people on the 5th floor, our friends the Grahams, felt it terribly. Their walls shook and swayed, and they were forced to bring old Mr Wilson, who had been laid up with congestion of the lungs, down to the ground floor . . .

"It was a farce, if it had not had at the time the awful and tragic element of the unknown, the *everything possible* in it, to hear the different exclamations of people. One lady on my étage I heard out-side repeating in an anguished cry for minutes, '*Mais, Madame, ma chambre! Mais ma chambre, ma chambre!*' I don't know yet what she meant, but she never said anything else at all. She had on her nightgown and *a blanket over her head*, nothing else."

Later in the afternoon, Nina and her daughter decided to take a drive to the seashore at Golfe Juan to distract their minds, "first seeking counsel from Mr Taylor in our husbandless condition as to whether we should remain here. Mr Taylor said there was no danger whatever in remaining as Cannes was not volcanic, and reassured us a great deal with his delightful cheery common sense but for all that the perspiration was pouring down his wife's face from fright . . . Nina thinks she will try to fix a sort of umbrella over Guy Colin's head to shield him from falling plaster. It was tremendous, Lydia says, just over her head and Guy Colin's, the first shock. Lydia thought it was people making a fearful noise 'right over my 'ead, and I kept calling out to 'em *shut up*! *Stop that noise!* till I saw it couldn't a been them Rooshians as has been packing the last three days and making that row I never *could* git 'im to sleep.'

"The thing that alarms us most is the bad way in which these great hotels are built. 'Ah, you see,' said our Chile or Pernambuco oracle, '*we* were all built for earthquakes, you're not.' Still the foundations we think must be good to have stood so well this morning's vibration. Our driver to Golfe Juan (our own Pierre whom we trust) was very funny when we asked him if he had heard the *tremblement de terre*. Of course he had, but he was fast asleep and thought it was his *belle-soeur*, calling him and scolding him for being so late. Delightful idea of the *belle soeur* this! Simply *becomes* an earthquake one morning, after having simulated one most of her life."

Nina's sense of humour, as we have seen, did not desert her during the crisis. Nevertheless, she was slightly annoyed when she got a rather untroubled letter from Frederick in reply to hers. "I see you have not the faintest idea of what we went through. All the better. We worded the telegram so as to keep your mind easy, but far from being a 'slight shock' as we said, we may tell you now it was a very violent one indeed, and lasted nearly a minute, which was awful I can tell you. Being suddenly and sharply woken up by a fearful and unaccountable noise like machinery all rattling in full swing and shaking your bed and your room, and yet knowing there was no machinery to account for it, and this horrible machinery not stopping, as it should do if it was merely some accident, but going on whilst you leapt up with your heart in your throat, calling to each other, trying to find your clothes, your candles, hearing distracted voices and rushings of people outside your door, and as yet not knowing in the least what it could possibly be! Realize it if you can. But you can't – for nobody that has not experienced earthquake *can* know what it is."

The *beau monde* of Cannes broke up after this experience. The season was ruined. In spite of her fortitude and sense of humour,

Nina never felt quite the same about Cannes, or anywhere else on the coast, again.

Her father and mother were long dead and her uncle William had died three years before, full of honours after spending vast sums of money on the restoration of St Giles Cathedral in Edinburgh, which had been in disrepair for three hundred years. Less than five years later Frederick, whose health had been getting steadily worse, died. Nina lived on, to see the marriage of her two other sons, Rudie and Freddy, and the new century, dying in my father's house at Bourne End. Directly after Frederick's death she decided to build herself a house in Scotland, in Portobello near her beloved Edinburgh, and on a journey to prepare this move she wrote to my father: "I find myself still going on saying suddenly to myself, 'Oh, I must tell Fred this – how this will amuse Fred – I must ask Fred what I ought to do.' And I get as it were a right down blow that knocks me over for the time. I feel it all more and more deeply as time goes on, instead of less. All the tiresome things that must crop up in a long companionship vanish utterly and forever – and only the dear old days of youth and happiness and mutual and delightful sympathy and comradeship remain."

The letters she exchanged with my father were particularly characteristic and vivid, and extended over several decades, following his career with loving and enthusiastic sympathy. But that is another story, perhaps, for another time.

Index

AGING, MONEY, AND LIFE SATISFACTION

Aspects of Financial Gerontology

Neal E. Cutler, PhD, is President and Scientific Director of the Boettner Institute of Financial Gerontology in Bryn Mawr, Pennsylvania. A member of the Board of Directors and Chair of the Research Committee of the American Society on Aging, Dr. Cutler is a Fellow of the Gerontological Society of America, and a Member of the Population Studies Center of the University of Pennsylvania. Previously he was Professor of Political Science and Gerontology at the University of Southern California, and Codirector of the Institute for Advanced Study in Gerontology and Geriatrics at the Andrus Gerontology Center. Dr. Cutler writes a bimonthly column on Financial Gerontology in the *Journal of the American Society of CLU and ChFC*.

Davis W. Gregg, PhD, is Chairman and founding Director of the Boettner Institute of Financial Gerontology in Bryn Mawr, Pennsylvania. From 1954 to 1982 he served as President of The American College in Bryn Mawr, where he is currently Distinguished Professor of Economics and Gerontology. In 1961 Dr. Gregg was awarded the John Newton Russell Memorial Award for outstanding service to the institution of life insurance. In 1979 he received the Solomon S. Huebner Gold Medal Award from The American College and in 1980 the Founders Gold Medal Award for Excellence from the International Insurance Society.

M. Powell Lawton, PhD, is Director of Research at the Philadelphia Geriatric Center in Philadelphia. He is also an Adjunct Professor of human development at Pennsylvania State University and Professor of Psychiatry, Medical College of Pennsylvania. He is the author of *Aging and the Environment, Planning and Managing Housing for the Elderly,* and the Editor of The Annual Review of Gerontology and Geriatrics, published by Springer Publishing Co. He was also the first editor of the American Psychological Association's journal, *Psychology and Aging*. Dr. Lawton's awards include the Kleemeier Award of the Gerontological Society of America, the Distinguished Contribution Award of the American Psychological Association's Division on Adult Development and Aging, the Career Award of the Environmental Design Research Association, the Ollie Randall Award of the Northeastern Gerontological Society, and the Annual Award of the Philadelphia Society of Clinical Psychologists.

Aging, Money, and Life Satisfaction

Aspects of Financial Gerontology

Neal E. Cutler, PhD
Davis W. Gregg, PhD
M. Powell Lawton, PhD

Editors

SPRINGER PUBLISHING COMPANY
New York

Springer Publishing Company, Inc.
536 Broadway
New York, NY 10012-3955

92 93 94 95 96 / 5 4 3 2 1

Library of Congress Cataloging-in-Publication Data

Aging, money, and life satisfaction : Aspects of financial gerontology
  / Neal E. Cutler, Davis W. Gregg, M. Powell Lawton, editors.
      p. cm.
    Includes bibliographical references and index.
    ISBN 0-8261-7700-X
    1. Old age—Economic aspects—United States—Congresses.
  2. Aging—Economic aspects—United States—Congresses.
  3. Retirement—Economic aspects—United States—Congresses.   4. Old
  age pensions—United States—Congresses.   I. Cutler, Neal E.
  II. Gregg, Davis W. (Davis Weinert)   III. Lawton, M. Powell
  (Mortimer Powell), 1923-   .
    [DNLM: 1. Aged—congresses. 2. Economics—congresses.
  3. Pensions—congresses   4. Social Security—congresses.   WT 30
  A26865]
  HQ1064.U5A63477   1992
  305.26—dc20
  DNLM/DLC
  for Library of Congress   91-5230
                                                                          CIP

Printed in the United States of America

In honor of
Joseph E. and Ruth Elizabeth Boettner

Contents

Foreword

This book on financial gerontology is the product of several distinguished scholars responding to a new-felt need in social science research. The story of this book is also the story of a research institute.

In 1986 the Boettner Research Institute was founded at The American College in Bryn Mawr, Pennsylvania. Its purpose was to discover linkages between the processes of aging and financial well-being and to disseminate its findings in all appropriate ways. A new term, *financial gerontology*, was identified for this pioneering effort. The contributions in this book are among the early papers prepared to advance this effort, including the annual Boettner Lectures, and the papers presented at the first Invitational Research Symposium held by the Institute at The American College in 1987 on "Financial Security and General Well-Being in the Life Course Perspective."

The Institute develops, sponsors, and conducts research, and disseminates information in the field of financial gerontology. This emerging field of study is concerned with the dynamics of financial security, well-being, and quality of life within and across generations. The Institute's purposes also include the study of ways of helping people establish and achieve appropriate financial goals throughout the life cycle; the encouragement of systematic social science research on the impact of both population aging and individual aging on financial well-being; the sponsorship of educational programs including public lectures, conferences, symposia, seminars, and other learning events for business, labor, government, and the general public; and the publication and dissemination of knowledge gained through research and educational programs.

As one who has spent a lifetime in the study of financial security for aging persons, I can commend this book to anyone who seeks a deeper understanding of the dynamics of the field of financial gerontology. Students and teachers, along with practitioners in financial services, pensions, insurance, estate and financial planning, will be informed by the new insights available in these pages. Because my own interest and efforts in the founding of the Boettner Institute began with the deliberations that led to its creation, I am proud and deeply honored to be asked to introduce this first book prepared by the Institute.

The Institute is named for and springs from the vision of Joseph E. Boettner, the person to whom the book is dedicated. He is a most extraordinary man. Now in his 89th year, his energy, enthusiasm, and receptivity to new concepts stand at a level exceeding that of most of those who have seen but half his years. His education has been lifelong, beginning with West Philadelphia High School, followed by evening school classes at the Wharton School of the University of Pennsylvania. Early in his career in life insurance he earned his Chartered Life Underwriter (CLU) diploma and designation. The challenges of his hearing disability sealed his commitment to education and resulted in a lifelong interest in strengthening the values of quality colleges and universities. He has been especially generous in his support of institutions of higher learning, especially those that seek to add to the store of knowledge as well as to transmit it.

Joseph Boettner's interest in new knowledge through research and his enlightened philanthropy have culminated in the formation of a new force in research and education, now named the Boettner Institute of Financial Gerontology. Its early success is promising. This book is tangible evidence of its reality.

Dan M. McGill, PhD, LLB, CLU
Founding Director and Chairman Emeritus
Pension Research Council
University of Pennsylvania

Acknowledgments

The editors would like to express their deep appreciation for the expertise and energies of the Boettner lecturers and symposium participants whose contributions included here begin to outline and define the exciting new field of financial gerontology. The blending of these contributions into a single book reflects the additional skills and diligence of many professionals to whom we are sincerely grateful including the editors of Springer Publishing Company, Kay Powell and her editorial staff at The American College in Bryn Mawr, editorial consultant Nina V. Kenney, and research assistant Kathleen L. Qualls.

Finally, we are especially grateful, to Helen L. Schmidt and Catherine Cardenuto, administrators of the Boettner Institute during the past several years, whose unfailing and skillful attention to task and detail, both large and small, have so centrally contributed to the success of the Boettner Institute as well as this book.

Contributors

David L. Featherman, PhD, President, Social Science Research Council, New York

Linda K. George, PhD, Professor of Sociology and Medical Sociology, Associate Director for Social and Behavioral Programs, Center for the Study of Aging and Human Development, Duke University Medical Center, Durham, NC

William C. Greenough, PhD,* Former President and Chairman, Teachers Insurance and Annuity Association-College Retirement Equities Fund, New York

George L. Maddox, PhD, Professor of Sociology and Medical Sociology, Chairman, University Council on Aging and Human Development, Duke University, Durham, NC

James N. Morgan, PhD, Research Scientist, Institute for Social Research, University of Michigan, Ann Arbor, MI

Matilda W. Riley, LHD, Associate Director, Behavioral and Social Research, National Institute on Aging, National Institute of Health, Baltimore, MD

*Deceased

xiii

The Emerging Dynamics of Financial Gerontology: Individual Aging and Population Aging in the New Century

Neal E. Cutler

APPROACHES TO THE DEFINITION OF FINANCIAL GERONTOLOGY

Although not yet a household phrase, *financial gerontology* identifies an area of basic and applied research that will affect much of American economics, policy, and family life during the next two decades. Since the 1950s the discipline of *gerontology* has emerged as one of the most rapidly expanding fields of social and biomedical research. The 1990 *Research Centers Directory* (Dresser & Hill, 1989) describes no fewer than 65 academic centers of aging and gerontological research in the United States alone.

Out of this expanding body of research comes the view that gerontology is a broad field of inquiry concerned not simply with old people but that includes analysis of the multiple *processes of aging*. The rapid growth that characterizes research in aging is found equally in the biology of aging, the psychology of aging, as well as the social sciences and aging (Birren, 1990). Yet even in the latter there is need for multidisciplinary inquiry. As the editors of the third edition of the *Handbook of Aging and the Social Sciences* clearly state, to understand the social context of aging requires "the systematic perspectives of a variety of broadly conceived social sciences" (Binstock & George, 1990, preface).

Research in financial gerontology, consequently, is based on the intersection of finance, business, and economic issues with the aging of individuals and the aging of society. Given the complexity of modern society, this overlap of gerontological and financial research not only identifies a new set of research questions but offers a lens through which many of the most fundamental questions of contemporary society can be viewed.

For example,

- The relationship of Social Security and employer pensions to individual and family retirement planning is dramatically magnified by the fact that greater numbers of individuals are living a longer span of years in retirement than was the case 10 or 20 years ago.
- A growing cultural emphasis on independence in old age means that an increasing number of older men and women will stay in their own homes for a longer period; although not all of them will require social and medical assistance on a regular basis in the home, an increasing number is likely to need such assistance.
- The aging and middle aging of 80 million baby boomers means that virtually all social programs and policies will experience substantial financial pressure, whether funded by public or private agencies, business or government institutions, and whether they are associated with the poor, the middle class, or the wealthy. Because the first baby boomer entered middle age in 1991 (see, e.g., Waldrop, 1991), and the last baby boomer celebrates her 100th birthday in 2064, the length as well as the depth of this demographic-financial-gerontological force is immense.
- Overall improvement in human longevity has dramatically expanded the number of multigeneration families in which older adult children are called on to provide a broad range of financial and nonfinancial care simultaneously to their maturing children and their aging parents. One study estimated that in 1900 the probability that a middle-aged couple would have *two or more parents still alive* was only 10%; by 1976 the probability was 47% (Uhlenberg, 1985).
- The financial situation of aging individuals and families, reflecting resources as well as obligations, has become increasingly complex including insurance, savings and investments, home ownership, multiple incomes, and multiple pensions. Consequently, the overall life satisfaction of aging persons is related not only to their objective income and wealth, but to how they perceive, fear, and understand the relationships among their wealth, health, health costs, and the degree to

which they subjectively understand and are satisfied with how their objective resources are being managed (Cutler & Gregg, 1991).

DUAL PERSPECTIVES: INDIVIDUAL AGING AND POPULATION AGING

Succinctly defined, financial gerontology is the emerging field of study concerned with the dynamics of financial security, well-being, and the quality of life during the life cycle and across generations (Gregg, 1990). It is a field of study that has a broad intellectual focus rooted in and guided by the theories, concepts, and data of basic and applied research in both gerontology and finance. As the preceding examples suggest, like gerontological and financial research more generally, financial gerontology embraces both a macroanalytic or population focus, as well as a microanalytic or individual concern with patterns of human attitudes, concerns, fears, needs, and wants.

Financial gerontology does not focus on the study of "old people" but on how the various *processes of aging* are related to questions of financial security and human well-being. Yet in focusing on *process* it is important to emphasize that both microprocesses and macroprocesses are involved—that is, we are concerned with two interconnected sets of studies, hypotheses, concepts, and data.

Individual aging, the microanalytic focus, is concerned with the several processes that describe how individual men and women develop, mature, and age. *Population aging*, the macroanalytic focus, refers to the number and proportion of older persons in a population, the demographic dynamics that produce these patterns, and the financial and social consequences of these patterns.

The two kinds of aging are not the same. For example, if average life expectancy of individuals already age 65 in 1990 becomes magically increased by 23 years from its current 17 years to 40 years overnight (individual aging), then the society as a whole might or might not become substantially older. The overall societal impact (population aging) of such a hypothetical change in individual aging would depend on the number of persons affected by this change.

For example, imagine a large country in which there are only 512 older persons. If these 512 men and women magically experience that sudden 23-year increase in their life expectancy, the policy implications of this individual aging change would not be especially profound. In other words, the financial and policy significance of individual aging rests largely on how it is "multiplied" by the force of population numbers.

By contrast, population aging can occur even in the absence of changes in individual aging. For example, the simple fact that about 80 million babies were born during 1946 to 1964 means that the number and percentage of 65-year-olds in the United States during 2011 to 2029 will create population aging, the magnitude of which is unique in human history. These trends and patterns will occur even if average individual life expectancy stays exactly where it is today.

There are other distinctions between individual and population aging. For example, individuals can only get older, whereas a population can actually get younger. The average age of the United States declined during the birth years of the baby boom as millions of persons age 0 entered the population. Other aspects of population aging of relevance to the study of financial gerontology can also be noted; for example, demographic experience to date suggests that a population becomes more female as it becomes older.

Issues of financial gerontology are directly affected by the fact that a population can become younger or more female. Such macrolevel changes are likely to signal controversies concerning basic social and economic allocation of scarce resources. "Scarce resources," in turn, include not only money but issues of fairness, access, and opportunity. For example, as an older population becomes more female because of the differential mortality and longevity of men and women, questions of geriatric medicine, home health care, and nursing home care finance and administration become female issues as much as they may be old-age issues.

Consequently, demographic imperatives help to identify and shape some of the most fundamental principles of private and public policy. The more general proposition is that financial gerontology must be sensitive not only to the relationship of individual aging to financial well-being, but also how the macrosocial and macroeconomic dimensions of population aging affect the financial as well as social opportunities of older men and women and their families.

COHORT CONTRASTS: AGE CONSCIOUSNESS IN AN AGING SOCIETY

Although individual aging and population aging are conceptually and empirically distinct, their interaction produces especially powerful dynamics. Although it is theoretically possible for a population to get older even if individual life expectancy is not increasing, in fact life expectancy at age 65 in the United States has been increasing (Taeuber, 1990).

More critically, we are now facing a situation in which individual aging and population aging are becoming dynamically intertwined in a way that is unique to human history. That is, we are entering a period—in many economically developed nations as well as in the United States—in which old-age life expectancy is increasing precisely at the time when baby boomers are entering their older years. Consequently, the presence of millions and millions of persons who are living longer (and retiring earlier) is producing a future condition of population aging characterized by unparalleled financial as well as social, cultural, and political implications (Cutler, 1991b).

There is perhaps an even more potent mechanism that links individual aging and population aging. The general principle at work here is that—as Matilda White Riley notes later in this book—*people do not age in laboratories, they age in society.* Economic, cultural, political, and historical events are all part of the societal context in which we age, and that affects both the content and consequences of our individual aging. Perhaps one of the most striking components of this experiential context, however, is population aging itself.

Researchers as well as practitioners working in financial gerontology should be sensitive to the following kind of question: To what extent and with what consequences is aging likely to "be different" for someone growing older in a society characterized by dramatic population aging in contrast to someone growing older in a society not undergoing population aging? As George Maddox appropriately notes in his chapter later in this book, old age is not new; societies have always had old people around. What is unique about contemporary society is that there are *so many* older persons.

Of course, we each age from adolescence to adulthood to middle age to old age. Surely such individual aging, however, was not the same for our parents and grandparents as for ourselves. The societal and historical context of individual aging in 1925 was for many reasons and on many levels different from what it will be in 1995. As Maddox's comment suggests, perhaps one of the most notable differences is that we are now beginning to experience a magnitude of population aging that was not even imagined in 1925. In turn, men and women who experience their individual aging in the context of population aging are likely to develop an age consciousness that affects their attitudes and expectations toward a broad array of financial and social issues (Bengtson, Cutler, Mangen, & Marshall, 1985).

Table 1.1 illustrates the degree to which the linkage between individual aging and population aging influences the content and direction of research in financial gerontology. Four individuals, labeled A to D, are identified in terms of their year of birth, the year of their 65th birthday, and the portion of their lives during which they lived with Social Security and Medicare. As used here Social Security and Medicare are meant to be symbolic of the more general programs and controversies that characterize a society experiencing substantial population aging.

Person A, born in 1870, was not affected by either Social Security or Medicare. By contrast, Person D lived her entire life in the context of Social Security and her entire adult life in the context of Medicare. As Linda George illustrates later in this book in her exceptional review of the life-satisfaction literature, the precise nature of how personal characteristics (individual

TABLE 1.1 Generational Cohort Calendar

Individual	Year born	Year age 65	Life-stage lived with Social Security and Medicare
A	1870	1935	—
B	1900	1965	Social Security from age 35
C	1925	1990	Social Security from age 10; Medicare from age 40
D	1945	2010	Social Security from age 0; Medicare from age 20

aging) and historical context (population aging) combine to produce vary-ing profiles of financial well-being is a central aim of systematic research in financial gerontology.

The more general proposition, however, is that although they are sepa-rable concepts, individual aging and population aging do combine in im-portant and powerful ways. When we consider the difference between grow-ing old in the 1920s and in the 1990s, probably the single most significant difference is that a person now entering older age is much more conscious of the financial and political as well as the health and personal aspects of aging, having lived most of his or her life in a society that has been antici-pating and responding to population aging. The ways in which people re-spond to their own individual aging are affected by a multiplicity of forces and factors including the society's response to population aging.

MULTIPLE APPROACHES TO FINANCIAL GERONTOLOGY

To understand more directly how the processes of individual aging and popu-lation aging penetrate the financial life of a nation and its citizens, several researchers have begun to develop an agenda for basic and applied research in a new field of inquiry that has come to be known as *financial gerontology*. Research in financial security has strong roots in finance and the social sci-ences. Thus, the emerging research efforts in financial gerontology draw broadly on concepts, methods, and data in such diverse basic and applied fields as demography, pension analysis, health care finance, savings and in-vestment dynamics, sociology, risk and insurance analysis, political science, retirement planning, and social psychology.

As an introduction to the multiple approaches to financial gerontology, this collection of public lectures and symposia papers brings together in a single book the results of a series of pioneering conceptual and empirical efforts. They are the product of a group of nationally eminent scholars who collectively represent both the gerontological and financial dimensions of financial gerontology.

The chapters in this book collectively identify some of the primary intellectual origins and policy concerns of financial gerontology. To more comprehensively portray this course of scholarly development, we note some of the research questions that are currently being developed as part of this emerging field of inquiry.

Population Growth

Any examination of the multiple connections among aging and financial issues begins with a basic demographic portrait of the gerontological landscape. It has been well documented and widely publicized that the older population of the United States has been increasing in both absolute and relative terms. What is less often acknowledged, however, is that *older age itself is very heterogeneous*, both behaviorally and demographically. Figure 1.1 portrays the percentage of the U.S. population for three older age groups during 1950 to 2025. Table 1.2 provides the population numbers and percentages for selected years.

It is apparent that aging is not a unitary demographic phenomenon. The different older age groups have somewhat different historical patterns and are of different sizes within the total population. The traditional 65+ age group shows the increase that has been generally portrayed in the public media, increasing from 12.6% of the total national population in 1990 (31 million) to a projected 19.6% in 2025 (59.0 million). The older-old (80+) is a much smaller group as a percentage of the total population, but it almost doubles in size from 4 million to 7 million during 1970 to 1990.

Figure 1.2 provides some indication of the growing overall importance of aging in American culture. Here we compare the numbers of three age groups: teenagers (age 10-19), middle agers (45-64), and the traditional definition of older age (65+). It is not difficult to recall the almost dominating influence that teenagers had on American culture in the 1960s and 1970s—from educational programs to crime and delinquency to popular music to protest politics. It is not difficult to see in Figure 1.2 the demographic basis for the economic and social influence of teenage culture.

TABLE 1.2 Three Older Age Groups—United States, 1950-2025

Age group (years)	1950 N	1950 %	1970 N	1970 %	1990 N	1990 %	2010 N	2010 %	2025 N	2025 %
45-64	30.8	20.3	42.0	20.5	46.7	18.7	78.6	27.9	74.5	24.8
65+	12.4	8.1	20.1	9.8	31.3	12.6	38.0	13.5	59.0	19.6
80+	1.7	1.1	3.7	1.8	6.9	2.8	10.6	3.8	12.8	4.3

N's in Millions; % = percent of total population.

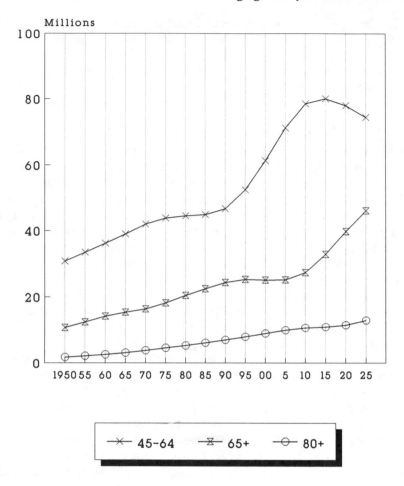

FIGURE 1.1 Three older age groups.

In a similar way we are perhaps only beginning to fully appreciate the impact of a middle-aged population of similar proportions during the next 10 to 15 years. Indeed, the two population bulges are the same birth cohort, the baby boomers, born 1946 to 1964. The great degree to which the members of this generational cohort influenced the whole nation as teenagers is likely to happen again when they are middle agers and then again later when they are older people. In his classic essay on "The Cohort as a Concept in the Study of Social Change," Ryder (1965) defines a cohort in

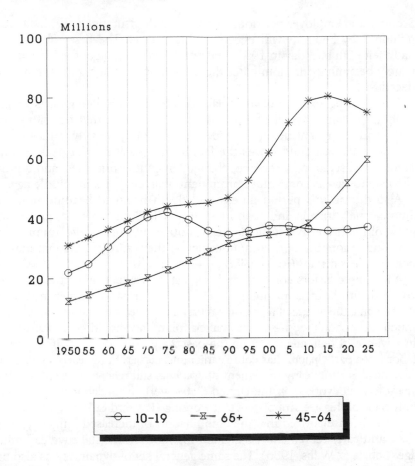

FIGURE 1.2 United States–Three age groups: teenagers, middleagers, and older-agers.

terms of its aggregate biography. Given its monumental size, the aggregate biography of the aging cohort of baby boomers is a story of financial, political, and cultural change of unprecedented national scope.

The Rapid Middle Aging of America

Although gerontology is usually identified with issues associated with old aging, it is fairly clear that the more dramatic growth during the next several years is in the 45 to 64 age group. Neither the size nor the timing of this trend should be a surprise. Before they become older and affect Social

Security and employer pensions, private health insurance and Medicare, 80 million baby boomers will become middle agers. The first baby boomers had their 45th birthday in 1991. The rapid middle aging of the United States is now beginning and dominates the demography of aging for the next two decades.

From the perspective of financial gerontology, middle aging is an especially important stage of life. It is during this period that decisions about work and retirement begin to be evaluated. Empty-nest dynamics become salient as the last child leaves the family home. Patterns of peak earnings, increased discretionary income, changed spending priorities, and a greater capacity to save become more prominent characteristics in middle age.

Also during this period illness and death begin to become noticeable among one's friends and "cohort mates." Children grow up, and parents grow old and die. We scan the death notices in our college alumni magazine and ignore the birth announcements; the reality of personal mortality becomes less distant (Karp, 1988).

All of these factors combine and interact to produce an active middle-age concern with financial planning. As David Featherman's chapter in this book documents, the nature of a person's retirement reflects economic behavior of a much earlier adulthood—so that financial planning should begin substantially in advance of retirement. During the past 25 years, retirement from full-time labor-force participation has come earlier and earlier. In the early 1960s, when the Social Security early retirement option was still relatively new, 80% of 62-year-old male workers in the United States were in the labor force. By 1985, only 51% of this age group were still working (Packard & Reno, 1988).

It has been theorized that the combination of increased longevity, empty nest, and early retirement has created the modern life-stage we call middle age (Schaie & Willis, 1986). The same general set of dynamics has also been described as the third quarter of life (Pifer, 1986), in which plans are evaluated and decisions made for the fourth quarter.

Thus the importance of middle aging to financial gerontology is found on several levels: Middle age is important financially in its own right; much of the decision making that occurs in middle age is concerned with financial, social, and health resource planning for older age. Additionally, the development of a new research focus on financial gerontology is also timely: As William Greenough notes later in this book, reasonable economic security for older persons is relatively new, having evolved in just the past 50 years.

That middle aging dominates the picture of aging for at least a generation is apparent from the demographic summary in Table 1.3, which contrasts the previous quarter century (1960-1985) with the new quarter century (1990-2015). The left-hand pair of columns indicates the average annual population in the United States in each of the two periods. The right-hand columns show the percentage change within each period for middle aging and older aging.

TABLE 1.3 Middle Aging versus Older Aging in Two Quarter-Century Periods—United States: 1960-1985 versus 1990-2015

Age group (years)	Average annual population in each quarter century		Change in each quarter century (%)	
	1960-1985	1990-2015	1960-1985	1990-2015
45-64	41,740	65,078	24.1	71.6
65+	22,020	35,918	71.1	39.9

Population numbers in 1,000s.

The data reinforce our intellectual and political images of the period: 1960 to 1985 was a period of substantial older aging, as the 65+ age group grew by more than 71% from 1960 to 1985; the 45 to 64 age group in this period grew by only 24.1%. In contrast, the maturation of the baby boomers makes the new quarter century a period of rapid middle aging. From 1990 to 2015 the 45 to 64 age group increases by 71.5%, whereas growth in the 65+ age group slows to 39.9%. As will be indicated subsequently, this general pattern is not unique to the United States but is characteristic rather generally of the economically developed nations of the world.

The Financial Status of Early Retirees

Recognition of these trends in middle aging and retirement leads to an exploration of the financial status of retirees. Financial gerontology is concerned with how population trends are likely to interact with individual patterns of retirement and financial resources. One recent project developed an analytic procedure for projecting the number of early retirees who are likely to have annual financial resources in retirement of $50,000 or more. Using the 1980 U.S. Census Public Use Sample, the research first identified all retired persons age 55 to 64, and inflation-adjusted their reported total household income to 1986 dollars (Longino, 1990).

A projection of the future size of this financially advantaged early retiree group, during 1990 to 2010, requires three factors: (a) the number of persons age 55 to 64 in the population during these years, (b) their rate of early retirement, and (c) the proportion of these early retirees who have substantial income (using here the criterion of $50,000 annually).

The first factor is directly available from U.S. population projections. For the other pair of factors, retirement and finances, the analysis assumed a modest increase above the 1980 census rates. Consequently, the simulation model simply increased the 1980 rate of early retirement by 5% and increased the 1980 rate of financially advantaged persons among early retirees by 5%.

These assumed 5% increases are probably conservative: Little evidence exists that the trend toward early retirement is abating, even in the presence of the legal elimination of mandatory retirement. Given the availability of Individual Retirement Accounts (IRAs), the extension and protection of pension coverage offered by the Employee Retirement Income Security Act (ERISA) since the mid-1970s, and the general public attention to financial aspects of aging, there may well be an increase in the proportion of future retirees who are financially advantaged (Easterlin, Macdonald, & Macunovich, 1990).

Overall, using available population projections of the 55 to 64 age group during 1980 to 2010, the research posed the following pair of "what-if" questions:

- What if the percentage of persons in this age group who choose to retire early increases by 5% over the 1980 rate of early retirement?
- Of this group of early retirees, what if 5% more of them, compared to 1980, have annual incomes of $50,000 or more?

Table 1.4 shows that even if 1980 rates of early retirement and financial advantage do not change, demographic growth alone will produce a 66% increase in the size of this group between 1990 and 2010. When the two modest 5% rate increases are combined with the population projections, the simulated increases are even more dramatic: The number of financially advantaged early retirees will increase by 77% during the 1990s, and an additional 135% in the subsequent decade. Clearly the challenge for research in financial gerontology is to identify these trends further; to understand the diversity of this group better; and to assess their needs, concerns, and plans (Cutler, 1991a).

TABLE 1.4 Financially Advantaged Early Retirees Simulations: 1990, 2000, and 2010

Increase in percentage of financially advantaged early retirees, caused by:		
Demographic change only:	1990–2000:	12.3%
	2000–2010:	48.4%
	1990–2010:	66.6%
5% rate increase in early retirement *and* 5% rate increase in affluence:		58.0%
Cumulative effect of both demographic and rate changes:	1990–2000:	77.4%
	2000–2010:	134.5%
	1990–2010:	163.3%
Age: 55–64; 1980 census baseline		
Income: $50,000 and above (in 1986 dollars)		

Aging Families, Health, and Personal Care

In the past few years health and health care financing have become the dominant issue on the agenda of our aging society. As part of this larger issue, social and medical policy have endeavored to minimize the unnecessary or premature nursing home institutionalization of older persons both for financial and humanitarian reasons. As the population ages there is increasing need for individual assistance in such everyday activities as getting dressed, eating, going to the toilet. If an older person has absolutely no one to provide such basic assistance, then the only solution may be that of entering the nursing home:

> One of the greatest indicators of long-term institutional care of elderly people is not medical need but, rather, the lack of social support when need arises. Older people with few or limited family relationships are prime candidates for institutionalization when they become sick. (Chappell, 1990, p. 440).

More generally, as James Morgan concludes later in this book, available social support and health are more significant causes of happiness than are wealth and income. Most of the time, the primary personal caregivers are the older person's own family members, the daughter or daughter-in-law in particular (Brody, 1981). The multiple burdens of this "sandwich generation" of middle-aged daughters is now receiving substantial national attention (e.g., Beck, 1990). Just as their teenaged children are about to leave the family home, their own parents may begin to require intensive personal care.

Not all families can provide this care. Increasingly the middle-aged daughter-mother is herself in the labor force. Residential mobility implies that not all elderly persons are near their adult children. Some middle-aged daughters may just not be physically, emotionally, or attitudinally capable of providing personal care on a daily basis.

Research must examine trends in the future supply-and-demand relationship of middle-aged caregivers to older persons who are in likely need of personal care. The financial gerontology perspective suggests that if the desired personal care is not available from within the family, then it will have to be paid for. Like health care more generally, payment for this kind of supportive care can be paid for by public programs, by personal financial resources, and by private insurance.

Such analysis has major implications for long-term care insurance—perhaps the most intensely discussed issue in recent debates concerning aging and health care. Within this discussion a key concern about currently available insurance policies has been the degree to which, and the circumstances under which, "long-term care" is broadly defined to include personal care provided at home—in contrast to such insurance being applicable only to placement of the older person in a nursing home (Christopherson, 1989).

Table 1.5 lists the five Activities of Daily Living (ADLs) that are often used as standard indicators of the dependency of older persons on the personal caregiving of another person (Katz, Downs, Cash, & Grotz, 1970). The working assumption is that if such care cannot be provided, the older person will have to be moved to a nursing home. As the data suggest, there is a dramatic increase in the need for personal care with advancing age.

What these national ADL rates do not indicate, however, is the likelihood that such care can be provided from within the family. To project the future *supply* of family-based personal care we use the number of women age 55 to 64 as a surrogate estimate of the daughters and daughters-in-law of elderly persons. To estimate the *demand* for personal care we multiplied the age-sex–specific ADL rates in Table 1.5 by the parallel age-sex–specific U.S. Census population projections.

TABLE 1.5 ADL Rates per 1000 Persons

Age	Total	Men	Women
Bathing			
65–74	35.2	33.4	36.7
75–84	80.9	68.2	88.8
85+	217.2	194.9	227.9
Dressing			
65–74	29.3	32.5	26.8
75–84	50.8	56.6	47.3
85+	132.3	126.5	135.7
Moving			
65–74	17.7	17.4	17.9
75–84	36.7	28.8	41.8
85+	89.6	66.7	99.1
Toileting			
65–74	12.4	13.6	11.4
75–84	29.3	22.7	33.4
85+	82.8	56.4	95.3
Eating			
65–74	6.3	8.5	4.7
75–84	15.3	17.6	13.9
85+	27.4	23.9	29.0
1 or more ADLs			
65–74	47.4	48.1	46.7
75–84	95.2	89.5	98.6
85+	238.8	218.8	247.7

Source: *Supplement on Aging*, 1984 Health Interview Survey.
Sample N (65+) = 11,497.

The results (Table 1.6) indicate that the greater ADL needs rate among men and women age 85+ combined with their demographic growth produces a substantial 173% increase in the likely need or demand for daily assistance and personal care during 1980 to 2010. By contrast, the growth in the number of middle-aged women as potential caregivers is only about one third the size of the growth in the need (Cutler, 1992).

Furthermore, even a ratio of about 4:1 may be optimistic considering likely changes in both the supply and the demand side of the caregiving equation. The actual number of caregivers may well be smaller than trends in the demographic supply of middle-aged women suggest, as increasing numbers of women enter the paid labor force, develop careers, and have salary and pension patterns that inhibit them from becoming full- or part-time caregivers.

On the demand side, an unintended consequence of improved health care technology and delivery may well be an increased number of older persons whose death (e.g., from heart attack, stroke, and cancer) is prevented or postponed, but who remain alive and somewhat ambulatory but in a more dependent condition.

A major symposium on this subject was published recently in the *Journal of Aging and Health* (Haan, Rice, Satariano, & Selby, 1991). The following summary by the symposium editors clearly points to a continuing future need for personal care to assist those elderly who have chronic disabilities and dependencies:

> Agreement appears to exist among the authors published here that an increasing proportion of the future disease burden will be taken up by nonfatal, chronic, often disabling conditions, such as cataracts and osteoarthritis. Furthermore, those saved from usually fatal conditions such as cardiovascular disease and cancer may suffer substantial levels of disability. (p. 136)

TABLE 1.6 Projected Need for Personal Care Persons with One or more ADL Limitations

Age group (years)	1980	1990	2000	2010	% Change: 1980–2010
65–74	737,139	869,412	863,487	996,042	35.1
75–84	735,990	945,052	1,142,015	1,159,308	57.5
85+	535,386	779,486	1,106,664	1,462,926	173.2
Total	2,008,515	2,593,949	3,112,166	3,618,276	80.1
Caregivers: women, age 55–64	11,551,000	11,260,000	12,601,000	18,257,000	58.1
Ratio of caregivers to care receivers	5.8	4.3	4.0	5.0	−12.3

International Patterns of Aging and Middle Aging

The financial impact of population aging is being felt throughout the world, especially in the economically developed countries (Giarini, 1990). Like their American cousins, European workers enjoy having the option of early retirement (Wartonick, 1980), causing their governments to have increasing concern about the financial burden of mature Social Security systems in the context of population aging (Liu, 1984).

The international significance of financial gerontology can be seen in the degree to which the patterns of aging identified in the United States are parallel to those found around the world (Gregg & Cutler, 1990). One of the greater similarities is the degree to which middle aging rather than old aging is the more notable population pattern during the next quarter century. Table 1.7, following the format of Table 1.3, compares the previous quarter century (1960-1985) with the new quarter century (1990-2015)—

TABLE 1.7 Middle Aging versus Older Aging in Two Quarter-Century Periods—Selected Countries: 1960-1985 versus 1990-2015

Age group (years)	Average annual population in each quarter-century		Change in each quarter century (%)	
	1960-1985	1990-2015	1960-1985	1990-2015
France				
45-64	10,983	14,146	10.4	36.3
65+	6,588	8,970	34.4	34.9
Sweden				
45-64	1,933	2,162	−4.6	14.7
65+	1,176	1,559	66.7	16.6
Japan				
45-64	21,199	33,961	82.1	3.1
65+	8,457	21,670	130.5	101.2
United States				
45-64	41,740	65,078	24.1	71.6
65+	22,020	35,918	71.1	39.9
More developed				
45-64	219,999	306,858	30.7	35.2
65+	109,140	177,753	67.7	44.6
Less developed				
45-64	363,247	803,624	77.2	119.2
65+	111,383	274,937	96.1	112.3
World				
45-64	583,246	1,110,482	57.7	91.5
65+	220,524	452,689	81.8	82.2

Population numbers in 1,000s.

for the middle- and old-age groups, for selected economically developed countries.

Although the size of the population numbers are different, the general patterns are similar. With the exception of Japan, the pattern found in these countries, and in the more developed and less developed country groups, are the same: 1960 to 1985 was a time in which the older (65+) age group had the larger growth. Comparing past with future, however, in each case (except Japan) there is an increase in the growth rate of the middle-aged group and a decrease in the growth rate for the older age group. This pattern is discernible even in the less developed countries, which are usually characterized by their high fertility rates and overall younger populations (Grigsby, 1991).

Japan is the only country in which middle aging was the dominant pattern of the past quarter century. This contrast with Japan directs us to an especially important dimension of financial gerontology. Much has been written during the past several years about the very low rate of personal savings in the United States, especially compared with Japan. Although the two countries and their national savings rates are often compared, there is typically less precision in the attention paid to differences in the age structure of the two countries—and the potential linkage between age and savings.

As mentioned earlier, at the individual level of analysis middle aging often includes such financial characteristics as increased earnings, changed patterns of spending, and a motivation to save and invest for the final quarter of life. Cross-national studies have also found evidence of a relationship between savings and middle age.

A Swedish study, for example, analyzed a sample of 20,000 individual tax returns in each of two successive years, comparing the imputed net savings for different age groups. It concludes that "the difference in the rate of savings between age groups is large enough to strongly indicate a higher 'savings ratio' in the age groups 50-65 than in the lower age groups" (Bentzel & Berg, 1983).

Demography, of course, is not the only factor that influences a nation's overall savings rate. A Japanese study noted that such factors as the structure of the Japanese Social Security system, the nature of retirement patterns and employment bonuses, and even religious-cultural factors all play their role in the evolution of personal savings practices (Shinohara, 1983). The author also finds evidence, however, that the high Japanese savings rate is in part a function of the concurrence of age and income dynamics in middle age.

A direct trend comparison of Japan and the United States is an appropriate way to conclude this overview of emerging research in financial gerontology. Figure 1.3 contrasts the percentage of middle agers in the two countries during 1950 to 2025. It is clear that middle aging in Japan began at least as early as the 1950s, whereas the United States does not begin a period of rapid middle aging until 1991—as the baby boomers enter middle age.

To the degree that the dynamics of middle aging do contribute to a propensity to save, then the comparative U.S.-Japan trends described in Figure 1.3 paint an optimistic picture for the United States. That is, whatever is contained in the population pattern that Japan has had for the past 25 years, the United States is about to get a lot of it. Clearly such concepts, hypotheses, and suggestive data as these direct us to a socially important and intellectually demanding agenda of research in financial gerontology.

THE BOETTNER INSTITUTE OF FINANCIAL GERONTOLOGY

The chapters in this book represent some of the initial efforts of a new research institute devoted to the definition and development of an emerging field of research: *financial gerontology*. The Boettner Institute of Financial Gerontology was established in 1986 with the view that human well-being and life satisfaction in the older years are strongly affected by financial well-being. In turn, financial well-being is not simply "money," but the relationship of objective financial resources to such subjective characteristics as the safety and certainty of financial resources, how well they are understood, and the confidence that older men and women and their families can have that, through public, private, and personal mechanisms, their financial status is secure.

The Boettner Institute takes as its mandate, therefore, a comprehensive conceptualization of financial gerontology as the study of the dynamics of financial well-being in the context of aging (and middle aging) during the life cycle and across generations. As the target is comprehensive, so must be the analytic tools; the work is broadly multidisciplinary and cross-disciplinary, as well as international in character. Especially innovative in the design of the Boettner Institute, has been the development of a program of systematic social science research deliberately connected to teaching and research in the fields of business and finance.

This unique combination of research activities and resources, representing social gerontology and financial services broadly conceived, is thus situated to learn from and contribute to both practitioner and academic constituencies. It represents an original institutional as well as intellectual contribution to the understanding of the financial dimensions of aging and human well-being. The chapters in this book include the 1987 to 1990 annual Boettner Lectures and related symposia papers. They offer the thinking, the analysis, and the writing of national scholars who themselves represent both academic and applied careers in the fields of both finance and aging.

Thus, this book suggests a forceful multiplicity of approaches to the study of financial gerontology.

45-64 as % of total population

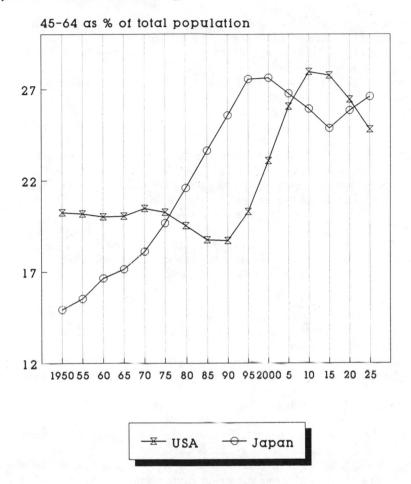

FIGURE 1.3 Middleaging: Japan versus United States.

REFERENCES

Beck, M. (1990, July 16). Trading places [Cover story]. *Newsweek*, pp. 48-54.

Bengtson, V. L., Cutler, N. E., Mangen, D., & Marshall, V. L. (1985). Generations, cohorts, and relations between age groups. In R. H. Binstock and E. Shanas (Eds.), *Handbook of aging and the social sciences*, (2nd ed., pp. 304-338). New York: Van Nostrand Reinhold.

Bentzel, R., & Berg, L. (1983). The role of demographic factors as a determinant of savings in Sweden. In F. Modigliani and R. Hemming (Eds.), *The determinants of national saving and wealth* (pp. 152-179). New York: St. Martin's Press.

Binstock, R. H., & George, L. K. (Eds.). (1990). *Handbook of aging and the social sciences* (3rd ed.). New York: Academic Press. (p.xv (is in preface)

Birren, J. E. (1990). Forward. In R. H. Binstock & L. K. George (Eds.), *Handbook of aging and the social sciences* (3rd ed., p. xiii). New York: Academic Press.

Brody, E. M. (1981). "Women in the middle" and family help to older people. *The Gerontologist, 21,* 471-480.

Chappell, N. L. (1990). Aging and social care. In R. H. Binstock & L. K. George (Eds.), *Handbook of aging and the social sciences* (3rd ed., pp. 438-454). New York: Academic Press.

Christopherson, D. L. (1989). Long-term care policies: The next generation? *Journal of the American Society of CLU & ChFC*, March, *XLIII* (2), 46-56.

Cutler, N. E. (1991a). Financial counseling with older adults. In S. R. Leimberg (Ed.), *Financial services professional's guide to the state of the art*, (pp. 10.11-18. Second Edition). Bryn Mawr, PA: The American College.

Cutler, N. E. (1991b). Older Americans Month, 1991: The value of diversity. *Journal of the American Society of CLU & ChFC,* May, *XLV* (3), 20-23.

Cutler, N. E. (in press). National estimates of functional limitation and the need for personal care in the older population, 1980-2010. In Bette R. Bonder (Ed.), *Occupational performance in the elderly.*

Cutler, N. E., & Gregg, D. W. (1991). The human "wealth span" and financial well-being in Older Age. *Generations,* Winter, 45-48.

Dresser, P. D., & Hill, K. (Eds.). (1989). *Research center directory* (14th ed., Vol. 2). Detroit: Gale Research.

Easterlin, R. A., Macdonald, C., & Macunovich, D. J. (1990). Retirement prospects of the baby boom generation: A different perspective. *The Gerontologist, 30,* 776-783.

Giarini, O. (1990). Introduction: The opportunities of the four pillars' strategy. *The Geneva Papers on Risk and Insurance* , *55,* 95-98.

Gregg, D. W. (1990). Introduction to "financial gerontology" column [Guest editorial]. *Journal of the American Society of CLU & ChFC*, November, *XLIV* (6).

Gregg, D. W., & Cutler, N. E. (1990). *Financial gerontology and the middle-aging of people and populations: Implications for future planning in insurance world-wide.* Paper presented at the annual meeting of the International Insurance Society, Paris, 1990.

Grigsby, J. S. (1991). Paths for future population aging. *The Gerontologist, 31,* 195-203.

Haan, M. N., Rice, D. P., Satariano, W. A., & Selby, J. V. (1991). Introduction: Living longer and doing worse? Present and future trends in the health of the elderly. *Journal of Aging and Health, 30,* 133-137.

Karp, D. A. (1988). A decade of reminders: Changing age consciousness between fifty and sixty years old. *The Gerontologist, 28,* 727-738.

Katz, S. T., Downs, T. D., Cash, H. R., & Grotz, R. C. (1970). Progress in the development of the index of ADL. *The Gerontologist, 10,* 20-30.

Liu, L. (1984). Social Security problems in Western European countries. *Social Security Bulletin, 47,* 17-22.

Longino, C. F. (1990). *Socioeconomic characteristics of retired persons in the United States with household income more than double the poverty level.* Bryn Mawr, PA: Boettner Institute of Financial Gerontology.

Packard, M. D., & Reno, V. P. (1988). A look at very early retirees. In R. Ricardo-Campbell & E. P. Lazear (Eds.), *Issues in Contemporary Retirement* (pp. 243–272). Stanford: Hoover Institution.

Pifer, A. (1986). The public policy response. In A. Pifer & L. Bronte (Eds.), *Our aging society* (pp. 391–413). New York: W. W. Norton.

Ryder, N. B. (1965). The cohort as a concept in the study of social change. *American Sociological Review, 30,* 843–861.

Schaie, K. W., & Willis, S. L. (1986). *Adult development and aging.* Glenview, IL: Scott, Foresman.

Shinohara, M. (1983). The determinants of post-war savings behaviour in Japan. In F. Modigliani & R. Hemming (Eds.), *The determinants of national saving and wealth* (152–179). New York: St. Martin's Press.

Taeuber, C. (1990). Diversity: The dramatic reality. In S. A. Bass, E. A. Kutza, & F. M. Torres-Gill (Eds.), *Diversity in aging* (pp. 1–45). Glenview, IL: Scott, Foresman.

Uhlenberg, P. (1985). Death and the family. In A. S. Skolnick & J. H. Skolnick (Eds.), *Family in transition* (5th ed., pp. 70–79). Boston: Little, Brown & Co. (Reprinted from *Journal of Family History,* 1980, *5,* 313–320).

Waldrop, J. (1991). The baby boom turns 45. *American Demographics,* January, 13(1), 22–27.

Wartonick, D. (1980). Social Security abroad: European attitudes toward retirement. *Social Security Bulletin, 43,* 26–28.

— 2 —

Aging in the Twenty-First Century
Matilda White Riley

It would be no news, of course, if I observed that aging in the 21st century will predictably be different from aging in the 20th. In the midst of all the other cataclysmic changes in this country and throughout the world, I almost hesitate to address such a topic as changes in aging.

Yet the changes are daunting. I have no crystal ball to dust off as an aid in considering them, but I *do* have some important observations to make. Among other changes, the increase in human longevity and its enormous implications for the aging process have to rank high. For the first time in history people are aging in a society where *most* people live to be old. In addition, although nearly three decades have been added to individual lives during the 20th century on the average, the entire world—and all our familiar social structures and institutions—are changing around these lives. These social changes affect people's lives in many dramatic ways that are still difficult for us to comprehend because we are part of them.

All this is well known. What *is* news is that social and behavioral scientists have begun to study these manifold changes, and to anticipate and debate the consequences for the future of the aging process and for its potential. That is, scientific research is providing many clues not only to what aging *may* be like in the future but also to what aging *could* be like if the potential is fulfilled. These clues require a revision of traditional views as to what aging means.

STRUCTURAL LAG

In this chapter I mainly discuss potentials. First, however, I want to tell you about a new insight that points to these potentials. This insight, recently

23

forged from research, defines one of the most perplexing problems of our time, the problem I call "structural lag." This concerns the mismatch between the two central changes before us here: (a) changes in individual aging and (b) changes in the structure of society that influence the ways individuals age. Although more and more people live longer than in the past and grow old in new ways, social structures have been slow to make room for them. These structures are still geared to the population of much younger people that characterized the 19th—certainly not the 21st—century.

Everyone can think of many personal anecdotes that illustrate this problem of structural lag, but I will tell about one closest to my own experience. Because my husband reached age 65 in 1973 he was required to retire as a top executive of a large national insurance company. He had to retire even though he was just reaching the peak of his vigor and his career. Jobs were for younger, not older, people. Of course, he is a special case, and during the intervening 17 years he has managed to create his own opportunities to be productive. These opportunities were not ready-made for him in contemporary society, however.

The point of this anecdote is that societal institutions are generally failing to make room for those many workers who, as they age, continue to be capable and are not yet ready for full retirement. Similarly, health care systems often fail to provide the supports necessary for the many older people who, even when frail, now want to function independently. Unlike roles for school children or young entrants into the labor force, few roles have been developed to fit workers or students who have grown old. Nor does society accord esteem and prestige to the significant productivity of older people's *unpaid* roles as homemakers or caretakers of the disabled. So I speak of this current mismatch as "structural lag" because the structure of social opportunities has not kept pace with the rapid changes in the ways that people are now growing old.

Clearly this mismatch is fraught with contemporary problems. Yet also within it lie untold promising potentials for the future. My message here is one of optimism. I shall argue that many of these potentials can become realities—that the mismatch can be reduced by diverse kinds of intervention. Intervention can occur through both public and private policies, changes in professional practice, and individual choices in everyday life. After all, the future does not just happen; it is created by human beings.

This is my vision: If the 20th century has been the era of increasing longevity, the 21st century will be the era of social opportunities for older people to age in new and better ways.

To explain this prediction I am going to explore various kinds of intervention (both deliberate and "naturally" occurring social changes). First, I shall discuss the potentials for aging—that is, how to optimize the already incredible strengths of people as they grow older. Second, and most critical for the 21st century, I shall consider the potentials for our outdated social structures—how to optimize the social opportunities for older people (and thereby to reduce the problem of structural lag). Third, I shall offer a conceptual framework that social scientists use as an aid to the understanding of individual aging, social opportunities, and the mismatch between them. Of course such understanding is essential to a scientifically grounded vision of aging in the future and to the changes needed for bringing this vision into reality.

OPTIMIZING INDIVIDUAL AGING

To begin with individual aging, let me call your attention to the unrecognized strengths and capacities of most older people. I shall destroy the myth that aging is exclusively a biological process. I shall ask you to think along with me that people do not grow up and grow old in laboratories, but rather in rapidly changing societies. I shall report evidence for the proposition that the aging process is not fixed; it is mutable and subject to intervention and improvement.

The Fallacy of Inevitable Aging Decline

Much research has demonstrated that the doctrine of "inevitable aging decline" is a fallacy—a fallacy initiated by faulty interpretation of cross-sectional data. Nevertheless, despite all the evidence to the contrary, this fallacious doctrine is still blindly accepted by many government policy makers, corporate executives, professional practitioners, and the public at large. The stereotype of inevitable decline remains stubborn; the very notion of aging seems to connote decrepitude, poverty, and misery (e.g., "afflicted with Alzheimer's disease," "imprisoned in a nursing home," or "dependent on medicine" as the only means of preventing either disease or institutionalization). Doctors are found to spend less time with older than with younger patients. Older people themselves take their aches and pains for granted, and assume—falsely—that they cannot learn new skills or ways of thinking (such as use of computers or complicated technologies).

The "Real" Aging Process: Neither Fixed, nor Immutable

Yet those who listen to the evidence will realize that it is simply not true that *because of age* all older people are destined to be ill, impoverished, cut off from society, sexually incapacitated, despondent, or unable to reason or to remember. Of course, everyone dies. Some older people—a minority—are seriously disadvantaged, and in need of personal and societal support. Most older people, however, function independently and effectively (see Figure 2.1).

Projections for the population 65 and older

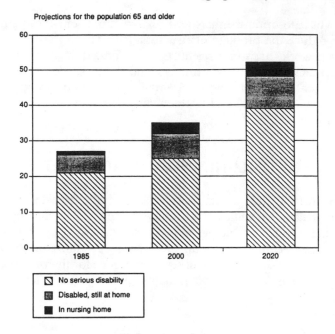

FIGURE 2.1 Increasing number of older people.

Projections for the population age 65 and older.
Source: Data supplied by Kenneth Manton and adapted with permission (Duke University).

The total number of people age 65 and older will predictably multiply in the 21st century as indicated by the rising heights of the bars in Figure 2.1; the large number of the healthy (bottom of each bar), however, will heavily outweigh the number of disabled or institutionalized people (top of each bar). Figure 2.1 underscores the first part of my message—that most older people are healthy and capable now, and will continue to be in the 21st century.

In this chapter I cannot focus directly on the critical problems of the minority who *are* irrevocably disabled or fatally ill. Rather I shall discuss "most" older people, who have even far greater and more diverse strengths and competence—in intellect, health, and interest in affairs—than are indicated in Figure 2.1 or recognized generally.

Moreover, the research evidence demonstrates that the aging process is variable—so that still greater strengths are possible. Social scientists are showing how the aging process varies with social conditions: how individuals grow old in widely diverse ways depending on their family life, socioeconomic status, and work conditions. Social scientists are also showing how the aging process changes over time as society changes. My grandmother at age 75 was very different from what I was at age 75, and my granddaughters will be still different when they reach age 75—because we were born at different times and grew older in different periods of history.

At a recent seminar at the National Institute on Aging a Danish researcher, Marianne Schroll, in reporting on some impressive cohort studies, showed a picture of a 70-year-old in 1984 and a 70-year-old in 1964 (see Figure 2.2). The contrast suggests how older people in Denmark have changed just during the last two decades.

Entire cohorts of people already old differ markedly from cohorts not yet old as to education, work history, standard of living attitudes, cultural tastes, diet and exercise, physical stature, age of menarche, experience with chronic rather than acute diseases, and so on.

Perhaps the most notable of all the historical alterations in the aging process spring from the unprecedented increases in longevity—which allow recent cohorts of young people to stay in school many years longer than their predecessors did, prolong retirement, postpone many diseases of old age, accumulate the experiences essential for wisdom, and extend family rela-

FIGURE 2.2 Are the elderly today "younger" than the elderly 20 years ago?

Source: Unpublished sketch by Marianne Schroll, Glostrup Center for Population Studies, 1964–1989, Denmark.

tionships, so that husbands and wives now typically survive together for 4 or even 5 decades or more. (For my husband and I next year will be our 60th year of marriage). It is these more recent cohorts who will be the old people of the 21st century.

Potentials for Intervention

In short, the aging process is mutable, and most older people are able to draw on widely diverse competencies—in health, intellect, and involvement in affairs. In addition (to reemphasize the point), there is significant potential for enhancing these strengths still further. Just consider what this means for the 21st century. Death is inevitable, but the nature of the aging process is not inevitable—after all, it is the quality of the later years that counts.

What kinds of intervention, then, might sustain or even enhance this quality in the future? Social and behavioral research has been producing some spectacular findings.

- Among older workers intellectual functioning improves with age if the work situation is challenging and calls for self-direction.
- Very old people whose performance on intelligence tests has deteriorated can be brought back to their performance levels of 20 years earlier if the social environment affords incentives and opportunities for practicing and learning new strategies.
- Memory can be enhanced if the impoverished context that often characterizes retirement is altered to include the stimulation of a rich and complex environment.
- Even slowed reaction time, long attributed to irreversible aging losses in central nervous system functioning, can be speeded up if the social situation provides training and consistent feedback.
- Changing the social environment in nursing homes to increase the sense of personal control and independence in aging patients can result in greater social activity, changed immune functioning, and perhaps even lowered mortality.

Moreover, even when alterations in behavior, life-styles, and social contacts are made late in life, such alterations can still reduce morbidity and mortality. To stop cigarette smoking at age 60, for example, can make a difference.

OPTIMIZING SOCIAL OPPORTUNITIES

So much for the incredible strengths and potential capacities of older people. Please note, however, that all these and many similar instances of intervention in the ways people age are characterized by one common theme: The older person's functioning is contingent on the social conditions. Bereft of social opportunities, resources, or incentives, older people cannot use or sustain their mental or physical strengths and capacities, and the "doctrine of inevitable aging decline" becomes a self-fulfilling prophecy. Thus, the root of the mismatch lies not in people's capacities or in the aging process itself, but in the lack of suitable social roles through which individuals can move as they grow older. Consequently, aging in the 21st century will depend on changes in society—on reduction of the 20th-century lag in social structures.

The Current Lag

Today's social structures and norms are the vestigial remains of the 19th century, when most people died before their work was finished or their last child had left home. Age 65 was established as the criterion for insurance eligibility in Germany back in the 1870s—yet age 65 is still used in many countries under today's utterly changed conditions of longevity. The older population is, of course, widely heterogeneous, but here are some examples of typical misfits between aging and social structures:

- For many decades now opportunities for older workers have been declining. Today less than half of men age 55 and older are in the labor force, a fraction that could drop to only one third by the start of the 21st century. For women, whose recent entry into the paid labor force will have untold consequences, the lag is even more pronounced. Yet survey after survey has indicated that many older workers wish to continue some kind of work—if the hours are flexible and the pay acceptable.
- In the family many older people are widows who live entirely alone. Those who are frail often lack social supports to maintain independent living in their own homes. Health care facilities are inadequate and costly, and people who are disabled often lack caretakers; many live in fear of destitution.
- Older people's place in society generally has aptly been called a "roleless role."

In sum, modifications in the role structure of society have indeed lagged behind the rapid changes in the process of aging—changes in the strengths, as well as in the numbers, of older people themselves. So far these structures have largely failed to aid older people in developing or expressing their remarkable potentials.

Potentials for Intervention in the Twenty-First Century

Nevertheless, research on social structures is beginning to show that, like the aging process, they too are mutable. Here again intervention to correct structural lag is found to be possible, and the possibilities in the 21st century are predictably far-flung. Consider a few scattered attempts at optimizing role structures for older people that are already under way and that give clear evidence of what is possible in the future.

In *education* opportunities are being made for older people either to teach (teaching adults who cannot read, for example, or immigrants who cannot speak English), or to go back to school. Nearly 1,000 colleges in the United States now accept students older than age 65.

In *leisure* opportunities are being made both for recreation and for more serious cultural pursuits. The Elderhostel movement is thriving worldwide, and retirement communities are increasingly located close to university facilities.

In the *household* opportunities for frail older people to remain independent are being improved through supportive community services, injury-proof housing design, and elder-friendly tools older people can use.

Throughout the *health care system* there are increasing demands for older people in the role of care*giver* (rather than care *receiver*).

At *work* there is increasing provision of part-time work, job sharing, and flexible hours. Some companies have model programs for "unretirement," that is, for rehiring retired employees. There are untold opportunities for moonlighting in work that is not officially identified in official employment statistics. There are increasingly varied and significant opportunities for many kinds of volunteer jobs.

And this is the right moment to mention *financial gerontology* as the focus of the Boettner Institute of Financial Gerontology. Already we have begun to witness the development of increasingly flexible contracts: contracts that combine insurance and investment features, contracts that contain stop-and-go provisions, contracts that anticipate changing financial requirements during the life course, contracts that give people increasing control over the traditional problem of economic security. These changes are harbingers of a 21st-century array of new financial instruments and arrangements.

All such structural interventions are producing new and more flexible roles, and wider options, for older people. Whether or not particular older individuals wish to remain in the economic mainstream of society or to be productive in the many unpaid and volunteer roles, one point is clear: Older people do not wish now, nor will they wish in the next century, to be disregarded, denigrated, or dependent.

Implications for All Ages

There is also another noteworthy point here. As such structural intervention develops in the next century it will have implications for people of all ages: young and (as in the Boettner Institute's emphasis) middle-aged—not *just* the old. Making room in a college classroom for older adults also affects the lives of traditional students who are younger. Any structural intervention, even though aimed at the old, will predictably have ramifications affecting how everyone grows older.

Indeed, I believe we can anticipate in practice in the 21st century what we once regarded as a purely visionary potential, the breakdown of the rigid age barriers that have traditionally divided societal roles into three parts: education in youth, work in middle age, and leisure in old age. Those "age-segregated" social structures may be giving way to more "age-integrated" structures—providing options for people during their lifetimes to intersperse periods of work with periods of education and leisure.

Furthermore, we can even begin to see signs of deliberate structural intervention to support this interspersing—to make it possible for people to move from school to work and later go from work back again to school; to change careers; and to spread leisure more evenly over the life course rather than concentrating nearly all of it in retirement. For example, some organizations are providing educational leaves from work, more portable pensions, or retraining for older adults and preparation for new occupations; others are allowing employees during their work lives to take several years of leave, to be spent—according to choice—in family care, for travel, or in continuing education.

Unintended Consequences

All these are heady portents of aging in the 21st century. One critical question remains, however: How can we ensure that changes and intervention undertaken today will optimize (rather than diminish) older people's opportunities for the future? This question requires far-reaching vision and the knowledge base essential for intervention, because intervention can sometimes have unintended and undesired consequences. For example, encouraging everyone to engage in physical exercise, though intended for lifelong strengthening of joints and muscles, may injure them instead; providing tender loving care in nursing homes, though intended as emotional support for older patients, may instead reduce independence and effective functioning; and encouraging older people to work may result in abuse of older workers.

Even elaborately designed kinds of intervention can turn out to have very little effect. For example, legislation to abolish age as a basis for mandatory retirement has failed to slow the trend toward retiring early.

Conversely, *failure* to intervene can exacerbate rather than reduce structural lag. For example, suppose the traditional trends are simply allowed to persist. A German scholar, Martin Kohli, has recently calculated the absurd outcome: Sometime in the second half of the 21st century society could arrive at a point when people, at the age of about 38, will move from the university directly into retirement! This is an absurd idea, to be sure (but I am not being absurd when I predict the end of nearly universal early retirement as we know it today).

The mission for social scientists, then, is to help guide intervention by providing not only a broad vision but also a firm scientific grounding for this vision.

CONCEPTUAL VIEW OF INTERVENTION

Toward this end a conceptual framework from the sociology of age is widely used for getting a handle on the future (as shown in Figure 2.3). It represents social space bounded by ages on the vertical axis and by dates on the horizontal axis. These dates indicate the course of history—past and future. Within this space two sets of lines crisscross each other. These refer to changes in aging and in social structures.

Aging

Consider first the diagonal lines, which refer to aging. They represent successive cohorts of people who were born in particular time periods and who are aging. As people age they move along the diagonal (see, e.g., Cohort A in Figure 2.3), across time and upward through the social structure; they pass through the successive roles in family life, school grades and work careers, retirement, and ultimately death. As they age they change biologically, psychologically, and socially, and they develop their individual strengths and capacities.

Moreover, because successive cohorts (the series of diagonals) are born at different dates and live through different segments of historical time, people in different cohorts age in different ways. Thus, a man born in 1890 (Cohort A) could scarcely have looked ahead to retirement at all, but a man born in 1950 (Cohort C, now 40 years old) can expect to spend one quarter of his adult lifetime in retirement.

The diagonals in Figure 2.3 are not purely abstract. They are used to aid understanding of "growing old in the 21st century"—because facts about the past lives of people now alive are already established. By tracing their lives into the future, we can use these facts to forecast how they will grow old.

Many facts are now available as guideposts to the future. In some ways future cohorts of older people will predictably be better off than their pre-

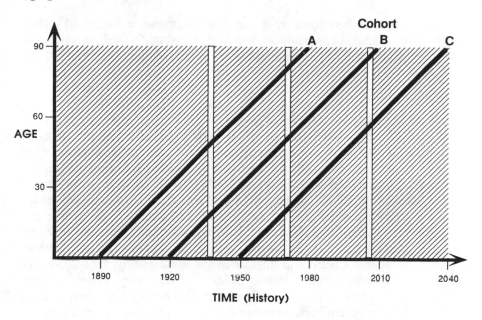

FIGURE 2.3 Conceptual framework: Aging and social change.

Source: Riley, M. W., Foner, A., & Waring, J. (1988). Sociology of age. In N. J. Smeiser (Ed.), *Handbook of sociology*, pp. 243-290. NY: Sage. Reprinted by permission.

decessors. For example, with improved nutrition, exercise, and reduced cigarette smoking in early life, they may well be less subject to heart disease when they reach later life. In other ways, however, the future cohorts of older people may be *less* advantaged than their predecessors: Their lives will reflect the deteriorating economic conditions of today and the increasing proportion of young people who are failing to meet acceptable standards of academic achievement.

Two trends among women are especially provocative: An increasing proportion of young women in each successive cohort has participated in the labor force, and an increasing proportion has also experienced a divorce. We sometimes think of these as negative indications for the future. Do they perhaps mean instead that, as these young women become the older women of the future, they will have acquired more skills than their predecessors for living independently? Will their early work experience have increased the future economic security of the many who will predictably live alone in the next century?

Given this wide variety of early life experiences, one point about the older people of the future seems certain: They will be widely heterogeneous (as indicated by their heterogeneity in health status, shown in Figure 2.1). Their needs for structural opportunities will be increasingly varied, and different types of people will call for different types of intervention.

Structural Change

In short, precisely what these older people will be like, how they will grow old, and what their needs will be will depend in part on their past lives. In large part, however, they will also depend on the changing structure of society. The perpendicular lines in the figure schematize this structure and its changes. Consider a past year, such as 1980. Here the vertical line is a cross-section slice through all the diagonal lines. This slice denotes the age structure at a single moment in history. It indicates how both the people and their social roles are organized roughly in age groupings, from the youngest at the bottom to the oldest at the top. Along this slice, one can imagine how people of all ages coexist and interact in the same society. In a family, for example, members of four different generations interrelate, either by forming close ties or by engaging in conflict. In another example, a nation's wealth can be distributed equitably between old and young, or—as some contend is already happening—so inequitably as to favor old people at the expense of children.

Over time, as society moves through past and future historical events and changes, one can imagine this vertical line moving—across the space from one date to the next. Over time, the age-related structures of opportunities are subject to social and cultural changes. Over time, the people in a particular age strata are no longer the same people; inevitably they are continually being replaced by younger entrants from more recent cohorts with more recent life experiences.

It is from these changes that the phenomenon of structural lag has been emerging. Today older people have become more numerous, better educated, and more vigorous than their predecessors back in 1940 or 1970; so far, however, few structural changes in society have been made for them. They are still generally treated as a disadvantaged minority—that is, they are handicapped by the lag. It is here that intervention will be especially crucial for the 21st century.

Asynchrony

One last—and I think intriguing—feature of Figure 2.3 is the inherent paradox of timing. Aging individuals are moving along the axis of the life course, the diagonal lines. Change in the structures of society (the moving vertical line), however, moves along its own axis of historical time. These two sets of lines are continually crisscrossing each other. Hence, they can never be perfectly synchronized. It is this asynchrony that accounts for the recurring mismatch between them—a mismatch that creates continuing pressures for intervention.

To return now to the critical question with which I began: How can the current lag be adjusted? How will structures change (or be changed) to foster the growing numbers, strengths, and heterogeneity of older people in the 21st century? The details are still dim; however, our conceptual diagram opens up glimpses into the future.

My view of the future can now be quickly summarized. We can discern a vision of a future society in which older people's lives are more varied, more open to choice, more rewarding. We can glimpse aging in a possible future society where lifelong learning will replace the lockstep of traditional education; a society in which ageist discrimination will no longer be a dominant force; a society in which entirely new arrangements for financial security will characterize the life course; a society in which retirement as we know it today will disappear and will be replaced by periods of leisure interspersed throughout life with periods of education and work; and a society in which the values of kinship and intimacy are matters of choice, not duty.

At this point the vision fades, to be replaced by the reality that these kinds of intervention have yet to be invented. I can, however, conclude with one sure prediction, theoretically grounded and empirically demonstrable: Capable older people and empty role structures cannot long coexist. Aging in the 21st century, in which the tension between the two must be continuously adjusted, will bear little resemblance to aging as we have known it in the 20th century.

END NOTES

A final word of credit, first, to the many works by colleagues and fellow social scientists on which my work has drawn; and, second, to themes of previous Boettner Lectures, which were brought out again in the following chapters.

The 1989 lecture on "Critical Policy Issues for Pensions," by my deeply missed friend William Greenough (see Chapter 3), showed how social changes affecting older people's financial security have been brought about through a "partnership of government, private sector, and individual efforts." Complementing such deliberate policy interventions, other changes influence older people's lives through latent processes that I call "cohort norm formation," with little awareness or overall control by the persons or agencies involved. For example, the remarkable century-long rise in women's participation in the labor force occurred through millions of separate decisions by individual women and individual employers, with members of each new cohort readier than their predecessors to accept the norm of women's occupational role. Such subtle forces will predictably combine with policies to shape the lives of older people in the 21st century.

Still more fundamental than the processes that change lives are the values that give meaning to these changes. In the 1987 Boettner Lecture another long-time friend and a coworker in the sociology of age, George Maddox (see Chapter 4), raised this question of values in his "Aging and Well-Being." George is concerned, as I am, not only with sociological principles for "inventing the future of aging" but also with what constitutes well-being—what in the best of all future worlds the good life can be. How can the quality of the added years be optimized in the 21st century? In addressing this question, George gave a "multi-faceted" definition of well-being that coupled longevity with "functional and economic independence, and happiness." Surely adequate health and income are central desiderata. Yet we must also ask: Are new societal values being forged even now by the cohorts of people who will be old in the next century—as they anticipate many years in retirement or, alternatively, look ahead to new careers with potentially lower financial rewards? Will older people's well-being also require opportunities for entirely new forms of productivity—including such activities as the exchange of experience and wisdom, the giving and receiving of social supports, esteem, and affection? Imponderable as such value questions seem, no examination of the potentials for aging in the 21st century can leave them out of account.

—— 3 ——

Critical Policy Issues
for Pensions

William C. Greenough

Reasonable economic security for America's elderly is very new. Only one work-ing lifetime ago 90% of Americans were dependent in their old age. They were America's poor poor—discriminated against and shoved aside, in less than good health. Much of this has changed dramatically in only half a century. The eld-erly are not affluent, but the proportion who are really poor is only about the same as in the general population. Although they are not yet in the mainstream of society, they are closer to it. They are also healthy longer.

What has changed during these decades? Social Security has taken effect, among other things.

The first Social Security benefits were paid in 1940. Yet by 1950 only 3% of the total income of elderly persons came from Social Security (Greenough & King, 1976, p. 18). Seven percent came from pension plans provided by private and public employers, 29% from assets, 11% from public assistance and veterans' benefits, and 50% from earnings. Today 38% of the aggregate income of the population age 65 and older comes from Social Security; 15% comes from occupational pensions, 17% from earnings, and 26% from as-sets (Grad, 1988). Looked at in terms of people instead of dollars, 91% of households with people older than age 64 now report receiving income from Social Security, 40% from an occupational pension, 20% from current earn-ings, and 67% from assets.

I have watched and been a part of efforts for better economic security for older Americans for almost 50 years. This Boettner lecture challenges me to take a comprehensive view of public policy issues on retirement security— what I believe we have done right in the past and what changes should be made. My objective will be to integrate all aspects of pensions and try to make recommendations that coordinate public and private efforts. Too big an assignment? Of course, but I plan to enjoy myself, recommending actions covering broad global trends and minutia with equal relish.

I shall present a number of, I hope, internally consistent and reinforcing recommendations for what needs to be done during the next wave of public action in the field of financial gerontology. They are the product of long experience and much thought, but in this lecture I do not have adequate time to support the conclusions with full reasoning or statistics.

My overall goal is to suggest a system of Social Security, private pensions, and personal savings benefits that will produce comfortable retirement security for Americans through economically and socially viable arrangements that strengthen the American economy.

THE NEED FOR RESEARCH

This brings me to my first comment on the future, a future in which the Boettner Institute of Financial Gerontology can play a significant role. Its chosen field of interest—financial gerontology—is a happy marriage of financial and human values in aging.

In coming months and years some portion of the intense concentration on financial well-being can be shifted toward learning more about the attitudes, expectations, hopes, and fears of middle-aged and older people about their financial security in old age. Public and private attitudes about Social Security, private pensions, taxes, insurance, work, and retirement, and questions of health, health care, and health cost all need additional systematic and innovative research efforts.

The "social demography" of aging is another needed item on the agenda of financial gerontology. We all recognize that the numbers of "older" persons (age 65 and older) in the United States have dramatically changed, from 4% of the population in 1900 (Greenough & King, 1976) to 13% in 1990 to a projected 17% in 2020 (Spencer, 1989). It is not just the gross size of this population that is relevant here, but who these people are: their employment history, their changing roles as men and women, and the opening or closing of economic opportunity for them.

Although I shall not discuss health benefits or catastrophic care, these issues are crucial factors in achieving true financial security in old age.

SOCIAL SECURITY

I believe that the Social Security system in the United States is, on balance, strong, well designed, and permanent. The 1983 Social Security amendments provided a sound enough framework, a liberal enough benefit schedule, and a fair enough tax treatment to justify public confidence. If we don't mess it up now, it will be there when our children are retired.

By far the most important long-term objective for the old-age, survivors, and disability insurance (OASDI), the wage-based part of Social Security, is for it to get and keep the confidence of the working population. In the 1970s and early 1980s public opinion polls showed an alarming lack of faith on the part of younger workers that Social Security would still be there when they retired. Several of the following recommendations are designed to achieve fair and equitable treatment of younger workers.

Financing

For half a century politicians have debated whether Social Security should be, or in fact can be, funded like private pensions. The answer has been to finance Social Security on a current-cost basis, with a contingency fund to bridge the gap between lower payroll tax receipts and higher benefit payments during periods of recession. When tax receipts exceed benefit payments, the excess is placed in special trust-fund obligations of the federal government.

A new aspect of this discussion has arisen recently: Should not Social Security build up a sizable reserve fund to meet the increasing benefit payments that will be required when baby boomers retire early in the 21st century? In the 1930s, there were 10 people in the age group 18 to 64 for each person age 65 and older. By 1960 the ratio of workers to beneficiaries had dropped to 5.1 and to 3.3 by 1985. Social Security actuaries estimate that it will stay above 3 workers per beneficiary during the next 20 to 25 years and then decline to about 2 during the following 2 decades as the baby boomers retire. Sounds like a perfect case for using the successful insurance principle of prefunding future estimated benefit obligations, does it not? Just invest the amount needed for prefunding the benefits in America's productive enterprises—General Motors, General Electric, General Telephone, General Signal, General Nuisance. All $2 trillion of it? Or $5 trillion? Or $12 trillion? If it were possible to accomplish this, it would be an intriguing example of how to achieve socialism without the bother of voting for it. The fact is, full or even substantial prefunding is not possible, because of the vast sums of money that would be withdrawn from consumption channels and the impossibility of transferring the necessary amount of goods forward to the next generation.

Wage Taxes and the Surplus

Social Security is a transfer system between generations and among recipients in one generation. Employment taxes are the largest tax load that most workers bear. How can we achieve fairness? The benefit schedules are heavily weighted, as they should be, toward workers with low earnings, and the tax rates are a flat percentage of wages up to the threshold level. This amounts to a progressive wage tax on workers when taxes are compared with benefits; that is, the recipient at the higher pay levels receives fewer benefits for the same amount of taxes. This is good public policy and is accepted by the American public.

The impact of the social security wage tax, however, shifts dramatically when the current taxes substantially exceed current benefit payments. When any considerable portion of the wage tax is diverted, through the trust fund, to the federal budget, that amount constitutes a regressive tax. It means that a flat percentage wage tax with a cap is partially financing the federal budget deficit—the government's regular operations, the military budget, and other components of the deficit. Two presidents and several Congresses in a row, taking highly political actions, have condemned, and then condoned and increased, the federal deficit and understated it by an amount equal to the excess Social Security tax receipts.

A year ago I started tossing on a pile in my office the plethora of suggestions for using the growing Social Security surplus. The pile is a foot high now. They are good suggestions: "Better schools—invest in our future human capital." "Finance Medicaid and Medicare and continuing care." "Day care." "Higher Social Security benefits." "Rebuild America's infrastructure—interstate highways, bridges, public buildings." Whichever of these worthy projects are implemented should be financed from general revenues or carry their own financing, not paid for with diverted OASDI funds "just because they are there." OASDI has not been financed by general revenues, and OASDI taxes should not be diverted to other uses through general revenues.

After much thought my conclusion is that Social Security taxes should be set at a level sufficient to meet about one year's benefit payments. No large surpluses or deficits should accrue.

The Retirement Age

One of the most powerful social and economic factors is the normal age for receiving full Social Security benefits. By good fortune all the forces line up on the same side, that of increasing the retirement age. The later retirement age would recognize the population's increasing health and life span, and public and congressional opposition to compulsory retirement ages. Postponement also takes into account our demographic trends, including the proportion of workers to retired persons, thereby helping keep the system financially in balance. The 1983 amendments gradually extending the normal retirement age to 67 by 2027 was a compromise. The President's Commission on Pension Policy, the Committee for Economic

Development (CED), and various other groups have generally advocated increasing the normal retirement age to 68 or 70, and phasing the change in earlier than 2027.

Raising the retirement age, however, will not have the desired financial effect unless the delayed retirement credit (the added benefit payment), scheduled to reach 8% a year in 2008, is rescinded. Politically it may be inadvisable to attempt to rescind the original 3% increase legislated in 1973, but at least the added 5% should be dropped. The provision represents confused analogies between social and private pensions. If the full actuarial increase–about 8%–is paid out to late retirees, there is no actuarial gain to the Social Security fund and no resulting solution to long-term financial pressures resulting from demographic trends. As to the argument that the 8% is needed as an incentive to delay retirement, several comments can be made. Why should social policy try to *induce* (as distinct from allowing) oldsters to continue in the work force? Are there not enough inducements already–the earnings from work, the desire to keep active, the generally higher wages of oldsters? The 8% "inducement" is an ill-advised provision of the Social Security law.

To sum up, I believe that at a convenient time the early retirement age under Social Security should be moved up from age 62 to age 65, and the normal retirement age of 67, which was specified in the 1983 amendments, should increase to age 68 and then to age 70. The changes should be phased in to coordinate with demographic changes. The delayed retirement credit should be repealed.

Means, or Needs, Testing

When Social Security amendments are being considered, well-intentioned people, from rich and high-income earners to "liberal" income redistributers, often ask: "Why should I get Social Security benefits; I don't need them? Just pay Social Security benefits to the poor." This is a misunderstanding of the whole idea of the great social income-transfer programs around the world, none of which have needs tests. They are not programs for the poor; they are programs to keep productive people from being poor. They are generational transfer programs, a government mechanism by which workers can, during their retirement, receive adequate income as a matter of dignified right, not charity. Those suggesting introducing a needs test probably think they are being generous; in a real sense they are being demeaning: "See how successful I am." They also are saying, although I doubt if they mean to, "If you want to beat the system, do not be thrifty; be sure to end up without funds, and then, but only then, the general public will take care of you as a charity case, along with those who are genuinely in need." The heart of Social Security is the receipt of benefits as a matter of right, related to previous productive employment, not charity. Means testing must never be introduced into the OASDI program.

The Retirement Test

Another controversial aspect of Social Security is the "retirement test" (also known as the "earnings test"). It is usually, but erroneously, stated in terms of workers who are under age 70 losing part or all of their benefits if their earnings from covered employment exceed a certain amount. Found in social income programs throughout the world, this is a sort of "presumed needs test." Therefore is it not bad? Does it not take away benefits that have been paid for? Does it not destroy incentive? Does it not lead to underground economy?

A major tenet of the Great Depression of the 1930s continues to be viable: Retirement benefits are to be paid to former workers who have withdrawn from the work force. Social Security is not a system to transfer income from young workers to old workers. Current Social Security tax rates were not designed to cover payments to all who continue to work beyond age 65. More important, there is no rationale for suddenly increasing a continuing worker's income substantially—that is, by the amount of Social Security benefits—the moment he or she reaches age 65 and then reducing it again sharply when actual retirement from employment occurs. That would be an expensive notch in income, costing many billions of dollars and not even being particularly useful in terms of life-income stream. The retirement test should not be eliminated, and indeed the age cap on the retirement test should be moved up from age 70 to at least age 75.

Taxing of Employee Contributions

A major policy objective for the future should be to defer income taxation on money contributed from wages to the Social Security system. (This should likewise apply to private pension contributions). It is especially inappropriate to include in taxable income those amounts that are being transferred from currently productive workers to those who are retired, and it could be a source of intergenerational stress. Young workers also have a right to be treated fairly in our society. The President's Commission on Pension Policy, the CED, and other organizations have recommended eliminating employee contributions to Social Security from current taxable income. This step could have been taken with style and effectiveness in conjunction with any one of the three first Reagan income tax cuts, but the opportunity was missed. Because the amount of tax revenue lost would be very large, nothing can be done until some future major tax realignment. As soon as financially feasible, employee contributions to Social Security should be removed from taxable income.

Should We Tax All Old-Age, Survivors, and Disability Insurance (OASDI) Benefits?

Strong pressures are developing to tax all Social Security benefits fully. This was the recommendation of the President's Commission on Pension Policy, the CED, and other studies—but only as part of a package that included eliminating taxes on contributions made by workers to Social Security. Until employee contributions are removed from taxable income, only half the Social Security benefits should be included in taxable income. For complex reasons this would be a better compromise solution than one that is frequently espoused—namely, taxing full benefits after the retiree has received back an amount equal to his or her contributions.

The Taxable Income Threshold

Social Security benefits are not includable in taxable income until other taxable income reaches $32,000 for married couples and $25,000 for singles. In 1983 it was a courageous decision to touch Social Security benefits with any taxation, and the threshold was a political compromise. This compromise, however, created an anomaly: Young, working, productive members of society have to include all their earnings in taxable income including the Social Security taxes they pay, whereas retired people, precisely because they are receiving transfer payments from the younger families, have a free ride with Social Security benefits up to the threshold level. This makes little sense. If the income threshold is removed, it will not hurt the poor, whose income is well below the threshold, and it will bring in appropriate revenue. The elderly will then be closer to being on the same footing as younger people regarding exemptions and deductions. At the present time many elderly people have a gratuitous extra tax exemption for their entire Social Security benefit. Eliminating the income threshold of $32,000 for married couples and $25,000 for a single person will remove another potential cause of intergenerational friction.

Escalation of Benefits

Social Security benefits are escalated by cost-of-living adjustments. This is appropriate and since 1974 has helped us avoid the biennial tinkering by Congress that had previously driven the system into financial trouble. In many countries the cost-of-living escalation of social benefits is limited—say, to 70% of the change in the cost of living—or is capped at a percentage or currency amount. If a change is ever considered, I think a different approach would be good. From time to time the cost of living goes up faster than wage rates. This means that young, productive members of society see their own incomes rising more slowly than those of the people to whom they are transferring their Social Security taxes. If any change were to be made in escalation, Social Security benefits should increase by cost-of-living increases *except* when wage rate increases are less, in which case the wage index would be used.

While I am on the subject of change let me emphasize my relief that Congress and the administration have, since 1983, generally left Social Security alone. Perhaps the Washington admonition, "Social Security is the third rail of politics—touch it and you are dead," really works well.

Changes in Social Security should be made in an omnibus bill at 5- to 10-year intervals, after careful study, and its provisions should be designed to be consistent with each other and not just a reaction to the political pressure group of the moment. The general thrust of these long-range proposals is to remove what I believe to be a present tilt against the young workers whose wage taxes support the system. This approach is against my own short-term interests, but perhaps this lends credibility to my recommendations. I believe everyone has a paramount interest in making sure that all generations are treated fairly to maintain strong support for the Social Security system.

PRIVATE PENSIONS

Let me set the stage for discussion of critical issues for private pensions by recounting how pensions developed in the college world, taken from my forthcoming book on the history of the Teachers Insurance and Annuity Association–College Retirement Equities Fund (TIAA-CREF). As Senator Jacob Javits said when he introduced the Employee Retirement Income Security Act (ERISA), "Perhaps we have something to learn from the colleges' pension plan." Pensions in the college world essentially started in 1906, with Andrew Carnegie's stunning announcement that he was giving $15 million to provide free pensions for college faculty members. These free pensions could be taken from employer to employer as long as the professor stayed within a specific group of 96 of the most prestigious colleges and universities in America. There were many things wrong with this pioneering system: The pensions were gratuities and not contractual; a gift of free pensions did not seem to bring out the most lovable characteristics of college professors; the mortality, interest, and salary assumptions were grossly inadequate. The plan was a defined-benefit final-salary plan, which meant there were indeterminate obligations supported by fixed and limited resources. Carnegie's $15 million should have been $100 million. Despite all the problems, portable, multiemployer pensions were born with that bold stroke.

When the Carnegie money predictably ran out in 1916, the college world and Carnegie organizations designed a successor plan, the TIAA, to provide

portable, immediately vested, fully funded contractual annuities, usually supported by equal contributions by the colleges and their staff members.

In the late 1930s, when I was an economics instructor and assistant to
the president of Indiana University, I began participating in the university's
retirement plan, contributing 5% of my $2,400 (a year, that is) salary to a
"portable, funded, fully vested" TIAA annuity contract. Sure enough, the TIAA
annuity contract was portable; in 1941 I took it and all of Indiana University's
contributions to it with me to my new employer, which happened to be
TIAA. I arrived at TIAA in the fall of 1941 to find a small ($125 million) but
respected limited-eligibility pension company.

Soon came World War II and then the Korean War, accompanied by painful inflation. As TIAA's economist I was particularly concerned about it, and
in January 1951 I suggested to our staff officers a new form of life annuity
based on equity investments. The chief executive officer appointed four task
forces—economics, actuarial, legal, and organizational—to implement the suggestion. Only eighteen months later, on July 1, 1952, TIAA placed in opera-
tion its new variable annuity plan, the CREF. This allowed participants to
benefit directly from common-stock investments in their retirement savings.
This was a highly controversial move in 1952, only 20 years after the deepest chasm of the Great Depression. Thirty-seven years later CREF has become a $35 billion giant, by far the largest single common-stock fund in
the world, equal in size to its older parent, TIAA. More than 1 million participants are covered by TIAA-CREF alone. When public-employee and other
plans are included, retirement coverage is available to 99% of college employees.

Developments in other types of employment have also been impressive.
Some 44 million American workers are covered by private plans, and well
over $2.3 trillion in 900,000 private pension plans support retirement in-
come. You probably all know the history of private pensions: originated by
American Express in 1875; copied by employers wanting to give gratuities
for long service; the start of a few public-employee plans; the rapid development of pensions after World War II and the Inland Steel Company case,
which made pensions a bargainable issue under the National Labor Relations Act; and the phenomenal growth throughout the 1950s, 1960s, and
early 1970s. All of this predated any serious government interest in super-
vising pension plans.

Until ERISA in 1974 the federal government gave little attention to pensions, and during the first three fourths of the 20th century state insurance
laws gave minimal attention to annuities and almost none to retirement plans
as such. Bank regulation was limited to trust accounts. Federal tax policy
addressed a few standards under which employers could deduct pension
costs as a business expense. This deductibility as a business expense is still
used as a basis for much of the federal regulation of pensions. The cost of

steel or aluminum or plastics used in building an automobile is deductible without restrictive conditions; the costs of farm produce purchased by a restaurant are deductible. In the case of pension plans, not only is deductibility conditional on many tests, but the tax is merely deferred until retirement. It is then levied on the individual, not the employer.

In the early 1970s a few factors simultaneously resulted in more federal interest in retirement security for Americans. Studebaker, a great old carriage-maker turned automobile company, went out of business after years of bragging in its advertising about its longtime, loyal, skilled employees, leaving all the employees under about age 55 bereft of their pensions. In 1972 Edwin Newman presented a celebrated NBC documentary on pensions titled "The Broken Promise," describing pensions lost through lack of vesting of benefits until an employee put in 20 or 30 years, of service and the lack of adequate funding of benefits even for those who were vested. The pension and insurance industries roundly criticized the program, but Senators Jacob Javits and Harrison Williams introduced ERISA.

For the past 15 years Congress and federal agencies have been vigorously withdrawing from the regulation of airlines, trucking, telecommunications, and savings institutions, with somewhat uneven results. The underregulation and, worse, the undersupervision of savings institutions is an event of impressive financial implications. We will have to be careful to learn the right lessons from these experiences when we turn to pensions.

One of the persistent features of our democracy is that it usually goes too far; this it has done with the regulation of the nonfiduciary provisions of private pensions. Americans are great overachievers, and they have done it again in the regulation of private pension plans. After ERISA, Congress followed in quick succession with ERTA, TEFRA, DEFRA, REACT, COBRA, OBRA, TRA, TAMRA, and, dare I add, CHAOS? There went the diversity of private plans, the flexibility and much of the freedom to innovate and to be different (a real trial for TIAA-CREF). There went the chance for reasonably simple, efficient-to-operate plans.

The main reason for suggesting less intrusive regulation of private pension plans is that government completely controls all the details of OASDI, which is providing well over half the benefits in America. The federal government determines who shall participate in OASDI (essentially all workers), when they shall participate and pay wage taxes (during employment), what the level of these taxes is, when participants are eligible for benefits (on retirement at specified ages, on disability, on death of wage earner), what the conditions for receipt of benefits are, and what the level of benefits is. For those whose needs are not met by these "matter of right" benefit programs, government provides vast systems of needs-tested benefits for the old, the young, and the middle-aged.

In all these programs government quite properly makes all the decisions as to income transfers—from higher paid to lower paid workers, from single to married, from smaller families to larger, from young to old, from richer to poorer. It is within the Social Security system that the objectives of social justice, fairness of distribution of income, and safety-net effectiveness are sought.

Within the private sector, however, the objectives of government action should be to help people achieve security in retirement, reward the thrifty, encourage the productive and innovative, and concurrently increase the capital formation of the country. In other words, the government's policies should stimulate the private sector to do its best to provide mechanisms for the maximum security of retired Americans. This it cannot do if it is walled in by detailed and narrow limits on every provision as the result of restrictive laws and regulations that are changed every year or two.

Too Much Regulation?

Are we overregulating private pensions? I believe the answer is not strictly enough as to fiduciary considerations and far too strictly as to employer-employee relationships. Perhaps we should step back from our preoccupation with various details of pension regulation and look at the broad picture of fiduciary responsibility, old-age financial security, capital formation, the right of individuals to make choices about their own earnings and savings, and especially the role and responsibility of government and the private sector in ultimate retirement security.

Government interest in private benefit plans should emphasize strict and competent regulation and supervision of fiduciary and funding aspects, assuring that whatever benefits are promised are actually paid. By the way, I mean strict and competent supervision of integrity. We want no savings-institution debacle in the pension business. I do not mean nit-picking, busy-work intervention but competent supervision. I do not mean substitution of a government department's investment judgment for that of the responsible pension-fund investment officer. The concept of the "prudent man" (now called "prudent expert" or "prudent professional") has worked well for a long time. Fundamentally ERISA's fiduciary requirements are designed to make sure that a pension plan's actions and investment activities are carried out in the best interest of plan participants and not for the interest of anyone else.

In passing ERISA, Congress took a long step toward assuring that whatever benefits were promised are actually paid. The emphasis on fiduciary standards, funding requirements, and earlier vesting are essential and must be retained. The effort to make readable information available to participants and achieve full disclosure is commendable. Reasonable availability of participation for long-term employees in all categories is also a proper area of government interest. There has been great improvement in all these aspects of private pensions because of government's mandate and encouragement.

I believe in insurance protection for individuals covered by pension plans. So I support the Pension Benefits Guarantee Corporation (PBGC), even though it does have problems, reflected in the fact that the original premiums were set at $1 and have now reached $16, and even higher for underfunded plans. That is a separate topic, however.

The federal government has a great interest in the health of private pension plans, both to provide capital and to meet the needs for retirement income that otherwise would fall on the public system. How should it balance this interest with its own regulation of private pension plans to achieve social goals? When does the necessary burden of regulation for public protection become unnecessary, onerous, too expensive, and counterproductive? Perhaps some illustrations are appropriate.

Undesirable Effects of Government Regulation

The Association of Private Pension and Welfare Plans recently published a 54-page list of improvements needed in government rules for private pension plans. Many other voices are starting to be heard, usually on specific rules or regulations. All I can do here is merely mention the remarkably complicated rules and regulations with respect to Social Security integration, most of the nondiscrimination rules, contribution limits, "top-heavy" tests, and other such complex mandates.

The federal government already requires employers to cover all employees by Social Security, at a total employer and employee cost of 15.02% of salary up to the threshold. Weighted benefits at the lower wage levels are expected to provide a socially acceptable level of retirement income. Is it appropriate for the federal government to also require that a 21-year-old man or woman be covered by an employer's noncontributory retirement plan, even if the person will not be vested for 5 years and retirement is more than 40 years away? Is this more socially desirable, for instance, than making additional education or training available, or reducing the costs of employment during the young, high-unemployment years? Would it not be better if the young people were making some of the decisions instead of being told that they must divert part of their earnings to their employer's retirement plan in their very early employment years? What is the effect of mandated coverage on America's competitive situation abroad and the loss of jobs to foreign production? Are we, in effect, telling some of our younger people, "Sorry, young worker, we have priced you out of the job market, but if you had a job we are protecting your rights by assuring your participation in the retirement plan that helped price you out of the market in the first place"?

On the other end of the age scale, government policy no longer permits compulsory retirement ages. Government regulations require continuation of contributions or benefit accruals during service after age 65. This sets up a Catch-22. Should employers establish retirement plans to provide adequate benefits at age 65, knowing that benefits will be redundant under federal benefit accumulation rules for people who retire at age 70? Or should they aim at a satisfactory benefit at age 70, knowing that the benefits at age 65 will be insufficient? Why should Congress insist on making these decisions uniformly for all employers and employees, many of whom just might be able to manage their own priorities quite well indeed? Where does public interest end and private choice begin?

Receiving Your Annuity

You have been saving for your retirement for many years. Be sure not to start your annuity income before age 59½ (with numerous exceptions), or you will pay an extra 10% excise tax. Do not start it after age 70½ (Why the one halfs?), or you will pay a 50% excise tax. Do not get too much income—you will pay a 15% excise tax if the benefit is too large. No, no, these are not new taxes—how dare anyone think they are?

If current proposals are implemented, people who continue to work beyond age 70½ will have to start receiving their pensions, and yet they and their employers will have to begin buying a new pension for them. Would it not be a good idea to reintroduce the useful concept of "constructive receipt" so that taxes can start at some point without forcing commencement of the annuity if employment continues?

Attention at the Department of Labor now is focused on the investment alternatives available in pension funding. When this extends beyond fiduciary responsibilities and into investment management, it is not a good area for government intervention. As an example, from 1906 to 1950 life insurance companies in New York were not permitted to invest in common stocks or other equities, and many restrictions were placed on other investments. This effectively prevented life insurance companies from meeting real needs of many policyholders, and TIAA had to get special legislation to start CREF. As another example, currently proposed regulations of the Department of Labor name specific fund types that are acceptable, thereby partially substituting its investment judgment for that of plan fiduciaries. Broad categories of investments appropriate for retirement savings are omitted entirely.

Moves by the government to restrict or mandate investments come at the same time as participant demands for greater flexibility in funding pension benefits. This represents a conviction that as Social Security plus private pensions plus individual savings become more adequate, there is less need to "protect people against their own bad financial judgment"—especially when such protection may prevent them from making good choices. Again, it is essential for government to protect the public by requiring honesty, full disclosure, antifraud measures, and fiduciary tests. It is questionable, however, whether government should go as far beyond that as it has.

To sum up, because government controls all aspects of the Social Security system, it should greatly reduce its present control over private pension plans. Government action should concentrate on fiduciary aspects, staying out of micromanagement of private-sector benefit plans such as mandating who shall participate, setting levels of benefit accruals and maximums on benefits, and making investment decisions other than fiduciary.

INDIVIDUAL SAVINGS

One of the casualties of the "no new taxes" political promise was the loss or major watering down of individual inducements to save for old age. The United States started out on the right road in the 1960s and 1970s with major incentives for individuals to save on their own. IRAs, Keoghs, and many specific programs were implemented and served well.

The purchasers of IRAs and other pension devices were and are merely deferring, not avoiding, taxes. Meanwhile they are contributing to capital formation while preparing for their own old age.

A congressional study, confirmed elsewhere, shows that the personal savings rate in America averaged a distressingly low 5.3% of disposable income in 1982 to 1986 and an even lower 3.7% since then. The rate fell to 3.2% in 1988, the lowest in 40 years. Savers contributed $38 billion to IRAs in 1986 but only half that amount the next year (*The New York Times*, 1989). The significant fact about IRAs is that they provide a share of the long-term capital needed to keep America productive while helping achieve the important social goal of building up adequate retirement funds. As IRA owners retire they pay their deferred taxes on benefits when received, while a new generation purchases IRAs and the circle repeats. Restrictions on early or loan withdrawals are appropriate to keep IRAs within the concept of sanctioned tax deferrals for retirement.

A regular part of America's social and economic philosophy should be to provide consistent long-term encouragement for private savings and savings through employer pension plans, IRAs, and other mechanisms.

Perhaps the time has come to reintroduce the recommendations in my 1964 Huebner Lecture at the University of Pennsylvania titled "Earned Retirement Income Tax Deferral." Under my plan every earner would be allowed to defer taxes on a given percentage of earnings—say 20% including personal savings, and any pension, profit-sharing, or bonus plan dedicated to retirement.

Indeed, someone should speak up for the American saver, the saver who defers consumption to be secure in old age. Artificially low interest rates and a lower value for the American dollar has hurt savers in three main ways:

- Lower real earnings on their savings
- Higher inflation, resulting from lower interest rates during some business phases
- Higher prices for imported goods (and foreign travel) because of the depreciating dollar

Perhaps part of the reason for the low rate of saving in America can be found here. Pension plans and private savings for retirement are the vehicle that transfers productive power from workers to pensioners, "from myself when young to myself when old." This process is the major source of long-term capital in America today—financing our industries and services, buildings, retailing, and other economic activities.

CONCLUSION

During the Great Depression we learned how to use the powers of the federal government to achieve social good. America has made great progress in the last half century toward individual financial security. This has come through a partnership of government, private-sector, and individual effort. The government sector is strong and inclusive.

The private sector is also strong, but in recent years the overenthusiastic interest of government in regulating the details of private benefit plans and private retirement savings is proving counterproductive. Growth is already slowing. In this Boettner Lecture we have stepped back a moment to contemplate whether the private sector, in decades to come, might be able to serve the American public better if it were unshackled now, if it were free to innovate, diversify, and set some of its own rules. I believe this would unleash strong forces leading to greater savings and retirement security.

REFERENCES

Effect of I.R.A.'s on Savings. (1989, September, 18). *The New York Times*.

Grad, S. (June 1988). *Income of the Population 55 and Over, 1986*. Social Security Administration Publication No. 13–11871, Tables 1 and 47.

Greenough, W. C., & King, F. P. (1976). *Pension Plans and Public Policy*. New York: Columbia University Press.

Spencer, G. (1989). "Projections of the population of the United States by age, sex, and race: 1988 to 2080." *Current Population Reports*, U.S. Bureau of the Census, Series P.25, No. 1018, p. 8. Washington, DC: U.S. Government Printing Office.

$$-4-$$

Aging and Well-Being
George L. Maddox

The achievement and maintenance of well-being are ultimate human concerns, and the relationship between age and well-being has been a major topic of research in gerontology. Current interest in celebrating our nation's age makes this an excellent time and place to remind ourselves of the past 2 centuries, during which Americans have pursued personal well-being as well as the general welfare—historically expressed as life, liberty, and happiness—with considerable success. It would be characteristically American to declare that we have pursued well-being successfully. Old age is the final arena in which we compete for the prizes that reassure us we have aged successfully personally and as a nation. We expect long life, functional and economic independence, and happiness.

There is something a bit oppressive about thinking of later adulthood as the arena for our final competition, after which we are judged to be successful or unsuccessful. Happily these days we are more likely to encounter discussions of aging well. Aging well has a softer sound if not a softer substance. Nevertheless, as scholars in anthropology have noted, our culture is relatively tough and demanding. We value and reward independence even in later life.

CONCEPTUALIZATION OF WELL-BEING

My education about how to conceptualize well-being began in the early 1960s. Cumming and Henry (1961) had provoked gerontological scholars with the observation that Nature in her wisdom had programmed older adults to achieve and maintain high morale (a positive sense of satisfaction or well-being) but had done so in a novel way. The only successful strategy to achieve this outcome was thought to be the process of disengagement, a mutually satisfactory withdrawal of older adults and the rest of society from social interaction. Two decades of debate have followed this novel proposition, and the major conclusion to be drawn is that Nature, for better or worse, provides no such single, simple route to well-being. Most older adults do indeed age well (Maddox, 1987), although they take a variety of routes. A more fruitful line of inquiry into the nature and determinants of well-being began in the mid-1960s with the work of Cantril (1966), Bradburn and Caplovitz (1965), and Bradburn (1969). Their work, in turn, was nicely combined in the work of Campbell, Converse, & Rodgers (1976) a decade later. How this coalescence of ideas about well-being was arrived at is worth describing briefly.

In sharp contrast to Cumming and Henry (1961), who sought the source of well-being within the individual, Cantril focused on externalities, on contextual factors that predict satisfaction with one's life. Cantril was a comparativist who began with the hypothesis that the substantive hopes and fears of individuals, and hence the factors related to their satisfaction, would be different cross-culturally. If this is a reasonable conjecture, then these hopes and fears must be established empirically, not assumed. Cantril explored patterns of human concerns around the world using what came to be called the Cantril self-anchoring ladder. People in different societies were asked to describe key dimensions of life at its best and worst. Then with the best and worst anchored in these personal descriptions, they were asked to place various factors nearer to the worst or the best on a 10-point "ladder." In effect these people were asked to express their degree of satisfaction with the achievement of relevant personal, social, and material goals. Cantril demonstrated that there was substantial variation in the importance of goals across societies and in the perception of personal achievement. Using the same logic Cantril asked whether the present was better or worse than the past and how the future was perceived. An observation of particular interest to gerontologists is that, in general, older adults in societies worldwide tended to report the highest degree of satisfaction of any age group and tended to have an optimistic view of their future.

Bradburn and Caplovitz (1965) took a different tract. Their focus was on mood and effect—happiness for short or perhaps psychological well-being. The new dimension of their work was the invitation to think of happiness not as the absence of negative affect, but the positive balance between the inevitable mixture of good and bad experiences that are the stuff of everyday life. Again gerontologists were interested in the finding that on balance psychological well-being is the rule, not the exception, in later life.

Enter Campbell and his colleagues. The concept of well-being proposed in *The Quality of American Life* (1976) synthesizes the work of Cantril and Bradburn. In this synthesis they capture a relatively cognitive and evaluative dimension of well-being in the dimension of *satisfaction*. Satisfaction in this case refers to the extent to which hopes and aspirations are perceived to be fulfilled. An affective dimension, *happiness*, concentrates on the balance between the positive and negative components of mood. Satisfaction and happiness are then merged into a scale of well-being. Perceptively Campbell and his colleagues (1976) anticipated that although satisfaction and happiness may be correlated, they are far from perfectly correlated. One can be satisfied with achievements but affectively unhappy, or one may be happy but dissatisfied. For the gerontologist there is the provocative suggestion that older adults tend to be more satisfied but less happy, whereas younger adults tend to be less satisfied but happier. More provocative still is the evidence that the only time in life during which satisfaction and happiness are simultaneously high is for married couples immediately before the birth of children and after the last child leaves home.

Research on well-being has also established the usefulness of recognizing the multidimensionality of satisfaction, as Cantril's experience led us to anticipate. Angus Campbell and his colleagues, for example, identified large dimensions of living that contribute cumulatively to one's sense of the quality of life. Many of these dimensions are intuitively obvious to a reflective person—income, health, family, neighborhood, community, and so on. Equally satisfied adults are not satisfied or dissatisfied with the same dimensions of their lives. Adults are not, and probably do not expect to be, equally satisfied with all dimensions of their lives. Adults are not, and probably do not expect to be, continuously happy. One does not achieve or maintain well-being simply or in a single way.

Surprisingly, gerontologists know more about the presence or absence of well-being in the later years than they know about how well-being is achieved and maintained. Furthermore, well-being is typically discussed, if at all, as an outcome rather than the dynamic predictor of the ability to cope and adapt. An alternative way of thinking about well-being has been suggested in a recent book by Antonovsky (1987), which takes a dynamic view of human well-being. While addressing directly how people stay healthy despite the inevitable assaults of life, Antonovsky has a great deal to say indirectly about well-being. We have been far too interested, he concludes, in studying pathogenesis (that is, the origins of adaptive failure) and too little in studying salutogenesis (the origins of adaptive adequacy). Health is not just an outcome; it is a general resource for resisting those chaotic entropic forces that lie just below the typically calm exterior of our existence. The key variable to be studied and understood, Antonovsky concludes, is a sense of coherence, whose three major components—comprehensibility, meaning, and manageability—are dynamically interrelated as people deal with the inevitable challenges of existence.

Antonovsky's book will surely provide a research agenda for gerontologists who read it. More than that, however, the book has a characteristic that is associated in my mind with greatness. While addressing complex social scientific issues, Antonovsky's writing is essentially free of jargon and insider talk. An educated layperson will have no difficulty in grasping his argument. Further, the book focuses on a theme that, in my view, has become a major challenge in gerontology—how to explain the heterogeneity of the aging processes, and the variety of coping and adaption processes observed among older adults.

The variety of experience among older adults and their expectations was the theme of my Kleemeier address to the Gerontological Society in 1986 (Maddox, 1987). My early research, which began with an attempt to understand how adults adapt in later years, impressed on me the importance of understanding and explaining heterogeneity. In a recent article in *Science,* Rowe and Kahn (1987) reach a similar conclusion. In fact, the first recommendation to gerontologists for future research is to explain heterogeneity in the processes of aging. Heterogeneity of the aging processes and in the experience of aging was certainly a fair description of my observations of older adults. The observed heterogeneity, I believe, has important theoretical and practical implications. In simplest terms, my view is that the observed heterogeneity is the outcome of dynamic synergistic interactions between persons and environments. Biological explanations of observed heterogeneity alone are insufficient; contextual factors external to human beings are also insufficient. The focus of gerontology must therefore be on people in context. Understanding aging and well-being provides as good an illustration of the issues as we will find.

A broad, multidimensional view of well-being, although consistent with reality, exacts its costs practically. In discussing well-being we risk having to discuss everything about human life. My objective in this lecture is more modest. We will discuss three revolutions that shed some light on the determinants of well-being: the demographic revolution in the age composition of populations, the revolution of knowledge about human aging, and the revolution of expectations as we think about inventing the future of aging. In conclusion some items for the future agenda of scientists and citizens in an aging society will be noted.

THE FIRST REVOLUTION: THE DEMOGRAPHIC TRANSITION

Individual aging and very old adults are not news. All societies have produced a few relatively old persons. Population aging is news, a modern triumph, as Robert Butler observed while he was director of the National Institute on Aging. This triumph was largely the product of what our colleagues in economics call externalities—that is, social and environmental factors that introduced public sanitation, encouraged personal hygiene, and ensured a relatively stable food supply. These externalities unlocked the biological potential of populations to survive childhood and to age.

Forecasting Dependency

Epidemiologists see this transition to aging societies as a consequence of the first revolution in public health. Clean water, adequate nutrition, personal hygiene, and public sanitation worked wonders. The most obvious implication of this revolution for health and health care was that the dominant form of disease shifted from acute to chronic, and a new imperative for long-term care could be forecasted. The second revolution in public health is now in process. This second revolution is the understanding that behavior and life-style constitute the dominant determinants of disease onset, course, and outcome. Externalities in the form of socially reinforced unhealthy behavior and life-styles that require modification have intruded on biomedicine's domain again (Maddox, 1985).

The demographic transition caught the imagination of the media early. The graying of populations became standard Sunday-supplement fare, and the tragedies associated with living too long in a world not designed for growing old have repeatedly been spelled out in graphic detail. Various accounts dispute just what the proportion of older people will be in the year 2020, and in any case demographers are rarely precisely correct in their projections. We know that the proportion will be high, in the range of 17% to 20%. Having settled that, we can declare with some confidence that the number of gray heads is largely irrelevant anyway.

What is relevant about an aging population is primarily the capacity of older adults now and in the future to function independently. The key issue is whether lengthening life expectancy will elevate rates of disabling dependency among aging populations. Figure 4.1 provides a convenient way to illustrate the issue: Although death is demonstrably being delayed, evidence that disabling morbidity is concomitantly delayed is distressingly problematic.

We know that mortality rates, even among very old persons, are continuing to decline in the United States. In Figure 4.1, the curve marked C is continuing to flex toward the right, moving toward the "rectangularizing" of the population survival curve that demographers often refer to. As the C curve moves to the right, what happens to curve A (morbidity or illness)? Is morbidity delayed? More important, what happens to curve B (the onset of disabling illness)? If the onset of illness and disability are not delayed as populations age, then the rates of dependency in older populations will rise. The facts of the matter are in dispute.

Katz et al. (1983) have framed the question usefully in focusing on the probability of disability-free years in later life, and have made useful but

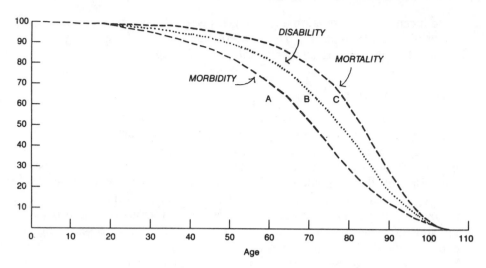

FIGURE 4.1 Factors in the Fries-anti-Fries debate about "rectangularization" of morbidity/disability/mortality curves.

tentative estimates based on cross-sectional evidence. The "independent years of life" concept is used to estimate how dependence increases after age 65, with the chances of becoming dependent at age 85 increasing to about 50-50 for the last 6 years of life. Hence, we would be well advised to pay more attention to the relatively very old if our concern is to anticipate society's responsibility to care for the dependent elderly. The so-called Fries-anti-Fries debate in gerontology is about whether this bleak projection can be countered or is being countered (White, Cartwright, Cornoni, & Brock, 1986). That is, can the distance between Curves A and B, and B and C in Figure 4.1 be compressed as populations age?

Fries's recommendation (1980) for understanding the relationship between age and dependency involves two basic propositions. The first is that life expectancy will tend to peak at about age 85. This, we now know, is demonstrably wrong. The second proposition is more interesting, complex, and hopeful: the onset of disabling impairments can be delayed so that the ratio of independent to dependent years in later life can be improved (again, see Figure 4.1). The evidence is really not yet conclusive on this hopeful proposition because we do not have the current evidence, much less the evidence on which to forecast the future with any confidence. The debate is consequential, however. A future in which Fries is proved to be wrong is sobering. The comment of Germaine Bree, the biographer of Albert Camus, comes to mind. Camus declared that God is dead, said Bree, but, she added, he seemed genuinely sorry. Those of us who declare Fries wrong will have occasion to be genuinely sorry if we are right. As populations age, the risk of dependency threatens well-being in a fundamental way.

Adaptation of Social Institutions

The current emphasis on counting older adults is misplaced in another way. A more important concern is the confrontation of an aging population with existing institutional arrangements for meeting needs. The real issues are how a society maintains income adequately for a population that produces many people who survive for 2 decades after they leave the workplace; how long-term care can be provided in a care system geared primarily for managing acute illness in high-technology hospitals; or how society can educate, house, and transport a population using mechanisms designed primarily for young persons. These questions cannot be begged by declaring that social institutions cannot adapt. All social institutions are negotiated and negotiable. Our social institutions can adapt, are adapting, and will probably continue to adapt more or less adequately.

The real issue is not to assume adaptive capacity of institutions, however, but to illustrate if not demonstrate that capacity through well-designed public policy. Economist Richard Easterlin (1980) suggested that the size of age cohorts matters because social groups compete for limited if not scarce material and social resources. Aging populations surely compete for scarce resources that are related to well-being. This point has not been missed by those who feel that a politically self-conscious older population may not develop or retain a commitment to intergenerational equity in the face of scarce social resources.

Older adults of recent decades have, in fact, lived in a relatively affluent world in which they have fared very well materially (Clark, Maddox, Schrimper, & Sumner, 1984). The continuation of this world is problematic, however. It is hardly surprising, therefore, that in the 1980s one encounters questions about generational equity in the allocation of social resources and advocacy in behalf of children and young adults. In recent national discussions we are hearing less about why we should do more for older adults and more about the needs of children and youth. Adequate public policy regarding achievement of generational equity should be informed by adequate information. Fortunately the demographic revolution has been matched by a revolution of information about the processes of aging and the experiences of aging. This information provides the basis for assessing the long-term relationship between aging and well-being for older adults. We will depend on advocates of children, youth, and young adults to present their claims vigorously.

THE KNOWLEDGE REVOLUTION

In the past quarter century—essentially during my professional lifetime—a knowledge revolution has occurred in gerontology and geriatrics. In characterizing the processes of aging and later life we have progressed dramatically from inherited mythology and informed guesses toward verifiable information. The sum of what we know and expect on the basis of reliable information lays the groundwork for reasonable optimism. We are certain that aging processes are to some degree mutable and, hence, can benefit from purposive intervention, for example. Perhaps more important, however, the way basic and clinical scientists conceptualize later life has been revolutionalized, and the evidence of that revolution is in the research cited in a recent overview article by Rowe, a physician, and Kahn, a psychologist (1987). Scientists and professionals in gerontology have rediscovered the relevance of an old maxim of experimental and clinical science: If you want to understand something, try to change it. Testing the limits of modifiability of human aging has become an appropriate goal.

An Ethical Caveat

But wait. There are ethical as well as legal reasons to be cautious about active intervention in aging processes. Purposive interventions must be assessed on their merits. My point is that we have changed the conversation about aging to include discussion of feasible, possibly beneficial interventions in aging. In summarizing the knowledge revolution I call your attention to four issues that illustrate my point: (a) the heterogeneity of older populations, (b) continuities in the aging process, (c) the modifiability of the aging process, and (d) the importance of the interactions between people and their environments. Each warrants brief development as it bears on the relationship between aging and well-being. Here is how current conversations in gerontology are proceeding these days.

Heterogeneity.   Capturing the essence of complex phenomena is difficult for scientists and laypersons alike. The layperson handles complexity by stereotyping; the scientist handles the problem by focusing on central tendencies. Either way, how do we capture the essence of, say, 26 million older adults in the United States and countless millions more worldwide? Are they poor, sick, depressed, isolated, or the contrary? Well, yes and no. It would be difficult to answer simply with confidence, although we know how ready we are to characterize *the elderly* at the slightest provocation. In fact, we may make such characterizations precisely to the extent that we are uninformed about just how much heterogeneity there is. Or we may characterize *the elderly* to fit our political agenda.

We now know a great deal about the heterogeneity among older adults and in the process of aging. The average life expectancy at birth worldwide varies enormously—from as low as 45 years to a high of more than 80 years. In the United States most persons older than age 65 have at least one chronic condition, but a majority of them (about 60%) have no disabling functional impairment; an estimated 15% have at least one disabling functional impairment, particularly after age 85, when the risk of disability reaches 50%. About 10% of older people are below the official poverty line in the United States, and another 10% to15% are below 125% of the poverty line. About 15% have above-average incomes. The risk of significant time in a nursing care facility during a lifetime is about 30%; 70% will live out their lives in the community. The risk of senile dementia of the Alzheimer's type is about 5% after age 65, about 20% at age 85. Older people are quite varied.

Although we might expect social and behavioral scientists to give attention to the heterogeneity of populations, such attention is less obvious for biomedically oriented scientists. Focusing on the central tendencies was, for example, very pronounced in the early reports of Nathan Shock (1977), the physiologist who popularized the observation that for all physiological systems, aging is accompanied by regression lines that are decidedly negative in slope (see Figure 4.2). Shock's intent was to remind us, presumably, that in the long run we are all dead. The more carefully we look, however, the more we become aware that at the same chronological age the variance around the central tendency is quite pronounced, and the slope of the regression lines for subcategories of individuals is quite varied. So although in the long run we are all dead, we do not get there in identical ways biologically or socially. In fact, within the last several years Nathan Shock himself has observed that his original presentation did not stress the heterogeneity of the aging process nearly enough.

So how can we account for such variation? Genetic potential is, of course, a factor. Social sciences appropriately emphasize a contextual variable—the essential material and social resources necessary for survival and development. Comparative demographics, which have demonstrated the differential population transformation across societies, suggest that population aging is probably explained less by biological potential than by the activation of that potential through the contributions of sanitation, personal hygiene, and a stable food supply. Societies are large-scale natural experiments in the efforts of the availability of resources essential for survival and growth. The abbreviated life expectancy at birth and high morbidity rates observed in developing countries tell this story effectively. Even within developed countries, however, the abbreviated life expectancy and higher morbidity of the poor also tell a story of what happens when essential resources are distributed unequally.

Although most older adults report a positive sense of well-being, its components are varied and the routes by which it is arrived at are different. Observe, for example, the patterns of morbidity and mortality as well as the distribution of well-being among older adults within the United States. Socioeconomic status (more simply, social class) is an index of the availability of resources known to be related to health and well-being. This observation leads to a second important conclusion from research—continuities in the processes of aging.

Continuities. What is past is prologue. In longitudinal research it is axiomatic that Shakespeare was right. The most powerful predictor of a variable at a second observation is the value of that variable at the first observation. One of the most commonly understood illustrations of this principle is found in the risk-factor concept. As popularly understood in discussions of cardiovascular disease, the probability of an unwanted event later in your life is related to the presence of risky (unhealthy) behavior or life-style earlier in your life. The risks factors for cardiovascular disease are now well known: smoking, drugs, faulty diet, inadequate exercise, stress. In a more general sense we lay down the trajectories of well-being in late life long before we are old. Note the emphasis on learned behavior in bringing on the risk factors that are most popularly discussed.

One needs to broaden the concept of risk, however. My recommendation to adults growing older, only partly in jest, is this: If you can avoid it, do not grow old poor, ignorant, or lacking a viable social support network. To put it positively, adequate income, education, and a mobilizable social support network predict a relatively positive experience in late life. I could go on to illustrate that how one relates to one's work and to one's family predicts adaptation to retirement and positive intergenerational relationships in later life. The basic point is understood, however. The fact that all studies of well-being demonstrate that socioeconomic status is positively related to perceived well-being hardly comes as a surprise. Indicators of socioeconomic status are literally the indicators of material and social well-being. They are factors whose distribution is socially and politically determined. In the lottery of life it is usually social groups, not Nature, that determine who is likely to win or lose. Well-being has social as well as personal determinants. A word of caution is required, however. Though material resources surely help, such resources alone do not ensure well-being.

Modifiability. In restating the maxim mentioned earlier—if you want to understand aging, try to change it—it is worth repeating my earlier word of caution. This is not a recommendation that we declare open season on older adults to demonstrate their capacity to change just for the sake of demonstrating that capacity. Grant me the awareness of ethical and legal restraints to make a point about modifiability of the aging process. A good recent review of relevant evidence on modifiability is found in Rowe and Kahn (1987) and in my own work (1987).

Let me illustrate the point with reference to Figure 4.2 and within the frame of reference provided by Nathan Shock's negative regression lines, which have characterized almost all observations about age-determined change—physiological, psychological, and social. Imagine a graph in which the ordinal represents some functional capacity (y) and the abscissa represents age (x) (see Figure 4.2). The slope of line a ... x defines what we usually mean by an age-related decline in functioning. If we observe that the intercept on some variable (y) for persons of a given age and note the variance and slope, what we find is that individuals at first observation at or below the mean (intercept) can, through interventions of various sorts, have

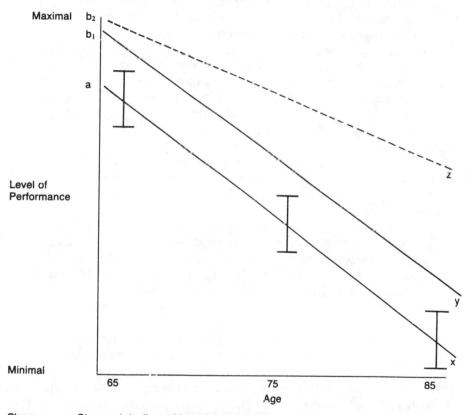

Slope a . . . x: Observed decline, with variance noted.
Slope b_1 . . . y: Hypothetical intercept is higher, slope is parallel to a . . . x.
Slope b_2 . . . y: Hypothetical intercept is higher, slope is less than a . . . x.

FIGURE 4.2 Observed and hypothetical decline of performance level following intervention.

their scores raised. In other words, it is never too late to benefit from train- ing: by exercise, in cognitive skills, and in interpersonal skills. In Figure 4.2 one could improve performance in some individuals at age 65 so that the initial performance level (a) moves to a higher level, b_1, or perhaps to b_2. Consider, for example, a standard intervention such as aerobic exercise in relation to cardiovascular functioning. Is it ever too late to achieve the known physiological modifications? The answer is no, but the time required to achieve the outcome is a bit longer. The exercise provides some side bene- fits, two notable ones in particular: maintenance of range of motion in joints and maintenance or improvement of positive mood. Exercise, in a word, provides physiological, orthopedic, and psychological benefits. Or take cog- nitive functioning. Psychologists Warner Schaie and Sherry Willis (1986) have summarized the implications of their research in this way: If you have a marker of cognitive functioning and follow the performance of people over 14 years you will note a decline in functioning, particularly in performance as contrasted with verbal skills. With modest training, however, one can re- turn healthy older adults to their earlier performance level. Or take the work of Rodin and Langer (1977; see also Rodin, Timko, & Harris, 1985) on self-concept and self-care. Disabled older adults in long-term care settings can be trained to expect to take additional responsibility for self-care and move toward taking that responsibility. Physiologist Bengt Arnetz (1985) demonstrates the same effect in Swedish studies, but as a psychophysiolo- gist he makes an additional comment. Social involvement in self-care pro- duces more measurable positive physiological response than conventionally measured perceived well-being.

It would be exciting if, through a variety of plausible, affordable interven- tions, the performance of older adults could be moved over the life course from the level represented in Figure 4.2 by line a ... x upward to line b_1 ... y or b_2 ... z. Even more exciting would be the implications of the changed slope of decremental decline illustrated by line b_2 ... z. We are not in a position to promise such an optimistic outcome. We are not in a position, however, to dismiss it either.

At the societal level there is no argument that the indexing of Social Secu- rity and the enactment of Medicare and Medicaid have diminished the prob- ability of impoverishment and decreased out-of-pocket expenses during the 1970s (Clark et al., 1984). Not enough, you may say. Probably so, but the issue here is not whether policy interventions promise rose gardens but whether interventions of a specific kind modify the experience and outcomes of aging. Demonstrably they do.

What difference does it make, however, if we know that interventions of various sorts can modify the aging processes and the experience of aging? What is the probability of enactment or action? Externalities—societal fac- tors in this case—are important.

Contexts.   Lawton and Nahemow (1973) brought into focus a tradition of personal-context fitting. The early work of these researchers sensitized us to the consequences of matching or mismatching individual capabilities and contextual opportunities. For a sociologist-epidemiologist, this is why having an economist's perspective, which calls my attention to the importance of the selective allocation of scarce resources, is so important. Similarly, years ago sociologists argued against the early formulations of the disengagement theory as internally driven behavior because the cross-national and socio-economic evidence suggested too much variability in the distribution of well-being to make universal, context-free outcomes believable.

The social policy interventions of the 1970s in behalf of older adults, such as the indexing of Social Security and the enactment of Medicare and Medicaid, inadequate as they may be, leave no doubt that such interventions make a difference in the material well-being of older adults (see Clark et al., 1984). Whether these programs make *enough* difference or whether they will be sustained in the future are relevant but different questions.

At this point, then, the modifiability of the aging processes is not just a matter of ethics regarding what kind of society we may dare to invent and pursue. Interventions are a matter of political consensus, will, and ingenuity in our society and in the organizations that serve us by implementing the societal objectives we wish to pursue. This is not to imply that in future political agendas we will achieve consensus and that we know the formula for allocating resources effectively to old and young. It is clear, however, that the options we prefer and implement will affect the future of aging.

A REVOLUTION OF HOPES AND EXPECTATIONS

The prelude to revolution and the commitment to inventing an alternative future is a fundamental change in expectations and hopes. The comedian Flip Wilson popularized the phrase "What you see is what you get." If what one sees is not existing reality but a vision (or alternative visions) of the future, then the context that the person wishes or intends to fit into may be an altered environment yet to be created. The expectation of the altered environment has as a corollary an alternative vision of the fulfillment we label well-being, both in its subjective and objective meaning.

Politically the environment in which we are aging has changed. A recent special article in *The New York Times* noted in its title, "Aging Is Not What It Used To Be." We do not have to accept or agree with the competing propositions that older adults are or are not a serious political force. The fact is that we have seen the substantial allocation of resources to income maintenance and health care that were not present previously. The national scientific research institutes devoted to addressing important health issues now include a National Institute on Aging. All professional societies, including those in medicine, have at least paid lip service to the relevance of an aging population to their professional mission. Foundations have announced an interest in aging—after 2 decades of avoidance. Voluntary organizations of older adults are visible, especially the American Association of Retired Persons (AARP), which has chosen to become an economic and possibly a serious political advocacy force for at least the American middle class.

The most interesting transformation, and the change that will ensure a continuing revolution, is the changed perception among older adults that history and the future are to be made, not simply inherited.

The issue, then, is to explore the limits of the possible. This is not a vacuous exercise in make-believe but an exercise that will involve serious negotiations between the generations about the equitable distribution of resources. These negotiations are primarily a political, not a scientific, exercise. The future of aging, therefore, depends substantially on the achievement of political consensus, the mobilization of political intentions and will, and the political ingenuity to shape the future of aging.

CONCLUSION

As we consider inventing the future, here are several items on my agenda as the future of aging and well-being in later life is explored.

- We need to investigate well-being not just as an outcome but as a predictor of the ability to cope and adapt in the face of the inevitable challenges of later life.
- We need to explore the variety of contexts that older adults with different personal and social resources can be fitted into so as to maximize appropriate independence for as long as possible.
- We need to monitor with increasing care not only the impact of societal institutions on older adults, but the impact on social institutions—particularly economic, health care, and family institutions.

Let me close with an observation about the future of aging that is adapted from the public-safety slogan of a decade or so ago. Drive carefully, the slogan went; the life you save may be your own. As we think about the future of aging, think carefully about the future you imagine and propose to construct; the future you construct may be your own. As we construct the future, we do so with confidence that the average expectation is a positive relationship between aging and well-being. It is the shape and distribution of well-being that are in our hands.

REFERENCES

Antonovsky, A. (1987). *Unraveling the mystery of health: How people manage stress and stay well.* San Francisco: Jossey-Bass.

Arnetz, B. (1985). Interaction of biomedical and psychosocial factors in research on aging. In P. Lawton & G. Maddox (Eds.), *Annual review of gerontology and geriatrics* (Vol. 5, pp. 56-94.) New York: Springer Publishing.

Bradburn, N. (1969). *The structure of psychological well-being.* Chicago: Aldine.

Bradburn, N., & Caplovitz, D. (1965). *Reports on happiness.* Chicago: Aldine.

Campbell, A., Converse, P., & Rodgers, W. (1976). *The quality of American life.* New York: Russell Sage Foundation.

Cantril, H. (1966). *The pattern of human concerns.* New Brunswick: Rutgers University Press.

Clark, R., Maddox, G., Schrimper, R., & Sumner, D. (1984). *Inflation and the economic well-being of the elderly.* Baltimore: John Hopkins University Press.

Cumming, E., & Henry, W. (1961). *Growing old: The process of disengagement.* New York: Basic Books.

Easterlin, R. (1980). *Birth and fortune.* New York: Basic Books.

Fries, J. (1980). Aging, natural death and the compression of morbidity. *New England Journal of Medicine, 303,* 130-135.

Katz, S., Branch, L., Branson, M., Papsiders, J., Beck, J., & Greer, D. (1983). Active life expectancy. *New England Journal of Medicine, 309,* 1218-24.

Lawton, P., & Nahemow, L. (1973). Ecology and the aging process. In C. Eisdorfer & P. Lawton (Eds.), *Psychology of adult developement and aging* (pp. 619-674). Washington, DC: American Psychological Association.

Maddox, G. (1985). Modifying the social environment. In W. Holland, R. Detels, & G. Knox (Eds.), *Oxford textbook of public health* (Vol. 2) (pp. 19-31). London: Oxford University Press.

Maddox, G. (1987). Aging differently. *The Gerontologist, 27,* 557-564.

Rodin, J., & Langer, E. (1977). Long-term effects of a control-relevant intervention with institutionalized aged. *Journal of Personality and Social Psychology, 35,* 897-902.

Rodin, J., Timko, C., & Harris, S. (1985). The construct of control. In P. Lawton, & G. Maddox (Eds.), *Annual review of gerontology and geriatrics* (Vol. 5, pp. 3-55). New York: Springer Publishing.

Rowe, J., & Kahn, R. (1987). Human aging: Usual and successful. *Science, 237,* 143-149.

Schaie, W., & Willis, S. (1986). Can decline in intellectual functioning be reversed? *Developmental Psychology, 22,* 223-232.

Shock, Nathan W. (1977). Systems integration. In C. E. Finch & L. Hayflick (Eds.), *Handbook of the Biology of Aging* (pp. 639-665). New York: Van Nostrand Reinhold.

White, L., Cartwright, W., Cornoni-Huntley, J., & Brock, D. (1986). Epidemiology of aging. In C. Eisdorfer *Annual review of gerontology and geriatrics,* (Vol. 6) (pp. 215-311). New York: Springer.

5

Economic Status and Subjective Well-Being: A Review of the Literature and an Agenda for Future Research

Linda K. George

Common sense tells us that financial security constitutes an important component of well-being. Nonetheless, American values about the importance of money and wealth and the moral worth of materialism often seem ambiguous and even contradictory. The same society that confers individual status largely on the basis of economic resources, accumulation of wealth, and conspicuous consumption has also spawned the adages that "money cannot buy happiness" and "the best things in life are free." Our cultural heroes include both the fabulously wealthy and those who reject materialism in favor of altruism and self-sacrifice. Thus, the degree to which financial security fosters general well-being and the specific ways in which it promotes life quality are less than self-evident.

At the most general level, this chapter concerns the relationships between financial status and overall well-being, especially individuals' perceptions of life quality. More specifically, the chapter focuses on the relationships among three factors—financial resources, satisfaction with financial resources, and subjective well-being—and the extent to which those relationships differ with age. Although these factors are of primary importance, they do not exist in a vacuum. Consequently, to the extent possible given space limitations, attention is also paid to the complex web of personal, social, economic, and historical contexts that underpin financial status and subjective well-being.

The chapter is organized into five major sections. The first three sections comprise a systematic review of previous literature on the relationships among financial resources, financial satisfaction, and subjective well-being. The first section provides conceptual and operational definitions of these variables and describes their distributions across time, age, and cohort. The second section summarizes information about the bivariate relationships among these concepts. The third section provides evidence about the robustness of the relationships among these variables in the context of multivariate models and explores the explanatory mechanisms underlying those relationships. In the fourth section, major conclusions about the relationship between financial status and subjective well-being are briefly summarized, and a theoretical case is made that these relationships may result from different processes for the elderly and the nonelderly. The final section presents an agenda for future research and includes a number of recommendations concerning profitable areas for further inquiry. Throughout the chapter, substantive conclusions are accompanied by identification of both the methodological difficulties that hamper firm judgments and the areas in which research evidence is so scant that confident conclusions are impossible.

DEFINITIONS AND DISTRIBUTIONS

In this section, the three concepts that constitute the major focus of this chapter—financial resources, satisfaction with financial resources, and subjective well-being—are examined individually. Each concept is defined both conceptually and in terms of its standard operationalizations. In addition, distributions of these variables are examined in terms of (a) aggregate historical trends during the past 20 to 25 years, (b) cohort differences, (c) patterns of change over time within cohorts, and (d) variability within the populations of interest (i.e., the elderly and the nonelderly).

Financial Resources

Conceptually, there is general consensus that financial resources include the total economic assets available to an individual. Thus, financial resources include income from all sources, savings, property, in-kind income, and so forth (e.g., Henretta & Campbell, 1978; Smeeding, 1990). Operationally, however, research seldom examines individuals' financial resources as defined in this way. More typically, income is used as a proxy for financial resources.

One of the often-debated methodological issues in research on economic status in general and the relationships between economic status and well-being in particular is the degree to which use of income measures distorts our understanding of financial resources more broadly defined (e.g., Crystal, 1986; Moon, 1977; Vaughan, 1980). On one hand, income is undoubtedly the best single indicator of disposable and liquid economic resources. Conversely, income is a single indicator—and consequently important differences in the economic resources available to individuals are ignored when income is used as the sole measure of financial resources. It is logical to expect that economic resources other than income are important for individuals' economic behaviors, satisfaction with financial matters, and even perhaps their perceived quality of life. Considerably more research is needed to understand the degree to which and the conditions under which income is a suitable proxy for financial resources.

There are well-documented age differences (between the elderly and the nonelderly) in both income and the broader concept of financial resources. Older persons have lower incomes, on average, than the nonelderly (e.g., Chen, 1985; Harris, 1986). Moreover, the relative importance of several sources of income varies between the elderly and the nonelderly. Compared with younger people, the elderly have smaller proportions of income from earnings and larger proportions from Social Security and private pensions (e.g., Chen, 1985; Clark & Baumer, 1985). In addition, older adults have an advantage in terms of tax regulations and thus are able to retain larger proportions of their total incomes (e.g., Vaughan, 1980; Crystal, 1986). Age differences also have an impact on financial resources other than income. Older adults are more likely than younger adults to own their homes and among homeowners older adults are less likely to have mortgages (e.g., Crystal, 1986; Streib, 1985). Age differences in other assets, such as stocks and properties other than personal residences, also appear to favor the elderly (e.g., Hurd & Shoven, 1982; Smeeding, 1990).

Important information about differences in economic resources between the elderly and the nonelderly is available, although nearly all of it is based on income rather than on financial resources as broadly defined. For the purposes of this chapter, four trends are especially pertinent. First, during the past 20 to 25 years, the economic status of the elderly, relative to the nonelderly, has improved dramatically (cf., Chen, 1985; Crystal, 1986; Duncan, Hill, & Rodgers, 1987; Harris, 1986; Preston, 1984; Smeeding, 1990). There is general consensus that during the 1960s the elderly were poorer, on average, than the nonelderly, but that this difference has disappeared by the 1980s. This improvement in the relative economic status of the elderly is observed in several ways, ranging from age-specific poverty rates (e.g., Chen, 1985; Crystal, 1986) to mean and median income levels (e.g., Duncan et al., 1987; Preston, 1984), and this pattern appears to be strengthened if income adjustments (e.g., for family size) are considered (Crystal, 1986; National Research Council, 1987; Radner, 1982; 1986).

Second, there are substantial cohort differences in economic status during later life. During recent decades, each new cohort has entered old age with greater levels of economic resources then previous cohorts. Consequently, increases in the relative economic status of the elderly observed during the past 20 years are largely the result of cohort effects (e.g., Duncan et al., 1987; Harris, 1986) rather than improvements in income maintenance policies for the elderly.

Third, and very important, the process of cohort succession that has led to an elderly population that is increasingly advantaged in relative terms masks a very different pattern at the individual level: Longitudinal studies clearly indicate that, within cohorts, economic resources decline with age (Duncan et al., 1987; Harris, 1986). This decline typically begins with retirement (Palmore, Fillenbaum, & George, 1984) and continues throughout old age. Moreover, there are relatively dramatic fluctuations in economic status over time during later life (Holden, Burkhauser, & Myers, 1986), and widowhood greatly exacerbates the typical decline in financial status (Holden et al., 1986; Zick & Smith, 1986). In contrast, the typical longitudinal pattern for younger and middle-aged adults is one of increasing economic status, although there are relatively dramatic fluctuations in financial status among this population also (Duncan, 1984; 1988).

A final salient point regarding financial resources concerns heterogeneity within the elderly and nonelderly populations. There is now strong evidence of greater income inequality among the older population than among the nonelderly population (cf., Crystal, 1986; National Research Council, 1987). Coupled with information about the economic status of the elderly relative to the nonelderly, this pattern suggests that efforts may be needed to reformulate national policies more along lines of need and less in terms of age. That is, recently even advocates for the older population have begun to suggest that efforts to redistribute financial resources among the older population may be more appropriate than a continued emphasis on the transfer of economic resources from younger to older cohorts (cf., Crystal, 1986).

Satisfaction with Financial Resources

The definition of satisfaction with financial resources is conceptually straightforward: It refers to subjective evaluations of the degree to which one's financial resources are adequate versus inadequate or bring satisfaction versus dissatisfaction (Andrews & Withey, 1976; Campbell, Converse & Rodgers, 1976). Although it has not been generally recognized in extant research, however, it appears that the specific method of operationalizing satisfaction with financial resources is consequential in terms of its distribution in the population—especially among older adults.

In previous research, three single-item measures have been used most frequently to elicit self-reports of satisfaction with financial resources: satisfaction with one's income, satisfaction with one's financial situation in general, and satisfaction with one's standard of living. Although few studies have included multiple measures of financial satisfaction and thus permitted comparisons of them, the limited information available suggests that they measure different aspects of financial satisfaction (e.g., Herzog & Rodgers, 1981). Satisfaction with one's financial situation appears to be the broadest of the three, eliciting evaluations of one's overall financial status. Satisfaction with income refers specifically to evaluations of the amount of money that one earns or receives from regular income sources. Satisfaction with standard of living refers to one's evaluation of the quantity and quality of goods and services purchased in the marketplace or otherwise at one's disposal.

Distributions of financial satisfaction measures are substantially different from the patterns observed for objective measures of financial resources, especially income. First, there is consistent evidence that older adults are more satisfied with their financial resources than young and middle-aged adults (Andrews & Withey, 1976; Campbell et al., 1976; Herzog & Rodgers, 1981). This pattern holds for all three dimensions of financial satisfaction, but age differences in satisfaction with standard of living are especially dramatic (Herzog & Rodgers, 1981).

Second, there is no evidence that financial satisfaction has increased among successive cohorts of older adults during the past 20 to 25 years—despite the fact that relative income levels increased substantially during the same interval. Indeed, data from the 1960s, 1970s, and 1980s consistently document that most older adults report high levels of satisfaction with their financial situations (e.g., Campbell et al., 1976; Herzog & Rodgers, 1981; Palmore et al., 1984; Streib & Schneider, 1971).

Third, there is no evidence from the limited longitudinal data bases available that financial satisfaction declines with age or time since retirement (Palmore, Burchett, Fillenbaum, George, & Wallman, 1985; Streib & Schneider, 1971). This pattern also contrasts with that for financial resources—as noted earlier, longitudinal studies consistently indicate that income (and perhaps other financial assets) declines during later life. Similarly, there is no evidence that financial satisfaction is subject to the rather dramatic fluctuations over time exhibited by objective measures of income.

Finally, and also in contrast to the pattern for financial resources, there is less variability in financial satisfaction among the elderly than among the nonelderly (Andrews & Withey, 1976; Campbell et al., 1976). Overall, then, financial satisfaction is distributed much differently from—and in many cases in patterns the opposite of—financial resources in terms of historical trends, cohort differences, longitudinal changes, and degree of age-related heterogeneity.

The emergence of scientific interest in measures of financial satisfaction appears to reflect two concerns. First, some investigators became interested in the role of financial satisfaction as an intervening variable between objective economic circumstances and quality-of-life outcomes (e.g., Andrews & Withey, 1976; Campbell et al., 1976; Liang, 1982). In essence, satisfaction with financial resources is viewed as one mechanism by which objective economic resources operate on perceptions of general well-being. Second, other investigators became interested in the issue of the *adequacy* of economic resources, pointing out that the same level of income (or other assets) can have very different implications for life quality depending on the varying needs of family units (e.g., Beck, 1982; Crystal, 1986; Strate & Dubnoff, 1986). For example, an annual income of $15,000 has very different implications in terms of income adequacy for a single-person household than for a household consisting of two adults and four minor children. From this perspective, financial satisfaction is viewed as one method of eliciting information about perceived income adequacy.

Although space limitations preclude a comprehensive examination of this issue, it should be noted that a variety of methods have been used to assess income adequacy. One of the simpler methods used to adjust income to needs is to control or make adjustments for family or household size (e.g., Crystal, 1986; Radner, 1982). Unfortunately, family size adjustments by themselves are inadequate for assessing income adequacy because there is no simple or straightforward method of knowing how to balance the greater economic needs of larger households against the "economies of scale" that accrue in multiple-person households. It is well known that income needs are not related to household size in a simple linear fashion. Moreover, specific parameters of family composition undoubtedly influence income needs. The presence of minor children, for example, appears to affect income adequacy over and above its implications for household size (for example, Vaughan & Lancaster, 1980).

The most common method of assessing income adequacy is to compare income to official budgets developed by federal agencies for policy purposes. Examples of budgets commonly used for this purpose includes the poverty lines published by the Social Security Administration (e.g., Orshansky, 1965) and the Census Bureau (e.g., U.S. Bureau of the Census, 1981), budgets based largely on dietary requirements and food consumption costs that are published by the Department of Agriculture (U.S. Department of Agriculture, 1975), and the budgets published by the Bureau of Labor Statistics (U.S. Bureau of Labor Statistics, 1982). Virtually all of these budgets are adjusted for family-household size and the age or working status of family members. Although these official budgets have served as the primary method of assessing income adequacy for more than two decades, they have been severely criticized as lacking validity by both researchers and policy makers. Indeed, dissatisfaction became so widespread that the Family Budgets Program of the Bureau of Labor Statistics was terminated in 1981.

As noted earlier, some investigators have also used financial satisfaction measures as proxies for income adequacy. Until recently, this approach was used almost exclusively by sociologists (e.g., Liang & Fairchild, 1979; Liang, Kahana, & Doherty, 1980). More recently, economists expressed interest in the use of financial satisfaction measures for constructing income equivalence scales (i.e., measures of the incomes needed by different kinds of households to generate equivalent standards of living) (cf., Colasanto, Kapteyn, & van der Gaag, 1984; Goedhart, Halberstadt, Kapteyn, & van Praag, 1977). Income equivalence scales based on measures of financial satisfaction determine the amount of money needed by families of different sizes and compositions to generate equal levels of financial satisfaction. These efforts have met with mixed results. On one hand, these studies suggest that subjective measures generate substantially different equivalence scales than objective measures and that some of the differences are meaningful in terms of what we know about economic status and family-household composition across adulthood (e.g., Goedhart et al., 1977; Strate & Dubnoff, 1986; Vaughan, 1980). Conversely, older adults appear to be so unrealistically satisfied with their income, that the low levels of actual income that can generate these high measures of satisfaction, according to many experts, are unreasonable and unrealistic for meeting the financial needs of older households (Vaughan, 1980). In essence, taking some of the estimates from these studies seriously would be to grossly underestimate the objective economic needs of older persons.

As documented below, financial satisfaction plays an important role in understanding both the determinants of subjective well-being and age differences in those determinants. Financial satisfaction is not synonymous with income adequacy, however. Moreover, the difference between financial satisfaction and income adequacy is especially discrepant for older adults. Methodologically, further effort is needed to develop valid measures of income adequacy that are distinct from financial satisfaction. Subsequent to the development of such measures, it would be useful to examine the relationship between income adequacy and financial satisfaction.

Subjective Well-being

Subjective well-being refers to the individual's perceptions of overall life quality (e.g., Andrews & Withey, 1976; Campbell et al., 1976; George, 1981; 1990). A variety of specific concepts and measures have been used to tap subjective well-being in previous research including life satisfaction, morale, happiness, and positive versus negative affect—with life satisfaction being the most frequently employed. On one hand, these indicators of well-being share important similarities: All of them are subjective and refer to the respondent's general affective state regarding life as a whole. Moreover, measures of these differing concepts tend to be highly intercorrelated (George, 1981). Conversely, there are also subtle differences among these indicators of well-being. Life satisfaction and morale tend to reflect long-term, relatively stable judgments of life quality, whereas happiness and affect measures reflect more transitory and short-term reports of mood (George, 1981).

Although the differences among measures of subjective well-being are important for some purposes, they appear to be largely irrelevant to the relationships among financial resources, financial satisfaction, and subjective well-being. Several previous studies include multiple indicators of subjective well-being (e.g., Andrews & Withey, 1976; Campbell et al., 1976); results of those studies do not suggest that the directions or magnitudes of the relationships between subjective well-being and economic resources or those between subjective well-being and financial satisfaction differ to any significant degree as a function of the way in which subjective well-being is conceptualized or operationalized.

There is limited evidence concerning trends in life satisfaction and other indicators of subjective well-being over time. Available evidence suggests that during the past 20 to 25 years, the life satisfaction of older adults has increased slightly relative to that of the nonelderly (Herzog & Rodgers, 1981; Rodgers, 1982). Thus in earlier studies, especially those conducted in the 1960s, older adults were somewhat less satisfied with their lives, on average, than middle-aged and younger adults. By the mid-1970s, however, older adults were equally satisfied or perhaps slightly more satisfied with their lives, on average, than younger people. This pattern, which has remained stable for more than a decade, is based on comparisons of cross-sectional surveys conducted during a 20- to 25-year period and is widely believed to represent cohort differences. During this same interval, the characteristics of the cohorts entering old age improved significantly in terms of average levels of economic resources, education, and health.

In terms of age effects, the longitudinal data available suggest that subjective well-being tends to remain stable during later life. Available data suggest neither systematic declines or increases in subjective well-being during later life nor temporal fluctuations such as those observed for income. Clearly, the subjective well-being of older adults (indeed, of all adults) is responsive to changes in life circumstances such as dramatic changes in health and the experience of widowhood (George, 1990). Nonetheless, in the absence of major personal and social dislocations, subjective well-being—especially measures based on long-term judgments of life quality—tends to remain quite stable throughout old age.

BIVARIATE RELATIONSHIPS

This section summarizes available evidence about the bivariate relationships among financial resources, financial satisfaction, and subjective well-being. Though information based on studies of multivariate models (reviewed in the next section) provides stronger evidence of the robustness of the relationships among these variables, bivariate correlations provide important data about the size and direction of the relationships and facilitate interpretation of the multivariate results. Throughout this section, attention is paid to the degree to which these bivariate relationships differ in magnitude for the elderly and the nonelderly.

Financial Resources and Subjective Well-Being

There is general consensus on theoretical grounds that financial resources will be positive and significantly related to subjective well-being—that higher levels of financial resources promote favorable perceptions of life quality. This hypothesis is well supported in available studies. A review of more than 20 studies that report the bivariate correlation between financial resources (as indexed by income) and subjective well-being (measured in a variety of ways) indicates that the range of those correlations is .12 to .43.

Though the relationship between income and subjective well-being is positive and often substantial in magnitude, a wide range of correlations has been reported in previous studies. One of the factors that explains this variation is the age range of the sample. Dividing the studies on the basis of age to the extent possible, the following pattern is observed in Table 5.1:

TABLE 5.1 Relationship Among Age, and Income and Subjective Well-Being

Age of respondents (years)	Correlation between income and subjective well-being
All adults	.15-.23
Age 59 and younger	.17-.43
Age 60 and older	.12-.33

This pattern suggests that, although income is positively related to subjective well-being for all adults, the relationship is stronger for the nonelderly than for the elderly. One study, based on a national probability sample of adults age 18 and older, focused explicitly on age differences in the relationship between income and subjective well-being (George, Okun, & Landerman, 1985). The three age groups used in that study were young adults (age 18-34), middle-aged adults (age 35-59), and older adults (age

60 and older). The correlation for the relationship between income and life satisfaction were .17 for the young adults, .43 for the middle-aged adults, and .20 for the older adults. These results suggest that the relationship between income and subjective well-being is considerably stronger for middle-aged than for younger or older adults.

It should also be noted that some studies suggest that the relationship between income and subjective well-being is nonlinear, with the relationship substantially stronger at the lower end of the income distribution (e.g., Vaughan & Lancaster, 1980; 1981). Substantially, this pattern suggests that income contributes directly to subjective well-being up to a threshold at which continued increments in income are less potent predictors of well-being. Methodologically, a nonlinear relationship between income and subjective well-being has two implications. First, sample composition may explain some of the variation in the size of the correlations between income and subjective well-being reported in previous studies (i.e., the size of the correlation will be influenced by the age distribution of the sample). Second, because none of the preceding studies included adjustments for a possible nonlinear relationship between income and subjective well-being, the correlations reported in previous work may underestimate the size of the true relationship.

Financial Satisfaction and Subjective Well-Being

There is also general consensus that perceptions of financial satisfaction should be positively and significantly related to perceptions of life quality. This hypothesis also has consistent support in previous studies. The literature review performed for this chapter identified 14 estimates of the correlation between financial satisfaction and subjective well-being. In all cases, the correlations were positive and statistically significant, ranging from .14 to .59.

There is wide variation in the size of the correlations between financial satisfaction and subjective well-being. Again, it appears that age differences in sample composition account for much of this variation. In studies of adults of all ages and studies restricted to the nonelderly, the correlations between financial satisfaction and subjective well-being range from .22 to .59. In studies based on samples of older adults (i.e., persons age 60 and older), the correlations between financial satisfaction and subjective well-being range from .14 to .29.

Financial Resources and Financial Satisfaction

The final bivariate relationship of concern is that between financial resources and financial satisfaction. Again, the clear expectation is that this relationship will be positive and significant. Interestingly, review of the literature reveals that few investigators report the size of the correlations between these measures, though several authors state that they are positive and substantial in magnitude (Andrews & Withey, 1976; Doyle & Forehand, 1984). Perhaps the best estimate of this relationship is the correlation of .23 reported by Campbell et al., (1976) in a national survey of American adults.

Results reported in previous studies do not permit a comparison of the size of the correlation between income (or other measures of financial resources) and financial satisfaction between older and younger samples. Vaughan's (1980) work on the use of subjective assessments of income adequacy to estimate family income equivalence scales, however, is very useful for understanding the degree to which differing levels of income lead to equal levels of financial satisfaction for older versus younger adults. As noted previously, income equivalence scales are developed to estimate the differing levels of income needed by different kinds of households to generate equivalent standards of living. The family income equivalence scales based on subjective assessments of financial satisfaction developed by Vaughan indicated that, depending on family size, households headed by individuals age 65 and older require only 30% of the income required by families of the same size headed by persons younger than age 65. Although Vaughan's results do not mean that income is less strongly correlated with financial satisfaction for older than for younger adults, they strongly document that older adults are equally satisfied with substantially lower levels of income than younger adults, even after adjustments for family size.

Vaughan and associates (Vaughan, 1980; Vaughan & Lancaster, 1980, 1981) also noted that the relationship between income and financial satisfaction is nonlinear. The form of this relationship suggests that financial satisfaction increases with higher levels of income until a threshold is reached; at that point, income becomes a less powerful predictor of financial satisfaction. Again, the potential nonlinear form of this relationship has been ignored in most previous research.

MULTIVARIATE MODELS

Financial resources (in the form of income) and, to a lesser extent, financial satisfaction have been incorporated into numerous multivariate models predicting life satisfaction and other measures of subjective well-being. This body of research is important to the topic of this chapter for two reasons. First, these studies permit us to assess the degree to which financial resources and financial satisfaction are significant predictors of subjective well-being, net of the effects of other relevant antecedents of perceived quality of life. Second, and more important, these studies augment our understanding of the mechanisms by which financial resources and financial satisfaction produce differing levels of subjective well-being.

The studies reviewed differ in terms of the age compositions of the samples employed. Some studies are based on cross sections of American adults (i.e., age 18 and older); others are based on samples of only older adults (i.e., age 60 or 65 and older). Comparisons of results based on samples that vary in age composition permit tentative conclusions about the degree to which the effects of financial resources and financial satisfaction on subjective well-being are equally robust across age groups and the degree to which the causal processes underlying those relationships vary with age or cohort.

Robustness of Relationships

Financial Resources and Subjective Well-being.   Twelve previous studies examined the relationships between income (a partial indicator of financial resources) and subjective well-being (measures of happiness, life satisfaction, and morale) in multivariate context (Beck 1982; Campbell et al., 1976; Doyle & Forehand, 1984; Elwell & Maltbie-Crannell, 1981; George et al., 1985; Horan & Belcher, 1982; Liang et al., 1980; Markides & Martin, 1979; Mutran & Burke, 1979; Mutran & Reitzes, 1981; Osberg, McGinnis, DeJong, & Seward, 1987; Usui, Keil, & Phillips, 1983). Four of the studies indicated that income had a significant effect on subjective well-being, even when several other determinants of perceived life quality were statistically controlled (Beck, 1982; Campbell et al., 1976; Doyle & Forehand, 1984; Usui et al., 1983). Six of the studies suggested that income did *not* have a significant direct effect on perceived life quality, net of other controls—though these studies consistently indicated that income had a significant indirect effect on subjective well-being via a variety of other, more proximate predictors (Horan & Belcher, 1982; Liang et al., 1980; Markides & Martin, 1979; Mutran & Burke, 1979; Mutran & Reitzers, 1981; Osberg et al., 1987).

Results from two of the studies were somewhat more complicated. In one study, separate multivariate models were estimated for three age groups, representing young, middle-aged, and older adults (George et al., 1985). Results from that study indicated that income had a significant direct effect on life satisfaction for young and middle-aged adults, but not for older adults. In that same study, however, income has a significant indirect effect on subjective well-being for all three age groups. In another study, separate path models of the determinants of life satisfaction were calculated for older men and women (Elwell & Maltbie-Crannell, 1981). The results indicated that income had a significant direct effect on subjective well-being for older men but not for older women. Again, however, for both subgroups, income had a significant indirect effect on life satisfaction via other predictors in the models.

Thus, available evidence is ambiguous and contradictory regarding the direct effect of income on subjective well-being. In all likelihood, whether income exerts a direct effect on subjective well-being depends on a variety of factors including sample composition and especially the specific configuration of other independent variables included in the model. In addition, recall that there is considerable evidence that the relationship between income and subjective well-being is nonlinear (e.g., Vaughan, 1980). Adjustments for potential nonlinearity between these variables were not included in any of the studies reviewed earlier. Consequently, the true relationship between income and subjective well-being may be underestimated in those studies. It should also be noted that at this point the only evidence available concerns the relationship between income and subjective well-being. Information about the relationships between subjective well-being and other dimensions of financial resources (or financial resources as operationalized in broader terms) is badly needed.

Regardless of whether the direct effects of income on subjective well-being are significant or nonsignificant in previous research, it is clear that the indirect effects of income are both statistically significant and substantively meaningful. Consequently, it would be ill advised to omit financial resources, as measured in some relatively objective way, from models of the determinants of subjective well-being during adulthood.

Financial Satisfaction and Subjective Well-being.   Six multivariate studies of the determinants of subjective well-being included financial satisfaction as a predictor of perceived quality of life. In all six studies, the effect of financial satisfaction on subjective well-being was statistically significant and substantial in size (Andrews & Withey, 1976; Campbell et al., 1976; Doyle & Forehand, 1984; Fengler & Jensen, 1981; Kozma & Stones, 1983; Liang, et al., 1980). Indeed, in one study based on a representative national sample of adults of all ages, satisfaction with standard of living was the strongest predictor of satisfaction with life—and there were 16 other measures of personal and social resources in the model (Campbell et al., 1976). In that same study, satisfaction with amount of savings also made an independent statistically significant and substantively meaningful contribution to the model. In studies restricted to samples of older adults, measures of financial satisfaction are generally equal to or only slightly less powerful than self-rated health in predicting perceived life quality. Only one study examined the degree to which other, more causally proximate predictions of subjective well-being mediate the effects of financial satisfaction. In that study, financial satisfaction remained a highly significant predictor of life satisfaction, although some of its effects were mediated by social integration (Liang et al., 1980).

A variety of specific measures of financial satisfaction have been used in the studies reviewed previously. Some studies elicit self-reports of satisfaction with one's general financial situation; others tap more specific dimensions of financial satisfaction, such as satisfaction with income or standard of living. Any attempt to identify patterns specific to particular measures of financial satisfaction is subject to substantial error, given the other differences across studies (e.g., differences in sample composition or in the configurations of other predictors in the models). Nonetheless, it appears that satisfaction with standard of living may be more strongly related to subjective well-being than other indicators of financial satisfaction (Andrews & Withey, 1976; Campbell et al., 1976; Herzog & Rodgers, 1981).

On the basis of available evidence, then, it appears that financial satisfaction is a statistically robust and substantively meaningful determinant of perceptions of life quality during adulthood. Again, investigators interested in understanding subjective well-being would be well advised to include financial satisfaction measures in their models.

Financial Resources and Financial Satisfaction.   On theoretical grounds, the relationship between financial resources and satisfaction with financial resources would be expected to be statistically significant and substantively large. In light of that, it is surprising that relatively few studies have put that hypothesis to empirical test—and, indeed, few studies of the determinants of subjective well-being have included indicators of both financial resources and financial satisfaction in the same model.

Six studies examined the relationships between income (one indicator of financial resources) and financial satisfaction in multivariate context (Campbell et al., 1976; Liang & Fairchild, 1979; Liang et al., 1980; Vaughan 1980; Vaughan & Lancaster, 1980; 1981). One additional study examined the relationship between socioeconomic status, a composite variable based in part on income, and financial satisfaction in the context of a multivariate model (Liang et al., 1980). Four of the six studies report statistically significant and substantively large relationships between income and financial satisfaction, net of other controls (Campbell et al., 1976; Vaughan, 1980; Vaughan & Lancaster, 1980, 1981). Similarly, in the one applicable study, socioeconomic status was strongly related to financial satisfaction, controlling on other relevant predictors (Liang et al., 1980). In two studies, however, the effects of income on financial satisfaction were reduced to nonsignificance when control variables were introduced (Liang & Fairchild, 1979; Liang et al., 1980). As described in detail subsequently, however, the nature of the control variables accounted for this pattern of results.

It should be noted that three studies indicate that the relationship between income and financial satisfaction is nonlinear (Vaughan, 1980; Vaughan & Lancaster, 1980; 1981). Because most of the preceding studies do not take this potential nonlinearity into account, some estimates of the strength of the relationship between income and financial satisfaction may be attenuated.

Explanatory Mechanisms

Thus far it has been established that the relationships among financial resources (typically income), financial satisfaction, and subjective well-being are robust across diverse samples and methods of measurements. Even if the direct effects of income and financial satisfaction are not consistently statistically significant, their indirect effects are theoretically important. What has not yet been addressed is how the effects of income and financial satisfaction on perceived quality of life are mediated by other variables and how those results reveal the causal processes by which income and financial satisfaction generate differing levels of subjective well-being. Available research sheds considerable light on these processes and explanatory mechanisms.

Mediators of the Impact of Income on Subjective Well-being. Six studies have identified factors other than financial satisfaction that mediate the impact of income on subjective well-being (Elwell & Maltbie-Crannell, 1981; George et al., 1985; Horan & Belcher, 1982; Markides & Martin, 1979; Mutran & Reitzes, 1981; Osberg, et al., 1987). The results of these studies are surprisingly consistent, especially in light of the fact that none of the investigators set out to replicate the findings of other researchers. In five of the six studies, the effects of income on subjective well-being were totally or substantially mediated by measures of activities (Elwell & Maltbie-Crannell, 1981; Horan & Belcher, 1982; Markides & Martin, 1979; Mutran & Reitzes, 1981; Osberg, et al., 1987). Operationalizations of activities varied somewhat across these studies. Most included indicators of participation in voluntary organizations, informal social contacts, and levels of involvement in preferred leisure activities. One study (Horan & Belcher, 1982) employed a measure of "cosmopolitan life-style," which was operationalized in terms of a specific set of leisure activities and consumer preferences.

One study did not fit the preceding pattern (George et al., 1985). In that study, the determinants of subjective well-being were examined for three age groups: young, middle-aged, and older adults. Results indicated that the effects of income on life satisfaction were not significantly mediated by any predictors (including activities) for the young and the middle-aged subsamples. In contrast, for the older group, the effects of income on life satisfaction were mediated by self-rated health. The results of this study—at least those for the older subsample—were not as discrepant as it might appear, however, in that the effects of health on subjective well-being were mediated largely by a measure of activities.

Taken as a whole, these studies suggest that the ways in which the effects of income on subjective well-being are mediated may differ somewhat across population subgroups. All the studies indicating that activities are the major avenue by which income affects subjective well-being were based on samples restricted to older adults. The one study that examined patterns of mediation within age groups suggested that activities mediate the impact of income on subjective well-being only for older adults (George et al., 1985). One other study, also based solely on a sample of older adults, reported that the effects of income on life satisfaction varied by sex (Elwell & Maltbie-Crannell, 1981). In that study, the effects of income on life satisfaction were totally mediated by activities for older women; for older men, activities substantially mediated the effects of income on subjective well-being, but income also had a significant direct effect on life satisfaction. Clearly the ways in which the effects of income on subjective well-being are mediated by other variables—especially subgroup differences in pattern of mediation—would profit from additional effort. In the meantime, however, it seems safe to conclude that for older adults much of the impact of income on subjective well-being can be explained by the positive impact of income on activity levels.

Not surprisingly, financial satisfaction has also been demonstrated to mediate substantially the impact of income on subjective well-being. More surprising is the fact that the mediating impact of financial satisfaction has been examined in only three studies. In all three of these studies, financial satisfaction largely mediated the effects of income on subjective well-being, but income retained a significant direct effect on perceptions of life quality also (Andrews & Withey, 1976; Campbell et al., 1976; Doyle & Forehand, 1984). It is perhaps worth noting that this similarity of findings emerged despite the fact that different dimensions of financial satisfaction were measured in the three studies: satisfaction with standard of living and with savings in the Campbell et al. (1976) study, satisfaction with income in the Andrews and Withey (1976) study, and perceptions that finances are a problem in the Doyle and Forehand (1984) study.

Mediators of the Impact of Financial Satisfaction on Subjective Well-being. Only one investigator examined the degree to which other, theoretically more proximate, predictors mediate the effect of financial satisfaction on subjective well-being. Liang and colleagues (Liang et al., 1980; Liang, 1982; Liang & Warfel, 1983) reported that some of the effect of financial satisfaction on perceived quality of life was indirect via objective and subjective social integration—with the former measure including organizational participation and other formal links to social structure and the latter measure tapping feelings of loneliness and social connectedness. Nonetheless, financial satisfaction also retains a significant direct effect on perceived life quality.

Given the limited attention that the potential mediators of financial satisfaction on subjective well-being have received in previous research, firm conclusions about this issue are precluded. It should be noted, however, that one of the reasons that this issue has received such limited attention is that most authors view domain-specific satisfaction measures (including satisfaction with financial resources) as the most proximate predictors of global life satisfaction (Andrews & Withey, 1976; Campbell et al., 1976). That is, some authors would undoubtedly argue that even to hypothesize that any variables mediate the effects of domain-specific satisfaction measures on global indicators of satisfaction with life would involve model misspecification. In the absence of longitudinal data of a very special kind, it is not possible to resolve the issue of how the antecedents of subjective well-being can best be modeled. At any rate, it remains unclear whether any predictors mediate—or should be expected to mediate—the effects of financial satisfaction on subjective well-being.

It is possible, however, that the effects of financial satisfaction on subjective well-being differ in strength for specific population subgroups. There is limited evidence of subgroup differences, though available evidence is inconsistent. Three previous studies examined urban-rural differences in the affects of financial satisfaction on subjective well-being measures in older samples. Two of the studies suggested that the effects of financial satisfaction on subjective well-being were significantly stronger for rural than for urban elderly (Kozma & Stones, 1983; Liang & Warfel, 1983); the other study suggested that financial satisfaction was a stronger predictor of life satisfaction for the urban elderly (Fengler & Jensen, 1981). Though the limited data available do not permit conclusions about subgroup differences, the topic is clearly one that would profit from additional effort.

Mediators of the Impact of Income on Financial Satisfaction.   At first glance, it may seem that the relationship between income and financial satisfaction is simple and direct; yet there is convincing evidence that such is not the case. First, as previously noted, the relationship between income and financial satisfaction is nonlinear (e.g., Vaughan, 1980). Second, and more theoretically important, some authors have designed studies to explain the relationship between income and financial satisfaction. The results of those studies are both interesting and complex.

Liang and colleagues successfully explained the relationship between income and financial satisfaction on the basis of two social-psychological processes: relative deprivation and perceived distributive justice. Two dimensions of relative deprivation were measured: comparisons of personal income levels to those of others (i.e., age peers) and comparisons of current to past income (Liang & Fairchild, 1979; Liang et al., 1980). Perceptions of distributive justice were measured in terms of the degree to which current income levels were viewed as fair and just (Liang et al., 1980). Results indicated that all three measures had statistically significant and substantively large effects on financial satisfaction. Indeed, once the effects of relative deprivation and perceived distributive justice were included in the models, the

direct effect of income on financial satisfaction was reduced to nonsignificance. Thus, Liang and colleagues concluded that the effects of income on
financial satisfaction are accounted for by individuals' perceptions of relative deprivation and the perceived fairness of their incomes.

Carp and Carp (1982) pursued a similar line of investigation. They began
with the hypothesis proposed by Campbell et al. (1976) as well as others (e.g.,
George, 1981) that satisfaction levels are a function of a comparison of personal aspirations to achievements—and the greater the discrepancy between aspirations and achievements, the lower the level of satisfaction. When Campbell
et al. (1976) put this hypothesis to empirical test, however, they found that
aspiration versus achievement theory operated only for young middle-aged
adults. Older adults failed to support the aspiration versus achievement theory
in two ways. First, older people reported levels of financial satisfaction far in
excess of their objective economic conditions. Second, for older people, substantial discrepancies between reported economic aspirations and actual levels
of economic resources often did not lead to financial dissatisfaction.

Similar to Liang and colleagues, Carp and Carp (1982) suggested that
perceptions of equity and fairness explain the relationship between income
and financial satisfaction in later life. Their research results supported this
conclusion. Compatible with the results of Campbell et al. (1976) aspirations versus achievements explained the relationship between income and
financial satisfaction for young and middle-aged adults; for older adults, perceived equity (and *not* aspiration-achievement theory) explained this relationship. Thus, young and middle-aged adults were satisfied with their financial
resources when their incomes were commensurate with their aspirations;
older adults were satisfied with their financial resources when they perceived
their incomes as just and fair.

Interestingly, there is limited evidence suggesting that perceptions of relative deprivation do *not* mediate the impact of income on subjective well-
being. Usui, Keil, & Durig (1985) reported that income and perceptions of
relative deprivation have independent and statistically significant direct effects on life satisfaction in a sample of older adults. Though it would be
dangerous to reach a firm conclusion on the basis of a single study, these
results suggest that relative deprivation and related psychological processes
moderate the impact of income on financial satisfaction but not the effect of
income on subjective well-being.

Though this body of research is limited in volume, there is considerable
evidence that the psychological mechanisms that translate income levels into
perceptions of financial satisfaction have been identified, at least in part. It
is also fascinating that these mechanisms appear to differ by age or perhaps
by cohort.

One additional issue merits brief mention. No extant studies have examined the degree to which income adequacy mediates the relationship be-

tween income and financial satisfaction, though some research suggests that several of the adjustments considered central to determining income adequacy (for example, family size) are significantly related to financial satisfaction (e.g., Vaughan, 1980). As noted previously, it appears that there are important conceptual and empirical differences between income and adequacy and financial satisfaction. The nature of these concepts and of their relationships to each other merits greater attention in future research.

THEORETICAL IMPLICATIONS

A considerable body of research has been summarized; it is now prudent to place this review in larger perspective. This section is intended to perform two tasks. First, the results of this review are summarized in broad terms. To minimize redundancy, the summary is restricted to two major points. Subsequently, a theoretical case is made that the distinction between status attainment and status maintenance helps to elucidate the numerous differences between age-cohort groups regarding the relationships among financial resources, financial satisfaction, and subjective well-being.

One major issue concerns the degree to which financial resources and financial satisfaction are robust determinants of perceived life quality. In this area, relatively straightforward conclusions can be reached. Financial resources, at least income, are clearly a determinant of subjective well-being. The relationship between income (as a partial proxy for financial resources as more broadly defined) and subjective well-being is not simple and direct. Nonetheless, it is clear that income operates directly or indirectly on subjective well-being. Similarly, perceptions of financial satisfaction are potent predictors of perceived quality of life. Thus for American adults, including the elderly, financial security (in the form of both objective economic conditions and perceptions of the adequacy of economic resources) is an important component of life quality.

Another major issue about which this review permits unambiguous conclusions is the question of whether there are age or cohort differences in the relationships among financial resources, financial satisfaction, and subjective well-being. This review identified at least four areas in which the elderly exhibit distinctive patterns relative to the nonelderly. First, both aggregate historical trends of relative economic status and longitudinal patterns of economic status within cohorts vary between the elderly and nonelderly—and the most important aspect of these patterns is that the aggregate trends lead to vastly different conclusions than do the longitudinal patterns. Aggregate historical trends indicate that, relative to the nonelderly, the economic status of the elderly has improved consistently during the past 20 to 25 years. In contrast, longitudinal patterns indicate that financial resources, especially income, decline over time among older adults and increase over time for younger and middle-aged adults. Both patterns are true, but the first represents a cohort effect in which successive cohorts of older adults enter later life more economically advantaged than their predecessors, and the latter represents an age effect within cohorts reflecting life-course differences in labor force participation and economic behavior more generally.

A second and especially important difference between older and younger adults is the relationship between income levels and financial satisfaction. Older adults clearly require substantially lower levels of income to report that they are satisfied with their levels of financial resources than do young and middle-aged adults. This pattern is important for both scientific and policy purposes. In terms of relatively basic research on the relationship between financial resources and subjective well-being, investigators need to recognize that older people require relatively small levels of economic resources to be satisfied with their financial lot in life. This issue is perhaps even more important for policy analysts. The amounts of income needed to elicit self-reports of financial satisfaction among the elderly are so low that policy makers dare not rely on reports of financial satisfaction as indicators of the amount of income needed to meet the objective needs of older persons.

Third, available evidence suggests that older adults employ somewhat different mechanisms than younger adults in making judgments about perceived income adequacy of financial satisfaction. For younger and middle-aged adults, financial satisfaction appears to be a function of the discrepancy between financial aspirations and economic achievements—the greater the discrepancy, the greater the dissatisfaction with financial resources. In contrast, for older adults, financial satisfaction appears to be a function of the degree to which older adults feel (a) deprived (relative to peers and to their past economic status), and (b) that they are receiving fair and just incomes. Thus, both interventions (e.g., income maintenance policies) and naturally occurring psychological accommodations (e.g., the accommodation processes described by Campbell et al., 1976) that lead to changes in financial satisfaction will differ for younger and older adults.

Finally, it appears that income operates differently as a determinant of subjective well-being for older and younger adults. The limited evidence available for younger and middle-aged adults suggests that the effects of income on subjective well-being are largely unmediated by life circumstances other than financial satisfaction. For the elderly, income is less likely to have a direct effect on subjective well-being; instead, income appears to promote subjective well-being for older adults via its role in increasing levels of activity and, to a lesser extent, fostering good health. We are left with the impression that income per se is important for perceived quality of life among nonelderly, whereas for older adults higher levels of financial resources are more important as means to desirable ends.

A common theme underlying these age or cohort differences in the relationships among financial resources, financial satisfaction, and subjective well-being may be the distinction between status attainment and status maintenance. This distinction was first proposed by Henretta and Campbell (1976) to highlight life-course differences in the determinants of economic status. They contended that for younger and middle-aged adults the central issue is the degree to which social background, and economic behaviors and orientations (as broadly defined) lead to personal economic achievements and mobility, whereas for older adults the key issue is the degree to which economic behaviors earlier in the life course permit older adults to maintain their levels of economic status relative to others in their cohorts.

As other investigators, including Myles (1981), have indicated, however, the concept of status maintenance can be usefully expanded beyond the issues addressed by Henretta and Campbell (1976). The distinction between status attainment and status maintenance may highlight age differences in orientations toward economic resources in a broader sense. Age differences in the levels of income required to generate financial satisfaction may reflect the fact that younger and middle-aged adults are concerned with making an economic mark for themselves and attaining higher economic status, if possible. Older adults, in contrast, may be satisfied as long as they can maintain acceptable life-styles.

The social-psychological mechanisms underlying reports of financial satisfaction may also reflect age differences in status orientation. The fact that younger adults' levels of financial satisfaction rest on a comparison of aspirations and achievements suggests that concerns about setting goals and meeting them are important economic behaviors in early and middle adulthood. Older adults' concerns about economic deprivation relative to age peers and, especially issues of fairness and equity, suggest that maintenance of economic position rather than increase in economic status is their major concern.

Path models of the determinants of subjective well-being across age groups lead to similar conclusions. For young and middle-aged adults, income has a direct effect on subjective well-being, suggesting that status attainment is an important basis of judgments about life quality. For older adults, income is more important because of its indirect effects via other antecedents of well-being (e.g., income is important for many older persons' perceived life quality because it allows them to sustain preferred levels of activity). Thus, when viewed more broadly, the distinction between status attainment and status maintenance may help to integrate and explain observed age differences in the relationships among financial resources, financial satisfaction, and subjective well-being.

AN AGENDA FOR FUTURE RESEARCH

Although we know a considerable amount about the relationships among financial resources, financial satisfaction, and subjective well-being, there are also several issues that would profit from additional effort. In this final section, six fruitful areas for future research are proposed. These recommendations vary considerably, both in the specificity with which the needed effort can be described and the degree to which the recommendations build directly on previous efforts.

Defining Financial Resources More Broadly

One issue that builds directly on previous efforts is the need for research that moves beyond simple measures of annual income. Financial resources clearly include more than money income, and levels of financial resources, as more broadly defined, vary both across age groups and within the older populations. Any or all of the conclusions reached in this chapter might be different had previous research included measures of financial resources as more broadly defined. If we are to understand thoroughly the relationship between financial security and general well-being, information about assets must be incorporated in future research.

The Thorny Issue of Income-Financial Adequacy

In the interests of both basic research concerning the impact of financial resources on subjective well-being and policy analyses of income maintenance policies, the issue of income-financial adequacy needs to be explored in greater depth. There is ample evidence that financial satisfaction is not an adequate proxy for income adequacy—especially for older adults. There are good reasons that current "objective" measures of income adequacy (e.g., poverty levels, budgets based largely on dietary requirements) are dissatisfying to both basic scientists and to policy analysts. Nonetheless, it seems clear that some form of objective or standardized system that includes adjustments for family size, age, and household composition, among other factors, will prove to be the most useful approach for assessing income adequacy.

The availability of satisfactory measures of income adequacy, independent of financial satisfaction, would permit important additional research. Social scientists would then be in a position to determine the degree to which income adequacy mediates the relationship between financial resources and financial satisfaction—a set of relationships that is important and obvious on logical grounds, but that has not been addressed thus far because of the lack of appropriate measures of income adequacy. Given proper methods of measuring income adequacy, policy analysts would be better able to develop income maintenance programs that ensure some level of equity and comparability across population subgroups.

Need for Longitudinal Studies

A major limitation of extant research that examines the relationships between financial security and subjective well-being is the absence of longitudinal data. Very little of what we know about these relationships is based on observations made over time. Indeed, the only points that we currently know on the basis of longitudinal data concern the dynamics of single variables: (a) that income declines during later life, and (b) that financial satisfaction and subjective well-being tend to remain stable during old age unless there are dramatic changes in objective circumstances. It is lamentable, but worth noting, that none of the studies examining the relationships between financial resources and subjective well-being reviewed in this chapter were based on longitudinal data.

At least four types of longitudinal studies are needed to understand better and draw accurate conclusions about the relationships between financial security and subjective well-being in later life. First, longitudinal studies are needed that document the ways in which life-course patterns, especially economic status and behaviors in young adulthood and middle age, affect economic status and quality of life during old age. On one hand, it is commonly recognized that financial status during later life is in large measure a function of economic achievements and decisions made earlier in life (e.g., Henretta & Campbell, 1976; O'Rand, 1990). Conversely, almost nothing is known about the specific processes by which earlier socioeconomic status translates into financial status and life quality during old age.

Second, longitudinal studies are needed that trace the trajectories of financial status and subjective well-being during later life and the ways those trajectories intersect and affect each other. A limited literature suggests that some of the assumptions that we frequently make about economic behavior in later life may be inaccurate or at least highly oversimplified. For example, some research calls into question the assumptions that (a) late life is typically a period of dispersion of assets and (b) older people are unlikely to invest financial resources in savings (e.g., Danziger, van der Gaag, Smolensky, & Taussig, 1982; Hamermesh, 1984; McConnel & Deljavan, 1983; Stoller & Stoller, 1987), Considerably more research is needed, however, to describe the ways in which older people handle their financial resources, how their financial resources wax and wane over time, and the implications of those dynamics for subjective well-being.

Third, better understanding of cohort differences related to financial security and subjective well-being in later life is needed. We already know that the increasing economic well-being of the older population relative to the nonelderly during the past 2 decades is largely a result of cohort differences. We also know that aggregate cohort differences can mask very different patterns of change occurring within cohorts. All of the research reviewed in this chapter was based on specific cohorts of adults measured at particular points in history. In the absence of longitudinal studies—or at least replications of extant research over time—we will not know the degree to which the patterns observed with considerable consistency thus far are cohort specific. For example, extant research suggests that younger adults' levels of financial satisfaction are based on comparisons of aspirations and achievements, whereas older adults' levels of financial satisfaction are based on perceptions of deprivation relative to age peers and judgments about fairness and equity. This difference in the way younger and older adults define financial satisfaction may reflect age or life-cycle differences in the mechanisms used to evaluate life quality, or instead it may reflect cohort differences in the references used to make evaluations of relative status. In the absence of longitudinal data, these competing explanations cannot be resolved.

A fourth and final contribution that would result from the use of longitudinal data is increased information about the degree to which variables of concern, especially financial satisfaction and subjective well-being, are sensitive to change. Currently, we do not know the degree to which changes in objective economic status are accompanied by changes in financial satisfaction and subjective well-being. Most scientists believe that satisfaction measures represent evaluations of personal well-being based on relatively long-term and stable time frames. Empirical data supporting these assumptions is scant, however. The best method of assessing the degree to which satisfaction measures are sensitive to change is to identify the degree to which they fluctuate in tandem with changes in objective circumstances.

More Intensive Examination of Heterogeneity Within the Older Population

Variability within the older population needs to be examined in greater detail, and extant knowledge about the heterogeneity needs to be more widely disseminated. It is my belief that most gerontological observers remain largely unaware of the economic heterogeneity within the older population—certainly the inaccurate perception that the elderly are at increased risk of poverty relative to the young remains the dominant assumption of the larger public. Yet the economic heterogeneity of the older population has potentially important implications for policies directed toward income maintenance during later life. Gerontologists now seem considerably more open to policy recommendations that would redistribute income from the high-income elderly to the low-income elderly (as opposed to redistributing income from the nonelderly to the elderly) than in the past. Nonetheless, before such recommendations are adopted, much more research is needed to establish guidelines for appropriate redistribution policies and to understand their implications.

A second issue related to heterogeneity among the older population concerns the need to examine in more detail the economic status general well-being of specific subgroups of the elderly. Three subgroups particularly in need of intensive examination are older women (e.g., Minkler & Stone, 1985; Smeeding, 1990), the chronically ill (e.g., George & Gwyther, 1986); and the widowed (e.g., Zick & Smith, 1986). Each of these subgroups faces increased risk of economic problems or exacerbated decline in economic resources relative to other older adults. More detailed examination of the dynamics of financial resources and well-being among these groups holds the promise of increasing our understanding of the conditions under which economic resources and subjective well-being are undermined in later life and of identifying subgroups appropriate for targeted policy interventions.

At the broadest level, increased examination of heterogeneity among the older population will improve our understanding of the factors that place certain older adults at great risk of economic problems in later life and undoubtedly will also contribute to the ever-present debates about age versus need as a criteria for public programs and policies (e.g., Neugarten, 1982). Indeed, recognition of the heterogeneity among the older population poses a major challenge to the rationale for the logic of age-based policies and programs.

Development of More Creative Approaches for Studying Financial Security and Subjective Well-Being in Later Life

The two final recommendations for future effort are considerably broader in scope than those previously described. In addition, they would require a greater change in direction than previous recommendations. One of the frustrations I experienced in reviewing available literature on the relationships among financial resources, financial satisfaction, and subjective well-being was the chronic and nagging sense that traditional methodological and statistical approaches, though useful for certain purposes, fail to reveal some kinds of important information.

In previous literature, two major statistical approaches have been used to examine financial status and general well-being in later life. Most commonly, correlational procedures, usually linear regression models, are used to estimate the relationships among financial resources, financial satisfaction, and subjective well-being in later life. Though these correlational techniques provide important information, they also have limitations—both inherent limitations and limitations consequent to the ways in which investigators have used them. As noted previously, unless adjustments are made—and they typically are *not* made—nonlinearities, especially threshold effects, in the bivariate and multivariate relationships among variables are ignored. Moreover, correlational techniques by themselves fail to shed light on some rather dramatic age-related differences in absolute levels of financial resources and well-being. For example, the correlations among income, financial satisfaction, and life satisfaction do not appear to differ to any degree across age groups. These relatively comparable correlations fail to inform us, however, of substantial and substantively important age differences—that older adults require only 30% as much income, on average, as younger adults to generate equal levels of financial satisfaction (Vaughan, 1980).

The other frequently employed statistical approach is to rely on measures of central tendency (e.g., comparing income means and medians across age groups) or other categorical measures (for example, using official poverty lines to compare the elderly and nonelderly in percentages of the poor). As Binstock (1986) noted, such measures "artificially homogenize population groupings and obfuscate understanding" because of their insensivitity to "issues of diversity, disaggregation, and distribution" (p. 60). Other investigators have noted similar problems with measures of central tendency (e.g., Quinn, 1985).

The limitations of such measures can be illustrated by examining a study by Holden et al. (1986). That study, based on 10-year longitudinal data of a national sample of older adults, indicated that cross-sectional studies greatly underestimate the true risks of poverty during later life. Indeed, the risk of becoming poor at some time during the 10-year interval was more than twice as great as the highest annual (i.e., cross-sectional) poverty rate. On one hand, this is a highly valuable study, documenting that conclusions based on cross-sectional data can be highly misleading—in this case, grossly underestimating the risk of poverty during later life. Conversely, the Holden et al. (1986) study may also be misleading because of its reliance on a categorical method of identifying the poor and the nonpoor. These authors identified substantial year-to-year fluctuation around a line of demarcation—that is, the poverty line—but they do not report cross-time correlations of income levels. In the absence of information about these correlations across time, we cannot know whether the authors have identified substantial changes in the ebb and flow of income during later life or are observing relatively modest fluctuations about a cutpoint.

Unfortunately, there is no obvious resolution to this issue. Perhaps the best that we can do is to be vigilant about the limitations of traditional statistical approaches and to incorporate examination of both correlational associations and absolute, metric levels of the variables of concern into our analysis and conclusions. In addition, this area is ripe for innovative methodological approaches that could provide a more comprehensive picture of the complexities among indicators of financial security and subjective well-being.

Neglected Aspects of Financial Security in Later Life

A final recommendation concerns the utility of exploring some aspects of financial security in later life that have been relatively neglected in previous research. One of the most unique aspects of financial security in later life—and also one of the most neglected—is the fact that older adults are in a unique position with regard to making financial plans and evaluating the adequacy of extant financial resources in light of uncertainty about future economic needs. As noted previously, most older adults report that they are satisfied with their *current* levels of economic resources and do not view financial hardships as a personal problem (National Council on Aging, 1981). Nonetheless, there is limited evidence that older adults fear that their financial resources will be inadequate to meet *future* needs. For example, the Older Americans Resources and Services (OARS) Multidimensional Functional Assessment Questionnaire (George & Fillenbaum, 1985) includes a battery of questions about perceptions of the adequacy of financial resources. This questionnaire has been administered in multiple sites in the context of multiple research designs. Research results based on the OARS Questionnaire consistently indicate that, although most older adults in a representative community sample report that their incomes are sufficient to meet current needs, 40% to 55% also believe that their incomes will not be sufficient to meet future needs—and many more will qualify their responses (e.g., by adding the stipulation that their incomes will be sufficient barring medical or other emergencies).

It might be argued that younger and middle-aged adults also fear emergencies and can envision circumstances under which their incomes would be insufficient for their needs—and, indeed, given that the OARS Questionnaire has not been administered to representative samples of the nonelderly, I cannot dispute that line of argument with empirical data. Nonetheless, I believe that older people are more concerned about their abilities to meet future financial demands than younger adults—and for good reasons. For one thing, evidence clearly indicates that the elderly are at much greater risk of needing money for major and long-term health care services than younger people. Moreover, older adults are less able than younger adults to alter their incomes or assets directly. It is my hypothesis that older adults' major concerns about financial security consist of fears that their economic resources will be insufficient for increased future needs generated by events such as illness or widowhood, and that their major challenge is to allocate rationally resources for a future that is uncertain in terms of both duration and level of need. Furthermore, I would guess that these concerns are especially salient to middle- and upper-income older adults.

Additional research is needed to define the financial concerns of older adults more clearly and to determine the degree to which those concerns are unique to later life (either in their presence or their frequency). It is likely that a focus on current financial status and general well-being, especially when ascertained from a static, cross-sectional perspective, ignores much of what the concept of financial security means to older adults.

In conclusion, available research documents that the links between financial status and subjective well-being are strong and robust during adulthood in general and during old age in particular. That same research provides considerable information about the degree to which and the ways in which financial resources affect subjective well-being. Additional research is greatly needed, however, to flesh out our understanding of the dynamics of financial status and general well-being, to provide a bedrock for informed policy decisions, and to identify what financial security means to older adults themselves.

REFERENCES

Andrews, F. M., & Withey, S. B. (1976). *Social indicators of well-being*. New York: Plenum.

Beck, S. H. (1982). Adjustment to and satisfaction with retirement. *Journal of Gerontology, 37*, 616–624.

Binstock, R. H. (1986). Perspectives on measuring hardship: Concepts, dimensions, and implications. *The Gerontologist, 26*, 60–62.

Campbell, A., Converse, P. E., & Rodgers, W. L. (1976). *The quality of American life*. New York: Russell Sage Foundation.

Carp, F. M., & Carp, A. (1982). Test of a model of domain satisfactions and well-being: Equity considerations. *Research on Aging, 4*, 503–522.

Chen, Y. (1985). Economic status of the aging. In R. Binstock & E. Shanas (Eds.), *Handbook of aging and the social sciences* (2nd ed.) (pp. 641–665). New York: Van Nostrand Reinhold.

Clark, R. L., & Baumer, D. L. (1985). Income maintenance policies. In R. H. Binstock & E. Shanas (Eds.), *Handbook of aging and the social sciences* (2nd ed.) (pp. 666–693). New York: Van Nostrand Reinhold.

Colasanto, D., Kapteyn, A., & Van der Gaag, J. (1984). Two subjective definitions of poverty: Results from the Wisconsin Basic Needs Study. *Journal of Human Resources, 19*, 127–138.

Crystal, S. (1986). Measuring income and inequality among the elderly. *The Gerontologist, 26*, 56–59.

Danziger, S., van der Gaag, J., Smolensky, E., & Taussig, M. K. (1982). The life-cycle hypothesis and the consumption behavior of the elderly. *Journal of Post Keynesian Economics, 5*, 208–227.

Doyle, D., & Forehand, M. J. (1984). Life satisfaction and old age: A reexamination. *Research on Aging, 6*, 432–448.

Duncan, G. J. (1984). *Years of poverty, years of plenty.* Ann Arbor: University of Michigan, Survey Research Center.

Duncan, G. J. (1988). The volatility of family income over the life course. In P. B. Baltes, D. L. Featherman, & R. M. Lerner (Eds.), *Life-span development and behavior* (pp. 317-358). Hillsdale, NJ: Erlbaum Associates.

Duncan, G. J., Hill, M. S., & Rodgers, W. (1987). The changing economic status of the young and the old. In National Research Council (Eds.), *Demographic change and the well-being of children and the elderly* (pp. 29-41). Washington, DC: National Academy Press.

Elwell, F., & Maltbie-Crannell, A. D. (1981). The impact of role loss upon coping resources and life satisfaction of the elderly. *Journal of Gerontology, 36,* 223-232.

Fengler, A. P., & Jensen, L. (1981). Perceived and objective conditions as predictors of the life satisfaction of urban and non urban elderly. *Journal of Gerontology, 36,* 750-752.

George, L. K. (1981). Subjective well-being: Conceptual and methodological issues. In C. Eisdorfer (Ed.), *Annual review of gerontology and geriatrics* (pp. 345-382). New York: Springer.

George, L. K. (1990). Social structure, social processes, and social-psychological states. In R. H. Binstock & L. K. George (Eds.), *Handbook of aging and the social sciences,* (3rd ed.), (pp. 186-200). San Diego: Academic Press.

George, L. K., & Fillenbaum, G. G. (1985). The OARS methodology: A decade of experience in geriatric assessment. *Journal of the American Geriatrics Association, 33,* 607-615.

George, L. K., & Gwyther, L. P. (1986). Caregiver well-being: A multidimensional examination of family caregivers of demented adults. *The Gerontologist, 26,* 253-259.

George, L. K., Okun, M. A., & Landerman, R. (1985). Age as a moderator of the determinants of life satisfaction. *Research on Aging, 7,* 209-233.

Goedhart, T. V., Halberstadt, T., Kapteyn, A., & van Praag, B. M. S. (1977). The poverty line: Concept and measurement. *Journal of Human Resources, 12,* 503-520.

Hamermesh, D. S. (1984). Consumption during retirement: The missing link in the life cycle. *Review of Economics and Statistics, 66,* 1-7.

Harris, R. J. (1986). Recent trends in the relative economic status of older adults. *Journal of Gerontology, 41,* 401-407.

Henretta, J. C., & Campbell, R. T. (1976). Status attainment and status maintenance: A study of stratification in old age. *American Sociological Review, 41,* 981-992.

Henretta, J. C., & Campbell, R. T. (1978). Net worth as an aspect of status. *American Journal of Sociology, 83,* 1204-1223.

Herzog, A. R., & Rodgers, W. L. (1981). Age and satisfaction: Data from several large surveys. *Research on Aging, 3,* 142-165.

Holden, K. C., Burkhauser, R. V., & Myers, D. A. (1986). Income transitions at older stages of life: The dynamics of poverty. *The Gerontologist, 26,* 292-297.

Horan, P. M., & Belcher, J. C. (1982). Lifestyle and morale in the southern rural aged. *Research on Aging, 4,* 523-549.

Hurd, M., & Shoven, J. B. (1982). Real income and wealth of the elderly. *American Economic Review, 74,* 314-318.

Kozma, A., & Stones, M. J. (1983). Predictors of happiness. *Journal of Gerontology, 38,* 626-628.

Liang, J. (1982). Sex differences in life satisfaction among the elderly. *Journal of Gerontology, 37*, 100–108.

Liang, J., Dvorkin, L., Kahana, E., & Mazian, F. (1980). Social integration and morale: A re-examination. *Journal of Gerontology, 35*, 746–757.

Liang, J., & Fairchild, T. (1979). Relative deprevation and perception of financial adequacy among the aged. *Journal of Gerontology, 34*, 746–759.

Liang, J., Kahana, E., & Doherty, E. (1980). Financial well-being among the aged: A further elaboration. *Journal of Gerontology, 35*, 409–420.

Liang, J., & Warfel, B. L. (1983). Urbanism and life satisfaction among the aged. *Journal of Gerontology, 38*, 97–106.

Markides, K. S., & Martin, H. W. (1979). A causal model of life satisfaction among the elderly. *Journal of Gerontology, 34*, 86–93.

McConnel, C. E., & Deljavan, F. (1983). Consumption patterns of the retired household. *Journal of Gerontology, 38*, 480–490.

Minkler, M., & Stone, R. (1985). The feminization of poverty and older women. *The Gerontologist, 25*, 351–357.

Moon, M. (1977). *The measurement of economic welfare.* Chicago: Academic Press.

Mutran, E., & Burke, P. J. (1979). Feeling "useless": A common component of young and old adult identities. *Research on Aging, 1*, 187–212.

Mutran, E., & Reitzes, D. C. (1981). Retirement, identity and well-being: Realization of role relationships. *Journal of Gerontology, 16*, 134–143.

Myles, J. F. (1981). Income inequality and status maintenance: Concepts, methods, and measures. *Research on Aging, 3*, 123–141.

National Council on Aging. (1981). *Aging in the eighties.* Washington, DC: National Council on Aging.

National Research Council. (1987). *Demographic change and the well-being of children and the elderly.* Washington, DC: National Academy Press.

Neugarten, B. L. (1982). Policy for the 1980s: Age or need entitlement? In B. L. Neugarten (Ed.), *Age or Need?* Beverly Hills: Sage.

O'Rand, A. M. (1990). Stratification and the life course. In R. H. Binstock & L. K. George (Eds.), *Handbook of aging and the social sciences* (3rd ed.) (pp. 130–144). San Diego: Academic Press.

Orshansky, M. (1965). Counting the poor: Another look at the poverty profile. *Social Security Bulletin, 28*, 3–29.

Osberg, J. S., McGinnis, G. E., DeJong, G., & Seward, M. L. (1987). Life satisfaction and quality of life among disabled elderly adults. *Journal of Gerontology, 42*, 228–230.

Palmore, E. B., Burchett, B., Fillenbaum, G. G., George, L. K. & Wallman, L. (1985). *Retirement: Causes and consequences.* New York: Springer.

Palmore, E. B., Fillenbaum, G. G., & George, L. K. (1984). Consequences of retirement. *Journal of Gerontology, 39*, 109–116.

Preston, S. H. (1984). Children and the elderly in the U.S. *Scientific American, 251*, 44–49.

Quinn, J. (1985). *The economic status of the elderly: Beware of the mean.* (Mimeo). Chestnut Hill, MA: Boston College, Department of Economics.

Radner, D. B. (1982). Distribution of family income: Improved estimates. *Social Security Bulletin, 45*, 9–28.

Radner, D. B. (1986). *Changes in the money income of the aged and nonaged, 1967–*

1983. (Social Security Administration Studies in Income Distribution, No. 14). Washington, DC: U.S. Department of Health and Human Services.

Rodgers, W. (1982). Trends in reported happiness within demographically defined subgroups, 1957-78. *Social Forces, 60*, 826-842.

Smeeding, T. M. (1990). Economic status of the elderly. In R. H. Binstock & L. K. George (Eds.), *Handbook of aging and the social sciences* (3rd ed.) (pp. 362-380). San Diego: Academic Press.

Stoller, E. P., & Stoller, M. A. (1987). The propensity to save among the elderly. *The Gerontologist, 27*, 314-320.

Strate, J. M., & Dubnoff, S. J. (1986). How much income is enough? Measuring the income adequacy of retired persons using a survey based approach. *Journal of Gerontology, 41*, 393-400.

Streib, G. F. (1985). Social stratification and aging. In R. H. Binstock & E. Shanas (Eds.), *Handbook of aging and the social sciences* (pp. 339-363). New York: Van Nostrand Reinhold.

Streib, G. F., & Schneider, C. J. (1971). *Retirement and American society: Impact and process*. Ithaca, NY: Cornell University Press.

U.S. Bureau of the Census. (1981). *Money income and poverty status of families and persons in the United States, 1980* (Current Population Reports, Series P-60, No. 127). Washington, DC: U.S. Government Printing Office.

U.S. Bureau of Labor Statistics. (1982). Family budgets, retired couples budgets. *Monthly Labor Review, 105*, 37-38.

U.S. Department of Agriculture. (1975). *Food plans for poverty measurement* (Technical Paper XII). Washington, DC: Department of Health and Human Services.

Usui, W. M., Keil, T. J., & Durig, K. R. (1985). Socioeconomic comparisons and life satisfaction of elderly adults. *Journal of Gerontology, 40*, 110-114.

Usui, W. M., Keil, T. J., & Phillips, D. C. (1983). Determinants of life satisfaction: A note on a race-interaction hypothesis. Journal of Gerontology, 38, 107-110.

Vaughan, D. R. (1980). *Using subjective assessments of income to estimate family equivalence scales: A report on work in progress* (ISDP Staff Memo). Washington, DC: Social Security Administration.

Vaughan, D. R., & Lancaster, C. G. (1980). Income levels and their impact on two subjective measures of well-being: Some early speculations from work in progress. *The 1979 Proceedings of the American Statistical Association*. Washington, DC: American Statistical Association.

Vaughan, D. R., & Lancaster, C. G. (1981). Applying a cardinal measurement model to normative assessments of income: Synopsis of a preliminary look. *The 1980 Proceedings of the American Statistical Association*. Washington, DC: American Statistical Association.

Zick, C. D., & Smith, K. R. (1986). Immediate and delayed effects of widowhood on poverty: Patterns from the 1970s. *The Gerontologist, 26*, 669-675.

6

Health, Work, Economic Status, and Happiness

James N. Morgan

There are many dimensions to the notion of financial security, almost as many as the dimensions of well-being. We provide some empirical data on wealth, health, work, and income from two data sets, the Panel Study of Income Dynamics (PSID) and the new study of Americans' Changing Lives (ACL), as well as some data on affective outcomes like happiness and satisfaction from the ACL Study.

We start with some general questions about the course of satisfaction with one's state of affairs throughout life and what influences that satisfaction. We have a dynamic model in mind in which initial health and physical and mental capacity permit activities that earn money, allow accumulation of wealth, fund adequate medical care and nutrition, and hence help determine future health, work, income, and satisfaction. Of course, there are many exogenous forces that affect people too, and indeed a major failing of social research is that none of our data bases has paid adequate attention to the relative importance of people's own choices and behavior versus their environment, opportunities, and exogenous events. Perhaps in our desire to avoid responsibility for those less fortunate, we look for reasons to blame them, seeking even to believe that their accidents or job loss or illness may well have resulted from their own carelessness rather than from random bad luck or an environment they could not escape.

Worse still, we have few data bases that allow us to examine related changes in health, income, wealth, and satisfaction during a long enough period for real changes to be visible above the "noise" of measurement error and random variation.

SOME OVERALL PROBLEMS OF ANALYSIS

We do have evidence that, other factors appearing equal, older people report higher levels of satisfaction and fewer complaints than younger people. It is not clear whether this is a generational difference, with more Calvinists in the older generations, adaptation and lowering of aspirations as people age, or a result of people changing those with whom they compare themselves. Older people may be less and less likely to compare themselves with "all others" and more likely to compare themselves with others of the same age, others of the same age who are worse off, or even others of the same age who have died (anything being better than that alternative). There may even be sample selection bias at older ages if the less satisfied die earlier.

There is a related methodological question about whether people's attitudes affect their behavior, which in turn affects their economic progress and health, which may in turn reinforce those attitudes in a cumulative life course of either improvement or deterioration. Studies with the PSID seem to show a different model, in which attitudes result largely from economic status and its changes and do not affect behavior or future changes in economic status (Duncan, and Hill, 1975).

Recent arguments about the stability of "personality" over time make us wary about just what various self-assessing questions are measuring: temporary volatile moods, responses to current situations, persistent attitudes, or stable personality traits.

Finally, if there are measurement errors or random noise in measures of anything that is measured periodically, this can cause a spurious appearance of negative autocorrelation. At the same time, persistent interpersonal differences may be producing what seems like a reinforcing "effect" of prior status across time when people are pooled in samples. (Heckman calls this "heterogeneity" masking real "state dependence" [Heckman, 1979].)

Given all these problems, what can we do to address the issue of satisfaction over the course of life? We can still look with cross-sectional data at the interrelationships among age, wealth, health, work, income, and satisfaction, hoping that the different age groups may roughly represent what happens to a single cohort as it ages, but keeping the problem of cohort differences in mind. We can think of a kind of "path analysis," in which current health and physical age affect the amount of productive activity a person does, which in turn affects his or her subsequent earnings. If health is consistently good and paid work consistently extensive, these facts should also affect wealth, and all these elements should affect people's satisfaction with life. Even better, we could account for current wealth first, then let it help explain health, work, and income. We do this using two data sets, one of which has no real satisfaction measure but much detail about health and wealth (PSID), and the other of which has much detail about paid and unpaid work, health, and affective outcomes like happiness and satisfaction, but much cruder measures of earnings, income, and wealth (ACL).

COMMENTS ON THE DATA

The ACL (American Changing Lives) study* oversamples blacks and people age 60 and older and, of course, uses weights to make population estimates unbiased. Missing data on crucial items, particularly those involving work hours or income, have been assigned using SEARCH-derived subgroups, thus minimizing error variance as compared with hot-deck techniques, which preserve it. Clustered samples, however, have larger-than-normal error variances anyway. Questions about work were separated in the questionnaire, leading to some obvious cases of double-reporting of the same hours in one place as child care and in another as housework. In a few cases paid work and housework were double-counted when people ran nursing homes or day care centers. Some arbitrary reductions or assignments were made in these cases.

The PSID originally oversamples low-income and minority families, and the oversampling of minorities, of course, continues while that of the poor attenuates. The sample, properly weighted for differential nonresponse and, in the case of family weights, for marrying into a sample family, remains representative. Most economic magnitudes are assigned, usually on the basis of SEARCH runs made on the prior year's data. The frequency of missing information is small in both studies, except perhaps for wealth estimates that are rough in any case. When people leave home and then return, they are carried as separate families in one household, but in these cases the family has been reassembled for estimating wealth. Because we want to look at individuals, we create separate files for wives, so the sample we deal with is a sample of husbands, wives, and single heads of families.

Once we start to look at the data, another problem presents itself: categorical or multiple measure. People can rate their health or satisfaction in five categories, or by using more or less, but the proper quantification should probably not use the categories of excellent (1) through good (3) to poor (5). Furthermore, respondents may list a whole set of adverse medical conditions or physical limitations, but we do not know how to weight the importance of these conditions if we want to combine them. Although we can count the hours people work, can we add paid and unpaid work to

*Americans Changing Lives Study is conducted by the Institute for Social Research, University of Michigan, and funded by the National Institute on Aging. Data available from the Inter University Consortium for Political and Social Research, P.O. Box 1248, Ann Arbor, Michigan 48106.

measure total work, and earned and unearned income to measure economic status? (Unearned income from capital is often more secure than earnings). Finally, are the relationships linear, even when one of the measures, like income or wealth, is skewed with a few very large numbers and another is bounded like work, or (even more) like homemaker's work, with many clustered at zero?

Our proposed approach is to keep things simple, make some arbitrary decisions about scaling, and let the data tell us about linearity of relationships on the argument that statistical refinements are unlikely to change our findings or even to change significance levels in any decisive way. (Anything worth looking at will show up in samples of the size we use and will be highly significant).

Hence, we may posit a path model, but we start with categorical regressions, which handle categorical explanatory variables and nonlinear effects neatly. We shall even use arbitrarily scaled dependent variables, believing—following Herman Wold's partial least-square approach (Wold, 1982)—that one could, by iterating back and forth, rapidly improve the scaling on both sides more safely than with maximum likelihood simultaneous estimation procedures like LISREL, where one cannot avoid statistical problems anyway, because there would be many dummy variables (1.0). In particular, using a geometric set of brackets for variables like income and wealth avoids heterogeneity and domination of estimates by a few extreme cases. The use of logs is difficult when there are some legitimate zero values, because the log of zero is minus infinity.

MODELS AND PROCEDURES

Many of the variables are either categorical (such as satisfaction) or so badly skewed that they cause statistical problems (e.g., wealth). We propose to categorize many things when they appear as explanatory variables and to quantify many things when they appear as dependent variables. For example, we propose to assign preliminary and arbitrary scales to factors like satisfaction, functioning health, or education. This has the advantage of handling nonlinearities and skewed variables neatly and easily, and focuses early on substance rather than on elaborate scaling procedures. In any case, two statistical facts help: First, differential weights on components of a measure (which is the same as differential scalings of categories) make very little difference unless the weights vary by factors of three or more; second, converting numerical estimates like hours or dollars into a few categories loses very little of the information $(1/ (1 + K^2)$, where K is the number of categories) (see Appendix of this chapter).

OVERALL PATTERNS

Both as description and as necessary "noise" to consider in further analysis, we look at differences among population groups characterized by sex, family size, and age. Use of our SEARCH program, a systematic simulation of a wise researcher ransacking the data, indicated that three family sizes, 1, 2, and 3 or more, plus gender were crucial in accounting for productive activity, along with age of the individual. We use family size realizing that some two-person families are not simple married couples, and that not all families of three or more have children in them, but asserting that the majority fit the stereotype. In addition, of course, through the life course individuals can marry, have children, see the children leave home, and survive a spouse's death in the standard life-cycle pattern. Fewer and fewer families fit this pattern, however, and although marital status and family size may be in part endogenous (subject to individual decisions), the relationships to work, health, and satisfaction are important whichever way the causation works.

Productive activities—health, wealth, and satisfaction, particularly health—are so dominated by gender, family composition, and age that it will always be necessary to consider them. Hence, at the beginning it is useful to look at the patterns. Table 6.1 summarizes by giving the means for the six gender-family size groups and the eta-squared measure of how much of the variance within each group is accounted for by six age categories. A mere 36 groups (six age groups within each of six gender-family size groups) can account for nearly half the variance in productive activity, paid or unpaid. More interesting, the importance of age differences varies widely, from almost none for the unpaid work of married women without children to half of the remaining variance in paid work hours by single persons of either gender.

Table 6.2 gives the age patterns of total productive activity of individuals according to gender and family size. It would appear that marrying decreases men's work and increases women's, but having children or any other people in the family increases work regardless of gender. The age pattern is clearly not linear, presumably dropping slowly as the children leave home and precipitously at retirement ages and beyond.

Table 6.3 focuses on unpaid work of all kinds: housework, child care, helping friends and neighbors, and volunteer work. Here the differential effects on men versus women of living with another rather than alone are still more dramatic. The effects of children on the age pattern are clearer, assuming that at the younger ages, at least, families of three or more are mostly those with children. It is obviously the women whose unpaid work increases when there are additional persons in the household.

Family size, however, varies with age in the usual life-cycle pattern, and health certainly declines with advanced age, so Table 6.4 shows the net ef-

TABLE 6.1 Effects of Age Without Gender and Family Size on Work, Health, and Satisfaction

| | Men | | | | Women | | | |
	Single person	Two persons	Three or more	All	Single person	Two persons	Three or more	All
Unpaid work mean	794	580	1,308	1,004	971	1,418	2,484	1,919
Eta-squared[a]	.014	.022	.138	.148	.036	.000	.132	.171
Paid work hours	1,448	1,358	2,078	1,762	759	887	1,094	978
Eta-squared[a]	.494	.388	.197	.374	.544	.356	.075	.211
Total worked mean	2,242	1,943	3,386	2,766	1,730	2,305	3,578	2,897
Eta-squared[a]	.418	.396	.273	.419	.346	.299	.204	.412
Total product mean ($)	29.96	22.98	43.75	35.11	18.20	26.16	43.87	34.40
Eta-squared[a]	.287	.275	.091	.232	.268	.221	.112	.284
Poor health mean[b]	2.36	2.40	2.11	2.24	2.54	2.44	2.26	2.36
Eta-squared[a]	.129	.147	.090	.130	.073	.094	.071	.085
Economic satisfaction mean[c]	5.36	5.76	5.17	5.39	5.40	.571	4.89	5.24
Eta-squared[a]	.000	.057	.029	.050	.108	.092	.011	.073

Source: National Institute on Aging, Americans' Changing Lives Study.
[a]Variance explained by six age groups. [b]Self-rating of health: 1 = excellent to 5 = poor (V915). [c]Satisfaction with finances minus difficulty in paying bills (V1302 − V1301 + 4).

TABLE 6.2 Total Annual Hours of Productive Activity by Age for Men and Women, Single Persons, Couples, and Families of Three or More

| | Men | | | | Women | | | |
Age (years)	Single person	Two persons	Three or more	All	Single person	Two persons	Three or more	All
Under 35	3,028	2,817	3,738	3,435	2,739	3,275	3,856	3,683
33–44	2,648	2,718	3,791	3,548	2,546	3,022	3,848	3,836
45–54	2,578	2,695	3,186	2,981	2,672	2,760	3,273	3,046
55–64	2,293	1,929	1,893	1,943	2,058	2,184	2,638	2,270
65–74	1,072	946	1,382	1,039	1,376	1,574	2,111	1,597
75+	1,076	601	635	711	1,054	1,236	1,015	1,120
All ages	2,242	1,943	3,386	2,766	1,730	2,305	3,578	2,897
Number of cases	278	507	573	1,358	527	835	897	2,259
Eta sauared (variance explained)	.418	.396	.273	.419	.346	.299	.204	.412

Source: National Institute on Aging, Americans' Changing Lives Study.

TABLE 6.3 Annual Hours of *Unpaid* Productive Activity by Age for Men and Women, Single Persons, Couples, and Families of Three or More

	Men				Women			
Age (years)	Single person	Two persons	Three or more	All	Single person	Two persons	Three or more	All
Under 35	823	696	1,552	1,264	665	1,451	2,830	2,446
33–44	669	714	1,480	1,308	782	1,369	2,536	2,243
45–54	738	598	936	816	820	1,423	1,974	1,699
55–64	844	493	720	602	1,092	1,451	2,064	1,540
65–74	745	501	669	568	1,082	1,452	1,787	397
75+	1,024	581	547	678	1,008	1,234	1,015	1,097
All ages	794	586	1,308	1,004	971	1,418	2,484	1,919
Number of cases	278	507	573	1,358	527	835	897	2,259
Eta sauared (variance explained)	.014	.022	.138	.148	.036	.000	.132	.171

Source: National Institute on Aging, Americans' Changing Lives Study.

fects of age, family size, health, home ownership, gender, and education on total work and on unpaid work of individuals. These are regressions with categorical predictors, so nonlinear effects are no problem. It is clear that age and family size remain powerful, whereas health, other factors being equal, loses most of its apparent effect on total work. Of course, we measure age more precisely than health so the statistical competition between them is unfair. Health never has much effect on unpaid work, which might tell us something about productive activity of older people—it is likely to be in doing things to care for self and others, usually unpaid. Conversely, im-

TABLE 6.4 Addictive Effects of Forecastable Characteristics on Productive Activity (Categorical Regressions)

	Total work hours		Unpaid hours	
	Eta^2	$Beta^2$	Eta^2	$Beta^2$
Age	.409	.240	.115	.055
Number in household	.232	.052	.191	.129
Health	.109	.020	.006	.000
Own home	.002	.009	.000	.005
Gender	.002	.008	.178	.190
Education	.093	.005	.017	.006
R^2 (adjusted)	.485		.417	

Source: National Institute on Aging, Americans' Changling Lives Study.
Note. Simple effects of health, family size, and education are partly attributable to age or gender.

provements in health, which would mostly affect older people, might appear to remove barriers that currently most affect paid work. Gender matters for unpaid work, the larger amount of which is done by women, giving them total work hours not much different from men. Perhaps most interesting is the impact of living arrangements on productive activity. Living with other people correlates with substantial increases in unpaid productive activity. Does this mean that if we could encourage more group living among the aged they would do more for themselves and each other, hence reducing the burden on the rest of society?

The table of total productive hours per year by age, gender, and family size can be used as the base for extrapolating future changes because we know there will be massive changes in the following:

- Age distribution of the population
- Distribution in each age group into single, two-, and three- or more-person families, which vastly affects their productive effort and the fraction of it that is paid for
- Health, particularly among older people, which also affects their productive activity (there is some doubt about potential health changes but change seems most likely for ages 55 to 65, affecting capacity to work)

In the future there will be more older people, and it is predicted that they will be healthier. There will be fewer families of three or more, particularly when the adults are age 20 to 25 or 45 or older, because of later marriages and few children being born.

It is clear that the main age effects occur at retirement and with advanced age. The effects of health on work were largest for men age 55 to 64, the period when they were getting out of paid work. We did some analysis using three age groups, divided at ages 55 and 65, but it became clear that we needed to look at men and women separately, too. Hence, we shall do the rest of the analysis separately with four age-gender groups: men under age 55, women under age 55, men age 55 or older, and women age 55 or older. We ran the regressions separately for each of the four groups, keeping age as a variable because it can easily have different effects during the earlier years than during the later years—for example, on wealth. It is after age 55 that paid work and health are likely to start declining or to decline much more rapidly.

Because so many of our variables are arbitrarily scaled or are combinations of other variables, Appendix A provides an alphabetical glossary defining them.

All three of the health measures deteriorate with age, but their relationship to work and happiness are not the same, so we keep them separate in what follows.

FINDINGS FROM THE NATIONAL INSTITUTE ON AGING–FUNDED STUDY OF AMERICANS' CHANGING LIVES

Table 6.5 gives the averages for all the variables for each of the four age-gender groups. All three health measures are, of course, worse after age 55 and they are also worse for men, particularly older men. (Other data always show young women and old men going to the hospital more, but the former includes having children so the interpretation is clouded.) The work hours are as expected. The affective measures show the men a little happier and more satisfied, for the most part, except that young men are less happy than young women. Age matters more, however, with uniformly higher positive reports at the older ages, particularly for satisfaction among women. The two age classes still leave room for age variation within them, so age is retained in the regression analyses of the four groups.

The simple correlations of the other variables with age within the two broad age groups for men and women reinforce the broad age patterns: Health is increasingly reported as poor (negatively correlated with age) even within the young age groups. All this information becomes evident when we look at the regression coefficients, with the added assurance that the effect is not spurious, so we turn to Table 6.6. Table 6.6 compresses the results from 32

TABLE 6.5 Means of Variables for Four Age-Gender Groups

Scale	Variables	Ages 25–54		Ages 55–98	
		Men	Women	Men	Women
5 = Poor	Health: self-rated[a]	2.03	2.15	2.73	2.74
4 = Good	Health: functioning	3.39	3.85	1.85	3.37
6 = Poor	Health: conditions[a]	0.55	0.74	5.94	2.13
	Age	37	37	67	68
0–1	Married	.75	.69	.79	.55
0.9	Number of others in family	1.62	1.89	0.40	.48
1–7	Education (bracket)[b]	3.34	3.02	1.95	1.91
0–1	Black	0.11	0.13	0.08	0.10
0–5,000	Paid work	2,173	1,317	787	372
0–5,000	Unpaid work	1,170	2,217	611	1,385
0–	Full income–equal adults	16,475	13,802	19,144	16,692
1–11	Efficacy	6.83	6.47	6.87	6.72
3–15	Happiness	9.33	9.57	9.71	9.67
−3–7	Satisfaction	3.67	3.61	4.31	4.18
1–8	Total-wealth class	5.72	5.78	6.21	6.18
1–9	Family income class	5.12	4.63	3.82	2.96
	N	730	991	628	1,265

Source: National Institute on Aging, Americans' Changing Lives Study.
[a]Higher is worse. [b]Bracket means not a continuous variable.

TABLE 6.6 Normalized Regression Coefficients for Four Age-Gender Groups[a]

	Dependent variables															
	Wealth		Health		Paid hours		Unpaid hours		Family income		Efficacy		Happiness		Satisfaction	
Explanatory variables	<55[b]	55+	<55	55+	<55	55+	<55	55+	<55	55+	<55	55+	<55	55+	<55	55+
Men																
Self-rated health	.05	.02	—	—	.09	.28c	.04	.08	.01	.10c	.19c	.29c	.09	.22c	.15c	.20c
Functional health	.05	.07	—	—	.11c	.06	.06	.06	.02	.00	-.09	.07	.06	.14c	-.06	.01
Health conditions	.04	.01	—	—	.11c	-.01	.02	.05	.06	.01	.09	.07	.07	.12c	.02	.05
Age	.31c	.00	-.22c	-.13c	-.33	-.44c	-.25c	-.06	.18c	-.14c	.11c	.10	.03	.17c	.16c	.09
Married	-.13c	.05	.11c	.04	.21c	-.02	.25c	-.20c	.25c	.18c	-.06	.00	.07	.18c	.20c	.32c
Number of others in household	-.01	-.05	-.13c	.00	.01	-.02	.23c	.08	-.08+	-.02	.04	-.08	.02	-.08	.06	-.04
Education	.11c	.32c	.18c	.13c	.10c	-.01	.05	.01	.32c	.26c	.00	-.01	-.04	-.03	-.03	-.12c
Black	-.01	-.09	.02	-.02	-.02	.01	.01	.03	-.06	-.03	.05	.07	-.12c	.08	-.09c	.00
Wealth			.08	.08	.07	.04	.00	-.02	.11c	.36	.02	.08	.00	.07	.02	.15c
Paid work							-.09c	-.18c	.32c	.27c	.06	-.11	.01	-.16c	.17c	-.06
Unpaid work					-.10c	-.13c			.05	-.01	.04	.05	.03	.03	.06	-.07
Income											.27c	.17c	.11	.08	.04	-.03
R² (adjusted)	.091	.135	.111	.051	.116	.342	.155	.066	.418	.584	.148	.198	.057	.226	.163	.185

110

Women																
Self-rated health	.05	.03	—	—	.12[c]	.09[c]	.03	.01	.14[c]	.11[c]	.23[c]	.23[c]	.21[c]	.28[c]	.19[c]	.16[c]
Functional health	.03	.00	—	—	.10[c]	.11[c]	.07	.22[c]	.03	-.01	-.11[c]	.10[c]	.00	.13[c]	.00	.02
Health conditions	.03	.11[c]	—	—	.00	.04	.03	.03	.00	.02	.00	.05	.03	.00	.01	-.01
Age	.19[c]	.00	-.13[c]	-.15[c]	.00	-.41[c]	-.15[c]	-.17[c]	.07[c]	-.12[c]	.07	.10[c]	-.03	.03	.15[c]	.17[c]
Married	-.06	.19[c]	.00	-.02	-.05	-.10[c]	.16[c]	.22[c]	.47[c]	.30[c]	-.02	.03	.08	.19[c]	.18[c]	.35[c]
Number of others in household	.05	.01	-.08	-.08[c]	-.05	.03	.28[c]	.25[c]	.00	-.07[c]	-.06	-.03	.03	-.01	.00	.03
Education	.16[c]	.29[c]	.14[c]	.23[c]	.16[c]	.11[c]	-.07[c]	-.01	.31[c]	.25[c]	.11[c]	.08[c]	.00	-.06	-.04	-.08[c]
Black	-.03	-.07[c]	.04	-.04	.00	-.01	-.03	-.03	-.07[c]	-.07[c]	.07	-.02	.08[c]	.01	-.10[c]	-.09[c]
Wealth			.05	.03	-.11[c]	-.07	-.11[c]	-.05	.15[c]	.34[c]	.04	.00	.05	.07	.05	.03
Paid work					-.38[c]	-.22[c]	-.34[c]	-.24[c]	.21[c]	.12[c]	.01	-.03	-.22[c]	-.25	.04	.08[c]
Unpaid work									.00	.04	.06	.02	-.01	-.03	.11[c]	.01
Income										.19[c]	.19[c]	.06	.17[c]	-.02	.11[c]	.09
R² (adjusted)	.051	.156	.048	.092	.259	.260	.346	.206	.513	.595	.129	.141	.135	.182	.155	.187

[a] Groups with frequencies:

	<55	55 or older
Men	730	629
Women	991	1,265.

[b] Years. [c] Significant (using $t > 2.5$) to allow for design effects.

multiple regressions, eight nested (sequential) dependent variables, examined separately for the four age-gender groups. This provides a kind of replication in some cases and an interesting differentiation in others.

Wealth can almost be considered exogenous in a cross section, but its accumulation during the early years of life, and for those with higher and more predictable incomes shows up in the importance of education and age (for those under age 55) in accounting for present wealth. (Remember, this is not pension rights or insurance or Social Security rights, but equity in house and other assets, sometimes called *bequeathable wealth*). Current health is important only for older women, where wealth may be allowing women with more health conditions to survive rather than poor health "causing" wealth. Marriage seems to decrease young men's wealth and increase that of older women. Note, however, that age effects in a cross section can easily be cohort differences, which may partly explain why wealth does not increase with age for the groups age 55 and older—younger people had higher real incomes.

We attempt then to explain self-rated health for which wealth does not appear to matter, but age does (negatively) and education does (positively). Interestingly enough, self-reported health appears to decline with age as much before age 55 as after, perhaps because it is limited to a 5-point scale that does not get worse than "poor"—that is, it is bounded. The regressions for functional health and number of (poor) health conditions are similar, with substantial negative age effects, larger before age 55 for several conditions. They are positively affected by education, especially among women.

We pair the next two dependent variables—paid and unpaid work—allowing each to help affect the other, in the belief that they compete for a limited time and capacity. This is an example of "seemingly unrelated regression" for which one proposed solution is to constrain the effects of paid work on unpaid work in one equation to be equal to the effects of unpaid work on paid work in the other equation. Actually, without constraint, they turn out almost the same in each of the four pairs of regressions. The competition for the person's time is clearly most intense for younger women, and indeed for women in general, as indicated by the stronger negative effects of unpaid hours on paid hours and vice versa. Because women report more total hours of work, time constraints should make alternative types of work more competitive with each other. Paid work is also affected by health—functional health for all but older men, self-rated health for all but younger men, and health conditions only for older women. Regression adjustments diminish the estimated effect of health on paid work, but it is the adjustment for education, not age, that accounts for the change. Young married men do more paid work, older married women do less, and the better educated do more, except for older men. Wealth discourages paid work of younger women, and, of course, after age 55 paid hours drop with age for both men and women.

Unpaid hours are driven by family considerations, with women, young married men, and people in families with other members (mostly children) doing more unpaid work. (Remember, in this study a wide variety of unpaid work was covered, but in fact housework and child care account for the bulk of it). Younger women in wealthy families who do less paid work also do less unpaid work. Most interesting, health appears to have little or no effect on unpaid work with the possible exception of the depressing effect of functional limitations on older women's unpaid work. There is evidence from time-diary studies that people exaggerate elements of their time allocations, particularly irregular ones, but that would not explain the lack of health effects on unpaid work. Perhaps health reduces the ability to perform at paid jobs, inducing some substitution of home production and housework. Poor health may increase the number of hours it takes to perform the same tasks.

On the positive side, however, one possible implication is that it may not be health problems that inhibit unpaid productive activities of older people but other problems that may be easier to resolve. Another implication, of course, of the strong impact of health on paid work is that improvements in health can have an impact on the total paid productive capacity of the country. Marriage increases the unpaid work of everyone except older men, for whom even having household members other than the wife does not induce more unpaid work.

Our measure of economic status is family income, which includes more than the earnings of the respondent. (The sample is of adults age 25 or older, even though we attempt to measure income and wealth for the whole family). Even so, the facts about one adult, who is usually a husband, wife, or single adult, account for half the variance in family income. We are now far enough along in our recursive model or causal chain so that wealth and health can have effects both directly and indirectly through health or work.

Background factors like education and marital status have powerful direct effects on income, but they also have indirect effects. More education leads to better health and to more paid work hours for everyone except older men and that, of course, increases family income. An abundance of other data has shown that education, for a variety of reasons, leads to less unemployment and more stable jobs. Being married increases paid work hours only for young men; it increases unpaid work for young men and all women, but decreases unpaid work of older men. None of this, of course, affects our measured income, because that excludes the value of unpaid work. Had we imputed a value to that work, then marriage would have increased economic status still more by inducing more unpaid work, except for older married men. Except for young men, it is self-rated health that directly affects family income, whereas neither health functioning nor an index of poor health conditions appears to affect family income. Those who do not trust self-reported health may argue that this result proves that people blame their market work failures on health. An equally convincing argument, however, is that people are better direct judges of their health than we are when we just ask about conditions or activity restrictions and create indexes. There is evidence in another study that self-reported health predicts longevity-mortality better than "more objective" health measures (McLossey & Shapiro, 1982).

Even questions about occupational disability cover only part of the way health can affect earning ability, and people whose work is primarily mental and does not induce physical labor can continue to work even with very poor health. Wealth seems to increase current income directly, of course, by producing interest and dividends (we do not count unrealized capital gains), but because individual differences persist, wealth may only reflect higher past incomes that continue to the present. The "effect" is greater among the older groups, where wealth is greater and also more varied.

We turn now to the effects on affective states, summarizing them with the use of three indexes that we have cavalierly labeled sense of efficacy, happiness, and satisfaction. We have omitted satisfaction with health from the satisfaction index because health and satisfaction with it decline substantially with age, whereas all the other satisfaction indexes increase with age.

We considered treating sense of efficacy as intermediate between all the other factors to the left and the final results—happiness and satisfaction— but decided to treat all three as affective states. One model would have sense of efficacy leading to other behaviors, such as taking calculated risks as an entrepreneur, that would cycle back through economic success and affect ultimate outcomes again.

We start discussing the affective outcomes with efficacy, on which there is a large theoretical literature treating it as a fairly stable but not unaffected attitude structure or even personality measure. Why do self-rated health and health functioning have opposite effects on efficacy, at least for young men and women? Indeed, why should good functional health lead, other factors being equal, to a lower sense of efficacy for young people? Could it be that those with functional limitations are proud of overcoming them or are denying their effects? Why should the number of poor health conditions or diagnoses have nonsignificant effects in the wrong direction?

More family income leaves all four groups feeling more efficacious, understandably, but wealth does not. Perhaps wealth is so badly measured that it provides a poor test. Even conceptually that standard of wealth is inadequate, because it excludes the value of social security and other pension rights, the value of life insurance, and the alternative security of good health insurance coverage. Efficacy goes up with age, significantly for young men and older women. Education produces a higher sense of efficacy but only for women.

Happiness is another matter. Health improves it, but only for older men and women. (This is consistent with a large literature on health and well-being.) Self-rated health makes everyone happier, though it is not significant for the younger men who have less variance in their reported health. People older than age 54 are happier, but only for the older men does happiness have a significant positive age correlation within the group. Young blacks are less happy, with black women having lower incomes than expected. Furthermore, income is associated with happiness, other factors being equal, only for the young. There is evidence from Juster's (1985) work that many people get more enjoyment out of their paid work than out of many other activities.

Hence, it is interesting to notice that although unpaid work has almost no effect on any of the affective states, paid work is negatively associated with happiness for all but the young men. The regression adjustments, especially for education, strengthen the negative effect of paid work on happiness. (We report later a SEARCH analysis of happiness that includes measures of social support as explanatory variables.)

The third affective outcome is an index of satisfaction over several domains (see Appendix A). Of the three health measures, only self-rated health retains significant effects on satisfaction in the multivariate context. Of course, some of this may be a result of response set (a tendency to see everything positively or negatively) or mood. Attitudes always correlate better with attitudes than with variables less sensitive to wording or mood. The age effect remains and is significant in three of the four groups, even allowing for sample design effects, again agreeing with many other reports. More education seems to go with less satisfaction, but only for those age 55 or older. Because each succeeding generation has more education than the last, a simple tendency for the well educated to be more critical and less satisfied might account for some of the simple age effect. The age effect remains, however, when regression "controls" for education. Three of the four groups have blacks who are less satisfied, understandably. In all groups, the married are substantially more satisfied, a testimony to the beneficial effect of marriage, or to a selection bias in which easily satisfied persons are more likely to marry and stay married. Strangely enough, economic status gets mixed reviews, with income increasing satisfaction only for young women, and wealth increasing it only for older men. The story is also mixed for the effects of work hours on satisfaction. Unpaid work increases satisfaction only for younger women, perhaps because children who cause the work also bring satisfaction. Why don't they also bring happiness or a sense of efficacy? (Perhaps because the children bring more disorder as well, making it more difficult to control one's life.)

Paid work increases satisfaction for young men and older women, even (insignificantly) reducing the satisfaction of older men. One possible explanation is that these degrees of satisfaction vary with age, and age is measured more accurately than the competing variables in the regression. It is a statistical fact that errors in measurement of an explanatory variable lead to underestimation of its power and significance.

Furthermore, with satisfaction we have another difficulty: If we regard the final criterion as human satisfaction, we face a methodological problem arising from a consistent tendency across many domains and countries for satisfaction to increase with age. (The only major exception is satisfaction with health.) Herzog and Rodgers (1981) have shown that some of this can be attributed to age differences in religiosity and in a tendency to give socially desirable answers, but accounting for differences in health or economic status *increases* the age pattern.

Religiosity in particular may reflect cohort differences, each succeeding generation being less religious and less likely to underreport dissatisfactions. Some of the age difference may, however, reflect adaptation to one's job, residence, or marriage—that is, sorting out one's life or settling for what one has. Herzog and Rodgers (1981) show a positive association of satisfaction with "tenure," reflecting adaptation to situations rather than mobility to improve them. These findings appear robust according to the scales and measures used and also across national boundaries. In Italy, Belgium, and Germany, however, the importance of economic deterioration with age apparently overwhelms the other forces increasing satisfaction with age.

We can deal with this problem in two ways. One is to introduce age as a correcting control in regression, reflecting cohort differences and adaptation to one's life. The difficulty is that age reflects and is highly correlated with many other factors, including income. Another possibility is to analyze the younger and older people separately.

Similar studies recording age findings have appeared recently: *The Quality of American Life: Perceptions, Evaluations, and Satisfaction* (Campbell, Converse, & Rodgers, 1986) and *Research on the Quality of Life* (Herzog & Rodgers, 1986). The latter tends to omit discussions of age for the most part, other than occasionally noting the tendency of satisfaction to go up with age, except for the chapter by Herzog and Rodgers, which suggests that some of the age effect may result from a different style of answering questions among older people—that is, an artifact.

FOCUS ON EXPLANATORY VARIABLES

We discuss the major results again for each explanatory variable, that is, by rows rather than columns of Table 6.6. When relevant, we shall point out that an apparently strong simple correlation must be treated as spurious because introducing the other variables simultaneously attenuated it to nonsignificance.

Self-reported good health increases paid work, particularly for men age 55 and older, when it can lead to later retirement. It has little or no effect on unpaid work, and appears to affect economic status (income) for everyone but young men, once the regression accounts for the demographics and the amount of paid work. Perhaps for young men health affects economic status largely through paid work.

High correlations between self-reported health and efficacy, happiness, and satisfaction indexes may well be partly response set, a tendency for some people to answer everything either positively or negatively. Attitudes always correlate better with attitudes than with anything else. The net effects are smallest on the happiness of younger people and largest on the efficacy of older men, perhaps reflecting health-induced retirement.

The other two health indicators—health functioning and the number of health conditions—have substantial simple correlations with paid work and with efficacy and happiness for older people, but in a multivariate framework few significant effects remain. It appears to be adjusting for education that produces this attenuation rather than adjusting for age. (The regressions were rerun omitting age). Functional health has net effects on paid work of the young and on their sense of efficacy, and it affects the happiness of older people. The number of health conditions affects the paid work of young men and their sense of efficacy, and appears to affect the happiness of older men.

Even within the two broad age groups, age affects the paid work of older people, which, of course, falls as they retire, and the unpaid work of younger people, which falls between ages 18 and 54 as the children grow up and leave home. Sense of efficacy rises as people mature, and their expressed satisfaction rises as they get used to their situation or perhaps because of cohort or generation differences in aspiration levels.

The next four variables all reflect combinations of opportunities available, constraints and pressures from past commitments, or social structures. Perhaps the more energetic are more likely to get married and have children. Living with others surely provides more opportunities and pressures to do unpaid work around the house (except for older men). Married men do more paid work and married women less. In the case of unpaid work the situation is reversed, to no one's surprise, with married women doing much more unpaid work and less paid work. Because men earn more and are less likely when unmarried to provide housing for others, married men (who have more dependents) are worse off than single men, and young married women are better off than young unmarried women, even controlling for the number of others in the household. For all the age-gender groups, marriage seems to be associated with more expressions of happiness and satisfaction, but with no difference in expressed sense of efficacy. Among those age 55 and older in particular, marriage seems to be associated with satisfaction with life. The skeptic might claim that this is selection bias, many of the dissatisfied having gotten divorced or never having married.

The term *others in the family* means mostly children for younger people and mostly parents, siblings, or other relatives for older people. The others clearly bring in less income or wealth than burden, for they decrease the full income—equivalent adult measure (not shown here), while increasing the amount of unpaid work, particularly for young women (with children). All these effects are expected and serve to assure us that our measurements of work are probably all correct. The effects of others on affective outcomes appears small, perhaps because the joy of having children around or the sense of doing one's duty by other family members offsets the economic burden.

Education is a proxy for more things than any other variable, perhaps, including earning power, stability of income, foresight and, hence, good health, and possibly critical facilities. Men with more education work more hours. For all four age-gender groups, education leads to better economic status, increasing income and wealth, and the planning that reduces family size. The relationships with affective outcomes are small, except perhaps for young women, in which case the better educated do more paid work and less unpaid work, and report feeling more efficacious. Controlling for income and work, the better educated are, if anything, insignificantly less likely to report themselves happy or satisfied, however.

Being black reduces opportunities because some prejudice persists, but it has an insignificant effect on economic status in our data once we adjust for age and education. Blacks, particularly the young ones, are less likely to say they are happy or satisfied.

There has been much recent discussion of the role of work in life satisfaction, and some evidence that people get enjoyment out of their work time, sometimes more than out of their leisure time (Juster, 1985). Indeed, when asked about perceived benefits from the process itself as distinct from its outcome in money or a clean house, people reported such benefits from the processes accompanying their jobs (per hour) at a higher level than from any other activities except child care and socializing. Of course, they put more hours into the job than into any of the other activities (Juster, 1985).

In our path model, work is an intermediate variable, affected by background factors and health, and in turn directly affecting economic status and affective outcomes. The data show significant positive direct effects of paid work on economic status of all except old women. The effects of paid work on affective outcomes are mixed. It increases efficacy and satisfaction of young men but appears to decrease the happiness of everyone except young men. It appears to reduce satisfaction of older men, perhaps because they would like to retire but cannot afford it, and to increase the satisfaction of older women, perhaps with late-blooming careers. The difficulty is not just that paid work increases income, reduces leisure, and also provides some direct satisfaction, but that for some it is of limited availability (they want more work), whereas for others it may be a burden (they want less or would like to work less if they could afford it). Relevant questions are asked in the PSID but not in the ACL study.

Unpaid work, however, does not improve economic status the way we measure it; indeed, it reduces economic status for young women. More important, unpaid work appears to have little effect on sense of efficacy or happiness. It increases satisfaction of younger women, perhaps because it involves their children, and decreases that of older men, who may find work around the house a burden. Failure to include the value of the unpaid work in the family income, however, means that we really do not allow the economic effects of unpaid work to appear. Conversely, unpaid work not only reduces paid work, which does have good affective outcomes directly and through income, but appears, other factors being equal, to have no good effects on any of the three affective outcomes for any of the four groups, except for the satisfaction of older women.

We have examined other economic status measures not presented here that combine income, wealth, needs, and leisure in rather arbitrary ways in the interests of keeping things simple. One adds an annuitized value of wealth to income, the annual amount one could buy with such income, and divides the total by the number of equivalent adults it supports. Annuitizing wealth tends to give it more importance to older people, unduly so if they have no intention of using it and are saving it for medical emergencies rather than bequests. The number of others in the family somewhat mechanically affects this economic status measure, and a measure that incorporates leisure (or total paid and unpaid work) also has automatic mechanical relationships to the work variables. Hence, we used income rather than income-needs, full income-needs, or "economic status," including leisure, and left a larger direct role for family size and an unconstrained examination of the effects of paid and unpaid work.

Finally, we can look at the direct effects of income on expressed affective states. Income has its expected strong positive effects on sense of efficacy and on happiness, significant for all except older women, and on satisfaction only for young women. We had thought of using the more comprehensive measure of well-being, which included the amount of free time left to enjoy income after it was earned, but the possibility that people enjoyed work more than leisure or that they might not be freely choosing how many hours to work for pay deterred us.

FOCUS ON HAPPINESS

George Maddox's Boettner lecture (see Chapter 4) emphasizing the crucial nature of social support reminded us that we had ignored a large variety of such measures in the ACL study and prompted the following additional analysis: Using an index of happiness that combined two 1 to 5 scales (see Appendix A) and ranges from 2 to 10, we ran our SEARCH program asking that the sample be sequentially divided using whatever factor produced the largest reduction in the remaining unexplained variance in "happiness." The result appears in Figure 6.1, which shows that it is the quality of the convoy of social support that matters first and foremost, and for both of the subgroups so defined, health matters next. Only for those with good health does income affect expressed happiness. For the others, further splits on health or social support dominate. One might object that attitudes always correlate better with other attitudes, if only because of mood or response set. One could also argue, however, that income is probably measured more accurately than health or social support and should appear more powerful for that statistical reason.

This has been a long story, and it would be only too easy to make it longer by putting in a curvilinear age-squared term, omitting age altogether, or changing the subgroup definitions. We prefer to aver that the main findings would be unaffected and to make some comparisons covering the first five columns of Table 6.6 with similar data from the 1984 interview wave of the PSID.

PANEL STUDY OF INCOME DYNAMICS FINDINGS

When we turn to the PSID, we have only health, work, wealth, and income to examine—no affective outcomes. Furthermore, the health of married women is reported by their husbands in most cases, which may explain why women appear less healthy in Table 6.7 than in Table 6.5, even though only one half of the older women are married (the other half report on their own health). The paid work hours agree well with the ACL data. The unpaid hours are solely housework, based on a single question, and again the husband reports on his wife's work. The numbers are far smaller than the broader concept based on many questions in the ACL study. Interestingly enough, the full income—equivalent adult measures, which we decided not to use in the multivariate analysis, are quite similar even though they are based on many questions about income and wealth in the PSID, and a single-income question and two wealth questions in the ACL. The averages are within 2% to 4% of each other for men and within 7% for women.

Table 6.8 provides the multivariate results. We are startlingly better able to account for wealth and health in the PSID, presumably reflecting more accurate measurements of both explanatory and dependent variables. The implication that wealth is measured more accurately with the longer sequence and perhaps more willing cooperation of the panel respondents might ex-

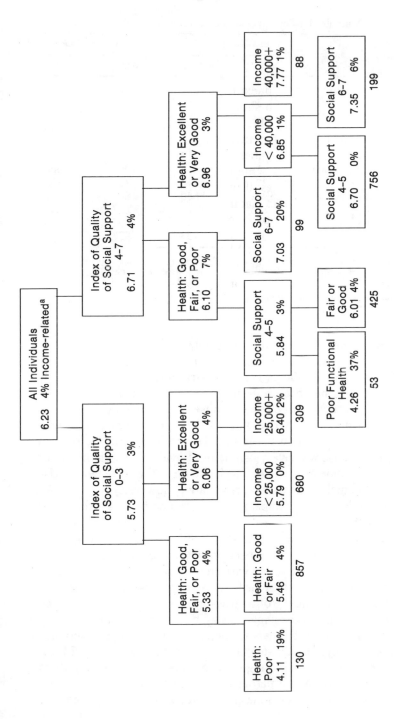

FIGURE 6.1 What makes people happy?

Happiness index—range, 2–10.

Ten final groups account for 13.5% of the variance. Only one tenth of that is from the two splits on income. No further split on anything could reduce the overall variance by as much as .5%—not gender, age, wealth, health, nor hours spent on unpaid or paid work.

[a]The percents of variance in the boxes are percents of the subgroup variance that could be accounted for by income, using all the income brackets available.

TABLE 6.7 Means of Variables for Four Age-Gender Groups

	Ages 18–54		Ages 55–98	
	Men[a]	Women[b]	Men[a]	Women[b]
Health rated by self or spouse	2.04	2.24	2.99	3.15
Age	36	36	66	68
Married	.78	.71	.83	.51
Number of others	1.48	1.65	0.49	0.34
Education (years)	13.0	12.6	11.1	10.8
Black	.09	.13	.08	.09
Paid work including commuting	2,218	1,255	964	408
Unpaid work	374	1,148	423	1,133
Full income–equal adult	16,361	14,860	19,883	18,001
Decile income-needs	5.06	4.76	5.12	4.35
Eight net worth classes	3.60	3.44	4.95	4.43
Number of cases	2,393	3,133	957	1,356

Source: Duncan, G. J., & Morgan, J. N. (Editors). (1975). Panel study of income dynamics. In *Five thousand American families: Patterns of economic progress.* Ann Arbor: University of Michigan, Institute for Social Research.
[a]Single heads or husbands. [b]Single heads or wives.

plain why wealth in the PSID also has uniformly strong and significant effects on health. Other than this, the main results are similar to those from the ACL study: good health increases paid work and, presumably, partly through it, income, income-needs, and full income–equivalent adult for all four groups. It has no significant effect on housework hours, however.

After age 55, age significantly reduces paid work but not housework. Economic status improves with age between ages 18 and 54, of course, for both men and women. Because we have a sample of individuals, single heads, or husbands or wives, families with a married head are in the table twice. (Use of individual weights makes the data representative, however.)

Again, marriage reduces men's unpaid housework and increases their paid work, and it does the reverse for women. Marriage also increases income more than needs, raising the income-needs variable within all four groups. As expected, having other family members present increases housework for women, decreases paid work for young women, and decreases income-needs by increasing the denominator. It seems to increase paid work of older men, but the causation may be going the other way—more hardworking older men either having more children they allow to stay home or providing housing for more relatives. Education appears to increase paid work for everyone, higher wages not leading to much substitution of leisure for money. Education decreases the housework of young women, presumably allowing them to pay others to do more of it, but perhaps also reflecting more efficient use of time and more time pressure because of paid work. Once again, of course,

TABLE 6.8 Standardized Regression Coefficients for Four Age-Gender Group Study

	Dependent variable									
	Wealth Bracket		Health[b]		Paid work and commuting		Housework		Income-needs decile	
Explanatory variables	< 55[a]	55+	< 55	55+	< 55	55+	< 55	55+	< 55	55+
Men										
Age	.47c	.00	−.26c	−.12c	−.10	−.49c	−.06	−.06	.11c	−.07c
Married	.17c	.19c	.02	−.05	.06	.00	−.04	−.14c	.05c	.06c
No. others in family	.05c	−.01	−.01	.03	.03	.10	.03	−.03	−.26c	−.11c
Education	.22c	.40c	.23c	.21c	.07c	.05	.04	−.04	.24c	.25c
Black	−.16c	−.14c	−.09c	−.06	−.05	.03	−.01	.04	.00	.01
Wealth			.16c	.21c	.28c	.11c	−.06	.03	.37c	.40c
Health**					.13c	.20c	.02	.09c	.04	.09c
Paid work							−.10c	−.19c	.27c	.23c
Housework					−.08c	−.11c			.00	−.03
R squared (adjusted)	.396	.270	.139	.159	.144	.441	.023	.046	.485	.583
Women										
Age	.43c	.08c	−.25c	−.18c	.02	−.47c	.04	−.18	.02	−.06c
Married	.32c	.30c	.03	−.08c	−.10c	−.06c	.16c	.32c	.20c	.14c
No. others in family	.04c	.06c	.01	−.03	−.07c	.02	.25c	.10c	−.16c	.01
Education	.22c	.42	.27c	.14c	.07c	.05	−.08c	−.03	.22c	.18c
Black	−.16c	−.18c	−.09c	−.07c	−.05c	.00	−.07c	−.05	−.05c	−.04
Wealth			.15c	.27c	.07c	.01	.03	.05	.47c	.46c
Health**					.05c	.13c	.03	.03	.05c	.04
Paid work							−.35c	−.18c	.19c	.20c
Housework					−.39c	−.26c			.03	−.03
R squared (adjusted)	.424	.344	.175	.180	.233	.283	.322	.235	.543	.543

Source: Duncan, G. J., & Morgan, J. N. (Editors). (1975). Panel study of income dynamics. In *Five thousand American families: Patterns of economic progress.* Ann Arbor: University of Michigan, Institute for Social Research.

[a]Years. [b]Sign reversed so 5 = excellent; 1 = poor. [c]Significant (using $t > 2.5$) to allow for design effects. [d]Groups with frequencies:

	18–54	55 or older
Men	2,397	957
Women	3,133	1,356.

paid work improves economic status as we measure it but housework does not, although this merely means that the benefits of housework are not included in the measure.

All in all, as far as we can cover the same ground with the PSID data, they neatly confirm the ACL data and give us confidence in their quality.

CONCLUSION

We have shown a reasonable pattern of relationship, arranged in a logical order from exogenous background factors like gender, race, and education, through intermediate factors like work and the resulting income, to outcomes of reported happiness or satisfaction. Replication for four groups—men and women younger than age 55, and men and women older than age 55—sometimes shows reasonable differences but mostly reinforces the main conclusions. Perhaps most important, it turns out that available social support and health have more effect than economic forces like income or wealth on making people happy.

We have attempted to put a dynamic life-course interpretation on static cross-section data. Clearly data on change would be better. The ACL study proposes to reinterview its sample, which would provide rich data on changes in status, behavior, and affective outcomes. The PSID contains data on change that will be vastly improved if, as proposed, the 1989 wave remeasures wealth, providing data on saving. The PSID data would also be significantly improved by the addition of even a few affective outcome measures.

REFERENCES

Campbell, A. C., Converse, P. E., & Rodgers, W. L. (1986). *The quality of American life: Perceptions, evaluations, and satisfaction.* New York: Russell Sage Foundation.

Dow, G. K., & Juster, F. T. (1985). Goods, time and well-being: The joint dependence problem. In F. T. Juster & F. P. Stafford (Eds.), *Time, goods and well-being* (pp. 397–413). Ann Arbor: University of Michigan, Survey Research Center, Institute for Social Research.

Duncan, G., & Hill, D. (1975). Attitudes, behavior, and economic outcomes: A structural equation approach. In G. J. Duncan & J. N. Morgan (Eds.), *Five thousand American families: Patterns of economic progress.* Ann Arbor: University of Michigan, Institute for Social Research.

Duncan, G. J., & Morgan, J. N. (Eds.) (1975). *Five thousand American families: Patterns of economic progress.* Ann Arbor: University of Michigan, Institute for Social Research.

Heckman, James J. (1979). Sample selection bias as a specification error, *Econometrica*, 47, 153–161.

Herzog, A. R., & Rodgers, W. L. (1981a). Age and satisfaction. *Research on Aging, 3,* 142–165.

Herzog, A. R., & Rodgers, W. L. (1981b). *Age and satisfaction: American and European data.* Eleventh International Congress of Gerontology, Hamburg, Germany.

Herzog, A. R., & Rodgers, W. L. (1986). Satisfaction among older adults. In F. M. Andrews (Ed.), *Research on the quality of life* (pp. 235–251). Ann Arbor: University of Michigan, Institute for Social Research.

Juster, F. T. (1985). Preference for work and leisure. In F. T. Juster & F. P. Stafford (Eds.), *Time, goods, and well-being* (pp. 333–351). Ann Arbor: University of Michigan, Survey Research Center, Institute for Social Research.

McLossey, J. M., & Shapiro, E. (1982). Self-rated health: A predictor of mortality among the elderly. *American Journal of Public Health, 72,* 800–808.

Wold, Herman (1982). Soft modeling: The basic design and some generalizations. In J. G. Joreskog & H. Wold (Eds.), *Systems under indirect observation: Casuality, structure, prediction.* Amsterdam: North Holland.

Appendix of Chapter 6
Definitions of Variables

ANNUITIZED WEALTH

This variable is the annual income purchasable with bequeathable wealth for expected life, assuming 3% interest on the remaining balance and using the longest of husband's or wife's expected lives. The result is the following multipliers in Table A1:

TABLE A.1 Annuitized Wealth for Man and Woman Based on Present Age

Age now (years)	Man	Woman
18–24	.038	.036
25–34	.042	.039
35–44	.047	.043
45–54	.057	.050
55–64	.073	.061
65–74	.108	.080
75+	.218	.128

CONTACT FREQUENCY

This variable is the sum of rescaled categories (0 for "never" to 5 for "more than once a week") of talking with friends, visiting friends, going to meetings, and having contacts in person by mail or telephone with children, mother, father. The range is 0 to 30, bracketed at 0 to 9, 10 to 13, 14 to 16, 17 to 18, 19 to 20, 21 to 22, 23 to 24, and 25 or more. (Inappropriate and No Answers were assigned 0.)

CONVOY NUMBERS

This variable is bracketed on C51, "About how many friends or other relatives do you have whom you could call on for advice or help if you needed it?" (This scale was 0, 1-2, 3-4, 5-6, 7-10, 11 or more.)

CONVOY QUALITY

This variable is the sum of rescaled classes of replies (1, "a great deal," to 5, "not at all") to questions about spouse or equivalent, mother or equivalent, father or equivalent, children, and friends, as to whether they "make you feel loved and cared for," "are willing to listen when you need to talk about your worries or problems," and (reversed) "make too many demands on you" or "are critical of what you do." (This scale can run from 0 to 100, and is bracketed at 0-54, 55-59, 60-64, 65-69, 70-74, 75-79, 80 or more. Inappropriate or No Answers were scaled 3 to neutralize estimates of average quality.)

ECONOMIC SATISFACTION

This variable is defined by the following question: "How difficult is it for you to meet the monthly payments on your bills?" (5, "not difficult," to 1," extremely difficult") plus 4 minus: "How satisfied are you with your financial situation?" (5, "not at all," to 1, "completely satisfied"). The range is 0 to 8.

EFFICACY

One point each was given for the following:

- Agreeing strongly or somewhat with
  - "I take a positive attitude toward myself."
  - "I can do just about anything I set my mind to do."
- Saying *yes* to
  - "Are you the type of person who plans for the future?"
- Saying *pretty sure* to
  - "Have you usually felt pretty sure your life would work out the way you want it to, or have there been times when you have not been sure about it?"
- Saying *carry out* to
  - "When you make plans ahead, do you usually get to carry out things the way you expected, or do things usually come up to make you change your plans?"

- Disagreeing strongly or somewhat with
  - "At times I think I am no good at all."
  - "All in all, I am inclined to feel that I am a failure."
  - "Sometimes I feel that I am being pushed around in life."
  - "There is really no way to solve the problems I have."
  - "I worry that something bad will happen to me."
  - "I worry that something bad will happen to one of my loved ones."

The range is 0 to 11.

EQUIVALENT ADULTS

This variable is the number of those age 18 or older in a family plus half the number under age 18.

FULL INCOME

This variable is the realized money income plus annuitized wealth.

HAPPINESS

This variable is defined by the question: "Have the changes brought about by your retirement been entirely good (5), mostly good (4), mostly bad (2), or entirely bad (1)?" (3 if not retired or not applicable) plus "These are the best years of my life." Strongly agree (5) to strongly disagree (1) plus "Life could be happier." The scale is strongly agree (1) to strongly disagree (5). The range is 3-15.

For the figure using SEARCH (Figure 6.1), the first (retirement) component was deleted, leaving an index that ran from 2 to 10.

HEALTH CONDITIONS

This variable is the number of the following conditions which are reported: arthritis, lung disease, hypertension or high blood pressure, heart attack, diabetes or high blood sugar, cancer or malignant tumor, foot problems (such as circulation, corns, or calluses), stroke, broken bones, urine out of control, poor or extremely limited vision (with glasses or contact lenses), poor or nonexistent hearing (with hearing aid). This scale is truncated, so the range is 0-6.

HEALTH FUNCTIONING

The variable is defined as follows:

1. *Severe*: In bed or chair most of the day because of health, or has a lot of difficulty bathing self, or cannot do it
2. *Moderately severe*: Has a lot of difficulty climbing stairs or cannot climb a few flights of stairs or walk several blocks
3. *Least severe*: Has a lot of difficulty doing heavy work or cannot do heavy work around the house such as shoveling snow or washing walls
4. *No functional impairment.*

SELF-REPORTED HEALTH

The variable is defined as follows:

ACL: "How would you rate your health at the present time? Would you say it is excellent, very good, good, fair, or poor?" (1 for "excellent" to 5 for "poor")

PSID: "Would you say your health in general is excellent, very good, good, fair, or poor?" (same scale as *ACL*).

INCOME

This variable is defined as follows:

ACL: After asking about nine sources of income, including food stamps, "If we include the income from all these sources, and add all of your (and your spouse's) earnings, what would your total income, before taxes, for the last 12 months add up to? Just give me a letter from the list on this page" (10 intervals).

PSID: Fifty-six questions on money income, edited, plus food stamps, plus the value of free rent for those who neither own nor rent.

LEISURE

This variable is defined as follows: sixteen hours a day after sleep and maintenance (5,840) minus total work hours, paid and unpaid.

OTHERS IN FAMILY

This variable is based on the number of people other than head of household and spouse, mostly children for those under age 55.

GENERAL SATISFACTION

For this variable, one point was given if the individual agreed strongly or somewhat with the statement "As I look back on my life, I am fairly well satisfied." One point was given for being completely or very satisfied with neighborhood, home, financial situation, being a parent, marriage, and job. To neutralize those without a spouse, children, or a job, subtract 1 if "not at all satisfied" or "not very satisfied" with parenting, job, or wife. (For those three, the scale is thus –1 if "dissatisfied," +1 if "satisfied," and 0 if "inappropriate.") The range is –3 to 7.

SATISFACTION WITH HEALTH

This variable is defined by the question: "In general, how satisfied are you with your health: completely, very, somewhat, not very, or not at all satisfied?" (not at all = 5). (This variable is not included in general satisfaction because it has the opposite age pattern.)

ECONOMIC SATISFACTION

This variable is defined by the questions: "How difficult is it for you to meet the monthly payments on your bills?" (5, "not at all" to 1, "very") minus "How satisfied are you with your present financial situation?" (1, "completely" to 5, "not at all") plus 4, so the range is 0 to 8.

WEALTH

This variable is defined by the questions:

ACL: "If you sold this house-apartment-farm today, how much money would you get for it (after paying off the mortgage)?" plus "Suppose you needed money quickly and you cashed in all of your (and your spouse's) checking and saving accounts, and any stocks and bonds and real estate (other than your principal home). If you added up what you got, about how much would this amount to? Just give me the letter from the list" (7 intervals, using midpoints.)

PSID: House value minus mortgage, plus 36 questions covering net equity in six types of wealth, minus "other" debt. Those not offering a dollar amount were asked in each case for an interval estimate.

WORK HOURS

ACL: Sum of nine components: regular paid work, irregular paid work, child care, housework, do-it-yourself work, volunteer work, helping others, chronic care of others, and crisis care of others. Questions in the components were as follows:

- Including paid vacation and sick leave, how many weeks altogether were you employed during the past 12 months? On the average, how many hours a week do you work on this job including paid and unpaid overtime?

- People pay each other to do work or chores instead of going to regular businesses. During the past 12 months were you paid to do any work of this sort that was not part of a regular job? (If yes, altogether, about how many hours did you spend doing paid work that was not part of a regular job during the past 12 months? (5 brackets given).

- About how many hours do you spend in an average week caring for the children who live here? (4 intervals given).

- Do you prepare food for meals or wash dishes? Do you do grocery shopping? Do you clean or vacuum? Do you do laundry? Do you sew and mend? Altogether, about how many hours do you spend doing these things in an average week?

- In the last 12 months did you yourself do any painting, redecorating or repairs on your home? Did you yourself do any work in your yard or other areas outside your home? (Please include things like mowing the lawn, weeding plants, or removing snow.) Did you yourself grow, freeze, or can any of your own food during the last 12 months? Did you yourself do any repairs on a car or truck that you own? Altogether, how many hours did you spend doing these things during the last 12 months? (Would you say "less than 20 hours," "20-39 hours," "40-79 hours," "80-159 hours," or "160 hours or more"?)

- Did you do volunteer work in the last year for a church, synagogue, or other religious organization? Did you do volunteer work for a school or educational organization? Did you do volunteer work for a political group or labor union in the last 12 months?

Did you do work last year for a senior citizen group or related organization? In the last 12 months, did you do volunteer work for any other national or local organization including United Fund, hospitals, and the like? About how many hours did you spend on volunteer work (of this kind/these kinds) during the last 12 months? (Would you say "less than 20 hours," "20-39 hours," "40-79 hours," "80-159 hours," or "160 hours or more"?)

• Now let us talk about help you may have given in the last year to friends, neighbors, or relatives who did not live with you. We are interested in help you provided during the last 12 months for which you did not receive payment. During the last 12 months did you provide transportation, shop, or run errands for friends, neighbors, or relatives who did not live with you? Did you help others with their housework or with the upkeep of their house, car, or other things? In the last 12 months, did you do child care without pay for persons not living in your household? Did you do any other things in the last 12 months to help neighbors, friends, or relatives who did not live with you? Altogether, about how many hours did you spend doing these things during the last 12 months? (same 5 intervals listed).

• Now I would like to talk with you about people who have trouble taking care of themselves because of physical or mental illness, disability, or for some other reason. Are you currently involved in helping someone like this by caring for them directly or arranging for their care by others? About how many hours did you spend doing this in the past year? (same 5 intervals).

• During the past 12 months, has anyone else you care about had a serious injury, illness, personal problem, or sudden crisis? Altogether, about how many hours did you spend in the past year helping him or her with his or her problem(s) or talking with him or her about the problem(s)? (same 5 intervals).

PSID: Edited from a sequence asking about illness, vacations, being out of the labor force. Then, how many weeks did you actually work on your main job in 1983? On the average how many hours a week did you work on your main job in 1983? Did you work any overtime that is not included in this? (If yes, how many hours did that overtime amount to in 1983?) (plus questions on weeks and hours per week for each extra job.) Add commuting time, edited from "About how much time does it take you to get to work each day, door to door?" (one way). Also add housework time, edited from, "About how much time do you (or your wife) spend on housework in an average week—time spent cooking, cleaning, and doing other work around the house?"

Warning: Time-diary evidence would indicate exaggeration of hours spent on any activity asked about, partly because people can do more than one thing at a time and partly because there is no adding-up constraint. Paid work is probably an exception because it is regular and fixed. Unpaid work in the ACL study was asked about in various places in the questionnaire, and in at least a few cases it involved obvious double-counting, which we truncated.

7

Development of Reserves for Adaptation to Old Age: Personal and Societal Agendas

David L. Featherman

Money does not buy happiness. I learned that aphorism at my mother's knee as she cautioned me against aspiring to great wealth as an ultimate goal in life. My mother's thinking reflected her working class setting of modest but stable income. Who needs the uncertainties and risks of great loss that arise from the inexorable temptation to turn seemingly boundless opportunities and fortune into larger material wealth? (See Brim, 1988, for a more sophisticated assessment of optimal aspiration setting and resetting through life, based on adaptation-level theories in social psychology).

The economist Richard Easterlin (1973) has cast the light of empirical study on my mother's aphorism (perhaps his mother's as well). Easterlin finds that although aggregate personal wealth in this country rises and falls according to the long and short cycles of the national economy, aggregate levels of reported happiness or subjective well-being remain rather stable. Such aggregate relationships imply that public morale or perceived economic welfare is highly relative. This suggests a psychology of accommodation or adaptation. My mother was apparently right, under one interpretation—namely that because most of us are never fully satisfied even with great wealth, then if happiness is what you want, be happy with what you have, even if it is not very much. She might have added with real wisdom, "Become happy with your life in its many facets despite the vagaries of your income; set your aspirations wisely."

What my mother did not tell me was that in empirical studies comparing individuals of wealth, poverty, or middle incomes, perceived well-being is not equally distributed. At least the rather low correlations suggest a slight tendency for material well-being to be associated with reported happiness (Campbell, Converse, & Rogers, 1976). The low correlations, however, also suggest that many of us do find happiness or well-being despite the level of income that characterizes us when survey takers count our material and mental welfare. Perhaps most of us find our happiness in the qualities of our familial and social ties, or in community service. Others may find happiness by helping another person who needs it, or by having a job that is not boring or demeaning. These possibilities are suggested in cross-sectional studies of subjective well-being, wherein familial and social relationships are the major source of perceived welfare (Campbell & Converse, 1972).

What also may underlie these low correlations in a population cross-section is a life-course shift in the standards we use to gauge our happiness, and perhaps even our financial well-being. In our young adulthood the prospects of gaining higher standards of living through decades-long improvements in our careers and employment circumstances may overshadow the fact that younger workers tend to be underpaid relative to their marginal productivities, whereas mature workers tend to be overpaid (Lazear, 1979). Achievement of worldly success is a culturally embedded value that motivates many of us. Comparing one's own life-style with that of neighbors is a gauge of family and personal status within one's inner circle of friends and coworkers (Coleman & Rainwater, 1978). Because of the normally expected upward drift of wage-based income over an individual's working life, there may be a disassociation between actual income and perceived well-being, at least before retirement and the elder years.

For the period beyond retirement, however, the relationship between income and well-being is open to even greater speculation. We know that individuals with higher preretirement incomes, better employment conditions, and more education during their adult years are also relatively better financed for normal and comfortable life-styles after retirement. This is true even after the reduction of income that comes from wage losses (but discounting catastrophic illness events). (See Henretta & Campbell, 1978, for national data and models of the continuity of relative socioeconomic attainment during the life cycle). This finding is consistent with others reported by Holden and Burkhauser (1987) from the Retirement History Study. They found that married couples who enter retirement with pensions have inflation-adjusted incomes of about 80% of their preretirement levels; during the first 8 years of retirement this income-replacement rate may fall to about 50% in real terms. Married couples retiring without pensions do a little worse, entering retirement with a replacement rate of 74% and falling to around 48% after about 8 years. Neither of these two groups were very likely to fall into income poverty (5% and 11%, respectively).

I take these studies as suggesting that despite a drop in wage income at retirement, the relatively more advantaged couples tend to remain so into and perhaps through most of old age. (The drop in wage-based income may stem from the difficulties of finding part-time wage employment or sustainable self-employment after retirement, but another factor could be less interest in working or in finding employment as retirement unfolds; see Fuchs, 1983.) The studies also suggest that the Social Security system and other public transfers assist married couples with or without pensions to avoid poverty and to buffer the impact of wage loss. Under these conditions the indicator of morale may shift away from income to other factors, such as health.

The most important link between financial well-being and perceived happiness during the life cycle may lie elsewhere—that is, not in the low measurable association between dollar and morale levels across persons and age groups. Rather, it may have more to do with the uncertain risks of rapid and large fluctuations in income. Many if not most households experience vacillating levels of income during a decade, and these changes are not confined to age-graded life points such as retirement. For example, Greg Duncan analyzed the continuing, annual Michigan Income Dynamics Panel that was begun by Jim Morgan in the late 1960s (Duncan, 1984; Duncan & Morgan, 1985). Duncan has reported that perhaps one third of American families encountered a large drop in living standards during the 1970s. Most of these events were not anticipated (unlike retirement), especially during the prime working years. Rapid changes in family income can and did affect psychological well-being (Duncan & Morgan, 1980; McLanahan & Sorensen, 1985) and the interpersonal dynamics of households (Elder, 1985). If, as Duncan concluded, the unanticipated volatility of family income during a decade is more the rule than the exception, then money cannot buy happiness. The predictability and perhaps controllability of an income level, however, might have a more direct relationship to perceived well-being. In any case, the connection between income and morale during the life course may in fact only become clear if we track and understand their mutual dynamics and the developmental psychology and sociology of individual and familial adaptations to change, volatility, and uncertainty. (See Brim, 1988, for a similar view, which states that "happiness" ensues from a complicated adjustment of aspirations to expectations through life in response to "wins and losses.")

The focus of the remainder of my chapter is directed at such adaptations to change, because I believe it is the development of personal and societal resources for adapting to unanticipated and as yet uncontrolled changes in the life course that is a major pathway to the successful aging of individuals and to a more optimal aging society. I suggest that the presence or absence of these resources are even more critical for adaptation to the challenges of later life. As a starting point I argue that the topic of financial security and well-being in old age may be a misleading conjunction. If the motivation behind the choice of this theme was to broaden our enlightenment of the road to successful aging on the presumption that financial insecurity was a special problem of the elderly and its solution would lead to greater well-being, then the motivation was only partly well-founded. To be sure the elderly are at risk of financial insecurity, through both voluntary and involuntary loss of work and wages, widowhood, chronic disease, or debilitation of self-care. It would be no fool's errand to secure the financial floor of independent living after retirement and to expand the means to peace of mind for the elderly as an important public goal for the state as a welfare securer during the life course (Mayer & Muller, 1986).

Yet in many respects the issue of the well-being of the elderly may not lie solely in the specifics of financial security. Even if the latter speculation is not correct, I am more certain that an understanding of the well-being of the elderly and of its expansion as a public goal may lie outside this realm. Studies of income-replacement levels (Danzinger, van der Gaag, Smolensky, & Taussig, 1984) and of the risks of entering poverty (Holden & Burkhauser, 1987) underlie my thinking on this point.

These studies emphasize two important facts about financial security that bear on well-being after retirement. First, those with better education, upper-level white-collar careers, pension plans, and a living spouse enter retirement with the necessary (if not sufficient) resources for replacing wages with part-time work and other financial sources that support or maintain their prior relative socioeconomic status and life-style as they live out old age (Henretta & Campbell, 1978). Income-replacement levels, although declining from roughly 74% among intact couples to about 48% during the first 8 or so years, do not place elderly married couples at unusual or high risk of poverty, either episodically or continuously. It must be noted, however, that risks to this normal pattern of security (including the maintenance of one's relative place within the status system of one's cohort) are unpredictable or unanticipated. For a woman, the death of a husband drastically raises the risk of falling into poverty, volatile inflation erodes the real value of assets, and catastrophic health care episodes may force the liquidation of home and other nonliquid assets.

In short, a practical problem-solving approach for the planning of financial security is no guarantee against financial insecurity or low morale. Men and women who have exercised rational choice and have had the good fortune to accrue pensions before retirement are marginally better off in the first years after retirement, especially if their spouse is alive and well. After the first decade the differences in income replacement between those with and without pensions is not great. Having remarried or remained in a long-term marriage may represent an asset toward well-being, but death of the spouse, especially an "early" death, puts widows at a great risk of financial insecurity that persists and deepens in old age.

My point is that most elderly in contemporary cohorts are financially secure, and if money could buy happiness, then their collective well-being should be rather high, *ceteris paribus*. There is an impressive range of events, mostly unpredictable as to onset and individual vulnerability, that place security and well-being at risk, however, even if the risk is unrealized for many (Fuchs, 1983; Rowe & Kahn, 1987). It is probably as much the uncertainties that surround the events such as a spouse's death, illness, inflation, and so on as it is the income losses themselves that erode the normal basis of well-being (Brim & Ryff, 1983; McLanahan & Sorensen, 1985). The elderly are not uniquely at risk of income insecurity, however, as Duncan (1988) reminds us in describing the pervasiveness through the life course of unpredictable income loss during a decade. Indeed, whereas the elderly in today's cohorts have the pay-as-you-go Social Security system to buffer some of these risks, many younger individuals and families, especially those without children, do not (Garfinkel & McLanahan, 1987; Preston, 1984).

THEMES AND COUNTERTHEMES: SECURITY AND WELL-BEING IN "POSTRETIRED" SOCIETY

I begin my remarks with the working assertion that the conjunction between financial security and well-being among the elderly is not a particularly illuminating one. At least it is not if one wants to understand how older persons might adapt more successfully to the multiple challenges of later life, or how a society might be better structured and equipped to deal with a larger postretired population. This bold assertion gains more force in life-span perspective, because it is my intent to argue that the financial and other well-being of the elderly is the fruit of seeds laid much earlier in life.

My proposal is that we not dwell narrowly on money or pensions, or how we finance the Social Security system, despite the obvious national and personal importance that these topics have for the elderly of today and tomorrow. Rather, the theme I wish to develop focuses on how we equip ourselves and our policy institutions with better tools to deal with the special developmental tasks of contemporary old age. The theme has special relevance for the personal and societal tasks that face our society as it moves into what I call the "postretired" era. By "postretired" I mean a society whose institutions reflect a population that is both aging and enlarging the fraction of the old and very old who are no longer at work in the labor force, or providing for their own care or the care of others (even if only temporarily in the long history of society; see Featherman, Smith, & Peterson, 1990).

My thesis has two dimensions—one is concerned with the individual life course, whereas the other refers to the institutional fabric of our changing society and its demographic transformations. As for the first dimension, along the adult lifeline we increasingly encounter "ill-structured" dilemmas rather than "well-structured" problems. These dilemmas are developmental tasks, if you will, that challenge our minds and bodies. At the same time our postindustrial society and its enlarging retired population also face increasingly greater dilemmas that defy easy technical solutions. The second dimension of my thesis suggests that these societal dilemmas that arise within a postretired society are also ill-structured tasks but for the development of society. I believe it is the individual's acquired capacities for resolving the ill-structured dilemmas of later adult life and old age that lies at the heart of well-being in old age. Likewise it is the capacity of society, and specifically its policy makers and leaders, to adopt a life-span developmental perspective—"long-range societal planning" (Michael, 1973)—that seems likely to optimize public welfare as society develops toward a mature postindustrial, postretired state.

It is the purpose of my chapter to illuminate the nature of a developmental resource—a resource both for the aging individual and for the aging society—that may provide a greater adaptive reserve as we individually and collectively face the challenges of the ill-structured world of old age and the future. In returning momentarily to the theme of this conference, I point out that the greater psychological effects of financial insecurity across the life course seem to come not from a direct tie to income levels but from unexpected and uncontrolled (or uncontrollable) changes in them, especially losses (Rodin, 1986; Shupe, 1985). Money does not buy happiness, but perhaps the individual and collective capacities—developmental reserves—to respond with resilience to unanticipated change or uncontrollable loss may provide the broader basis of individual well-being, both financial and otherwise, and of public welfare. I would also state plainly at the outset that what follows is a preliminary statement of my own thoughts about these relationships, and I am much indebted to others who earlier have suggested the inputs to these themes as I now develop them (see Featherman et al., 1990, for a fuller exposition of these themes and a related theory of adaptive competence).

DEVELOPMENTAL TASKS IN LATER ADULT LIFE

Let me begin by sketching the problems of later adult life—the tasks and dilemmas that face men and women as they become disengaged from full-time paying jobs and other major roles in the mainstream institutions of our society, and enter for good or ill what I shall call the life period of old age. Other students of human development also tend to define life periods in functional terms—that is, by the qualitatively different sets of problems that persons in each "season" of life must solve or master. They must do so to progress or adapt normally within the cultural and historical context of society's understanding of appropriate age-based behavior (Hagestad & Neugarten, 1985; Riley, 1985). (I will set aside the important academic debate of the questions: Are these life "stages" real or merely heuristic abstractions? Is development during the life span, whether broken into qualitatively different phases or not, inherently progressive and universally patterned for all persons within a given society? These functional terms define sets of so-called developmental tasks [Havighurst, 1956; Oerter, 1986]).

One of the more difficult tasks faced by the elderly is that of securing financial and other well-being, as it is for younger adults as well. For the elderly, however, it is embedded as a component of what I see to be a more major developmental task that is unique to later adult life and old age—namely, retirement into "productive" leisure. By productive leisure I refer in part to Jim Morgan's work (chapter 6) and his collaborative research with Bob Kahn about self- and other-care, and related community service, support-giving, and self-maintenance–providing behaviors. This productivity, although usually unpaid, is part of the untallied economic contributions of the elderly to the total national product and toward their own welfare. Without it the costs to society of an enlarging postretired population would be much greater, and the quality of life for the rest of us even without these costs in the balance would be lower. By productive leisure, however, I also refer to the transformation of individuals' productive capacities, or their direct transfer, from expression within the paying jobs of the work force and unpaid ones in family and kin care into self-defined pursuits that maintain or enlarge one's personal sense of worth or mental health.

I do not think that I need to dwell on the importance of the transition from a place in the productive economy with its direct ties to financial and other levels of well-being to securing material welfare and esteem after retirement. I do want to emphasize the developmental significance of this transition, however. Though men are tending to retire at earlier ages (and women appear to be working until later ages), retirement remains an important developmental watershed at the boundary of old age as a life period. It marks the passage from participation in the mainstream and well-structured institutions of adult society to the ill-structured social statuses of elderhood. These statuses are without benefit of institutional settings and acknowledged roles with titles and clear expectations for appropriate behavior (Rosow, 1985). It becomes measurably more difficult within contemporary arrangements of old age for the retired to gain wage-based financial security because of the unorganized diversity of part-time work as "consultants" and "advisers," and other honorific statuses that lack any organizational basis. The retired may also work in a secondary economy in which self-employment is a risky, transitory, and declining occupation. This is an important point because it is through formal organizations and our membership in them that our financial, health, and perhaps social ties tend to be acquired and secured for the duration. American postindustrial society can be viewed as a society of burgeoning organizations and emergent interorganizational systems that regulate the access and supply of welfare (Mayer & Muller, 1986).

The Social Security system is a possible exception that makes the point for the elderly and old age. In our construction of a pay-as-you go system Social Security payments represent a centralized (function of the state) transfer of money from workers within employing firms to aged or certain disabled former workers currently without these organizational attachments, and the means of implicit contracts, unions, and other market mechanisms of welfare negotiation and provision for what remains of their lifetimes as permanently detached nonworkers.

Even for those older workers who do remain in the conventional labor force, some are channeled into work roles that lack any specific duties at dead-end/make-work jobs, or are "kicked upstairs," which effectively reduces the structure of accountability, daily routinization, and definition of tasks to be performed that anyone cares about (Rosow, 1985). Popular reports of current "golden parachute" career buyouts and "plateauing" of managerial careers allege that the private sector is trimming its upper echelon of positions in the organizational charts to be competitive in a slow-growth economy. One effect is that large cohorts of middle-level managers will find even fewer upper-managerial roles and vice-presidencies—for example, forcing firms to dismiss middle-aged and older workers (say, beyond age 55) into a marketplace of highly uncertain financial prospects for the remaining working years (Bardwick, 1986).

In short, the developmental task of retirement or disengagement from "productive labor" involves a set of transitions during a usually extended period that, even without the complications of ill health or involuntary choice about timing (Atchley, 1983), challenge the developmental reserves of the older adult. Most of us do not know how to address these problems, and our system of formal and informal education provides little to no training or preparation, even though it could do so (Montada & Schmitt, 1986). Retirement, broadly defined, is an ill-structured task. As a process retirement stretches over an increasingly broad age range, involves loss of formal roles and attachments to formal organizations that provide a base for personal identity and family welfare, and leads toward a "tenuous" social designation or honorific status as a "retired person" (Rosow, 1985). The major element of the developmental task of retirement is how to replace the loss of work roles and other organizational attachments. Such replacement must entail both the reality of productivity and a public and self-acknowledgment that these productive behaviors are indeed of high social and personal value. This task is extremely difficult in a society of organizations that so tightly associates productivity with formal roles and the economy of dollar-denominated services.

Retirement is only one of the developmental tasks of old age. Another is the assembly of a "convoy" of life partners whose instrumental, emotional, and other support-giving exchanges may be a key factor in coping with stressful challenges to health through life but increasingly so in the later years (Kahn & Antonucci, 1980; Rodin, 1986). Another, more intrapsychic task is managing and preserving a sense of continuity of "self" (Kaufman, 1986). Yet another and perhaps final task is dealing with the problems of becoming institutionalized or hospitalized in frail health yet controlling the circumstances and conditions of one's death (Marshall, 1981). The latter task is especially difficult in a society of organizations. Today's medical technology and personnel are supremely efficient in sustaining vital functions even at high financial and perhaps personal costs. The economy, technology, and professionalization of the medical industry seems to lead to ever-more complex forms of organized service provision. Ironically personal control over the terms of one's death in such a highly well-structured organizational environment appears to be a very ill-structured task for the elderly (Baltes & Werner-Wahl, 1987).

All these developmental tasks, and gerontologists and developmentalists will not agree on an exhaustive listing of them, share the property that I have called ill structured versus well structured. The distinction has been made in the decision-making and cognitive problem-solving literatures, and it has had importance for basic cognitive and policy sciences as well as practical organizational decision making (see Churchman, 1971; Kitchener, 1983; and Peterson, 1985, the latter for a review of a wide range of literature).

For our purposes the distinction between well-structured and ill-structured life problems is like the distinction between puzzles and dilemmas (Kitchener, 1983). In a puzzle, like a jigsaw or crossword puzzle and even chess, the one best and only solution is sought. The puzzle solver does not consider alternative solutions or new rules of the game. One does not question the validity of the assumptions on which the game is based; one does not reshape pieces of the puzzle or decide that the shape of the overall result can be nonsquare or nonrectangular, for example. Indeed, well-structured problems, like balancing a checkbook, are guaranteed if one persists in applying standard rules or techniques as provided. In the real world of "nongames," such as educational and occupational careers within bureaucratic organizations, the problems of the first half of life are filled, albeit not exclusively, with relatively more well-structured tasks.

By contrast, ill-structured problems, such as I have described as rising in prevalence during the last quarter of life, defy the one-best-solution approach based on close means-ends relationships and techniques-based solution systems. They are more like dilemmas than puzzles. They are dialectical problems with contradicting ends and purposes, relative solutions, and ambiguous end points that often change in form and salience as we pursue them. As C. West Churchman puts it:

> In the richer problems of everyday life, one rarely finds that the problems can be constructed as a puzzle, and one of the most difficult aspects of realistic problem-solving is the determination of whether or not a solution has occurred. . . . Another way of saying the same thing is that in social problems like pollution and poverty there is no authorized source for terminating the inquiry. (Churchman, 1971, p. 144)

If the life world of the elderly is composed of many more ill-structured dilemmas than well-structured problems, what resources or reserves are required to cope with them effectively? If the balance of problems of life management changes during the life course as one moves from large organizational, bureaucratic settings toward a more atomistic, roleless context after retirement, what are the appropriate preparations for these new challenges or new developmental tasks? Clearly financial preparations may be important, but I want to focus instead on a different basis of preparation that lies in qualities of mind that are brought to the solution of problems in everyday life and in life management in later adulthood and old age.

I want to argue that the disjunction between the balance of well-structured and ill-structured problems in the first and second halves of life make it normally difficult for many elderly to adapt successfully. Older adults are not well prepared for the challenges of old age by the sociological nature of prior life experiences of well-structured problem solving. Are there some adult-life contexts, however, that do provide apparently greater developmental reserves for the transitions from well- to ill-structured problems? I believe there are, at least within the world of some work and career lines that my research group is beginning to study (although there may be other domains, such as family life, wherein similar positive preparations may be engendered). At this early stage of our research we are conceptualizing and studying the developmental connection between some jobs and work careers, the management of careers of high expertise, and comparatively more successful aging in postretired life. Before laying out our rationale and some preliminary findings, let me turn briefly to a general description of development and developmental reserves as we use these ideas in our work (see Featherman, 1987; Featherman, Smith, & Peterson, 1990).

DEVELOPMENT AS GAINS AND LOSSES
OF ADAPTIVE COMPETENCE THROUGH LIFE

We subscribe to the view that development occurs when there is a change in adaptive capacity (Baltes, 1987; Featherman, 1987). That is, human development involves capacities and responses to challenging conditions that confront the person with several alternatives: (a) to adapt mind and behavior to the newly prevailing circumstances, (b) to deploy one's collective resources to change prevailing conditions, or (c) to leave the context for a more optimal fit between self and context. (Here I draw on an approach to competence or intelligence as adaptive processes between changing individuals and their changing environments; Berg & Sternberg, 1985; Featherman et al., in press). In any event, development combines a simultaneous and inevitable interplay of both growth (gains) and decline (losses) in function (Baltes, 1987). The relative pattern of gains and losses can vary through life for a given individual and at any age for individuals with different biographies and positions in society.

This view of development is related to Waddington's (1975) evolutionary approach to epigenesis. As illustrated by Waddington's metaphor of the epigenetic landscape, development proceeds from a condition of undifferentiated globality to differentiated specialization of function—that is, to a channeling. The particular pathway taken by Waddington's ball (the person) as it descends the epigenetic landscape and becomes channeled is described in the metaphor by the dual force of gravity and of the channels of the landscape. Respectively, these forces refer to (a) the genetic potential for particular developmental outcomes that are expressed cumulatively; and (b) the social and cultural structures, and the developmental tasks of different life courses. Just as the ball loses undifferentiated plasticity as it begins its descent and gains specialized competence as it becomes channeled, so the developing person acquires adaptive capacity through genetic and sociocultural channeling of gains and losses during the life course. Specialization as an adaptive response to environmental challenges leads simultaneously to both gains and losses. This is an important point for what follows.

Specialization

This process of gains at the cost of losses lies at the core of developmental change. As Baltes (1987) and others have noted, any one moment in the life course or history of development may involve a prevalence of declines over growth rather than vice versa. Hypothetically this may be the case in the very latest phases of life, when at least in our Western cultural images and belief systems we tend to emphasize "aging" as net processes of loss over the fewer perceived instances of growth (Heckhausen, Dixon, & Baltes, 1989). Not all developmental change leads by necessity to growth in adaptive capacity from the viewpoint of the person. Loss of resilience in the central nervous system in advanced old age, even in the face of lifelong neuronal capacities for self-repair and dendritic growth (Cotman & Peterson, 1987), as well as death itself, provides concreteness. The comparison between the poorly nourished and impoverished ghetto child and the suburban affluent counterpart reminds us, however, that the balance of gains and losses at any age or for a particular person or racial group need not amount to overall growth. Not all channeled courses of the sociocultural and genetic landscape lead to equally adaptive capacities in persons over life, given prevailing social and cultural institutions, and the genetics of individual differences. The complexities of developmental functions across life reflect human genetic and social systems of diverse opportunities and constraints.

Developmentalists who analyze these complex patterns of adaptational gains and losses in mental, behavioral, and social context through life currently puzzle over their balance in the later years. George Maddox's chapter addresses the evolutionary and contemporary functions and dysfunctions of population heterogeneity that result from this complexity in human development. For gerontologists such as myself who try to understand old age as a life-span developmental phenomenon, the substantive arena of cognitive functioning has proved to be rather suggestive, if not fully enlightening, about resources for successful aging within a life world of ill-structured dilemmas. What I want to stress unequivocally from my understanding of cognitive development is that the outcomes are interactive products of our biology, social institutions, and individual wills or self-expression. Let me focus, however, on that part of cognitive development that seems to reflect an important relationship between intelligence and problem solving through adulthood, as influenced by the socially and culturally channeled life course.

First, adult intelligence is not what intelligence tests measure. Rather, as a general feature of mind it is "mental activity involved in adapting to a change in one's environment in order to produce an optimal fit between oneself and the environment" (Berg & Sternberg, 1985, p. 343). Intelligence, so defined, seems to evoke and engender rather different adaptational capacities and behaviors when the "landscape" of developmental tasks is well structured (e.g., during childhood and adolescence, or the school-going years) than when it becomes rather more ill structured. Thus psychogerontologists point out that scholastically oriented intelligence tests tap capacities and impose constraints of speeded memory performance that are functionally linked to success in school and in the work force. Yet these very tests and the "primary mental abilities" they assess may not diagnose the most salient range and depth of competencies that equip older adults for greater or lesser success at their central developmental tasks, like "productive" nonpaid work, loving, self-managing, and taking care of others (Dittmann-Kohli, 1988; Labouvie-Vief, 1982; Willis & Schaie, 1986).

Second, the "special" mental resource of later adulthood that reflects apparent individual differences in adult intelligence seems to be the content of knowledge rather than the mechanics of information processing. The most successfully aging, in these intellectual terms, may derive success from rich knowledge or *expertise* (Glaser, 1987). Expertise includes the faculties for discerning when and how to apply facts and procedural knowledge. The most successful aging may be able to recognize, consciously or not, that "solving" well-structured problems and ill-structured ones call for different approaches. Let me describe this expertise and the model of mind that gerontologists believe to underlie it (see Baltes, Dittmann-Kohli, & Dixon, 1984, and Berg & Sternberg, 1985, for similar models of mind and important inputs to my own conceptions).

MENTAL PRAGMATICS AND INTELLIGENT ADAPTATION IN LATER LIFE

Under one life-span model of the developing mind the conceptual distinction between the *pragmatics* and the *mechanics* of information processing and problem solving is crucial, especially to understanding the cognitive reserves for adaptation in later life (see Baltes et al., 1984). For many years psychologists have observed that tested abilities, such as in memory tasks and rapid processing of logical relationships, appear on average to decline after midlife. They have also noted that these same abilities are widely distributed within a cohort, so that many elderly up to age 80 may do as well on these tested abilities as the typical young adult, especially when speed of response is not a feature of the testing situation. Furthermore, memory and some other primary mental abilities can be retrained and restored among the very old, suggesting that in the normally aging adult there is an untapped reserve of these abilities that may be unrealized in contemporary environments (Baltes & Willis, 1982). When there are real average declines, they seem to involve tests that tap the mechanics of intelligence—that is, the architecture of the brain as an information processor. (Tests of "fluid" intelligence may be assessing this facet of mental functioning; see Horn & Donaldson, 1980.) Recent research in Berlin suggests that there may be biological declines in the mechanics of cognitive processing, if one is tracking the upper limits of these basic information processing functions in the elderly (Baltes & Kliegl, 1986).

By contrast, the pragmatics of cognition are like the software rather than the hardware of mind, and include the information content of factual and procedural knowledge. Pragmatics also include the "executive system" that guides storage and retrieval of this information, and that governs when, where, and how to use it. The "executive system" is best described as knowledge about knowledge and knowledge about the conditions of applying what one knows. If the content of mind is cognition, then these executive, guidance, and application systems are metacognitions (Flavell, 1979). (Psychometric tests of "crystallized" intelligence may be tapping these pragmatics; see Baltes et al., 1984; Horn & Donaldson, 1980).

Using this distinction between pragmatics and mechanics some geropsychologists describe hypothetically different developmental histories for each of these major cognitive systems. In adulthood the average developmental course of mechanics is probably decline, whereas for pragmatics it may be gain or maintenance. Thus, if the adaptational success of the older adult is a reflection of differential intelligence, then it follows that expert performances at the developmental tasks of old age are more likely to rest on an extensive reserve of pragmatics. Such instances of successful aging may be based on the cumulative history of experience and training that has expanded this developmental reserve. This hypothetical conclusion is most credible when one compares the equally expert performances of older and younger adults, where it can be assumed that a theoretical decline in the mechanics of the mind will disadvantage the older but perhaps be overridden or offset by compensation through extraordinary applications of the pragmatics of the mind (Perlmutter, 1988; Salthouse, 1987). That is, the extensive informational systems of the elderly may enable some of them to compensate for performance loss that can arise from the biological aging of the undiseased brain (Cotman & Peterson, 1987).

Among the instances of pragmatics in mental functioning that gerontologists are now studying as potential assets in successful aging is wisdom. Wisdom is an elusive concept to define, because it has wide usage in philosophy, literature, and religion as well as in behavioral science (Clayton & Birren, 1980). The concept of wisdom may prove to be intractable to empirical inquiry. In one scientific effort, however, Paul Baltes, Jacqui Smith, and others at the Max Planck Institute for Education and Human Development in Berlin are testing individual differences in wisdom among young and very old adults. They believe that wisdom, as part of mental pragmatics, possibly emerges only later in life. It is an adaptational resource that may compensate for losses in other cognitive systems (in addition to being an asset in its own right). Baltes et al., (1984) define cognitive wisdom with several assessment criteria that are applied in coding and rating responses to vignettes that present typical life dilemmas.

- Expertise (including descriptive and procedural knowledge) in the fundamental pragmatics of life
- Interpretive and evaluative knowledge about the significance of this content domain (life problems like coping with financial trouble)

- Contextual richness (breadth) of problem definition and solution
- Uncertainty and relativism (especially complexity, difficulty, and variability) of problem situation and definition
- "Good" (effective, practical) judgment and the ability to give "good" advice

The Berlin research is looking at the possibility that on these wisdom tasks their older subjects will perform far better than the younger ones at tasks that call for cumulative life experiences (i.e., life dilemmas that evoke special knowledge). On the tests of speeded memory performance, however, the young will outperform the old. If these hypotheses are credible, then wisdom may be a basis for functioning productively in later adulthood. Not only may wisdom be a factor in the positive mental adjustments to the inherent changes of old age, but it may also provide a means of assisting others to adjust as an instance of social support.

What I find fascinating about the Berlin effort to make wisdom a tractable scientific construct is a certain parallel between their operational definition and a distinction made between planning and problem-solving orientations in my own research about how workers respond to work tasks and work career management, a subject to which I now turn. What is intriguing is the possibility that cognitive "wisdom" and what we call "reflective planning" may be tapping very similar aspects of mental pragmatics. If so, then perhaps by studying the developmental history of this reflective planning orientation we can gain some understanding of the development of wisdom. If the planning orientation proves to be a rather generic cognitive orientation that arises and is applied outside the domain of work and careers per se, then perhaps it too is a basis of positive adaptation and successful aging within a life world of ill-structured dilemmas.

PLANNING ORIENTATIONS, PROBLEM SOLVING, AND THE WORK WORLD

Several years ago James Peterson (1985), an industrial engineer and a postdoctoral trainee in my research group, was studying the educational and occupational histories of engineers. He wanted to understand the basis of two types of careers or career lines that engineers in his national sample undertook—careers beginning and remaining within engineering, and careers in planning and design that branched off from engineering as a separate career line, but apparently only after midlife. Furthermore, Peterson wanted to analyze the origins and distribution of two orientations planning at work that these engineers and planners-designers were reported by the literature to apply. Our work group calls these "reactive" and "reflective" planning

(Nadler, 1981; Peterson, 1985; Rittel & Webber, 1973). Using an 88-item index to discriminate novices (licensed practitioners) from experts (national and international award winners) and engineers from planners-designers, Peterson constructed a measure of the two orientations. He found that between 85% and 90% of the engineers and planners were "pure types." In other words, novice and expert engineers tend to be "reactive" or tactical planners, whereas former engineers who are now in planning and design jobs tend to use "reflective planning" or strategic planning in handling work tasks. How did they get that way? Why should two sets of engineers, both educated in similar curricula and beginning their working lives in similar jobs develop different orientations toward problem solving at work-related tasks? The answer is unclear with data in hand, but Peterson and I have some speculations and work in progress (with Nadler, Marks, Caldwell, and Smith) that may illuminate these origins and their possible relevance to different pathways of successful adaptation to postworking life (see Featherman, 1990; Featherman & Peterson, 1986; and Featherman et al., 1990, for fuller exposition) (see Figure 7.1).

First, let me provide a brief overview of how I see these two planning orientations toward work as potentially different cognitive orientations toward problem definition and solution search. Both reflective planning and reactive plan-

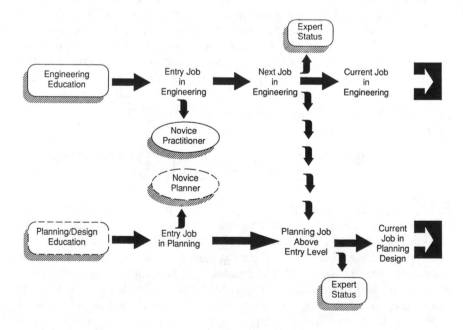

FIGURE 7.1 Study of adaptive competence in two career lines: How is expert status gained and maintained?

ning are instances of what cognitive scientists call *epistemic cognitions* (Kitchener, 1983); they represent instances of the management, guidance, and application of the metacognitive systems in the mind that I referred to earlier. Epistemic knowledge or expertise enables the problem solver to monitor the essential nature of problems and the truth value of alternative solutions (Kitchener, 1983). It includes the individual's awareness of the limits of his or her knowledge—that is, that some things can be known, whereas others cannot. Epistemic knowledge involves the certainty of one's factual and procedural knowledge and the criteria by which one knows that one knows. It also includes the mental or heuristic strategies an individual uses to define the limits of a problem solution (Kitchener, 1983, pp. 222-223).

Reactive and reflective planning are qualitatively distinct, albeit related, epistemic approaches to defining and solving problems, at least the problems at work. Within engineering careers especially problem solving is approached epistemically with the reactive, tactical orientation. Expert engineers most frequently search for one optimal technical solution, use quantitative evaluative criteria, employ lawful generalizations about ineluctable means-ends relationships, see problems as falling into generic types, and focus narrowly on the discrete technical puzzle to be solved without reference to the wider human values or ultimate purposes and assumptions behind the "puzzle." Reactive problem solving in this sense is like doing good research to solve a problem that is defined by someone else.

By contrast the epistemic approach to problems more typically deployed by planners and designers is somewhat more eclectic, strategic, and selective. That is, reflective planners selectively deploy reactive problem solving within the context of reflective planning (Nadler, 1981). Perhaps it is most accurate to say that planners do reflective planning that incorporates but goes beyond the narrower limits of reactive problem solving. The reflective planning orientation questions the universal validity of the one-best-technical or optimizing solution system. The planning orientation, used most effectively by expert planners in our data, acknowledges that discrete problems or puzzles are nearly always nested within ill-structured or fuzzy human purposes that are to be served. Therefore, problems are cast not as puzzles whose solution is guaranteed if one but follows lawful technical mechanics; rather, they are viewed as dilemmas. The task in problem solving for the planner is to evaluate means and ends, and to integrate this information into a practical, albeit conditional, solution. This cognitive and behavioral task may involve interactive solutions in a time-line processing approach that sometimes entails the means of technical optimization theories, but at other times draws on social systems analysis, or hermeneutics, or other options.

Our research on the origins of these two orientations toward work is in a very preliminary stage. We believe that they arise among engineers as related but qualitatively distinguishable epistemic approaches to problems and solutions for two reasons: one is rooted in work and career experience, and the other lies in personality and mental "traits." Work demands in engineering and the curriculum of engineering schools promote skills in reactive planning and tactical problem solving. One can assume that individuals are drawn into engineering as a career if they tend to solve problems in the traditional model of logical, technical optimization. Likewise planning and design careers present very different social and technical aspects in the common tasks of those jobs; those who rise to acknowledged expertise in these fields are surely both selected on the reactive planning orientation in their thinking and have been trained on the job. Yet what is curious is how the two cognitive orientations arise within a cohort that is exposed to undergraduate education in engineering, taught to problem solve in traditional ways, and embark commonly on engineering careers that foster the problem-solving rather than the planning orientation. We cannot now answer this question of origins.

Let me return, however, to the relevance of these work and career orientations to cognitive wisdom and ultimately to intellectual resources for successful aging.

THE REFLECTIVE PLANNING ORIENTATION, COGNITIVE WISDOM, AND SUCCESSFUL AGING

In the course of Peterson's (1985) doctoral research on the careers of planners and engineers, he and I noticed the similarity between the cognitive orientation of reflective planning and cognitive wisdom, as the latter was defined by the Baltes and Smith research in Berlin (Featherman & Peterson, 1986). It is possible to express both constructs of planning and wisdom as expert knowledge systems having to do with solving ill-structured or "fuzzy" problems in the real world of people and values, as well as of technical and material phenomena. Both recognize and accept the importance of arriving at strategic solutions contextually, conditionally, and existentially. Both view the attainment of solutions as a process of successive approximation by using "opportunistic planning" (Scholnick & Friedman, 1987), in which the object of the solution—the person to be helped, the self, the problem to be solved—is part of the solution system. That is, personality, values, and wider human purposes are always part of the solution rather than disturbances of it. The problem solver cannot work effectively as an "outside expert" who solves the problem without extensive input from those who are affected by the problem and its solution.

In the technical terminology of cognitive science I suggest that both cognitive wisdom and the planning orientation are epistemic executive systems in the mind that organize and direct how problems are defined and solutions are sought (in a highly automatized way for those of high expertise [Sternberg, 1985]). Put more plainly and to the point, the reflective planning orientation, like cognitive wisdom, may be part of the developmental reserve within the intelligence of some older adults that enables them to adapt with comparatively greater success to the challenges of ill-structured tasks in later life. In our research we are attempting to show that persons who are high (or low) on cognitive wisdom are also high (or low) on the reflective planning orientation. Naturally we must also establish that reflective planning that is expressed phenotypically as an approach to problems and solutions in work and careers is a generic orientation that can be evoked in other life domains. We know how to measure the expression of reflective planning as distinct from reactive or tactical planning among engineers; we must develop more general measuring tools for other work-related settings and for the problems of life that evoke wise or unwise behavior and advice giving. These research tasks are large challenges.

Let me close this section about successful aging of the person, however, with my rationale for pursuing these scientific challenges in the course of trying to understand why the reflective, strategic planning orientation rather than the reactive, tactical one may provide greater adaptive advantage in old age. In the course of doing so I want to comment on the importance of seeing this connection in a life-span perspective. That is, successful adaptation to the qualitatively unique problems (developmental tasks) of old age may be rooted in cognitive systems that are differentially developed in certain but not all work careers during adult life. (This is not to suggest that successful aging, in the vein of Rowe & Kahn, 1987, rests wholly on cognitive resources, or, that the planning orientation emerges only via paid work careers.)

In our research we note that engineers who achieve peer-acknowledged expert status are like planners and designers of equal expertise in their field in one respect. Both sets of experts have developed extensive expertise in career management. Specifically, we believe we are identifying a set of career-management practices based on specialization, optimum deployment of specialized expert knowledge, and the activation of compensatory mechanisms of conservation of effort or the substitution of one set of specialized knowledge for another to restore expert status that may be at risk of obsolescence or inappropriateness to the job. We are creating measurement tools for each of these subprocesses to understand how careers of high achievement are attained within engineering and selected other career lines. It is our assessment, based on very preliminary data, that such strategies of adaptation to the challenges of careers during the working life signal the development of what we call *adaptive competence* regarding building and maintaining high competence at productive paid labor (Featherman et al., 1990). If you will, think of adaptive competence as one adult form of intelligence. That is, *adap-*

tive competence is the differential ability to respond with resilience to the challenges of daily life including changes in one's own mental and behavioral limitations, and in the social and physical ecology of the environment. Getting to the top of one's career and staying there, being and staying productive, and making strategic adjustments in self- and work environment is what adaptive competence in working life is about, according to our research.

Our research hypothesizes that experts in career management will be comparatively better equipped for successful aging in postretired life than will those who retire as "novices," *ceteris paribus.* Experts have apparently developed greater adaptive competence than their same-aged counterparts who end their careers as, in our data, practitioner engineers without national or international awards for high expertise in engineering and career management skills. (Incidentally such career management skills may involve the strategic use of highly specialized assistants and subordinates in project teams to get one's work accomplished. Thus, skills in career development of self and others become consolidated). We believe that adaptive competence, developed within the working career by experts, may transfer and be applied to the much more ill-structured life world of postretirement as a developmental advantage for successful aging. Why? Because the mechanisms of specialization, optimization, and compensation that make up high adaptive competence in work careers can be applied to problem solving in life career management—applied to the developmental tasks of making a transition into retirement, managing the challenges of unstructured roles, and meeting the uncertainties of unexpected change.

Let me take you one step further into our ongoing research, however, for I believe our group is addressing a promising connection between what goes on in some (and I stress the word "some") working lives and careers and the possibilities for successful aging—that is, for vitality and resilience of the kinds Linda George and Jim Morgan are addressing, for the "high end" of the distributions of individual differences in functioning that George Maddox has described. To repeat, we do believe that expertise in career management, at least in some careers, can provide a developmental reserve for adapting successfully to later life's dilemmas and challenges. Career experts should age more successfully than novices or practitioners.

We also are pursuing the idea that among both expert engineers, and expert planners and designers, however, we can make a further prediction at the individual level of who will be comparatively more successful in handling postretirement. We think the key variable is whether or not the person approaches problems and their solutions with reflective planning. Specifically, we believe that experts at career management who approach tasks and career issues with a reflective rather than a reactive planning orientation have a special adaptive advantage in finding solutions to the many ill-structured tasks of retirement and postretired life. By contrast, we expect to find that career experts who through their work are accustomed to solving problems with a reactive planning approach, although adapting well to some of the more well-structured tasks in later life, will be less equipped to cope with the many ill-structured ones.

Our rationale for these expectations is laid out in other writings (Featherman, 1987; Featherman & Peterson, 1986; Featherman et al., 1990). It is based on research in cognitive psychology (some with children, others with adults), however, showing a link between persons' experiences with different types of tasks and problematical challenges to intellect, on the one hand, and qualitatively different knowledge systems or expertises in problem solving on the other hand (Glaser, 1987; Hatano & Inagaki, 1983; Kitchener & Wood, 1987). It also is based on research in organizational and occupational sociology. The upshot of this multidisciplinary research base for our work is that the kinds of jobs and work settings in which engineers are employed lend themselves to the nurturance and reinforcement of "routine expertise," whereas the career line of planning and design, taken by former engineers at midcareer or later, tends to foster "adaptive expertise" (Hatano & Inagaki, 1983). These are qualitatively different intelligences, if you will, that equally bright individuals may have as a function of a long-term career in handling qualitatively different kinds of problematic challenges and solution systems. Therefore in our pilot research about these ideas we are examining the following kinds of questions:

1. Do expert planners do a better job of anticipating the transition into retirement and adjust better to it than novice planners and even the expert engineers who take a tactical problem-solving, reactive planning approach?
2. Is there a positive correspondence between the reflective planning orientation toward work and career-related problems, on the one hand, and measures of cognitive wisdom, like those developed by the Berlin group, on the other?
3. On other measures of successful aging, including psychosocial ones such as subjective well-being as well as health-related ones (Rowe & Kahn, 1987), are experts in career management at a higher level than those who are less expert? Are planners and designers as a group doing better than the engineers? Are those with a reflective planning orientation in both groups surpassing those with a reactive, tactical orientation?

As these questions are answered, and if the outcomes bear out our hypotheses, then we will have taken a big step toward understanding at least some of the life-course antecedents of successful aging. Of course, the research in progress only involves two career lines, and we cannot say on that slim basis that work life in general promotes these different outcomes. We have chosen these two career lines, however, as prototypes of the kinds of organizational and sociological properties that should provide a critical test of our ideas. If our work progresses well, and as we extend it to other work and nonwork contexts of adulthood, we will have made a connection between those personal developmental assets that may underlie financial security and mental well-being across the life-span. We will have linked qualities of adaptation to early and middle adult life to those that seem requisite for successful encounters with later life and old age.

This research program and these general objectives provide the rationale for my belief that the conjunction of financial security and well-being in later life is to be understood in life-span terms as having roots in much earlier adulthood. Yet I do not want to leave the impression that I believe successful aging for the individual lies entirely within the realm of personal developmental reserves, like adaptive competence and other adaptive capacities. Successful aging within the context of a changing, postretired society is not an outcome of individual work history or wholly a matter of prudent initiative by the person through the life-span. Instead, successful aging is inevitably an outcome of the interaction between personal agency, experience, and the properties of the interpersonal, organizational, and historical context of the life course. Thus, to close my observations I want to comment on what might be called the successful aging of a postretired society and to connect this process with successful aging of the individual. The connection involves the planning orientation, taken generically, and the prevalence of ill-structured problems at the societal and individual life-course levels.

SUCCESSFUL AGING IN A POSTRETIRED SOCIETY

In discussing very briefly a postretired society I do not wish to engage in futurology or to resketch the essence of a postindustrial society (Bell, 1973; see Featherman et al., 1990, for a fuller treatment of this societal construct). Neither do I wish to paint the broad and now obvious landscape of the "graying" society with its low fertility and mortality and consequently rapidly growing (in a proportionate sense) very old age stratum. It has been many years since Keyfitz (1973) forecast the social and economic impacts, and provided formal demographic models of a stable population at or below (as we now are) replacement levels. So most of us here, scientists and policy makers alike, are aware of these facts and their sociodemographic bases (see Sweet & Bumpass, 1987, for an explanation of the fertility side of this demographic base, which is the more important historically and potentially more volatile in the future).

Most of us also know that the relative density (if not also the absolute size) of the postretired population continues to increase under present demographic conditions. This is especially so for men in America, who tend to opt for early retirement. Women still retire earlier, perhaps reflecting a joint spouse decision to spend a potentially lengthier postretired life together. The shift toward earlier retirement, although it may reverse itself if the state reorganizes the incentive-disincentive mix through tax laws and Social Security limits, currently runs counter to mandatory retirement statutes that have expanded the years of permissible employment. Perhaps as working women of middle-aged adult cohorts, many more of whom will be divorced than their predecessors, reach the retirement decision point, they will decide differently from their male contemporaries.

If the fraction and size of the postretired population increases, and if the social world of such persons remains as filled with "tenuous" and "informal" positions and roles as today (Rosow, 1985), then the prevalence of ill-structured problems at the individual level will aggregate toward higher levels in society. Even if the state-initiated policies toward the aged change in response to the growing political force of interest groups of older, educated active voters (Bengtson, Cutler, Mangen, & Marshall, 1985; Guillimard, 1983), the policy challenge of arranging for a wider experience of "successful" as distinct from "usual" aging (Rowe & Kahn, 1987) in the population is likely to remain unaddressed.

My contention is that our federal, state, and private-sector planning efforts for the impending postretired society are not optimally suited to the challenges of the times. As strategies for our collective adaptation to our contemporary environment, they seem suboptimal; in my view they do not increase our adaptive capacity. Conventional planning efforts leave us ill-prepared for constructing the societal conditions for successful aging. Their insufficiency is as great in this arena as they are for finding and implementing solutions for other ill-structured problems in America, like a growing urban underclass in the face of plenty for others. To my perhaps naïve eyes our planning efforts seem largely piecemeal and responsive to short-run political pressures from partisan considerations, well-financed interest groups, and current trends to defederalize public welfare provisions. Other critics of the making of public policy, in general, have identified other roots of the problems facing modern governments (and private bureaucracies, for that matter). The difficulties may lie in the conventional ways in which a complex "society of organizations" defines and seeks solutions to problems in the course of what we euphemistically call societal planning. This conventional mode of planning may become inappropriate during times of rapid and fundamental societal transformation, as I suggest we are seeing as we "gray," "postmodernize," and face the other more ill-structured dilemmas of a postretired society. Conventional planning, based on reactive problem solving per se, may not serve our postretired interests well when the dilemmas of collective resource allocation require reflective solutions based on fuzzy constructs like "intergenerational equity" or planning horizons suggested by intergenerational equity through the practice of distributive justice through the life-span (Daniels, 1988). Old solutions, even conventional ways of defining what is a problem and arriving at solutions, may not equip us collectively for the adaptational challenges at hand.

Take for example this assessment written by E. Dunn (1971):

> The principal problem of social organization that confronts advanced societies . . . can best be seen by contrasting the organizational consequences of normal problem solving and paradigm shifts. In normal problem solving, system reorganization is purposive, anticipatory, and controlled. In contrast, paradigm shifts have historically been primarily reactive, unanticipated, and uncontrolled. They tend to arise out of a reaction to exogenously and endogenously generated boundary crises. They are frequently unanticipated by the management elite of the system. The reorganization is often defensive in character—that is, it is directed toward preserving and extending the life of the system in the face of change rather than taking the form of a directed self-transformation in pursuit of some high-order goal.
>
> We appear to have arrived at a point in social history where this kind of uncontrolled social transformation is taking on a rate and form that seem to threaten the viability of the social process itself. The reason for the special nature of the threat in advanced societies is the fact that we have formalized and mastered the process of normal problem solving in the physical sciences and in the design of physical systems to the point that this very process is generating an accelerated and escalating series of boundary crises for established social systems. (Dunn, 1971, cited in Michael, 1973)

If Dunn's assessment about the insufficiency of normal societal planning, a mode of logicorational problem solving taken from the physical sciences, is correct today as it may have been in the early 1970s, then I can draw together two ideas. The first is that successful aging for the individual may rest in part on the development of cognitive and behavioral capacities for coping with ill-structured dilemmas through a reflective, strategic planning orientation. The second is that a similar strategic versus tactical approach (reflective versus reactive planning), embedded within the societal planning process for the present and future volume of uncharted dilemmas of the postretired society, may optimize the societal conditions for individuals to age successfully. Michael has labeled such an approach "long-range societal planning." The latter idea is consistent with the view that governmental planning that is truly a strategic, reflective approach may add to the likelihood of individuals' aging successfully because its policy time line considers the full life-span. It also may do so because true planning is conscious of the need to find interactive, opportunistic, and transactional solutions as different cohorts enter adulthood and old age (see Brim & Phillips, 1988, for an example of this kind of policy approach when applied to childhood as a life period).

So, let me conclude my observations by developing the speculative idea that "long-range societal planning" may be the policy-level analogue to reflective planning at the individual level. "Long-range societal planning" may be a necessary condition for the successful aging of a postretired society and as a societal-level complement to the successful aging of individuals.

LONG-RANGE SOCIETAL PLANNING
VERSUS PROBLEM SOLVING

In his book *On Learning to Plan—and Planning to Learn* Donald N. Michael (1976) forecast, with guarded optimism, that governmental agencies and major corporations would be forced to plan differently for the future than they had in the past. Faced with the piecemeal and often unsuccessful results of applying wholly techno-rational problem solving and "social engineering" solutions to the dilemmas of our times, he predicted that planners would be forced toward a shift from the paradigm of conventional, tactical planning to new modes of strategic thinking. Michael saw what, to him, were encouraging signs that a "future-responsive societal learning" process of strategic planning (what we call *reflective planning* at the individual level) might be on the horizon. Through the application of the philosophy to the practice of policy planning and implementation, Michaels wrote that future-responsive societal learning would enable a society of organizations to engage in "directed self-transformation." Long-range societal planning, based on future-responsive societal learning strategies, would enable society to adapt more successfully to the fuzzy and ill-structured dilemmas of modern times and to improve the quality of life for citizens.

Michael wrote his manuscript in the late 1960s and early 1970s, before the 1973 oil embargo, stagflation, Reaganomics, yuppie-style consumption, and a stock market driven by buyout and merger mania. It was a time when governmental agencies still held a mandate for optimizing human welfare and when the private sector focused on developing the capacities of its work force as a basis of economic productivity. Although Michael's forecast, in hindsight, seems overly optimistic, I believe his analysis of the need for a new strategic-planning approach and the reasons for its unlikely adoption are important as we think about the dilemmas and challenges of a postretired society.

Critics in the management sciences and industrial engineering join Michael's assessment of the poor performance of conventional, tactical problem solving as a basis of societal planning, especially for innovation (Gross, 1970; Nadler, 1981; Rittel & Webber, 1972; Schon, 1967). The problem with tactical or reactive planning in a world of fuzzy or ill-structured problems goes beyond any basic limitations of tactical problem solving as a strategy for scientific or technical innovation. Although modern decision theory and technology have developed cybernetic algorithms for some limited types of fuzzy problems, these models of artificial intelligence and optimal "satisficing" have proved to be of limited value when applied to complex problems like poverty and environmental pollution that are inherently involved with human welfare. These critics of conventional tactical planning identify several problems with this approach including the "elitist, top-down [system of planning] which assumes that planners hold a monopoly on expertise" (Michael, 1973, p. 17). According to Michael the "social engineering" approach underlies the "war on the problem" mentality in which the nature of the problem is rarely questioned (i.e., the assumption that everybody knows what the problem of a graying society is, what poverty is) and in which the only issue is how to solve the problem as given—given to the experts whose specialized technical knowledge provides the essential components of the ultimate solution.

Michael, among others (e.g., Nadler, 1981; Rittel & Webber, 1972), suggests a new approach of strategic rather than tactical planning: future-responsive societal learning. Its six elements compose a continuous feedback system of learning (see Argyris, 1976, regarding "double-loop learning" for a similar idea) that involves the planner as well as others in the planning organization (i.e., the governmental agency) and problem-policy-affected persons in the social and physical environment:

1. Live with and acknowledge great uncertainty.
2. Embrace error.
3. Seek and accept the ethical responsibility and conflict-laden interpersonal circumstances that attend goal-setting.
4. Evaluate the present in the light of anticipated futures and commit [oneself] to actions in the present intended to respond to such long-range anticipations.
5. Live with role stress and forego the satisfactions of stable, on-the-job, social group relationships.
6. Be open to changes in commitment and direction as suggested by changes in conjectured pictures of the future and by evaluations of on-going activities. (Michael, 1973, p. 18)

The rationale for future-responsive societal learning as an informed approach to problem solving is that it fosters an examination of both what the problem is and what the solutions might be. It suggests that rational or technical social engineering may play a part in arriving at some solution, but does so only after several constructions and comparisons of a variety of mental models of "the problem." This experiment in model synthesis involves divergent thinking, novelty, and the ability to see all the permutations of a given problem. It entails a "transactional" sifting through of ultimate and often conflicting purposes, societal goals, and other ends that are the settings of societal problems (for example, the welfare of the aged and the welfare of children in a postretired society; see Preston, 1984). Only after this process of examining ends or purposes can an examination of means be achieved and technico-rational tools be deployed. Even then, long-range societal planning based on future-oriented societal learning calls for a continual monitoring of the policy and a reinvoking of the future-responsive societal learning solution algorithm as new information about success and failure becomes available on a time-line basis.

It is also important to the rationale for future-responsive societal learning, however, that the relevant expertise for reflective planning not lie exclusively in the minds and hands of policy specialists and technical experts. The relevant expertise may not be confined to technical knowledge per se, but must lie in a wider appreciation for pluralistic futures, purposes, and human values that are not part of conventional political wisdom or of scientific paradigms. The process of divergent thinking that runs in tandem with convergence to define and solve ill-structured societal problems may ultimately be a collective, societal, and more democratic process of problem solving than is suggested by the so-called social engineering model of today's "war on problems" approach to tactical planning. As a more communal, democratic algorithm of problem solving, this approach is much more prone to conflict, evidence of error and dead-ends, and apparent uncertainty.

And "there's the rub." Michael (1976) and other critics of conventional policy and tactical planning efforts based on reactive problem solving are aware of the organizational, social, and psychological constraints on the realization and deployment of "long-range societal planning" and the learning approach that underlies it. Conflict and uncertainty extract high costs and are politically unattractive. Decision makers and managers in organizations are trained, if only by the rigors of career advancement, to hide errors or adopt rather more conservative, well-tested strategies that minimize the attribution of mistaken judgment. Expert knowledge, usually based on scientific information, legitimizes decisions and is an accepted basis of separating the "public" from "professionals." It is difficult to construct, implement, and evaluate policy in a democratic mode without incurring costly inefficiency and protracted indecision. Yet, social science technology for changing organizational decision making toward a learning approach to planning for long-range change (i.e., strategic planning) rather than short-run expedience (i.e., tactical planning) is not well developed. Neither is there a basic knowledge system for fostering or developing in persons a reflective approach to problems and solutions that is not reduced to reactive problem solving (Friedman, Scholnick, & Cocking, 1987; Yussen, 1985).

Despite these constraints in our social psychology and in the organization of decision making, does Michael's (1976) analysis of the inappropriateness of conventional technical planning for tomorrow's ill-structured future have relevance for building toward a successfully aging society? I think it does. To me his argument greatly complements my own about the individual resources for successful aging in a person's later years. Let me close by summarizing the ways that reflective problem solving in the aging person and long-range societal planning by decision makers in an aging society complement one another.

REFLECTIVE PROBLEM SOLVING AS PERSONAL AND SOCIETAL RESOURCE FOR INDIVIDUAL AND SOCIETAL WELL-BEING

The postretired society of the next decades poses many challenges for the elderly as individuals and for the creation of an equitable public policy of welfare that enhances financial security and psychological well-being over the entire life course. Many of the challenges are linked to the demographic aging of society, which will transfer a growing portion of the population into a rather ill-structured world of informal and tenuous roles and social statuses. It is this ill-structured context of old age that is problematic, for it presents the individual with greater uncertainty about material and psychological outcomes than in other life periods. This relative absence of formally organized life course "scripts" accounts, in part, for the wider variation in measured attributes of mind and behavior among the elderly than in other periods, such as childhood and adolescence.

Planning for the future always offers the challenge of imagining options in the face of high uncertainty and rapid change. In a postretired society, however, the challenges of uncertainty and the sheer number of feasible outcomes are amplified by the weight of an aging population shifting the balance of political attention and pressure toward defining new conditions for old age. Establishing and maintaining public policies that would restructure the life world of old age will have to contend with the special problem of a potential imbalance, however temporary, between the needs of the old and the needs of the young. The challenge of preparing for a postretired society undoubtedly includes a recasting of the policy horizon from short-range to long-range planning and from an age-period–specific set of policies to a set based on a dynamic model of the human life course and distributive justice over cohorts' life-spans (Daniels, 1988).

In both instances, individuals' capacity to adapt with success to the uncertainties and ill structure of old age and the ability of policy to adapt to the demographic, socioeconomic, and ethical dilemmas of a postretired society present historically unprecedented developmental tasks. I suggest that one resource for both sets of tasks—one that raises the adaptive potential within the context of ill-structured dilemmas—is the planning orientation of reflective planning that I have described in my presentation. For individuals it offers a reserve of intellectual or cognitive functioning that promotes a search for alternative futures as well as for alternative means to selected goals. When deployed by policy makers and managers, it fosters long-range societal planning that includes a continuing learning or feedback process about the impacts and implications of decisions for all age groups and for cohorts over their life-spans.

There is no panacea for preparing for unpredictable futures. No one resource, psychological or material, is the magic bullet. Yet the setting of mind to task is a step toward preparation. In this case, the epistemic orientation of reflective problem solving—the reflective planning orientation—seems to offer a developmental reserve for coping with the uncertainties that we face and with the challenges of structuring that future. It is a frame of mind that may offer beneficial advantages in a postretired society. Our research is currently directed toward an understanding of how this frame of mind can be developed in the natural conditions of work and in some careers. We hope to learn how it might be engendered as a developmental preparation for the tasks of later life through deliberate intervention and training at earlier points in the life course. We also must learn how to deploy this orientation within organizational settings and in decisional roles within them, despite well-documented resistance from organizational dynamics and ego-defensive systems. The research agenda is just in its infancy.

The rationale for the scientific exploration of these possible links between mind, society, and welfare is clear and pressing. Money cannot buy happiness, but who would deny that a sense of well-being and financial security are personal life goals for many of us? Yet, both financial security and perceived well-being are ephemeral, transitory conditions in most lives; continuity in them is perhaps rarer than change. Nevertheless, for a hard-core minority in our society, basics like safe housing and minimal nutrition are absent each day; for them, mere survival and not the volatility of happiness is continually at risk. Both the persistent core of deprivation within an affluent society and the ephemeral security of well-being among the comparatively more affluent majority pose ill-structured developmental challenges to the welfare of society and each individual. In facing these ill-structured, seemingly unsolvable dilemmas, not all frames of mind equip us equally well. For the challenges of both development through the whole life span and societal change into the future, learning to plan and planning to learn seem like sound investments for increasing adaptive competence.

REFERENCES

Argyris, C. (1976). Single-loop and double-loop models in research on decision making. *Administrative Sciences Quarterly, 21*, 363–377.

Atchley, R. (1982). Retirement as a social institution. *Annual Review of Sociology, 8*, 263–287.

Baltes, M., & Werner-Wahl, H. (1987). Dependence in aging. In L. L. Cartensen & B. Edelstein (Eds.), *Handbook of clinical gerontology* (pp. 204–221). New York: Pergamon Press.

Baltes, P. (1987). Theoretical propositions of life-span developmental psychology. *Developmental Psychology, 23*, 611–626.

Baltes, P., Dittmann-Kohli, F., & Dixon, R. (1984). New perspectives on the development of intelligence in adulthood: Toward a dual-process conception and a model of selective optimization with compensation. In P. B. Baltes & O. G. Brim, Jr. (Eds.), *Life-span development and behavior* (Vol. 6, pp. 34–78). New York: Academic Press.

Baltes, P., & Kliegl, R. (1986). On the dynamics between growth and decline in the aging of intelligence and memory. In K. Poeck, H. Freund, & H. Gaenshort (Eds.), *Neurology* (pp. 1–17). Heidelberg: Springer-Verlag.

Baltes, P., & Willis, S. (1982). Plasticity and enhancement of intellectual functioning in old age: Penn State's ADEPT. In R. Cray & S. Trehub (Eds.), *Aging and cognitive process* (pp. 353–389). New York: Plenum.

Bardwick, J. (1986). *The plateauing trap: How to avoid it in your career—and in your life.* New York: American Management Institute.

Bell, D. (1973). *The coming of post-industrial society.* New York: Basic Books.

Bengtson, V., Cutler, N., Mangen, D., & Marshall, V. (1985). Generations, cohorts, and relations between age groups. In R. Binstock & E. Shanas (Eds.), *Handbook of aging and the social sciences* (2nd ed., pp. 304–338). New York: Van Nostrand.

Berg, C., & Sternberg, R. (1985). A triarchic theory of intellectual development during adulthood. *Developmental Review, 5*, 334–370.

Brim, O. G., Jr. (1988, September). Losing and winning. *Psychology Today*, pp. 48–52.

Brim, O. G., Jr., & Phillips, D. (1988). The life-span intervention cube. In E. M. Hetherington, R. Lerner, & M. Perlmutter (Eds.), *Child development in life-span perspective* (pp. 277–299). Hillsdale, NJ: Erlbaum.

Brim, O. G., Jr. (1992). *Ambition: How we manage success and failure throughout our lives.* New York. Basic Books.

Brim, O., Jr., & Ryff, C. (1983). On the properties of life events. In P. Baltes & O. G. Brim, Jr. (Eds.), *Life-span development and behavior* (Vol. 3, pp. 368–388). New York: Academic Press.

Campbell, A., & Converse, P. (Eds.). (1972). *The human meaning of social change.* New York: Russell Sage.

Campbell, A., Converse, P. E., & Rogers, W. L. (1976). *The quality of American life.* New York: Russell Sage.

Churchman, C. (1971). *The design of inquiring systems: Basic concepts of systems and organization.* New York: Basic Books.

Clayton, V., & Birren, J. (1980). The development of wisdom across the lifespan: A reexamination of an ancient topic. In P. Baltes & O. G. Brim, Jr. (Eds.), *Life-span development and behavior* (Vol. 4, pp. 104–137). New York: Academic Press.

Coleman, R., & Rainwater, L. (1978). *Social standing in America*. New York: Basic Books.

Cotman, C., & Peterson, J. (1987). *Aging*. Unpublished manuscript, University of California, Irvine, CA.

Daniels, N. (1988a). *Am I my parents' keeper: An essay on justice between the young and old*. New York: Oxford University Press.

Daniels, N. (1988b). Justice between age groups and health care for the elderly. [Special issue]. *Journal of Medicine and Philosophy, 13*, 1–3.

Danzinger, S., Van der Gaag, J., Smolensky, E., & Taussig, M. (1984). Implications for the relative economic status of the elderly for transfer policy. In H. Aaron & G. Burtless (Eds.), *Retirement and economic behavior* (pp. 175–196). Washington, DC: Brookings Foundation.

Dittmann-Kohli, F. (1988). *Self and meaning of life: Central domains of personality development in adulthood*. Unpublished manuscript, Max Planck Institute for Human Development and Education, West Berlin.

Duncan, G. (1984). *Years of poverty, years of plenty: The changing economic fortunes of American worker and families*. Ann Arbor, MI: Institute for Social Research.

Duncan, G. (1988). Volatility of family income over the life course. In P. Baltes, D. Featherman, & R. Lerner (Eds.), *Life-span development and behavior* (Vol. 9, pp. 318–359). Hillsdale, NJ: Erlbaum.

Duncan, G., & Morgan, J. (1980). The incidence and some consequences of major life events. In G. Duncan & J. Morgan (Eds.), *Five thousand American families—patterns of economic progress* (Vol. 8, pp. 183–240). Ann Arbor, MI: Institute for Social Research.

Duncan, G., & Morgan, J. (1985). The panel study of income dynamics. In G. H. Elder, Jr. (Ed.), *Life course dynamics* (pp. 50–74). Ithaca, NY: Cornell University Press.

Eastearlin, R. (1973). Does money buy happiness? *Public Interest, 30*, 3–10.

Elder, G., Jr. (1985). *Life course dynamics*. Ithaca, NY: Cornell University Press.

Featherman, D. (1987). *Work, adaptive competence, and successful aging: A theory of adult cognitive development*. Lecture given at the World Congress of the International Society for the Study of Behavioral Development, Tokyo, Japan.

Featherman, D., & Peterson, J. (1986). *Adaptive competence in work careers: Socialization for successful aging*. Poster session presented at the annual meeting of the Gerontological Society of America, Chicago.

Featherman, D., Smith, J., & Peterson, J. (1990). Successful aging in a "post-retired" society. In P. Baltes & M. Baltes (Eds.), *Successful aging: Perspectives from the behavioral sciences* (pp. 50–93). Cambridge: Cambridge University Press.

Flavell, J. (1979). Metacognition and cognitive monitoring: A new area of cognitive-development inquiry. *American Psychologist, 35*, 906–911.

Friedman, S., Scholnick, E., & Cocking, R. (1987). *Blueprints for thinking: The role of planning in cognitive development*. Cambridge: Cambridge University Press.

Fuchs, V. (1983). *How we live*. New York: Basic Books.

Garfinkel, I., & McLanahan, S. (1987). *Single mothers and their children: A new dilemma*. Washington, DC: Urban Institute.

Glaser, R. (1987). Thoughts on expertise. In C. Schooler & K. Schaie (Eds.), *Cognitive functioning and social structure over the life course* (pp. 79–94). New Jersey: Ablex Publishing Corporation.

Guillemard, A. (1983). *Old age and the welfare state.* Beverly Hills: Sage.

Hagestad, G., & Neugarten, B. (1985). Age and the life course. In R. Binstock & E. Shanas (Eds.), *Handbook of aging and the social sciences* (2nd ed., pp. 35-62). New York: Van Nostrand.

Hatano, G., & Inagaki, K. (1983, April). *Two courses of expertise.* Paper presented at the Conference on Child Development in Japan and the United States, Stanford, CA.

Havighurst, R. (1956). Research on the developmental task concept. *School Review: A Journal of Secondary Education, 64,* 215-223.

Havighurst, R. (1982). *Development tasks and education.* New York: Longman.

Heckhausen, J., Dixon, R., & Baltes, P. (1989). Gains and losses in development through adulthood as perceived by different adult age groups. *Developmental Psychology, 25,* 109-121.

Henretta, J., & Campbell, R. (1978, March). Wealth as income in status attainment models. *American Journal of Sociology, 83,* 1204-1223.

Holden, K., & Burkhauser, R. (1987). *The risk and timing of poverty after retirement* (Final Report to the AARP-Anders Foundation). Madison: University of Wisconsin-Madison, Institute on Aging and Adult Life.

Horn, J., & Donaldson, G. (1980). Cognitive development in adulthood. In O. G. Brim, Jr., & J. Kagan (Eds.), *Constancy and change in human development* (pp. 445-529). Cambridge, MA: Harvard.

Kahn, R., & Antonucci, T. (1980). Convoys over the life course: Attachment, roles, and social support. In P. Baltes & O. G. Brim, Jr. (Eds.), *Life-span development and behavior* (Vol. 3, pp. 253-286). New York: Academic Press.

Kaufman, S. (1986). *The ageless self.* Madison: University of Wisconsin Press.

Keyfitz, N. (1973, July). Individual mobility in a stationary population. *Population Studies, 27,* 335-352.

Kitchener, K. (1983). Cognition, metacognition, and epistemic cognition: A three-level model of cognitive processing. *Human Development, 26,* 222-232.

Kitchener, K., & Wood, P. (1987). Development of concepts of justification in German university students. *International Journal of Behavioral Development, 10,* 171-185.

Kohn, M., & Schooler, C. (1983). *Work and personality: An inquiry into the impact of social stratification.* Hillsdale, NJ: Ablex.

Labouvie-Vief, G. (1982). Dynamic development and mature autonomy. *Human Development, 25,* 161-191.

Labouvie-Vief, G. (1985). Intelligence and cognition. In J. Birran & K. W. Schaie (Eds.), *Handbook of the psychology of aging* (2nd ed., pp. 500-543). New York: Van Nostrand.

Lazear, E. (1979, December). Why is there mandatory retirement? *Journal of Political Economy, 87,* 1261-1284.

Marshall, V. (1980). *Last chapters: A sociology of aging and dying.* Belmont, CA: Wadsworth.

Mayer, K. U., & Muller, W. (1986). The state and the structure of the life course. In A. B. Sorenson, F. Weinert, & L. Sherrod (Eds.), *Human development and the life course* (pp. 217-246). Hillsdale, NJ: Erlbaum.

McLanahan, S., & Sorensen, A. B. (1985). Life events and psychological well-being over the life course. In G. H. Elder, Jr. (Ed.), *Life course dynamics* (pp. 217-238). Ithaca, NY: Cornell University Press.

Michael, D. N. (1973). *On learning to plan—and planning to learn.* San Francisco: Jossey Bass.

Montada, L., & Schmitt, M. (1986). Issues in applied developmental psychology: A life-span perspective. In P. Baltes & O. G. Brim, Jr. (Eds.), *Life-span development and behavior* (Vol. 4, pp. 2-32). New York: Academic Press.

Nadler, G. (1981). *The planning and design approach.* New York: John Wiley & Sons.

Oerter, R. (1986). Developmental task through the life span: A new approach to an old concept. In P. Baltes, D. Featherman, & R. Lerner (Eds.), *Life-span development and behavior* (Vol. 7, pp. 233-265). Hillsdale, NJ: Lawrence Erlbaum Associates.

Perlmutter, M. (1988). Cognitive development in life-span perspective. In E. M. Heatherington, R. Lerner, & M. Perlmutter (Eds.), *Child development in life-span perspective* (pp. 191-218). Hillsdale, NJ: Erlbaum.

Peterson, J. (1985). *Personal qualities and job characteristics of expert engineers and planners.* Doctoral dissertation, University of Wisconsin-Madison, Madison.

Preston, S. (1984). Children and the elderly: Divergent paths for America's dependents. *Demography, 21,* 435-458.

Riley, M. (1985). Age strata in social systems. In R. Binstock & E. Shanas (Eds.), *Handbook of aging and the social sciences* (2nd ed., pp. 369-402). New York: Van Nostrand.

Rittel, H., & Webber, M. (1974). Dilemmas in a general theory of planning. *Design Methods Group-Design Research Society Journal, 8,* 31-39.

Robinson, P., Coberly, S., & Paul, C. (1985). Work and retirement. In R. Binstock & E. Shanas (Eds.), *Handbook of aging and the social sciences* (2nd ed., pp. 503-553). New York: Van Nostrand Reinhold.

Rodin, J. (1986). Aging and health: Effects of the sense of control. *Science, 233,* 1271-1275.

Roscow, I. (1985). Status and role changes through the life cycle. In R. Binstock & E. Shanas (Eds.), *Handbook of aging and the social sciences* (2nd ed., pp. 62-93). New York: Van Nostrand Reinhold.

Rowe, J., & Kahn, R. (1987). Human aging: Usual and successful. *Science, 237,* 143-249.

Salthouse, T. (1987). Aging, experience and compensation. In C. Schooler & K. W. Schaie (Eds.), *Cognitive functioning and social structure over the life course* (pp. 142-158). Norwood, NJ: Ablex.

Scholnick, E., & Friedman, S. (1987). The planning construct in the psychological literature. In S. Friedman, E. Scholnick, & R. Cocking (Eds.), *Blueprints for thinking* (pp. 3-38). New York: Cambridge University Press.

Schon, D. (1983). *The reflective practitioner.* New York: Basic Books.

Shupe, D. (1985). Perceived control, helplessness, and choice: Their relationship to health and aging. In J. E. Birren & J. Livingston (Eds.), *Cognition, stress, and aging* (pp. 174-197). Englewood Cliffs, NJ: Prentice Hall.

Sternberg, R. (1985). Human intelligence: The model is the message. *Science, 230,* 1111-1118.

Sweet, J. A., & Bumpass, L. L. (1987). *American families and households.* New York: Russell Sage Foundation.

Waddington, C. (1975). *Evolution of an evolutionist.* Edinburgh, Scotland: Edinburgh University Press.

Willis, S., & Shaie, K. W. (1986). Practical intelligence in later adulthood. In R. Sternberg & R. Wagner (Eds.), *Practical intelligence: Origins of competence in the everyday world* (pp. 236–270). New York: Cambridge University Press.

Yussen, S. (1985). The role of metacognition in contemporary theories of cognitive development. In D. Forrest-Pressley & G. Waller (Eds.), *Contemporary research in cognition and metacognition.* Orlando: Academic Press.

—8—

Human Wealth-Span: The Financial Dimensions of Successful Aging

Davis W. Gregg

NATURE OF WEALTH-SPAN

This chapter introduces the concept of human wealth-span and demonstrates its relevance to the financial dimensions of successful aging. Wealth-span, like *life-span* and *health-span*, suggests a dynamic lifelong process in which the course of later life is affected by earning, spending, and savings decisions taken earlier. Of particular relevance to older aging—and again parallel to life-span and health-span—the developmental nature of wealth-span suggests that financial well-being can be affirmatively influenced by actions taken even in the later years of life.

In their seminal article, "Human Aging: Usual and Successful," Rowe and Kahn (1987) propose the concept of *health-span* as an extension of the idea of life-span. The core of their health-span concept concerns the utility of interventions. Rowe and Kahn suggest that most health-related behavior— for example, changes in diet or exercise—even if made in the later years of a person's health-span, can yield improvements in health. Thus, the authors call for major efforts to increase the health-span, on the order of the revolutionary increase in the life-span that has occurred during this century. The goal is to maintain full physical and psychological functions as nearly as possible to the end of life.

By analogy we suggest the idea of the individual *wealth-span* (Gregg, 1987). Ideally a person should have excellent diet and health habits from the earliest possible age. In the same way, an individual ideally should have good

169

financial habits at an early age. Yet such behavior often does not occur in either context. For wealth-span behavior in particular, it may not be economically possible for many modest-income families to undertake the future-oriented savings or investment that the ideal case might define. Indeed, Social Security and employer pensions are often seen by younger workers as their only possible means of retirement savings. As suggested earlier, subjective financial well-being may reside in knowing that Social Security and pension credits are accruing safely and "almost painlessly."

Conversely, as Table 8.1 illustrates, even modest-income households are likely to have resources beyond Social Security. Consequently, new or modified financial behaviors, even initiated in later life, are likely to have positive effects. The authors' recent analysis of the "middle aging" of people and populations (Gregg & Cutler, 1990) identifies four sets of dynamics that characteristically occur during middle age and that suggest the importance of a wealth-span developmental perspective on setting the financial stage for the final years of life. The sets of dynamics are (a) retirement and retirement preparation; (b) empty-nest and related family dynamics; (c) peak earnings and increased capacity for savings and investment; and (d) illness, mortality, and the imperative to plan for death and beyond.

This analysis suggests, in other words, that there is a strong set of relationships among objective financial resources, wealth-span as a developmental paradigm for understanding financial behavior during the life cycle, and middle age as an especially dynamic phase of the wealth-span. These relationships can serve as the framework for a variety of financially relevant interventions—more commonly referred to as financial planning.

The image of estate planners, tax counselors, and investment advisors is often that they provide "interventions" relevant primarily to society's upper class. Yet, as the research of our institute and others (Crown, Mutschler, &

TABLE 8.1 Characteristics of Retirees Age 65 to 74 with Income Double the Poverty Level but Less than $30,000

Number	3.95 million
% of all retirees, age 65-74	33.3%
% of all double-poverty retirees, age 65-74	63.4%
Mean years of schooling	10.6 years
% with 1+ years of college	19.5%
% married	72.1%
% who own their home	81.7%
% receiving Social Security	88.3%
% receiving interest, dividends, rental income	51.9%
% receiving pensions, annuities, other nonwork income	40.2%
Median total household income in 1986 dollars	$19,265

Source: 1980 U.S. Census. Dollars in 1986 constant dollars.

Leavitt, 1987) is beginning to document, many middle-class families in the middle-aging phase of their wealth-span increasingly find themselves with modest to considerable wealth. Indeed, in *Voices of Experience*, a summary and analysis of the volunteered statements of a national sample of modest-income annuitants, the dominant comment was, "I wish I had begun to plan my finances earlier" (Milletti, 1984).

Ironically, because these families probably do not think of themselves as wealthy, they are unlikely to have been deeply involved, during the course of their wealth-span, in the "management" of their slowly accumulating wealth—over and above usual practices of spending and saving. Yet home equity, life insurance, and pension survivorship benefits have the effect of pushing many middle-aging families into meaningful and often unanticipated wealth. In some cases, of course, the unexpected outcome is the "semi-millionaire widow."

In sum, it is precisely this kind of family for whom the concept of wealth-span is particularly relevant. Interventions that are made in even the later stages of the wealth-span can help to preserve current and future wealth and arrange for its most desired use by the older householders and their heirs.

Financial well-being in older age is a function not only of objective income and wealth, but of the psychological satisfaction that comes from confidence in the understanding and management of that wealth.

Through a combination of private efforts and opportunities, public programs and guarantees, and inflation and demography, increasing numbers of individuals and families will find themselves in a position of relative and perhaps unexpected wealth in their middle and old age. The concept of wealth-span, and the capacity for change, intervention, and development that this concept implies, provides a crucial opportunity for the increased financial well-being of older individuals in the broader context of societal economic security.

As continuing efforts proceed, and new and higher goals in life-span and health-span are achieved, so will efforts be initiated to achieve a revolutionary increase in wealth-span—*the maintenance of full financial function as nearly as possible to the end of life.*

I think the main factor of retiring is being financially able to retire. Then you won't have to just sit around and not be able to do the things you used to do when you were working and had a regular paycheck. To be able to buy the things you need—for entertainment, travel, home needs, and health.[1]

[1]The importance of wealth and finance to the preparation for and living in retirement will be suggested in the several inserts in this chapter quoted from *Voices of Experience: 1500 Retired People Talk about Retirement* by Mario A. Milletti and published by TIAA/CREF in 1984. The voices quoted are of college and university personnel in the TIAA/CREF retirement system.

FINANCIAL GERONTOLOGY RESEARCH

An exploration of the relationship of the wealth-span concept to the concepts of life-span and health-span directs our attention to research that embraces both aging and finance. Such research aims to understand the impact of financial well-being on the quality of life, and the processes by which persons making informed financial decisions can improve their life-span and health-span. A basic goal of such analysis is to encourage interest in the human wealth-span concept among researchers and practitioners with the ultimate objectives of helping persons acquire and manage financial resources for achieving life-span goals.

The impact of money on well-being is not a new subject. Much work, for example, has been done in the poverty area (e.g., Smeeding, 1990). Somewhat less is known about consumption habits and their relationship to wealth and income (e.g., Moschis, 1987). Far too little is known, however, of the dynamics of financial well-being and life quality within and across the generations. More needs to be learned of how the financial dimension of life affects the physical and psychological dimensions, and vice versa. All these actual and hypothesized interrelationships should be examined across the entire range of income—not just the poor or the wealthy (e.g., Longino, 1991). There are countless questions to be addressed.

- What is "financial well-being"? How much wealth is enough? What is the linkage between financial well-being and other forms of well-being?
- What are the attitudes of people toward various forms of "wealth," toward alternative sources of "income"?
- What is the role of society (employers and governments) in providing financial security?
- On what kind of information do people make financial decisions? From whom and from where do they get the information and counseling?

Save as much money as you can to be independent.

Exploration of such questions will go a long way in linking the professional world of financial services and the research world of gerontology. More generally, we believe that the economic and financial perspective will be of substantial value in the quest for a greater understanding of successful aging.

It seems timely and reasonable, as the human life-span and health-span are lengthening, that parallel efforts be made to seek a revolutionary improvement in the *human wealth-span*, defined as "*the maintenance of full financial function as nearly as possible to the end of life.*" Such efforts entail the cooperation of researchers and organizations in the public and private sectors.

ECONOMIC SECURITY: A COMPELLING GOAL

Fundamental to the development of sound research on the human wealth-span is an understanding of the individual-level attitudes and behaviors underlying the concept. It can be argued that the need for security is fundamental and that economic security is a compelling goal for most persons. The goal can be defined only for a given person at a given time. For a nation or a society, criteria of economic security will vary with economic development. Although merely adequate food, clothing, and shelter may be the central goal in less developed nations, far more may be expected and even demanded by most persons in more developed societies.

Security is a many-faceted concept with economic, social, psychological, and other cultural and personal dimensions. To a teenager, security may be "walking-around money" for a Saturday night date. To one of immense wealth, security may include yachts, planes, castles, and jewels.

The etymology of "security," the Latin *securus*, means "without care," and is suggestive of broad human implications. Security can be thought of as peace of mind and freedom from uncertainty. Insecurity is characterized by feelings of doubt, anxiety, fear, worry, and apprehension.

There is strong evidence that most men and women have a preference for security. The Swiss philosopher Tournier (1965) argues that this preference is traceable to a universal principle applicable to the whole of nature: There is a tendency for all things to continue in their mode of existence. In the physical world, there is the law of inertia. In biology, there is the dominance of habit and reflexes. Tournier speaks of the two instincts of man: one being the instinct "of adventure, movement, discovery, risk-taking and progress"; the other, the instinct "of repose, repetition, security and stability." He argues that "customs, usages, and the whole of civilization rest on the instinct of stability" and observes that the "modern social ideal of security and the tremendous increase in insurance express this urge to eliminate all kinds of risk" (p. 156).

The only thing I might do differently is to start a sensible, safe investment plan sooner.

Whatever the genesis of the human instinct for security, it appears that behavior is inexorably related to needs and wants. Thus, one is led to speculate that personal insecurity results from the inability or the uncertainty of individuals, whatever their situations, regarding the satisfaction of one or more of their needs or wants.

Two general observations seem pertinent. First, human needs, desires, and wants are infinite, whereas the power to fill them is finite. One eminent social scientist observed that

> Man is a wanting animal and rarely reaches a state of complete satisfaction except for a short time. As one desire is satisfied, another one pops up to take its place. When this is satisfied, still another comes into the foreground. It is a characteristic of the human being throughout his whole life that he is practically always desiring something. (Maslow, 1943, p. 87)

Thus, if we accept the concept that insecurity derives from the individual's inability or uncertainty regarding the satisfaction of his needs, we must conclude that man will always be faced with problems of insecurity—a conclusion that seems consistent with the realities of life.

Life at both extremes of the security scale, total insecurity and perfect security, seems unrealistic. The real issue for human growth and happiness, and for societal advancement, relates to the optimal degree of security and the optimal methods of achieving that objective.

A second observation is that any analysis of security in terms of needs or wants is incomplete without recognition of a ranking, a hierarchy, or a priority of human needs. Human motivation is highly complex. Yet, a carefully developed and widely recognized theory of human motivation (Maslow, 1970) sheds meaningful light on an individual's quest for economic security.

Accepting the fact that man is a perpetually wanting animal, Maslow (1970) argues that the appearance of a need rests on prior situations, on other predominant needs, and that needs and desires, to be understood, should be arranged in hierarchies of preeminence. Graphically, he argues that,

> We should never have the desire to compose music or create mathematical systems, or to adorn our homes, or to be well-dressed, if our stomachs were empty most of the time, or if we were continually dying of thirst, or if we were continually threatened by an always impending catastrophe, or if everyone hated us." (Maslow, 1943, p. 88)

HUMAN NEEDS AND ECONOMIC SECURITY

Economists as well as psychologists, gerontologists, and other social scientists are concerned with the nature and satisfaction of human needs. As an academic discipline, economics is defined as the study of how individuals and societies can and do choose to allocate and use their limited resources to produce, distribute, and consume goods to satisfy human needs (Samuelson, 1989).

I wish I learned more about handling my financial affairs or had found an advisor I could trust.

It has been noted that human beings naturally strive to attain some desired level or degree of personal security, and this quest engages many and varied efforts. Economic activities are included among this vast array of security-oriented activities including risk taking, work, consumption, and saving. The acquisition of economic goods for immediate use, or to hold as part of personal wealth, command a great deal of a person's time and energy. Indeed, it may be argued that the economic dimension of most individuals and families' lifetime endeavors is a central pursuit. Economists tend to speak largely in terms of economic needs, whereas psychologists identify a hierarchy of human needs. There is no conflict here, however.

The assumption of a hierarchy of needs gives meaning and depth to the single perspective of the economists. In short, we engage in economic activities for a variety of reasons other than sustenance of self and family. Consider an analogy with happiness: The U.S. Constitution guarantees the "pursuit of happiness" and not happiness itself. So it is that for some of us at least some of the time, as Linda George documents so well elsewhere in this book, the *pursuit* of economic well-being reflects a subjective, psychological need that is separate from, albeit related to, the objective financial resources of economic well-being.

Several conclusions seem evident. First, all economic actions taken by individuals are for the ultimate purpose of satisfying human needs, not all of which are manifestly financial or economic, and thus provide some degree of security. Second, economic security can be defined as the attainment of feelings of certainty, peace of mind, comfort and fulfillment through the acquisition, ownership, and use of economic goods. Third, the extent to which a person's needs are being met and personal feelings of security attained will vary over time. Fourth, the general search for personal and family security is inextricably connected to the broad totality of individual, community, and societal needs in a complex manner.

Fundamentally, however, the economic dimension of security is psychologically and socially linked to all needs, economic and noneconomic, in a direct or less direct way for most people most of the time, in most societies of the world. Furthermore, to suggest that this linkage varies in nature and intensity during the life cycle is not only an eminently plausible (and researchable) hypothesis—it speaks to the natural and inevitable connection among the concepts of wealth-span, health-span, and life-span.

In summary, then, are the following points:

1. Economic security mechanisms have a fundamental role to play in satisfying most of a person's basic needs, whatever the level of priority or preeminence.
2. In each category of human need, the perceived minimum tends to rise as the person's wealth grows.
3. A person is concerned not only with present needs but with future needs.

4. A person is concerned not only with personal needs, but with family needs, church, college, community, and the like.
5. A person's needs are relative, and as he or she moves up the ladder of living standards, they seek increased protection through economic security mechanisms to prevent a fall from this higher point while attempting to satisfy the next level of needs.
6. Any institution, private or public, concerned primarily with serving the needs of individuals through economic means should include all of these aspects in its perspective of the concept of security.

ANTICIPATED AREAS OF BASIC AND APPLIED RESEARCH

For the human wealth-span concept to come alive as a basic dimension of financial gerontology, knowledge is needed in several categories.

1. *Life-span of an individual*: The biological and behavioral characteristics of the life-span of an individual from birth to death are understood generally. The economic characteristics are less understood. The basic economic profile is known for most persons in the sense that infanthood is the time of total dependence on others, with incremental independence until the 20s when many become financially independent. The return toward dependence begins for some after retirement from work; if disability occurs, substantial (even total) dependence may recur in the last years of life.
2. *Economic profile of individual life cycle*: Greater knowledge is needed about the maturational economic profile of individuals. This would include such financial "milestones" as when income and wealth might first flow to an individual, through inheritance or family allowance, childhood "odd jobs," teenage "entrepreneurial" activity, and the like. The role of securing and increasing wealth through interest-bearing savings needs to be better understood. From the late teen years, more sophisticated knowledge is needed about income-expenditure and asset-liability realities.

At a very early age, endowed with my present wisdom, I would have saved more, much more, so that the simple fact of compound interest would have provided for an uncomplicated financial future.

It may be hypothesized that, in the vocabulary of the human wealth-span, "maturity" is signaled when a person initially begins to confront such choices as postponing current pleasure for future satisfactions, and when there is understanding of the role of credit and the relationship between current debt and future obligations.

Our understanding of life-cycle patterns in economic and consumer behavior at the individual level of analysis is beginning to catch up with knowledge of the developmental and aging processes in such related areas as social learning and political behavior. For example, we know that the maximum earning years typically come at ages 45 to 55, and that the role of saving and the "magic of compound interest" become important substantially earlier. During the middle-aged period it becomes even more significant to project ahead to retirement years and to the special economic needs associated with cessation of earned income, the potential of disability, and higher health care costs. Middle-aged financial planning may also initiate an evaluation of the family's financial capacity to engage in travel, avocations, charity, and other such often-postponed activities now possible because of the availability of time and money.

Although a developmental and life-cycle analysis of economic and consumer socialization has recently been published (Moschis, 1987), a parallel paradigm for the study of cohort patterns of financial and consumer behavior remains to be developed. The general model of variations in individual aging in different historical circumstances, which Matilda White Riley so clearly articulates earlier in this book, is certainly applicable to how individuals respond, via their concerns and planning, to their own financial security.

For example, certainly it is plausible to hypothesize that a 55-year-old born in 1916 (and who entered the labor market at age 18 in 1934) will respond to the concerns and anxieties of older age financial security differently from a middle ager born in the middle of the baby boom in 1956. Their "starting positions" in life are different; their historical, demographic, and economic experiences are different; and their outlooks on entering middle age and anticipating older age are different. Further, the societal and public policy context of the financial environment they will encounter in their older years will be different.

In short, to use the basic theme of this chapter, we should expect that wealth span experiences and expectations will be substantially different for different generational cohorts. Again, the conclusion is that we need to understand, conceptually and empirically, not only the aging and life-cycle dimensions of the human wealth-span, but the generational and societal circumstances in which men and women develop, age, and change.

Retirement provides freedom for a person to pursue his interests, provided he has been fortunate enough to have been blessed with average or better health. Financial planning over a lifetime is essential to enjoy this freedom.

3. *Financial services world and financial planning process*: An understanding
   of the human wealth-span must include not only life-cycle needs and
   the pattern of wealth flow for individuals, but also the financial
   institutions available to serve these needs. These institutions include
   commercial and trust banks, life and health insurance companies,
   savings and investment firms, mortgage companies, installment credit
   companies, Social Security and Medicare, corporate pension firms, and
   others. In addition, substantial numbers of professional practitioners
   engage in financial and estate planning important to those who need
   financial guidance. Among this group are financial advisors, attorneys,
   tax specialists, accountants, insurance professionals, trust officers, and
   the like.

We are dealing here with rather substantial complexities on "both sides
of the table"—in which the older person and the financial adviser are at the
table. As the previous paragraphs suggest, the range of institutions and professional specialties relevant to financial planning is very broad (e.g., see
Leimberg, 1991). Simultaneously, the range of experience, resources, knowledge, needs, hopes, and fears on the part of the older citizens-consumers-
clients is equally broad. In an earlier analysis of the wealth-span concept
(Cutler & Gregg, 1991), it was found, for example, that even families with
modest financial resources often have such a multiplicity of sources or
streams of income and wealth that they should use systematic financial planning both before and during retirement.

In this context the challenge for financial gerontology is to design and
execute research appropriate to the task of acquiring systematic knowledge
of "both sides of the table," and how they react to each other, so that the
financial planning relationship is more successful. We recognize that there
are more than simply "two sides" in the relationship. Also at the table (or at
least "in the same room") are such other interested parties as government
agencies and the family of the client-consumer.

THE CLINICAL APPROACH
TO FINANCIAL GERONTOLOGY

As indicated at the outset, the chapters in this book aim to identify the emerging research agenda of a new research institute: the Boettner Institute of
Financial Gerontology. The goals of the enterprise, institutional and scientific, include both basic and applied research. Our aims include the creation of knowledge that will contribute to the interest and capacity of financial services professionals to improve the lives of middle-aged and older men
and women.

As we know, a commencement is both an end and a beginning: the graduation from school and the beginning of a new period in one's life. We conclude this discussion of the intellectual origins of the wealth-span concept and the science of financial gerontology with a brief description of a new venture: the exploration of the clinical approach to financial gerontology. At its most general level this activity embodies the general educational and public-service goals of most educational institutions: *to help people help people*. The clinical approach aims to bring together professionals in the fields of financial services on the one hand, and gerontological services on the other.

More specifically, the clinical approach aims to improve the quality of financial advice and service, which is made available to older people and their families. There is, to be sure, an abundance of financial information that is relevant to the diversity of financial circumstances found within the growing older population. Financial advisers and counselors, some of whom see themselves as specializing in an older clientele, are found among tax lawyers, financial planners, insurance advisers, accountants, stock brokers, bankers, health finance counselors, and others. The belief, however, is that although the technical quality of the financial information may be first-rate, less widespread among these professionals is the capacity to provide the information in a way that is optimally responsive to an older population.

To be sure, in financial gerontology as in all of geriatrics and gerontology, we must continually acknowledge the vast diversity within the older population (Taeuber, 1990). This group (age 65+) will number between 31 million and 35 million men and women during the next 10 years. Because they vary by income, wealth, education, race, gender—and age—financial services professionals must be both informed about general patterns of financial gerontology as well as responsive to unique circumstances and individual differences. Statistical or historical stereotypes are especially dysfunctional in financial gerontology.

A couple in their 80s, married for close to 60 years, recently mentioned that their financial adviser was especially keen on ensuring that their children would be well protected financially from the perspective of the parents' estate. The couple had to point out, however, that their children were themselves in their middle 50s and did not really need such protection. Older people are not all alike.

The specific research goals of clinical financial gerontology concern developing and improving not simply financial information, but the quality of the *process* by which information and advice about financial dynamics and products are made available to older persons. This research focuses on the systematic exchange of knowledge, experience, and insight between two important groups: financial service professionals and gerontological service professionals. Examples of this latter group are persons who work for community agencies, senior centers, and planning agencies, and who routinely assess the various needs of older persons.

The working hypothesis is that through the *interaction* of these two groups financial professionals can learn more about the gerontological nature of their clientele, and gerontologists can learn more about the role that financial planning plays in the wealth-span attitudes and behavior of older persons.

During the focus-group interactions, the financial and gerontological service providers will discuss and assess a structured set of "case examples" of older persons with prespecified financial, family, and personal characteristics. During the first phases of the research, the Institute will empanel several groups of specialists (researchers in relevant fields as well as service practitioners) who will, first, identify the gerontological and financial principles that should be confronted in the focus group interactions and, second, develop the case examples. The case examples will represent a broad range of older individual and family situations.

If I had to do it over, I would put more money into retirement.

In this way the groups of financial and gerontological specialists will assess older case examples representing different family configurations, different income and wealth profiles, different occupational and ethnic situations, and, of course, different age group and cohort membership ranging from middle-aged remarriages with new babies to older old widows with 60-year-old children.

Traditionally, professional advisers in the fields of insurance, investment, and financial services generally perform three functions for older clients: They assess needs, suggest goals, and offer advice and plans for connecting the needs with the goals. One of the more apparent "missing links" in this chain of knowledge and skills in financial planning is the fact that the financial circumstances of middle-aged and older persons are embedded in a network of both generational experiences and family relationships.

The main focus of financial services professionals is, of course, on financial issues, just as the primary concern of gerontological and geriatric practitioners is with the social and health concerns of older persons. A concern with the wealth-span of aging persons—with wealth-span implying the goals of successful intervention in later stages of the life cycle—requires both financial and gerontological knowledge.

The financial decision-making environment of younger persons, for example, is usually confined to their immediate family. For middle-aged and older men and women, however, there is greater desire for, and even reliance on information and opinion provided by grown children and other family members. Similarly, wealth-span analysis, planning, and intervention are also dependent on an array of information concerning government policies and programs such as income tax, estate tax, Medicare, and Social Security; and on "institutional wealth" information concerning pensions, and life, health, and long-term care insurance.

Ultimately, the financial and gerontological evaluation of an older person's or couple's wealth-span, including both obstacles and opportunities, is a complex function of current and future financial resources, current and anticipated health, and the financial, social, and even geographical structure of family. Consequently, to assist and advise aging persons most effectively, both financial and gerontological counselors must learn from each other's experience, knowledge, and skills—which collectively represent the research goals of the Boettner Institute's clinical approach to financial gerontology.

DEMOCRATIZATION OF FINANCIAL SECURITY

Increasing human longevity and increasing numbers of older and middle-aged men and women are among the great stories of our recent history. Although old age was not too long ago the preserve of the few and the wealthy, we have recently begun to experience what Robert Butler (1989), founding director of the National Institute on Aging, has called "the democratization of old age." To this we would add that so too we see the expanding distribution of a comfortable retirement income to a larger number of men and women in the form of pensions, individual retirement arrangements, Social Security, home equity, and investment assets (Crown, et al., 1991; Easterlin, MacDonald, & Macunovich, 1990)—a situation that we might call "the democratization of financial security" in old age.

In this important context we are happy to offer the field of financial gerontology, the study of the dynamics of financial security, well-being, and the quality of human life within and across generations. Although these general issues have been with us for a while, the explicit approach that characterizes financial gerontology—a combination of the dynamism of gerontology and financial services research and education—is quite new. It is to this dynamic endeavor that we dedicate this commencement.

REFERENCES

Butler, R. (1989). *The inside of aging.* Paper presented at The Brooksdale Leadership Conference, San Diego, California.

Crown, W. H., Mutschler, P.H., & Leavitt, T.D. (1987). *Beyond retirement: Characteristics of older workers and the implications for retirement policy.* Waltham, MA: Brandeis University, Heller Graduate School, Policy Center on Aging.

Crown, W. H., Longino, C. F., & Cutler, N. E. (1992). Income vs. wealth: Net worth and the economic status of the elderly.

Cutler, N. E., & Gregg, D. W. (1991). The human "wealth span" and financial well-being in older age. *Generations, 15,* 45-48.

Easterlin, R. A., Macdonald, C., & Macunovich, D. J. (1990). Retirement prospects of the baby boom generation: A different perspective. *The Gerontologist, 30,* 776–783.

Gregg, D. W. (1987). *The wealth span: A promising dimension for gerontological research,* (Invitational Research Symposium). Bryn Mawr, PA: Boettner Institute of Financial Gerontology.

Gregg, D. W., & Cutler, N. E. (1990). *Financial gerontology and the middle-aging of people and populations: Implications for future planning in insurance world-wide.* Paris: International Insurance Society.

Leimberg, S. R. (Ed.). (1991). *Financial services professional's guide to state of the art* (2nd ed.) Bryn Mawr, PA: The American College.

Longino, C. F. (1991). *Socioeconomic characteristics of retired persons in the United States with household income more than double the poverty level.* Bryn Mawr, PA: Boettner Institute of Financial Gerontology.

Maslow, A. H. (1943). Preface to motivation theory. *Psychosomatic Medicine, 5,* 87.

Maslow, A. H. (1970). *Motivation and personality* (2nd ed., pp. 38-45). New York: Harper & Row.

Milletti, M. A. (1984). *Voices of America.* New York: Teachers Insurance and Annuity Association and College Retirement Equities Fund.

Moschis, G. P. (1987). *Consumer socialization: A life-cycle perspective.* Lexington, MA: Lexington Books.

Rowe, J. W., & Kahn, R. L. (1987). Human aging: Usual and successful. *Science, 237,* 143-49.

Samuelson, P. A., & Nordhaus, W. D. (1989). *Economics* (13th ed., pp. -). New York: McGraw-Hill.

Smeeding, T. M. (1990). Economic status of the elderly. In R. H. Binstock & L. K. George (Eds), *Handbook of aging and the social sciences* (3rd ed., pp. 362-381). New York: Academic Press.

Taeuber, C. (1990). Diversity: The dramatic reality. In S. Bass, E. Kutza, & F. Torres-Gil (Eds.), *Diversity in aging* (pp. 2-28). New York: Scott, Foresman.

Tournier, P. (1965). *The adventure of living,* p. 156. New York: Harper & Row.

Winter, M., et al. (1989). *Determinants and consequences of changes in income, assets, and expenditures among older Americans.* Ames: Iowa State University, Department of Family Environment.

Index